Economic Theory

Equilibrium and Change

Economic Theory
Equilibrium and Change

M. BURSTEIN

Esmée Fairbairn Professor
of the Economics of Finance and Investment
University of Warwick, England

John Wiley & Sons Ltd
London . New York . Sydney . Toronto

Library of Congress catalog card No. 68-57663

SBN 471 12537 7

Printed in Great Britain by J. W. Arrowsmith Ltd., Bristol, England.

For BRUM, take it for all and all

Preface

1

I wrote this book because I like to write books, but I hope that *Economic Theory* is useful.

1) It systematically analyses phenomena familiar to the Acceptance World and the Street, but inaccessible to most scholars.
2) Economics, since I encountered it in 1940, has experienced a technological explosion permitting deeper penetration along a wider front. However there has been poor communication between the new technocrats and traditional practitioners. They do not seem to be learning much from each other. So I am trying to do some brokerage. Blessed is the peacemaker?

2

The preparation of this book has improved my grasp of certain material which I insecurely apprehended in *Money*.[1] Thus modern economics finds as *bêtes noires* the *dévots* of comparative-statics *cum* general-equilibrium who seemed to be in command in 1957, opposed by Mrs. Robinson and others who argued that comparative statics was for the most part unable to handle material dredged up from *Life*. For example: to state Pareto-optimum theory correctly is usually to bar practical interpretations of its experimentally-undiscernable variables. To make a harshly accurate statement of the dynamics of *tâtonnement* is to shove traditional stability analysis into a corner.

Once economic statics and dynamics are stated *exactly*, Thornton, Wicksell, Robertson and Keynes—somewhat rephrased—fit easily into an economic–dynamics freed from obsession with the stability properties of equilibria. Furthermore, upon the general-equilibrium obsession becoming dissolved, macroeconomics can be built up around properties of decision making in modern industry instead of abstract producers, thus restoring Marshall's insights to serious economic theory.

vii

Formal economics, then, encourages us to turn again to old masters. It also arouses interest in the views of subtly informed men of affairs, partly because proper economic dynamics, explaining the motion of ongoing systems, must be fed with material which can be supplied only from practical knowledge.

3

Modern economics has done much more than sap neo-classical general-equilibrium theory and receive welfare economics whilst reviving defunct gods. Exposing inconsistencies and lacunæ whilst linking up hitherto unconnected topics,* it has coalesced such matter as Lagrange-multiplier theory, dualism, Kuhn-Tucker theory and linear inequalities. It has created a whole new field of analysis of optimization, a side effect being a revitalized production-theory meshed with engineering science.

'Socialist' economics has been reopened. Once it is understood that 'general competitive equilibrium' is a mathematical notion, not a description of an event, it becomes clear that socialist and non-socialist economies are alike from the standpoint of price theory. Still alternative social institutions may affect significantly disequilibrium market behaviour as well as innovation and information exchange.

4

The book starts from square one, viewing economic theory from a modern vantage whilst preserving the dialogue with the past through exploitation of the calculus. Hopefully, abstract reasoning thus will illuminate a practical subject. Admittedly the book hangs on an abstract formulation, abjuring association of its symbols with data, thus sinking into the blend of the abstract and the intuitive which has made economic theory so bastard a subject. For example, readers' intuitions will associate the prices of the theory with personal experience.

The abstract formulation is this:

Two strands of thought dominate economic theory: optimization; the laws of motion of economic quantities. The techniques of analysis of the first strand primarily concern maximization of value-weighted sums over feasible (often convex) sets and lead up to equilibrium theory through fixed-point theorems. Theoretical discussions of economic dynamics traditionally have centred on stability properties of artificial *tâtonnement* solutions. Once the harsh confines of such analysis become understood—and only rigour makes this possible—one wishes to build up a 'dynamic theory of policy' relying heavily on the line Wicksell-Keynes-Harrod-Robinson, never comfortably nested in equilibrium analysis. The techniques of analysis of this second strand are from differential equations. The second strand is much looser than the first, encompassing more, but less securely.

---

*Striking examples are relationships revealed between dualism and the law of merger (cf. Chapter 7, Appendix) and between the dynamics of *tâtonnement* and money-supply theory (cf. Chapter 13).

Chapter 6, concerned with realities making pure-competition theory inappropriate as a basis for macroeconomics, introduces some stylized facts, but otherwise few facts are introduced. Andronow and Chaikin offer a *raison d'être*:

> In every theoretical treatment of a physical phenomenon, considerable idealization of the true properties is unavoidable. One may classify a system as linear, conservative or otherwise, as a system with so many degrees of freedom, etc. All such assertions are idealizations. Real systems are neither linear nor conservative, nor do they have a finite number of degrees of freedom, since they cannot be described with absolute precision by mathematical relations. Therefore a strict classification can be applied only to abstract schemes obtained from appropriate idealizations.[2]

The book has little econometric content. I merely limn the problems of setting up an estimating scheme uniquely associating with a particular linear structure. Only the identification problem, together with necessary underpinning from the theory of linear estimation, is considered. Identification here is important mostly because it sharpens up the problem of *interpretation* of observations as abstract variables of theories.

Some treatment of stochastic processes is essential in the book's scheme. Rigorous economic theory almost always has been deterministic. The economist should understand that to interpret stochastic events through deterministic theories, as he does, is somewhat eccentric.

5

I hope that I have accomplished at least this much:

1) a statement of modern general-equilibrium theory for Everyman, including a thorough consideration of *tâtonnement* and its dynamics, together with the thrust of Markov chain theory;
2) a harsh examination of utilitarianism;
3) a careful statement of the short run and long run in production theory;
4) clarification of stock-flow economics;
5) insertion of activity analysis into the heart of the theory of the firm, sustaining the transition from 'orthodox' theory by a careful statement of the relation of Lagrange multipliers to dualism;
6) a statement of *brain drain* theory, escaping from sterile pure-competition/Cobb-Douglas aggregate-production-function formulations;
7) integration of imperfect-competition theory with new developments in 'information cost' theory and with Keynesian economics;
8) integration of the theory of finance with the theory of the firm, leading to restoration of single-valued criteria for producers;
9) a statement of monopoly theory as a special case of programming;

10) an association of vertical-merger theory with *non-tâtonnement* dynamics and dualism;

11) elaboration of a dynamic theory of policy, founded on interpretation of Keynesian economics eschewing equilibrium and transcending the statical theory of policy *à la* Tinbergen;

12) a reconsideration of money-supply theory, leading to rehabilitation of Bank Rate and a rigorous interpretation of availability (of credit) theories;

13) clarification of nuances of application of general-competitive-equilibrium reasoning to socialist economies;

14) development of the deep implications of divorce of macroeconomics from general-equilibrium and even from disequilibrium;

15) insertion of the Pontryagin Principle into standard optimization theory.

6

Long ago I was impressed by the attraction of economics as applied mathematics to otherwise recalcitrant engineers. Then in 1965–6, as visiting professor of mathematical economics at Birmingham, I had an excellent opportunity to test my didactic theories on a variety of students excellently equipped mathematically but with little knowledge of economics—an opportunity repeated in 1967 at Warwick. It has become clear to me that the rigour of modern economics is itself a powerful didactic force—that here too a mainspring of science is the sense of beauty and the love of order.

7

I owe much to BRUM. And I also have many personal intellectual debts, three so profound that I prefer to state them specifically. Tadek Matuszewski forced me to take up modern price theory and his incorrigible opposition to orthodox—certainly to English—economics provoked what has been a fruitful reconsideration of my core-positions. Mitchell Harwitz has been my tutor and premier colleague—and then there is Robert Clower.

1. M. Burstein, *Money*, (Cambridge, Mass.: Schenkmann Publishing Co., Inc.; 1963).

2. [A. Andronow and C. Chaikin, *Theory of Oscillations* (Princeton: Princeton University Press; 1949), p. 3.]

1st *January* 1968   M. BURSTEIN

Contents

PART I

Introduction

CHAPTER 1

Scope and Method

1. ECONOMIC THEORY

This book is about economic theory. It deals with formal properties of abstract constructions whose arguments are labelled prices, outputs, money-supply, income, employment, etc. Thus consider a *model* for the rth market:

$$f^r(p_r; \alpha_r) = 0 \qquad (1)$$

The root of equation (1) $\bar{p}_r$, may be labelled the *equilibrium price* (or the roots the equilibrium prices) of the rth commodity. The function f^r is an *excess-demand function* defining the difference between quantities deemed desired to be demanded and supplied on p_r and parameters α_r (α_r being a vector), including prices of other commodities, indexes of tastes, etc.

'Market' is a highly abstract concept. An economic market is not an agora. It is a complex of events anent transactions in a given commodity class. The definitional spiral is endless. What is a commodity? 'A commodity ... is defined by a specification of all its physical characteristics, of its availability date, and of its availability location'.[1] 'Price' is an attribute of the primal concept, commodity.

It is perhaps natural to think of the prices, outputs, etc., of economic theory as symbols for 'real' events—for sense-perceptions often said to make up 'the real world'. Thus p_r might be interpreted as the price of asparagus to be delivered at New York at date t, a price which will be reported later in the *New York Times*. But, no, it is better not, at least until econometrics is considered (cf. ¶1.3). Contrast Lord Bertrand Russell's definition of matter:

'My own definition of *matter* may seem unsatisfactory: I should define it as what satisfies the equations of physics.'[2]

Economic theory reasons about data spaces defined with reference to abstract commodities instead of the matter of physics.

3

Finally, just as 'market' events are perceived abstractly, so are the actions of individuals. A consumer essentially is interpreted as *a consumption set on which preferences are being made*, a producer as *a production set on which profits are being maximized*. So, in economic theory, micro-decisions are interpretations of mathematical operations such as max $\mathbf{p} \cdot \mathbf{x}$ over $\mathbf{X}$.

2. PARTIAL (ISOLATED) AND GENERAL EQUILIBRIUM; COMPARATIVE STATICS

Only in the Markov theory of Chapter 9 (Appendix) do we pursue statics in a really satisfactory way. Only there is equilibrium explicitly analysed as a special state of a dynamical system. Indeed, for the most part, the equations solved for statical equilibrium in this book cannot be interpreted dynamically except through artificial devices (cf. ¶1.5 §§5 *infra*). Unfortunately we thus reflect much the greater part of the literature on economic statics.

§2

Economic statics contrast the partial (i.e. isolated) with the general equilibrium of abstract systems. Contrast equations (2) with equation (1).

$$f^r(p_r; \alpha_r) = 0 \tag{1}$$

$$f^1(p_1, \ldots, p_n; \xi) = 0$$
$$\cdots\cdots\cdots\cdots\cdots\cdots \tag{2}$$
$$f^n(p_1, \ldots, p_n; \xi) = 0$$

Equations (2) might better be written:

$$\mathbf{f}(\mathbf{p}, \xi) = \mathbf{0} \tag{3}$$

where $\mathbf{p}$ is the vector $(p_1, p_2, \ldots, p_n)$, ξ the vector $(\xi_1, \xi_2, \ldots, \xi_m)$ and $\mathbf{f}(\mathbf{p}, \xi)$ the vector $(f^1(\ ), \ldots, f^n(\ ))$.

The context makes clear whether a row- or column-vector is meant. For matrix-multiplication purposes, $\mathbf{p}$ will be a column vector unless it is specifically noted otherwise.

Equation (1) suggests the Marshallian method (after Alfred Marshall):

'[Marshall fixed] attention ... not upon the whole economy, but on a sector (it had better be a rather small sector) of it: the partial equilibrium of the single "industry" ... [A]s Marshall never tired of emphasizing, the theory made no claim to be a *precise* theory; it would be quite sufficient if [its] assumptions ... were very approximately true.'[3]

In order to be effective even in its own terms, the Marshallian method—

when applied, say, to an hypothetical and idealized asparagus market—would require that this market be small enough for its *interdependence* with the rest of the hypothetical economy to be neglected with little loss of accuracy. The Marshallian method well might handle an idealized New York asparagus market, surely the Chipping Sodbury market, whilst the Walrasian method (after Léon Walras), based on the simultaneous solution of equations (2), would be too cumbersome.

The Marshallian method cannot yield up consistent results except at a point of general equilibrium: α_r includes values for $p_1, \ldots, p_{r-1}, p_{r+1}, \ldots, p_n$ whilst α_{r+1} includes values for $p_1, \ldots, p_r, p_{r+2}, \ldots, p_n$.

On the other hand, the Marshallian method surely would be unworkable, even at this thought-experiment level, if a market's interdependence with the rest of the economy could not be ignored. Witness the American automobile industry or Monaco's tourist trade.

The methods of partial- and general-equilibrium in economics are not *categorically* different:

'Logically the determination of output of a given firm under pure competition is precisely the same as the simultaneous determination of thousands of prices and quantities. In every case *ceteris paribus* assumptions must be made. The only difference lies in the fact that in the general equilibrium analysis of, let us say, Walras, the content of the historical discipline of theoretical economics is practically exhausted. The things which are taken as data for that system happen to be matters which economists have traditionally chosen not to be in their province....'[4]

Indeed, as time has passed, economic theorists have focussed increasingly on statical versus dynamical analysis rather than on the forms of statical analysis represented by partial- and general-equilibrium.

§3

Comparative statics concerns effects of changes in data on solutions. For example, having solved equations (2) for $\bar{p}$ relative to the initial data, the vector $d\bar{p}$ is to be determined relative to parameter changes $d\xi$ comprising a change in data. Totally differentiating equations (2) and noting that $(\partial f/\partial p)$ and $(-\partial f/\partial \xi)$ are matrices

$$(\partial f/\partial p)\, d\bar{p} = (-\partial f/\partial \xi)\, d\xi \tag{4}$$

The partial derivatives are evaluated at a specific point $(\bar{p}; \xi)$, the initial solution, so that equations (4) are merely a set of linear equations in the unknowns dp, $d\xi$ being a vector or arbitrary increments. If the errors of these linear approximations approach zero in the limit, satisfaction of equations (4) assures equilibrium.

The increments might have to be very small. Specifically, in the neighbourhood of $(\bar{\mathbf{p}}, \xi)$ the family of $(n+m+1)$ dimensional hypersurface $f''(\mathbf{p}, \xi) = E^r$ is to be represented by the family of hyperplanes $\Sigma_s f_s^r \, dp_s + \Sigma_q f_q^r \, d\xi_q = E^r$ and the approximated solution space in the neighbourhood of $(\bar{\mathbf{p}}, \xi)$ is comprised of points $(\mathbf{dp}, \mathbf{d\xi})$ such that $(\mathbf{dp}, \mathbf{d\xi})'(f_s^r, f_q^r) = 0$.

The simulated function space is spanned by the vectors $(f_1^r, 0, \ldots, 0), \ldots, (0, \ldots, 0, f_{n+m}^r)$ yielding up the family of hyperplanes when summed and weighted respectively by $dp_1, \ldots, dp_n, d\xi_1, \ldots, d\xi_m$. Of course, $(\mathbf{dp}, \mathbf{d\xi})$ implies a specific $(\mathbf{p}, \xi)$ since differentials are being taken around $(\bar{\mathbf{p}}, \xi)$.

Denote the determinant, the Jacobian, of the matrix of coefficients of the left-hand side of equations (4) as Δ and the cofactor of the element belonging to the sth row and the rth column as Δ_{sr}.

$$\begin{vmatrix} \partial f^1/\partial p_1 \ldots \partial f^1/\partial p_n \\ \ldots\ldots\ldots\ldots\ldots\ldots \\ \partial f^n/\partial p_1 \ldots \partial f^n/\partial p_n \end{vmatrix} = \Delta, \text{ a Jacobian} \qquad (5)$$

Using Cramer's rule and taking up a case in which ξ_1 and no other parameter changes:

$$d\bar{p}_r/d\xi_1 = \sum_{s=1}^{n} (-\partial f^s/\partial \xi_1)\Delta_{sr}/\Delta \qquad (6)$$

Equation (6) crystallizes the method of comparative statics: it associates changes in equilibrium values of dependent variables having parametric changes, with changes in data.

Finally, a series of obvious substitutions permits equation (3) to be written:

$$\bar{\mathbf{p}} = \mathbf{F}(\xi) \qquad (7)$$

For a linear system A and B being matrices of coefficients and $\mathbf{A}^{-1}$ the inverse matrix of A, $\mathbf{A}\bar{\mathbf{p}} = \mathbf{B}\xi$ and $\bar{\mathbf{p}} = \mathbf{A}^{-1}\mathbf{B}\xi$.

§4

Illustrating the method of comparative statics in an isolated market, the quantity demanded of the rth commodity is defined by $100 - 2p_r$ whilst that supplied is $3(p_r - \tau)$, τ being a unit tax paid by suppliers. Equilibrium requires that

$$(100 - 2p_r) - 3(p_r - \tau) = 0 \qquad (8)$$

$$\bar{p}_r = 20 + 0.6\tau \qquad (9)$$

$$d\bar{p}_r = 0.6 \, d\tau \qquad (10)$$

A unit increase in the tax-rate leads to a 0.6 unit increase in equilibrium price.

Equation (7) ignores problems of *boundary conditions*. Thus we usually require that prices be non-negative or, if negative, that they be in accordance with disposal costs. And negative-output might be forbidden by the theory.

3. MACRO-EMPIRICAL FOUNDATIONS

(¶1.5 may be read before ¶¶1.3, 4.)

A graphic device illustrating the work of ¶1.3 is a *phase space*.[5]

In Chapter 6 we apply this concept to a theoretical analysis of the problem of 'optimal unemployment', relying on the dynamical theory of gases. Cf. Sir James Jeans, *The Dynamical Theory of Gases* (New York: Dover Publications, Inc.; 1954), 4th ed. The central notions were developed by J. W. Gibbs in his method of statistical mechanics. Cf. esp. R. B. Lindsay and H. Margenau, *Foundations of Physics* (New York: Dover Publications, Inc.; 1957), pp. 218–220.

Thus, if we become concerned with the prices and outputs of n commodities, we may work with a Euclidian space spanned by $2n$ Cartesian co-ordinates—one for each price and output—or with 2 n-dimensional spaces if, as is common, we wish to deal with a commodity-space *and* a price-space. The *state* of the system at instant t is then represented by a point in the phase space—a $2n$ vector. There are a number of ways in which the system's experience can be represented: correspondences can be drawn up between points in the phase space and *time*, represented by a 1-dimensional continuum (that of the real line); *world-points* can be plotted in an $n+1$ space analogous to space–time continua in physics. As for the first alternative, compare Andronow and Chaikin:

'["Our particular situation" is such that] its state is determined at any time t by the values of $\mathbf{x}$ and of its velocity $\dot{\mathbf{x}}[= \mathbf{y}]$. The phase space will then be a phase plane. . . . The point $\mathbf{M}(\mathbf{x}, \mathbf{y})$ is referred to as the *representative point* of the system. Thus the phase plane represents the totality of all possible states of the given system. As t varies . . . , $\mathbf{x}, \mathbf{y}$ will be functions of t: $\mathbf{x} = \mathbf{f}(t)$, $\mathbf{y} = \mathbf{g}(t)$, and $\mathbf{M}$ will describe a path π. The two equations . . . are of a type known as *parametric equations*. [They] represent also a *motion* on the path, that is to say a certain mode of describing the path as time varies. . . . The complete path represents the actual history of the system throughout all time. The totality of all the paths represents all the *possible* histories.'[6]

As for the second alternative, compare Hermann Weyl:

'[referring to "the structure of space and time"] The possible space–time or *world-points* form a four-dimensional continuum. . . . All simultaneous world-points form a three-dimensional *stratum*, all world-points of equal location a one-dimensional *fiber*. . . .

One attributes furthermore to time and space, a *metrical structure* by assuming that equality of time intervals and congruence of spatial configurations have an objective meaning. The statements of Euclidian geometry describe the spatial structure in greater detail. . . [T]he graphical time table of the motion of a body travelling with uniform speed along a straight line will be an inclined straight line. On this *world-line* lie those, and only those, space–time places which are occupied by the body in the course of its history.'[7]

Note well that we do *not* refer to representations of world-lines in Minkowski spaces, as is commonly done in relativity-physics. Minkowski spaces contain an imaginary coordinate, that for time in physical applications. Cf. G. Y. Rainich, *Mathematics of Relativity* (New York: John Wiley & Sons, Inc.; 1950), Chap. 2, esp. p. 52.

Next we distinguish between deterministic and non-deterministic theory, i.e. dynamical and statistical theory.

'In discussing the distinctive features of all dynamical laws and theories one must focus attention first upon their most salient characteristic: their implication of strict determinism.'[8]

Consider a 1-dimensional phase space suitable to a crude model of national income determination:

$$Y_t = \alpha + \beta Y_{t-1} \tag{11}$$

Say that parameters α and β are 100 and 0·9. Another datum, an initial condition, is required before the system can be started up: $Y_{-1} = 900$, the analysis beginning at $t = 0$. Then $Y_0 = 910$. We can see intuitively that $\lim_{t \to \infty} Y_t = 1000$ and that the structure calls for $Y_{t+1} = 1000$ if $Y_t = 1000$. (Compare the *absorbing states* referred to in the appendix to Chapter 9.)

Equation (11), upon being equipped with a structure, calls for a unique series of events, for a unique collection of *world-points* belonging to the 2-dimensional income-time space built up from the 1-dimensional phase space. The model is *deterministic*.

We soon shall see that empirical science, whether or not deterministic, requires *operational definitions*:

'We may illustrate ["the new attitude toward a concept"] by considering the concept of length. ... To find the length of an object, we have to perform certain physical operations. The concept of length is therefore fixed when the operations by which length is measured are fixed. ... In general, we mean by any concept nothing more than a set of operations; *the concept is synonymous with the corresponding set of operations*. If the concept is physical, as of length, the operations are actual physical operations ... or if the concept is mental, as of mathematical continuity, the operations are mental operations, namely those by which we determine whether a given aggregate of magnitudes is continuous.'[9]

Now empirical or experimental economics would have had a smooth path if economic theory had been theory about measurements, but, traditionally, it has not been such—and the theory of this book is not such. Traditionally, economic theory has much resembled the *Elements* of Euclid. In theory producers and consumers, sets on which profits or utility are being maximized, reach conclusion much as do isosceles triangles. Doubtless the theory of general competitive equilibrium or statical Keynesian income theory were suggested by Life and, doubtless, they have helped us cope with Life, but they are not mathematical specifications about relationships between operationally defined variables. The consumers, producers, prices, etc., of neoclassical economics are observationally indiscernible; IS and LM curves cannot rigorously be defined in calendar time. So *econometrics* has made a more-radical departure than many of its practitioners appear to have realized. The variables of econometrics are operationally defined and have little metaphysical relation to those of traditional theory, even if denoted by the same symbols.

Empirical economics concerns confidence bounds for phase paths of operationally defined variables. *So empirically useful economic theory must be able to accommodate stochastic events and, to that extent, be non-deterministic.* Non-determinism can arise in quite different ways:

1) There will occur errors of observation, calculation and reportage, i.e. *errors in the variables*, even under a perfect theory. Doubtless there is also an analogue in economics to the *Uncertainty Relations* of Heisenberg.

> '[The] general conclusion ... implies the impossibility of knowing with precision and at the same time, the position and state of a corpuscle.'[10]

Professor Popper is uneasy about Quantum Theory and Heisenberg's *Uncertainty Relations* in particular. Cf. Karl R. Popper, *The Logic of Scientific Discovery* (New York: Science Editions, Inc.; 1961), Chaps. 8 and 9. The text below suggests that *test* and *falsification* have not been vital in economic theory partly because implications of almost all economic theories are falsified by economic events not within their direct purview.

2) Recalling Professor Samuelson's remarks: no feasible economic theory can comprehend all of the influences on economic data; no feasible economic theory can predict exactly the world-line even of perfectly measured variables. There may be *errors in the equations*.

As it happens, most work in empirical economics is based on errors in the equations, whilst the great mass of non-quantum physics is based on errors in the variables, but this difference does not even occasion enough concern to be included in ¶1.3 §§3.

§ 2

Agreed, we could simply estimate the structures of deterministic models under some criterion of goodness of fit with observations. Indeed the hypothesis yielding up the highest R^2 could be accepted, others being rejected—but then no systematic conjecture could be made about the properties of predictions based on deterministic hypothesis A, relative to those of deterministic hypothesis B, for data set 2 regardless of their performances for data set 1. Systematic assertions require at the least the specifications of underlying stochastic processes of ¶1.4 §§1. Indeed all that can be said rigorously is that the data falsify both A and B.

So we must build non-deterministic models in order to be able systematically to conceive of initial data, giving rise to alternative subsets in phase space. We must develop formal criteria for accepting and rejecting inherently imperfect hypotheses.

Note that the text has distinguished between non-deterministic theory and non-deterministic hypotheses.

§3

Econometrics properly belongs to the theory of stochastic processes. It turns up a mass of material, centred on 'economics versus physics as empirical subjects'. It exposes the gulf between the variables of most of pure economic theory and data (often denoted by the same symbols and defined through physical operations) used in econometric work.

Whilst there are not categorical differences between empirical economics and physics—ideally their methodologies would be the same—important differences do exist, encompassing:

1) aggregation;
2) subjectivity, including expectations;
3) tropism.

The components of physical *aggregations* are much more uniform than are the components of counterpart economic aggregations. Compare collections of oxygen atoms with non-white United States households in 1967. The upshot for economics is the *aggregation problem*:

'A serious gap exists between the greater part of rigorous economic theory and the pragmatic way in which economic systems are empirically analysed. Axiomatically founded theories refer mostly to individuals. ... Empirical descriptions of economic actions ... are nearly always extremely global: they are confined to the behaviour of groups of individuals. ... What are the connexions between the functional relationships postulated by the economic theories of individual households and the relationships for groups ... postulated by the empirical research worker?'[11]

Indeed *aggregation bias* is common.[12]

Economic decision units must, in all but the special case of pure competition, be conceived to optimize relative to *subjective* data such as probability distributions of sales possibilities. Indeed *expectations* are highly important in empirical economics. It is possible (!) in physics to ignore expectations. The (perhaps stochastic) properties of physical particles can be verified with great precision whilst economic behaviour reflects *opinions* about the parameters of processes external to the actors (externality varying from economic particle to economic particle) and future disturbances to the process. So:

1) experiments on economic-actors (particles) might not be worthwhile unless they are hypnotized into believing that the experimental context is that of 'real' life;

2) in the imperfect nature of things, a model's structure is apt to be dislocated by feedback (as it seems to the economic experimenter) when it is set amongst the pigeons (economic data) long enough. This is because the experiences—the particular sample of events drawn from the population of possible event-samples—of economic actors are likely to change their behavioural-structure;

3) events in the domains of psychology, sociology, etc., are likely to affect economic behaviour in many ways at any time. Equivalent domains, relative to physics, are not known (aside, perhaps, from revealed religion) and apparently need not be invented;

4) behaviour of economic particles is affected by their watching each other (thus fads, mass hysteria, Terrors, etc.).

Economic-actors are *consciously tropistic* as they respond to data, which is sometimes subjective, whilst pursuing calculated optimizing behaviour. Of course, many thermodynamical phenomena can be explained through a criterion calling for minimization of temperature-dispersion amongst homogeneous matter. And the world-distribution of elephants doubtless could be explained through maximization of a collective pachydermic utility function. $\partial U/\partial x_i$ doubtless it would be negative if x_i were mice-density.

§4

Notwithstanding 'aggregation, subjectivity and tropism', Einstein and Infeld came close to defining our subject, i.e. econometrics *cum* experimental-empirical economics:

> 'The laws of quantum physics are of a statistical character: they concern not one single system but an aggregation of identical systems. They cannot be verified by measurement of one individual, but only by a series of repeated measurements.
>
> Radioactive disintegration is one of the many events for which quantum physics tries to formulate laws governing the spontaneous transmission from one element to another.... According to our present knowledge, we have no power to designate the individual atoms condemned to disintegration.... There is not the slightest trace of a law governing their individual behaviour. Only statistical laws can be formulated, laws governing large aggregations of atoms.... Quantum physics abandons individual laws of elementary particles and states *directly* the statistical laws governing aggregations, and its laws are for crowds and not for individuals.'[13]

The Theil and Einstein–Infeld excerpts may not appear to be consistent from the standpoint of econometrics, since Theil starts from laws governing individual behaviour. However, the excerpts are consistent. It is the lack of uniformity amongst the equivalent of oxygen atoms in economics which requires that aggregation be studied in order to understand how the object of interest—estimates of macroparameters—might become biased. Cf. R. G. D. Allen, *Mathematical Economics* (London: Macmillan & Co.; 1956), pp. 697–701.

4. ECONOMETRICS

We may plunge directly into our work: application of *statistical inference* to estimation of parameters of economic models and, inferentially, to prediction.

> 'In statistical inference proper, the model is never questioned.... *We always assume that one of the structures of the model exactly represents the actual process* by which the values of the observed quantities have been determined. The methods of mathematical statistics do not provide us with a means of specifying the model....
>
> This basic limitation on the scope of statistical inference is of no serious importance for models whose assumptions are not very restrictive. But in econometrics the complexity of phenomena, the impossibility of experimentation and the scarcity of data impose the choice of fairly restrictive models.'[14]

We shall take up only two econometric subjects: *the theory of linear estimation* (merely touched on) and *identification* (treated rather more fully).

§2

Taking up *the theory of linear estimation* (à la Malinvaud), and noting that ¶1.3 is confined to linear models, we focus on *Problem P*:

PROBLEM P. 'Given an observation on the random vector $\mathbf{x}$, its covariance matrix $\mathbf{Q}$ and the linear subspace $\mathbf{L}$ which contains its mean $\mathbf{y}$, estimate the position of $\mathbf{y}$ in $\mathbf{L}$.[14]

Of course, $\mathbf{y}$ and $\mathbf{x}$ in $\mathbf{y} = \mathbf{a} + \mathbf{bx}$ well may be logarithms.

Glossing this description, the expected value of a vector of random variables can be denoted:

$$\mathbf{y} = E(\mathbf{x}) \tag{12}$$

The covariance matrix is defined:

$$\mathbf{Q} = E[(\mathbf{x} - \mathbf{y})(\mathbf{x} - \mathbf{y})'], \tag{13}$$

noting that the product of n-vectors $\mathbf{z}$ and $\mathbf{z}'$, $\mathbf{z}$ being a column vector, is an $n \times n$ matrix. Finally, 'by definition, a set $\mathbf{L}$ in a vector space is a *linear manifold* or equivalently a *vector subspace* if, for any real number α and any vectors $\mathbf{y}^1$ and $\mathbf{y}^2$ of $\mathbf{L}$, $\alpha\mathbf{y}^1$ and $\mathbf{y}^1 + \mathbf{y}^2$ belong to $\mathbf{L}$'.[14]

We are to focus on *linear estimators*, that is on functions $\mathbf{f}(\mathbf{x})$ such that $\mathbf{f}(\mathbf{x}^*)$ is to be 'our estimate of $\mathbf{y}$ when $\mathbf{x}^*$ is the observed value'[14] and, again following Malinvaud, such that:

$$\mathbf{f}(\mathbf{x}^1 + \mathbf{x}^2) = \mathbf{f}(\mathbf{x}^1) + \mathbf{f}(\mathbf{x}^2) \tag{14}$$

$$\mathbf{f}(\alpha\mathbf{x}) = \alpha\mathbf{f}(\mathbf{x}) \tag{15}$$

for all vectors $\mathbf{x}$ and scalars α. We note that, if $\mathbf{G}$ is a matrix, then the linear function $\mathbf{f}(\mathbf{x})$ can be represented by $\mathbf{G}\mathbf{x}$, yielding a column vector, of course.

A crucial result is this: if $\mathbf{G}$ is selected relative to the n-vector $\mathbf{x}^*$, taking note of problem P, so that there is minimized

$$\sum_{i=1}^{n} \left\{ [x_i^* - f(x_i^*)]^2 \right\}$$

then the resulting estimate of $\mathbf{y}$ will, amongst other things:

1) have minimum variance amongst all unbiased linear estimators;
2) have zero correlation with the residual vector $\mathbf{x} - \mathbf{f}(\mathbf{x})$; and, if $\mathbf{x}$ is normally distributed:
3) be normally distributed;
4) be distributed independently of the residual vector (i.e. exhibit zero covariance with it).

This leads up to the *raison d'être* of ¶1.3 §§1: *the optimal properties of the method of least squares*,[14] partly explaining why least squares is a bread-and-butter estimating technique. Very briefly, optimality here is to be defined relative to the propositions of *statistical decision theory*. Statistical decision theory associate losses with estimation errors, and since the errors are stochastic, so must be the loss function of the estimator. A criterion may be the expected value of the loss, the *risk*. Symbolically, where $\mathbf{h}_j$ is an estimator and $\bar{\mathbf{y}}$ and $\bar{\alpha}$ the true values of $\mathbf{y}$ and the characteristic α,

$$R(\mathbf{h}_j; \bar{\mathbf{y}}, \bar{\alpha}) = E\{\mathbf{Pr}[\mathbf{h}_j(\mathbf{x}) - \bar{\mathbf{y}}; \bar{\mathbf{y}}, \bar{\alpha}]\} \tag{16}$$

Of course, in general, estimator $\mathbf{h}_1$ will not dominate $\mathbf{h}_2$. In general, risks associated with the techniques will be higher in the one case for one parametric specification and lower for another. This leads us towards a still narrower criterion, viz. the greatest value attained by risk-function for admissible values of $\mathbf{y}$ and α. And we shall classify an estimator as *minimax* if *supremum* (just defined) does not exceed that of any other in its class. However, a *minimax* estimator might not be *admissible*: a particular estimator is said to be *admissible* in a certain class of estimators if there exists no other estimator belonging to that class 'less risky' for any combination of $\bar{y}$ belonging to L and α.

'We now confine ourselves to the case where the loss is a positive definite quadratic form of the components of the estimation error $y^* - \bar{y}$.'[14]

We have been forced to change Malinvaud's notation, emphasizing that his expression, $\hat{y} - y$, is standard and ordinarily would be used here. For a definition of a positive-definite quadratic form, cf. ¶3.4 §§7 *infra*.

Then it becomes possible to denote the loss as $(y^* - \bar{y})'W(y^* - \bar{y})$ where W is a positive definite symmetric matrix (an example of a symmetric matrix is $\begin{pmatrix} 10 \\ 01 \end{pmatrix}$. This done, keeping in mind that ours is Problem P, we find that:

1) least squares is both *minimax* and admissible amongst linear estimators;
2) least squares is both *minimax* and admissible amongst regular unbiased estimators when x is normally distributed.

For the definition of regular estimators, see H. Cramér, *Mathematical Methods of Statistics* (Princeton: Princeton University Press; 1946), Chap. 32 §§3, pp. 477–487.

At the least, the reader will want to command the technique of least squares estimation in order to move comfortably in econometric literature.

§3[15]

Taking up *identification*, consider data on wheat-prices and wheat-sales in Country A, plotted as in Fig. 1. Surely it is natural to try to fit a

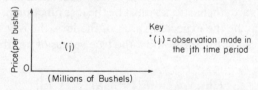

Fig. 1.   Wheat in Country *A*.

curve to the data. It is inconceivable that simple curves such as ordinary straight lines, or straight lines on a log-log grid would fit the data *perfectly*. Indeed even if an nth order polynomial were fitted to the $n + 1$ observations recorded in Fig. 1, some future observations would lie outside of the serpentine curve. Of course, we have seen that 'the impossibility of experimentation and scarcity of data' force empirical-economics into especially crude formulations, that the rôle of *error* is important in economics, or should we say grossly important, bearing in mind the rôle of indeterminism in physics as well as economics.

While it is plausible enough to stipulate that error arises from imprecise observations (errors in the variables), we shall emphasize errors of specification (errors in the equations).[16] Thus, letting wheat pass into the guise of the rth commodity, an econometrician defining the quantity demanded of the rth commodity at date t on its current price, lagged national income, and a vector of other current prices, may write:

$$q_{rt}^d = f(\mathbf{p}_{rt}, \mathbf{p}_{0t}, Y_{t-7}) + u_t \qquad (17)$$

or

$$q_{rt}^d = a + bp_{rt} + c_1 p_{0t} + \ldots + c_n p_{0nt} + eY_{t-7} + u_t \qquad (18)$$

Equation (18) is a simple linear hypothesis. In both equations, u_t is a random *disturbance term* with an expected value of zero.[17]

The disturbance term reflects random changes in taste and other excluded variables, e.g. p_s not in $\mathbf{p}_0$.

Now econometric theory is concerned with limitations on inferences which properly can be drawn from curves of the form

$$q_t = a + bp_t + cY_t + u_t \qquad (19)$$

fitted to scatters like that of Fig. 1.

More precisely, inferences are to be drawn from the parameter-estimates yielded up by the process relative to the data.

Perhaps a student who has estimated parameters a, b, and c and the variance of u will write:

$$q_t^d = \hat{a} + \hat{b}p_t + \hat{c}Y_t + u_t \qquad (20)$$

He will have made a mistake.

Can the parameters of a *structural relationship*, a relationship framed in the language of economic theory, be *identified* from data? Not necessarily —for unless the model is shaped in certain ways and unless appropriate assumptions are made about properties of disturbances, some or all parts of the model might be unidentifiable.

A demand relation, unlike the grin of a Cheshire cat, does not enjoy a life of its own. It must be part of a system in which demand-forces and supply-forces interact.

For simplicity, the text deals with an isolated market. The limitations of this approach already have been explained. One realizes that identifiability is a property of a model.

Thus let equations (21) and (22) comprise a model:

$$q_t = a + bp_t + u_{1t} \qquad (21)$$

$$\text{S1}$$

$$q_t = a + bp_t \qquad\quad + u_{2t} \qquad (22)$$

Equation (21) defines the quantity demanded and equation (22) that supplied of a very perishable food. Simultaneous satisfaction of equations (21) and (22) implies that demand is equal to supply.

u_{1t} and u_{2t} are numbers representing demand-disturbances and supply-disturbances at date t, numbers which cannot be directly observed as can p_t and q_t. Of course, the sense in which p_t and q_t can be observed is rather special. It is the sense in which operations can be executed by clerks charged with calculating the appropriate numbers.

S1 stipulates that observations are being taken on cleared markets. The procedure would be nonsense if there were queues of unsatisfied borrowers or if goods were rotting on shelves at prevailing prices.

If **S1** holds, so does equation (23):

$$q_t = \frac{a+c}{2} + \frac{b+d}{2} p_t + \frac{u_{1t} + u_{2t}}{2} \qquad (23)$$

which can be written:

$$q_t = e + fp_t + v_t \qquad (24)$$

Indeed, equation (25) holds:

$$q_t = \lambda_1 a + (\lambda_2 c/\lambda_1 + \lambda_2) + \lambda_1 b + (\lambda_2 d/\lambda_1 + \lambda_2) + \lambda_1 u_{1t} + (\lambda_2 u_{2t}/\lambda_1 + \lambda_2) \qquad (25)$$

where λ_1 and λ_2 are positive multipliers. Unfortunately, equations (23), (24) and (25) are observationally indistinguishable from equations (21) and (22)—which are observationally indistinguishable from each other. Each fits the data as well as any other. As a result, a statistical procedure estimating parameters maximizing the likelihood of the sample observations leads to the conclusion that there are an indefinitely large number of estimates, including all the convex linear combinations of a and c and of b and d, each doing as good a job as any other.

§4

How can the putative influences of interdependent economic forces be separated out? How can a model be made identifiable? Start with **S1**, but now assume that demand is influenced by current income, z_{1t}, whilst supply is influenced by last period's rainfall, inscribed at date t as z_{2t}. Denote q_t as y_{1t} and p_t as y_{2t}. System **S2** follows

$$y_{1t} - by_{2t} - gz_{1t} \qquad\quad - a = u_{1t} \qquad (26)$$

$$\text{S2}$$

$$y_{1t} - dy_{2t} \qquad\quad - hz_{2t} - c = u_{2t} \qquad (27)$$

Normalize equation (27) on y_{2t}, say by dividing through by d, and make some obvious notational changes:

$$y_{1t} + \beta_{12}y_{2t} + \gamma_{11}z_{1t} \qquad = u_{1t} \qquad (28)$$
$$\text{S2}$$
$$\beta_{21}y_{1t} + \quad y_{2t} \quad + \gamma_{22}z_{2t} = u_{2t} \qquad (29)$$

After some straightforward substitutions, the equilibrium values of the endogenous variables, y_{1t} and y_{2t}, can be expressed as functions of the exogenous variables z_t. Equations (30) and (31) comprise the *reduced form* of **S2**.

$$y_{1t} = \pi_{10} + \pi_{11}z_{1t} + \pi_{12}z_{2t} + v_{1t} \qquad (30)$$
$$\text{S3}$$
$$y_{2t} = \pi_{20} + \pi_{21}z_{1t} + \pi_{22}z_{2t} + v_{2t} \qquad (31)$$

The πs are linear combinations of the coefficients of **S2**. More generally the reduced form of the system $\mathbf{B}y_t + \Upsilon z_t = \mathbf{u}_t$ is $y_t = -\mathbf{B}^{-1}\Upsilon z_t + \mathbf{B}^{-1}\mathbf{u}_t$, i.e.,

$$\mathbf{y}_t = \pi z_t + \mathbf{v}_t \qquad (32)$$

The maximum-likelihood estimates of the βs and γs can be expressed in terms of the reduced-form coefficients. The algebraic connexions between 'true' values of structural and reduced-form parameters have been described by J. Johnston.[18] Multiply equation (31) by β_{12} and add to it equation (30) obtaining

$$y_{1t} + \beta_{12}y_{2t} = (\pi_{11} + \beta_{12}\pi_{21})z_{1t} + (\pi_{12} + \beta_{12}\pi_{22})z_{2t} + (v_{1t} + \beta_{12}v_{2t}) \quad (33)$$

Recall from the note preceding equation (32) that $\mathbf{v}_t = \mathbf{B}^{-1}\mathbf{u}_t$ i.e., $\mathbf{u}_t = \mathbf{B}\mathbf{v}_t$, i.e.,

$$\begin{bmatrix} u_{1t} \\ u_{2t} \end{bmatrix} = \begin{bmatrix} 1 & \beta_{12} \\ \beta_{21} & 1 \end{bmatrix} \begin{bmatrix} v_{1t} \\ v_{2t} \end{bmatrix} \qquad (34)$$

Specifically, $u_{1t} = v_{1t} + \beta_{12}v_{2t}$.

Since $u_{1t} = v_{1t} + \beta_{12}v_{2t}$, both equations (28) and (33) are true and, since z_{2t} does not appear in equation (28):

$$-\gamma_{11} = \pi_{11} + \beta_{12}\pi_{21} \qquad (35)$$
$$0 = \pi_{12} + \beta_{12}\pi_{22} \qquad (36)$$

Once estimates of the variables π have been obtained, equations (35) and (36) can be solved for maximum-likelihood estimates of β_{12} and γ_{11}:

$$\beta_{12} = -\pi_{12}/\pi_{22} \qquad (37)$$
$$\gamma_{11} = (\pi_{12}\pi_{21} - \pi_{11}\pi_{22})/\pi_{22} \qquad (38)$$

Similar expressions can be obtained for β_{21} and γ_{22}, the other structural parameters.

S2 is an identifiable system. S2 is the only structure compatible with the reduced form S3. It is impossible for any other structure to associate with S3 on equally favourable terms. Comparing equation (39) below, the proof centres on the existence or not of a non-singular matrix $\mathbf{A}$ (thus $\mathbf{A} \neq \mathbf{I}$), such that $\mathbf{AB}$ and $\mathbf{A\Upsilon}$ observe all the *a priori* restrictions known to be satisfied by $\mathbf{B}$ and $\mathbf{\Upsilon}$ (otherwise $\mathbf{B}$ and $\mathbf{\Upsilon}$ are arbitrary) and so that $(\mathbf{A\hat{B}}, \mathbf{A\hat{\Upsilon}})$ as well as $(\mathbf{\hat{B}}, \mathbf{\hat{\Upsilon}})$ maximize the likelihood of the sample of endogenous variables (y), given the exogenous variables (z).

Exogenous variables are determined outside the model. The maximum likelihood is $\Pr(\hat{v}_1) \cdot \Pr(\hat{v}_2) \cdot \ldots \cdot \Pr(\hat{v}_n)$, where $\hat{v}_s$ is a vector of estimates of the disturbances in the sth reduced-form equation over the T periods of observation.[19]

A pair of structures with the same reduced form have equal likelihood. If the structures $\mathbf{By}_t + \mathbf{\Upsilon z}_t = \mathbf{u}_t$ and $\mathbf{ABy}_t + \mathbf{A\Upsilon z}_t = \mathbf{Au}_t$ have the same reduced form and if $\mathbf{\hat{B}}$ and $\mathbf{\hat{\Upsilon}}$ are maximum-likelihood estimates, then $\mathbf{A\hat{B}}$ and $\mathbf{A\hat{\Upsilon}}$ also are maximum-likelihood estimates. Thus,

$$\mathbf{ABy}_t + \mathbf{A\Upsilon z}_t = \mathbf{Au}_t \tag{39}$$

The reduced form of equation (37) is

$$(\mathbf{AB})^{-1}(\mathbf{AB})\mathbf{y}_t + (\mathbf{AB})^{-1}\mathbf{A\Upsilon z}_t = (\mathbf{AB})^{-1}\mathbf{Au}_t \tag{40}$$

That is:

$$\mathbf{y}_t = -\mathbf{B}^{-1}\mathbf{\Upsilon z}_t + \mathbf{B}^{-1}\mathbf{u}_t \tag{41}$$

Rewrite the reduced form of S2, i.e. S3:

$$\mathbf{y}_t = -\mathbf{B}^{-1}\mathbf{\Upsilon z}_t + \mathbf{B}^{-1}\mathbf{u}_t \tag{42}$$

Equations (41) and (42) are identical! Obviously identifiability requires that there should not exist an arbitrary non-singular matrix $\mathbf{A}$.

Systems like S1 are not identifiable. Now, following Johnston, consider the system

i)
$$y_{1t} + \beta_{12}y_{2t} \qquad\qquad = u_{1t} \tag{43}$$

ii)
$$\beta_{21}y_{1t} \quad + y_{2t} + \gamma_{21}z_{1t} = u_{2t} \tag{44}$$

Note that:

$$\mathbf{\Upsilon} = \begin{pmatrix} 0 \\ \\ \gamma_{21} \end{pmatrix}$$

Here the system's restrictions require that:

iii)
$$\mathbf{A} = \begin{bmatrix} 1 & 0 \\ a_{21} & 1 - a_{21}\beta_{12} \end{bmatrix} \tag{45}$$

$A^* \neq A$ violates the requirement that $\beta_{11} = 1 = \beta_{22}$ and that $\gamma_{11} = 0$. (Note that the other coefficients yielded up by the transformation are observationally indistinguishable from those of the original model.) Equation (44) is not identifiable: a_{21} being arbitrary, an infinity of equations of the form of equation (44) lead to the same reduced form and are equally plausible statistically.[20]

Keeping in mind that the exact equivalence of equations (41) and (42) is at the heart of the matter, consider the *a priori* restrictions obeyed by B and Υ in **S2** and to be imposed on AB and $A\Upsilon$: $a_{12} = 0 = a_{21}$; $a_{11} = 1 = a_{22}$.

z_1 appears only in equation (28) and z_2 only in equation (29). The coefficients of y_1 in equation (28) and y_2 in equation (29) are unity.

Thus,

$$A = \begin{pmatrix} a_{11} & a_{12} \\ a_{21} & a_{22} \end{pmatrix} = \begin{bmatrix} 1 & 0 \\ 0 & 1 \end{bmatrix} \tag{46}$$

The only permissible transformation of **S2** which has the reduced form **S3** is:

$$IBy_t + I\Upsilon z_t = Iu_t \tag{47}$$

S2 is *exactly identified*.

§5

Econometrics must be concerned with the authority of one as against another explanation of data. Witness the identification problem. But it is not obvious that model-building is necessary or even desirable. It is possible that observation without theory, based on meticulous compilations of patterns of leads and lags (e.g., lightning and thunderclaps—or announcements of intentions to purchase refrigerators and purchases) could build up a solid basis for economic policy whilst elegant formulations would fail, frustrated by the complexity of economic forces. Still the history of science vindicates formal model-building.[21]

'Facts' depend on theories. Hopi Indians, clinging to a brutally simple religion, might conduct econometric studies estimating the parameters of their gods' collective preference function and concluding that prolonged drought implies divine yearning for fresh slaughters of maidens. Other theories, different but not inherently more scientific, would, from these data, call for cloud-seeding. It would not occur to the Hopis to challenge their religious hypothesis, just as it never would occur to us to adopt it. Value-structures affect scientific theories. Furthermore, the kinds of data we collect depend on our theories. Economists convinced that 'the supply of money' is fools' gold will not squander funds on money-supply data collection. No, economic theory is not a set of hypotheses about the 'real world'. Economic theory concerns a data space which is itself an object of choice by economists.

For a concisely excellent discussion of the methodology of economic theory (specifically in connexion with the truth of the theory's antecedent conditions), see D. V. T. Bear and D. Orr.[21] Their bibliography is highly valuable.

5. OPTIMIZATION AND MARKET BEHAVIOUR

Economic theory concerns conscious decision-making and trading in markets, however idealized. Since a decision ideally is based on one's best choice, it is not surprising that much economic literature concerns maximization or minimization of a criterion (profits, costs, tax yields, etc., subject to constraints (wage rates, demand conditions, technology, etc., for the firm; wealth and income, commodity prices, etc., for the household).

The mathematical conjugate of economic theory as one of optimization is the theory of extremal methods, including constrained maximization. For example, the theory of production may be boiled down to:

$$\max x_1 \tag{48}$$

subject to:

$$f^j(x_1, x_2, \ldots, x_n) \le c_j \qquad j = 1, 2, \ldots, m \tag{49}$$

$$x_2 \ge x_2^0, x_3 \ge x_3^0, \ldots, x_n \ge x_n^0 \tag{50}$$

In the simplest case each of the n activities—a particular way of doing things—yields but one output, that is to say, a different output in each instance. In the simplest case—the one underlying our example—the intensity at which the ith activity is operated, x_i, may be used as a measure of the output of the ith commodity. The activities absorb capacities c. For example, $f^r(\mathbf{x})$, defines the absorption of the rth capacity (e.g. machine-hours of a certain type) on the outputs. Inequalities (49) require that capacity constraints be obeyed; inequalities (50) require that outputs $x_2^0, \ldots, x_n^0$ be achieved. Adhering to a fruitful model distinguishing sharply between the theories of household choice and the firm, the firm can be stipulated as maximizing a value-weighted sum $\mathbf{p} \cdot \mathbf{y} - \mathbf{w} \cdot \tilde{\mathbf{y}}$ subject to $f(\mathbf{y}, \tilde{\mathbf{y}}) = 0$, where $\mathbf{p}$ and $\mathbf{w}$ are vectors of prices of outputs and inputs, $\tilde{\mathbf{y}}$ is a vector of factor purchases and $f(\mathbf{y}, \tilde{\mathbf{y}})$ is the implicit form of the production function defining the frontier of feasible inputs–outputs.

§2

Price—a value attributable to, but not intrinsic to, a commodity. The approach of economics to decision theory is bottomed on price. The firm's criterion or objective typically is defined in 'money' terms— the household is constrained by the costs of what it buys against the revenues from what it sells.

The difference between money as an abstract unit of account and as a class of property performing monetary functions is discussed in M. L. Burstein, *Money* (Cambridge, Mass.: Schenkman Pub. Co. Inc.; 1963), Chap. 1.

Furthermore, many economic problems, e.g., maximization of a revenue function over a set of feasible outputs, can be analysed with *Lagrange multipliers.*

Social welfare problems usually are technocratic. Social and, as it happens, individual 'welfare' are defined on commodities which are consumed or produced. Perhaps the stock of some commodity at the end of the planning interval is to be maximized, subject to required intermediate consumptions and terminal levels of other stocks.

A Lagrange function is of the style

$$f(\mathbf{x}) - \lambda_1 g(\mathbf{x}) - \lambda_2 h(\mathbf{x})$$

or

$$f(\mathbf{x}) + \lambda_1 g(\mathbf{x}) + \lambda_2 h(\mathbf{x})$$

where $g(\mathbf{x}) = 0$ and $h(\mathbf{x}) = 0$ are constraints on the maximization of $f(\mathbf{x})$, $\mathbf{x}$ being a vector. The Lagrange multipliers, λ_1 and λ_2, are treated as unknowns to be solved for through the equations

$$f_i(\mathbf{x}) + \lambda_1 g_i(\mathbf{x}) + \lambda_2 h_i(\mathbf{x}) = 0 \tag{51}$$

$$g(\mathbf{x}) = 0 \qquad h(\mathbf{x}) = 0$$

where f_r is the partial derivative of f with respect to the rth element of $\mathbf{x}$.

It will become clear that satisfaction of the Lagrange conditions for a relative extremum does not assure that a global extremum has been attained.[22]

In the solutions of these *primal problems*, the values of Lagrange multipliers can be interpreted as marginal values of constraints—as the rates at which the solution-value increases with relaxations of constraints, e.g. that on freight-car capacity. Accordingly, when the *objective function* is expressed in dollars—a revenue function is an example—the Lagrange multipliers can be interpreted as prices, here as resource rentals. Even when the *objective function* is not expressed in value terms—a utility function would be an example—ratios $\bar{\lambda}_r / \bar{\lambda}_s$ can be interpreted as *relative prices.*

Each primal problem associates with a *dual problem* solving explicitly for the Lagrange multipliers, the marginal values of the primal constraints. The upshot is especially interesting when decision units are optimizing with respect to value-weighted quantities. Thus, consider the analysis of competitive equilibrium. Cost-minimizing, profit-maximizing traders assure that a competitive equilibrium will obey the dual constraints. To say this is to say that prices of resources and of outputs will be such that imputed resource-values will exhaust the value of final outputs and that activities which are not cost-justified will not be undertaken. Moreover, identical resources receive identical imputations wherever employed in a competitive equilibrium. Finally, deep relationships between the concepts of prices and Lagrange multipliers or *positive normals* yield up important *optimality* properties to be studied in Chapters 5 and 10.

§3

Market! Economic decisions are harmonized or revealed to be discordant in markets. The upshot, when translated into the language of the model of pure competition, is the theory of general competitive equilibrium. Competitive equilibrium—in a sense a mathematical notion—reflects an economic thought-experiment in which households and firms, responding to *parametric* prices, unconsciously bring about new price constellations through effects of their behaviour on bids and offers until, perhaps, an equilibrium is achieved. The theme goes back at least as far as Adam Smith: the invisible hand of competition.

> 'He generally, indeed, neither intends to promote the public interest, nor knows how much he is promoting it.... [a]nd he intends only his own gain, and he is in this, as in many other cases, led by an invisible hand to promote an end which was no part of his intention.'[23]

However, 'competition' has come to be an abstraction in economic theory, not a description.

§4

As a theory of the laws of motion of such variables as prices and outputs, the mathematical conjugate of economic theory is differential or difference equations. In a simple case time derivatives $\dot{\mathbf{p}}$ may be defined on $\mathbf{p}$ so that the appropriate system is a set of simultaneous differential equations:

$$\dot{\mathbf{p}} = \mathbf{f}(\mathbf{p}) \tag{52}$$

If equations (52) possess an integral—defined on time of course—one could, upon being supplied with initial conditions, grind out the system's state for tomorrow and tomorrow and tomorrow...

§5

It is important to understand that, although the techniques and formalizations of economic theory lead up to a useful dichotomization—optimization versus laws of motion—the two branches belong to the same trunk. Thus, in any intertemporal economic theory each decision-unit plans temporal sequences of actions, deemed to be optimal relative to his data and expectations. Generally speaking, maximization of a criterion, such as the present value of a programme, calls for a particular time-path for each decision variable, including outputs and perhaps prices. In this way systems, such as equations (52), are linked up with optimization theory.

Having cautioned against excessive apartheid between our two branches of economic theory, we may now emphasize how alternative approaches to the analysis of systems such as equations (52) *do* differ. Indeed we shall discover that theories of economic-dynamics worked out in historical (calendar) time—as against logical (meta) time—lead to results which verge upon being qualitatively different from those of, say, the pure theory of competitive auction markets. Modern income theory is a good illustration.

Very briefly, the great bulk of neo-classical economic theory—including that of such advanced writers as Arrow, Debreu, Hurwicz, and McKenzie —concerns auction markets equilibrated through a process of *tâtonnement*. The *tâtonnement* transpires in meta-time, so that in neo-classical theories the calendar-time required for market-adjustment can be ignored. Trading at false prices is not to occur or can be ignored. Hence, it becomes possible to distinguish categorically between *ex ante* quantities planned for sale or purchase and quantities emergent in market equilibrium at the completion of *tâtonnement*. The former are but notional even in pure theory. It follows that the functions $\mathbf{f(p)}$ of equations (52) are functions of excess-demands calculated from plans reported by hypothetical firms and households optimizing criterion functions relative to $\mathbf{p}$, the price-vector announced by the 'auctioneer' (*le crieur*). Accordingly $\dot{\mathbf{p}}$ pertains to prices cried out by the 'auctioneer' *and* that an unstable equilibrium here would be a state such that departure by *le crieur* from $\bar{\mathbf{p}}$ would prevent *him* from returning to $\bar{\mathbf{p}}$ so long as he were to adhere to his dynamic-rules ($\dot{\mathbf{p}} = \mathbf{f(p)}$)—in other words the auctioneer would then go crazy.

POINT. The dynamics of *tâtonnement* concern a meta-time, not calendar-time. Hence necessarily they are but notional. At the same time, the notional history of *realized* prices of an economy operating under *tâtonnement* would concern only realizations of transactions occurring in market-equilibrium.

Upon dropping *tâtonnement* and working out dynamical theory in calendar-time, there becomes appropriate what Professor Clower has called a *dual-decision process*. This leads up to a result for purely-competitive markets very much like that which would be generated by a model of 'all-round monopoly'.

The text's analysis verges on Keynesian economics in which households and firms are concerned with how much they will be able to sell at going prices (and indeed may *quote* these prices) as well as with levels of prices facing them. The *consumption function* is a good example of Keynesian theory. Neo-classical households choose their incomes. (Compare the discussion of *fixprice* theory of Chapter 9 and of money-supply theory in Part IV.)[24]

Specifically, the trader must take account of the possibility that he will not be able to accomplish his plan—optimal relative to **p**—that he might not be able to accomplish desired sales and/or purchases. Of course, this is a fact of life for anyone customarily *quoting* prices in markets in which he trades. A monopolist (or, of course, a monopolist-monopsonist) always must work out his programme against a background of subjective probabilities attributed to quantities he may be able to sell or buy at quoted prices. He must contemplate the possibility of having to run down his inventory, of refusing orders and of seeing extraordinary queues form up if he quotes too low and/or underestimates demand-schedules. If he quotes too high, his inventories are likely to swell, his order book to dry up, etc. Note well that these problems, either of achieving desired realizations at prevailing prices or guessing underlying demand-supply conditions correctly when quoting prices, are entirely foreign to traders in competitive auction markets whether or not false trading *à la* Marshall and Hicks is permitted.

There is immediately suggested a reinterpretation, if not reformulation, of equations (52) along these lines:

1) it becomes attractive to interpret **p** and **ṗ** as data of the sort published in the *Economist* and the *New York Times*;
2) since expectations of realizable events presumably are affected by experience and since the history of the process matters for other reasons, lagged values for prices, outputs, sales, etc., should be included in equations (52) whether these are interpreted *ex ante* or as in (1) above.

Of course, the upshot is to supply a calendar-time interpretation for economic dynamics and, hence, a basis for an econometric theory of economic dynamics.

Note that my distinction between calendar- and meta-time is *not* that of Prof. Samuelson between the time-variable of dynamic and that of historical systems. Cf. Paul A. Samuelson, *Foundations of Economic Analysis* (Cambridge, Mass.: Harvard University Press; 1947), pp. 313–317. Samuelson's problem concerns systems in which calendar dating matters, as against those in which all that matters is time elapsed since date t. Historiographically, we might compare Sir Lewis Namier with Arnold J. Toynbee. On the other hand, Prof. Joan Robinson's distinction between *logical-* and *historical-time* is very close to my own. Cf. Joan Robinson, *Essays in the Theory of Economic Growth* (London: Macmillan & Co. Ltd.; 1962), pp. 23–29, a profoundly important piece of analysis. I have struggled with this problem in the past. Cf. M. L. Burstein, *Money* (Cambridge, Mass.: Schenkam Pub. Co. Inc.; 1963), Note K to Chap. 5A, pp. 237–238.

For an excellent-discussion of the history of *tâtonnement*, see Don Patinkin, *Money, Interest, and Prices* (Evanston: Row, Peterson & Co.; 1956). Also William Jaffé, 'Walras' Theory of *Tâtonnement*: A Critique of Recent Interpretations,' *Journal of Political Economy*, Vol. 75, No. 1, Feb. 1967, pp. 1–19.

As will become clear, emphasis on *tâtonnement* necessarily accompanies *rigorous* neo-classical theory: hence its rôle in the work of Arrow, Debreu and others. Marshall, working more informally, did *not* specify *tâtonnement*. Quite to the contrary! Cf. Sir John Hicks, *Capital and Growth* (Oxford: The Clarendon Press; 1965), pp. 52–54.

Professor Hicks prefers a more or less Marshallian approach to the *tâtonnement*. Cf. J. R. Hicks, *Value and Capital* (Oxford: The Clarendon Press; 1946), 2nd ed., pp. 127 and 129. He considers effects of trading at 'false' (non-equilibrium) prices in the course of a Hicksian Monday, preferring *not* to stipulate that the adjustment process transpires in our notional-time. Rather he assumes that

'the transactions which take place at "very false" prices are limited in volume. If any intelligence is shown in price fixing they will be.'

He then argues that effects of false trading are analogous to income effects and that any resulting indeterminacy is of the sort which can be produced by income effects.

Thus neo-classical excess-demand functions cannot be interpreted as such except in the meta-time of *tâtonnement*. Professor Hicks *does* point out that 'false trading' leads to shifts in asset positions, parametric for $f(p)$, but the real problem is much more serious. In a *disequilibrium* economy *à la* Clower, or in a world of all-round monopoly, traders treat parameters of probability distributions of realizable *quantities* as parameters for their decision-process. Thus Keynes!

I have suggested earlier that Keynesian theory might better be studied through a model of all-round monopoly. Cf. M. L. Burstein, *Money*, footnote 27, p. 666. A very early formalization, in a value-theory context, of all-round monopoly is in Joan Robinson, *The Economics of Imperfect Competition* (London: Macmillan & Co. Ltd.; 1938), Chap. 27, 'A World of Monopolies'. (The author remarks on the relationship of her analysis to 'full employment' of factors of production, but not in a way which is of interest to us at this point.) See also A. C. Pigou, *The Economics of Stationary States* (London: Macmillan & Co. Ltd.; 1935), Chap. 41, 'All-Round Monopoly....' Here Professor Pigou verges upon but does not attain what I should view as the central ground, namely the distinction between the *objective* constraint posed by the vector p in idealized competitive markets and the *subjective* evaluation by 'monopolists' of their sales possibilities now and in future.

§6

It may be said with some truth that the effect of ¶1.5 §§4–5 is to empha-size the importance of *disequilibrium* in economic theory. However, this 'truth' might cause harm unless it is understood that *disequilibrium* is *not* an inherent property of a given set of economic data, but instead can only be defined relative to a theoretical model. Thus compare Lindsay and Margenau:

'However, to have a clear understanding of a physical concept like matter is not at all equivalent to the assumption that there is a "real" world behind our sense-perceptions which is responsible for the existence of matter.... There is scarcely any use in believing in a real material world behind physical phenomena unless it is a permanent, unchanging affair toward the knowledge of which we progress with slow but certain steps. But our knowledge of it is based naturally on the prevailing physical theories....'[25]

Economic intuition also can be put into play. Consider a 'Harrodian' model (cf. Part IV). Parameters s and v might be specified so that the warranted rate of growth is 3 per cent per annum. Alternatively, values might be assigned which lead up to a warranted rate of 2 per cent. Now consider data exhibiting a 2 per cent growth rate. Do these data display 'equilibrium'? Clearly the answer depends on the structure assigned to the model. It would seem that *equilibrium* in economics cannot have precise meaning outside of the notional state of universal pure competition in auction markets.

§ 7

By way of summary, economic theory in its optimizing mode's neo-classical guise concerns decision-makers. These may be maximizing value-weighted sums defined on commodity spaces but confined to sets of feasible-outputs; or they may be preference functions, also defined on commodity spaces but subject to restraints on expenditure values. An extension of economics as a theory of optimizing behaviour—*welfare economics*—evaluates economic actions in terms of groups of preferences defined on commodity spaces and constrained by functions, which similarly define and which limit the possibilities of collective action. Perhaps in its positive guise macrodynamics is the polar opposite of welfare economics. It attempts to ascertain the laws of motion of economic quantities, trying to predict quantitatively-defined future states of the economy relative to initial conditions. Macrodynamics is rooted in differential equations as against the extremal methods of the other branch of the science.

Of course, differential equations have a rôle in optimization-theory. For example, one might wish to maximize an intertemporal criterion subject to constraints expressed as differential equations as can be done through, say, Pontryagin's Maximum Principle. Consider this guise for intertemporal maximization by a monopolist (cf. Chapter 7 *infra*). To be more precise, then, we wish to distinguish between problems of optimization in the sense of programme-formulation and problems of prediction of data of the sort reported in the *Economist*—quite apart from the desirability of the predicted results. As a matter of fact, the techniques of analysis of the first class of problem *have* differed markedly from those used for the second class along the lines stated in the text.

We avoid the positive-economics/normative-economics dichotomy partly because 'optimization' is a word of art and does not apply 'good' or 'desirable'. 'Optimization' is a mathematical notion.

CHAPTER 1—APPENDIX: ON STATIONARY STATES

Sources include: J. S. Mill, *Principles of Political Economy* (London: Longmans, Green & Co.; 1909), Ashley Edition, esp. Book IV, Chap. VI; A. C. Pigou, *The Economics of Stationary States* (London: Macmillan & Co. Ltd.; 1935); Joseph A. Schumpeter, *History of Economic Analysis* (New York: Oxford University Press; 1954), pp. 963 ff.; F. Zeuthen, *Economic Theory and Method* (Cambridge, Mass.: Harvard University Press; 1955), esp. Chap. 23, pp. 139–142.

This appendix is not a treatise on economic stationary states, but rather a note on their methodology, emphasizing crucial positions taken in Chapter 1. Perhaps the single most important point concerns effects of imputation of criterion-functions to the particles under study on the validity of certain quasi-physical models.

§2

It is important to distinguish between the rôle which has been assumed by the stationary state in classical and Keynesian economics on the one hand and in more-or-less neo-classical economics on the other. In the one case, the stationary state culminates an historical process contemplated in a grand speculation. There are close links between the stylized history of the classical writers and the (perhaps regrettable) 'euthanasia of the *rentier*' passages of *The General Theory*.[26] In the other case, stationary state analysis develops through at least two branches:

1) the heuristic efforts of Marshall and Pigou to isolate certain problems in resource allocation;
2) rather recent work in the wake of the seminal article of Archibald and Lipsey,[27] dealing with full-equilibrium states along lines much like those of certain physical theories or of Markov chain theory.

§3

As it happens, we shall pick no *methodological* quarrel with the classical-Keynesian stationary state analysis and propose to dismiss it here with a few revealing quotations.

'It must always have been seen, more or less distinctly, by political economists, that the increase in wealth is not boundless: that at the end of what they term the progressive state lies the stationary state, that all progress in wealth is but a postponement of this, and that each step in advance is an approach to it.... The richest and most prosperous countries would very soon attain the stationary state, if no further improvements were made in the productive arts, and if there were a suspension of the overflow of capital from those countries into the uncultivated or ill-cultivated regions of the earth.'[28]

'Let us assume that steps are taken to ensure that the rate of interest is consistent with the rate of investment which corresponds to full employment.... On such assumptions I should guess that a properly run community equipped with modern technical resources, of which the population is not increasing rapidly, ought to be able to bring down the marginal efficiency of capital in equilibrium approximately to zero within a single generation; so that we should attain the conditions of a quasi-stationary community....'[29]

'Now, though this state of affairs [i.e. a very-low pure rate of interest]
would be compatible with some measure of individualism, yet it would
mean the euthanasia of the *rentier*, and, consequently, the euthanasia of the
cumulative oppressive power of the capitalist to exploit the scarcity-value
of capital. . . .'[30]

Very briefly, failure to set up an *all-inclusive* concept of capital—one including human and
non-human agents of production—is likely to cause one to make an invalid application of
the law of variable proportions. One is likely to conceive of accumulation of capital leading to
a more significant change in proportions of applied productive agents than in fact occurs.
After all, there is no reason why investment in human and non-human agents should not be
carried on simultaneously—nor has the rôle of the 'original and indestructible powers of the
soil' proved to be as important as Ricardo suggested.

Correct analysis of the 'all-inclusive nature of capital' appears first to have been stressed
significantly in modern analysis by Professor Frank H. Knight. See also Milton Friedman,
Lectures in Price Theory (Chicago: The Aldine Press; 1965), 'Capital and Interest'.

§ 4[31]

It is not easy to deal with the heuristic 'stationary' analysis of Marshall
and Pigou. Eschewing rigour, they ingenuously claim merely to be
trying to aid our intuitions. Professor Pigou considers 'three degrees of
stationary states':

'First, the system of industry as a whole may be stationary, while the several
industries that compose it are in movement. Secondly, every separate
industry may be stationary, while the individual firms in it are in movement.
Thirdly, individual firms as well as individual industries, may be stationary.'[32]

Roughly speaking, the first degree is that of a stationary system *à la* Mill.
The second degree puts us down within the heartland of Marshallian
economics, leading us to take up one by one industries in long run
equilibrium. The third degree leads up to one of the more stimulating
facets of Marshall's work, the growth (decay) and equilibrium of the
firm, each firm being considered to be nested within an industry facing
a given demand curve.

¶1.A §§4 is to peter out rapidly and for a reason which leads straight into
¶1.A §§5. Marshall and Pigou, mostly concerned—certainly in this aspect
of their work—with value, not accumulation, sought out a didactic
device to illustrate how relative values (including factor-rewards) would
become established under tranquil conditions. Indeed Marshall was
diffident about using the stationary state device. In truth he employs it
rather clumsily and mostly to show that, stipulating highly-elastic long run
industry cost curves,

'[i]n a stationary state then the plain rule would be that cost of production
governs value.'
'This state obtains its name from the fact that in it the general conditions
of production and consumption, of distribution and exchange remain
motionless; but yet it is full of movement; for it is a mode of life. The average

age... may be stationary; though each individual is growing up towards his prime, or downwards to old age.'[33]

On the other hand, Marshall and Pigou would not touch with a barge-pole the stipulations necessary to transform a theoretical economic stationary state into a counterpart of a physical stationary state.

It is obvious from Pigou's work, *including its notes*, that he was well aware of the physical analogues to economic stationary states.

Marshall and Pigou emphasized that households were biological entities whose preferences were ceaselessly changing because of economic history. Consumption-behaviour was to be constant only in a vague aggregative sense. A Marshallian industry could be stationary only in a very special sense:

'Of course we might assume that in our stationary state every business remained always of the same size, and with the same trade connexion. But we need not go so far as that; it will suffice to suppose that firms rise and fall, but that the "representative" firm remains always of about the same size... and that therefore the economies resulting from its own resources are constant: and since the aggregate volume of production is constant, so also are the economies resulting from subsidiary industries in the neighbourhood, etc. ...'[34]

Marshall would not yield an inch to 'the fiction of a stationary state' which he did not absolutely have to yield in order to establish his propositions about long run normal prices under tranquil conditions!

It is apparent then that the neo-classical stationary state *à la* Marshall and Pigou, is not meant to be a rigorously stationary process in which appropriate operations, albeit those of a thought-experiment, lead to precisely the same measurement-values again and again and again.

§5

Cf. M. L. Burstein, *Money* (Cambridge, Mass.: Schenkman Publishing Co. Inc.; 1963), pp. 756–763, in part reproducing R. W. Clower and M. L. Burstein, 'On the Invariance of Demand for Cash and Other Assets,' *Review of Economic Studies*, Oct. 1960. It will become obvious that ¶1.A §§5 is sceptical about the foundations of Clower–Burstein, granting that we appear to be correct on our own stipulations. Perhaps 'pensive' should be substituted for 'sceptical'.

Recall the discussion in Chapter 1 of the aggregation problem in econometrics. It has relevance for, say, a problem of estimating aggregate demand for cash balances relative to various data-specifications. Now consider a problem of predicting how the distribution of the proportions of cash balances of households, classified by income, might be affected by one or another parametric change over various intervals. No new methodological issue is raised. *Now* consider the last-mentioned problem in a thoroughly disaggregated context: we are to consider distribution of cash balances amongst households taken up one by one, each represented by a demand function rooted in preference analysis. Serious methodo-logical issues now arise. Amongst other things, the relevant stationary state analysis becomes much tighter and, alas!, probably rigorously inadmissible.

There are at least three ways in which 'biology' affects the theory of economic processes *worked out over calendar time*:

1) preferences of economic actors are affected by the interaction of ageing and experience of the economic process in ways that cannot be known 'now' ('I' today am different from 'me' tomorrow; cf. related textual discussion) so that it is chimerical to represent a given actor at calendar-date t by a behaviour-function, rooted in preference analysis, assigned to him for calendar-date 0;
2) as an economic actor passes through his life cycle, he will vary his consumptions and accumulations (e.g., saving in middle-age and dis-saving in old-age), even under a putative original plan, so that no 'particle' at any time ever intends to repeat date t's economic acts at date $t+1$, quite aside from (1) above;
3) in general, some of the actors will die before the process reaches date h whilst others will have become entitled to make economic decisions, so that it is mechanically impossible to work out a dynamic process in calendar time for a given collection of economic actors unless, perhaps, they are to be immortal eunuchs (but cf. (1)).

Economist-liberals are oddly vague about what is a household and what is an individual. (Cf. ¶10.2 §§2 *infra*.) Of course, the distinction is not important for our immediate, non-normative, discussion.

Thus we cannot construct as an analogy to a problem in completely-disaggregated preference-orientated economic dynamics a collection of objects in a bottle arranged in equilibrium in a certain way. The bottle is shaken. Ideally, after a time, the original equilibrium arrangement is restored. Crudely, the lusty wenches and bold jack-a-napes of date 0 may be dry-dugged and grey-bearded at date t. Nor is there *any* valid analogy which occurs to me for a thought experiment in calendar time.

We conclude, then, that systems of the form $\dot{x} = f(x)$ where x_j may be a vector of excess-demands by the jth household, identified by a preference-function from the onset of the analysis, are not meet for full-equilibrium (stationary state) analysis—partly, and very crudely, because the mortal households in the long run simply will all be dead.

'*In the long run* we are all dead.' The context is *not* an attack on Protestant Virtue. Rather Keynes is earnestly urging economists to study transitional phenomena in connexion with the Quantity Theory of Money, stipulated broadly to be valid.[35]

Of course, the conclusion of ¶1.A §§5 fully justifies the shyness of Marshall and Pigou towards stationary states, whilst jeopardizing more ambitious full-equilibrium analyses. More constructively, ¶1.A §§5 reminds us that:

> '... Quantum physics abandons individual laws of elementary particles and states *directly* the statistical laws governing aggregations and its laws are for crowds and not for individuals.'[36]

Thus, if economists choose to do stationary state theory, we reckon that they should heed at least these caveats:

1) aggregation *à la* Marshall and Pigou is in order. Appropriate entities are such as 'the proportion of households headed by males aged 34–37 owning Shell shares';
2) and following from (1), stationary state theory properly concerns only the most coarse features of preference analysis and, in any serious sense, mostly eschews it;
3) and following from (1) and (2), demand-analysis (for example) is, for 'stationary-state' purposes best *not* rooted in aggregation of micro-behaviour. Certainly disaggregation to the level of households appears to be inappropriate.

The implications appear to be rather farther reaching but are gracefully suppressed throughout the book.

Finally, there is perhaps a moral to be drawn from this appendix. After all, nobody ever has collected, or even concocted, data revealing a stationary economic process. Stationary state theory truly belongs only to an imaginary realm.

All the trouble comes when theorists leave this realm's meta-time.

Render therefore unto Theory
The things which are Theory's.

Consider related topic, *the neutrality of money*. Monetary-neutrality also can be meaningful only in meta-time. Cf. M. L. Burstein, *Money* (Cambridge, Mass.: Schenkman Publishing Co. Inc.; 1963), Chap. 14C, pp. 749–763. Cf. also, Franco Modigliani, 'The Monetary Mechanism and Its Interaction with Real Phenomena,' *The Review of Economics and Statistics*, Feb. 1963 (Supplement), pp. 79–107, esp. §II, pp. 83–88.

REFERENCES

1. G. Debreu, *Theory of Value* (New York: John Wiley & Sons; 1959), p. 30.
2. Bertrand Russell, *A History of Western Philosophy* (New York: Simon & Schuster; 1945), p. 658.
3. John Hicks, *Capital and Growth* (Oxford: The Clarendon Press; 1965), pp. 49–50.

4. Paul A. Samuelson, *Foundations of Economic Analysis* (Cambridge, Mass.: Harvard University Press; 1947), p. 8.

5. Cf. D. W. Bushaw and R. W. Clower, *Introduction to Mathematical Economics* (Homewood, Ill.: Richard D. Irwin, Inc.: 1957), pp. 51–53.

6. A. A. Andronow and C. E. Chaikin, *Theory of Oscillations* (Princeton: Princeton University Press; 1949), p. 7.

7. Hermann Weyl, *Philosophy of Mathematics and Natural Science* (New York: Atheneum; 1963), pp. 95–96. (Originally published by Princeton University Press, 1949.)

8. Lindsay and Margenau, *Foundations of Physics* (New York: Dover Publications, Inc.; 1957), p. 189 and note pp. 188–201.

9. P. W. Bridgman, *The Logic of Physics* (New York: Macmillan; 1927), p. 5.

10. Louis de Broglie, *The Revolution in Physics* (London: Routledge & Kegan Paul; 1954), p. 207 and note pp. 205–211.

11. H. Theil, *Linear Aggregation of Economic Relations* (Amsterdam: North Holland Publishing Co.; 1954), p. 1.

12. Cf. R. G. D. Allen, *Mathematical Economics* (London: Macmillan & Co.; 1956), Chap. 20, and E. Malinvaud, *Statistical Methods of Econometrics* (Chicago: Rand McNally & Co.; 1966), pp. 117–135.

13. A. Einstein and L. Infeld, *The Evolution of Physics* (New York: Simon & Schuster; 1942), pp. 299–302.

14. E. Malinvaud, *Statistical Methods of Econometrics* (Chicago: Rand McNally & Co.; 1966), p. 64 and note Chapter 5 and pp. 139, 140, 143, 168–171, in context of §2.

15. Cf. Franklin M. Fisher, *The Identification Problem in Econometrics* (New York: McGraw-Hill Book Co.; 1966). Also T. C. Koopmans, 'Identification Problems in Economic Model Constructions,' Chap. 3 (pp. 27–48) of W. Hood and T. Koopmans, ed., *Studies in Econometric Methods* (New York: John Wiley & Sons Inc.; 1953), best known as Monograph 14.

16. Cf. A. Goldberger, *Econometric Theory* (New York: John Wiley & Sons Ltd.; 1964), pp. 282–284.

17. Cf. J. Johnston, *Econometric Methods* (New York: McGraw-Hill Book Co.; 1963), Chap. 1.

18. J. Johnston, *Econometric Methods* (New York: McGraw-Hill Book Co.; 1963), fn. 6, p. 244.

19. Cf. J. Johnston, *Econometric Methods* (New York: McGraw-Hill Book Co.; 1963), p. 242 ff.

20. J. Johnston, *Econometric Methods* (New York: McGraw-Hill Book Co.; 1963), pp. 245–246.

21. D. V. T. Bear and D. Orr, 'Logic and Expediency in Economic Theorizing,' *The Journal of Political Economy*, April 1967, pp. 188–196.

22. Cf. R. Courant, *Differential and Integral Calculus* (New York: Interscience Publishers Inc.; 1936), Vol. 2, pp. 188–203.

23. Adam Smith, *The Wealth of Nations*, 1776, Book 4, Chap. 2 (p. 423 of the Modern Library edition of E. Cannan's edition, issued in 1937).

24. Robert W. Clower, 'The Keynesian Counter-revolution: A Theoretical Appraisal,' pp. 103–125 of F. H. Hahn & F. P. R. Brechling (eds.), *The Theory of Interest Rates* (London: Macmillan & Co. Ltd.; 1965).

25. R. B. Lindsay and H. Margenau, *Foundations of Physics* (New York: Dover Publications Inc.; 1957), pp. 2–3.

26. Cf. especially J. M. Keynes, *The General Theory of Employment, Interest and Money* (London: Macmillan & Co. Ltd.; 1936), pp. 220–221 and 374–377.
27. G. C. Archibald and R. G. Lipsey, 'Monetary and Value Theory: A Critique of Lange and Patinkin,' *Review of Economic Studies*, Oct. 1958. Also the Symposium on Monetary Theory published in the *Review of Economic Studies*, Oct. 1960.
28. J. S. Mill, *Principles of Political Economy* (London: Longmans, Green & Co.; 1909), Ashley Edition, p. 746. (Mill goes on to emphasize that economic welfare and economic growth are not the same thing.) Cf. also Chapter 2 *infra*.
29. J. M. Keynes, *The General Theory of Employment, Interest and Money* (London: Macmillan & Co. Ltd.; 1936), p. 220.
30. J. M. Keynes, *The General Theory of Employment, Interest and Money* (London: Macmillan & Co. Ltd; 1936), pp. 375–376.
31. Cf. Sir John Hicks, *Capital and Growth* (Oxford: The Clarendon Press; 1965), Chap. 5.
32. A. C. Pigou, *The Economics of Stationary States* (London: Macmillan & Co. Ltd.; 1935), p. 81.
33. A. Marshall, *Principles of Economics* (London: Macmillan & Co. Ltd.; 1920), 8th ed., pp. 366–367.
34. A. Marshall, *Principles of Economics* (London: Macmillan & Co. Ltd.; 1920), 8th edn., p. 367.
35. J. M. Keynes, *A Tract on Monetary Reform* (London: Macmillan & Co. Ltd.; 1923), p. 80.
36. Einstein and Infeld, *The Evolution of Physics* (New York: Simon & Schuster; 1942).

CHAPTER 2

Introduction to General-equilibrium: Endowments, Techniques and Tastes

1. INTRODUCTION

Modern economics has developed from two strands of thought never properly integrated. The 'classical' strand, represented by such writers as Ricardo and Marx, illuminates macrodynamics but obfuscates value theory. The 'neo-classicals', including Cournot, Walras and Marshall, broke open value theory but either ignored macrodynamics or got it wrong.

§2

Classical economics ignores choice theories. Economic actors—workers, peasants, landowners, *entrepreneurs*—either save or consume all of their incomes. So for the classical economist economic development is importantly affected by how income is distributed. The classical model is highly aggregated. All commodities are put into one or two pigeon-holes, another reason why choice theory became neglected. The classical model is dynamical. Classical economics is a theory of economic development based on a highly stylized 18th and early 19th century historical perspective. Marx, for example, was interested in a special dynamical problem: how might capitalist systems break down? He never solved his problem correctly, but he did lay a foundation for Keynes, Harrod and other 20th century economists emphasizing the relationship between the level of economic activity and economic growth.

§3

Neo-classical economics is especially concerned with *allocation* of resources between activities at a moment in time.

34

The activities being contemplated and the products being traded can occur in the future however.

Neo-classical economic actors are landowners-labourers-*rentiers*-capitalists. So distribution plays a lesser rôle in neo-classical than in classical economics, and, since allocation is in its bones, neo-classical theory ideally is highly disaggregated, dealing with countless commodities. The *pièce de résistance* of neo-classical theory is *general-equilibrium*, a state in which the actions of firms and households are optimal relative to prevailing prices and consistent with each other. Since equilibrium is an equipoise of conflicting forces, neo-classical theory does not readily encompass motion, but, instead, has developed a method of comparative statics treating parameter-changes, a method keyed to thought-experiments which cannot be interpreted in calendar time.

2. THE RICARDIAN BACKGROUND

What were the stylized facts confronting European economic historians *circa* 1800? Workers and peasants, condemned to penury by their adamant sexuality, had lived close to a margin of subsistence from time out of mind. The aristocracy, including the Crown, lavishly spent the proceeds of their vast rental incomes on consumption goods, including châteaux and wars. Much of the labour force serviced unproductive consumption. The frugal bourgeoisie, augmented by exceptional agronomist aristocrats (a prototype being the great von Thünen) comprised the *entrepreneur* class, living simply, devoting much of their incomes to accumulation of productive capital.

In the upshot an economy unwilling or unable to import food would eventually confront a barrier imposed by the limited supply of arable land. Eventual economic stagnation would then be unavoidable. And the significant economic struggle was between urban or rural capitalists and landowners: was national income to be ploughed back or consumed? Workers and peasants earned the same meagre average income in any event. A larger accumulation of capital merely meant that more workers and peasants could be supported at an ineluctable margin of subsistence.

R. Tawney and M. Weber argued that Calvinism promoted economic growth. The Tawney–Weber hypothesis appears to be easily refutable but too attractive to be discarded. Cf. R. H. Tawney, *Religion and the Rise of Capitalism* (New York: Harcourt, Brace & Co.; 1926) and Max Weber, *The Protestant Ethic and the Spirit of Capitalism* (New York: Charles Scribner's Sons; 1930).

I do not recall general refutations of the Tawney–Weber hypothesis, but that paragon of common sense, the late Pieter Geyl, surely has punctured it in the Dutch context. Cf. Pieter Geyl, *The Revolt of the Netherlands* (London: Ernest Benn Ltd.; 1958), esp. pp. 16–17.

§ 2

Rephrasing the conclusions of ¶2.2 §§1 :

1) in classical economics, distribution (between landowners and capitalists) and growth are inextricably linked;
2) in a *closed* system the land barrier must become a clog on growth.

In Britain early in the 19th century the land-barrier loomed quite close. It seemed important to the classical economists to repeal the Corn Laws (i.e. to remove tariffs on grain importations) in order to postpone stagnation and, as cereal prices inevitably fell, to redistribute income from landowners to *entrepreneurs*.

§ 3

Classical writers, notably Ricardo, specified an agricultural technology which might be described as peasant-*cum*-plough working on land, subject to diminishing returns. Labour-capital inputs are doses of labour-capital. Each dose consists of a peasant working with a standard outfit of equipment. Thus the data of Fig. 1. Annual (net) corn production (x)

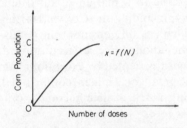

Fig. 1.   Corn Production

is a function of the number of doses (N). Corn production increases with N at a decreasing rate: $f''(N) < 0$: incremental yields fall as more labour-capital works against the fixed quantum of land or, more realistically, as inferior land is brought under cultivation and superior land is worked harder.

The subsistence wage rate is w^0 bushels per annum and is affected by sociology while reflecting requirements of infants and other unproductive members of families. The distance 0A in Fig. 2 measures w^0. It is clear that in equilibrium no more than 0B doses will be employed on the land : the 0Bth dose barely yields enough extra corn to feed the 0Bth peasant.

If full weight is accorded to Malthusian population theory, a giant step can be taken. Roughly speaking, an indefinitely large supply of labour is stipulated to be available at w^0, neglecting such motes as gestation

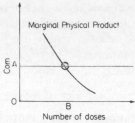

Fig. 2.   Wage Rates and Productivity

periods and transformation of infants into labourers. Furthermore, the prevailing wage rate cannot long be anything but w^0: if $w > w^0$, the labour force will increase by leaps and bounds as the birth rate rises and the death rate falls; if $w < w^0$, the labour force will decay rapidly as the birth rate plunges and the death rate soars. The supply of labour is perfectly elastic at w^0. Next note that, even if the rent of capital were zero, it never would pay rural *entrepreneurs* to use more than 0B labourers at $w = w^0 = 0A$: the $(0B+1)$st dose yields less than 0A bushels per period. It follows from Fig. 1 that the upper limit of grain (corn) production for a society with the land area and technology so far stipulated is 0C bushels per period.

Additional inferences can be drawn. Consider the expression

$$\frac{0C - w^0(0B)}{w^0} \tag{1}$$

$w^0(0B)$ is the corn-consumption requirement of the rural labour force.

Expression (1) defines the upper limit of the number of labourers who ultimately can be supported in the manufacturing sector. Denote the quotient by 0D. What about manufacturing technology? Neglect land as an input in manufacturing. One labourer working with a standard outfit of equipment yields one unit of manufactures per period. Maintaining the zero-interest-rate assumption and neglecting depreciation, the price of a unit of manufactures, measured in corn, would be w^0 in equilibrium. Competition amongst manufacturers would drive down this price to w^0.

The value of aggregate product, measured in bushels of corn, ultimately would be $0C + w^0 0D$ and $0B + 0C$ machines would have been accumulated when the economy passed into the stationary state. The manufactures would then be consumed by the landowners whose rental income, measured in corn, would be $0C - w^0 0B$. The wage bill in manufacturing, equal to manufacturing proceeds, would be equal to landowner expenditures: $(0C - w^0 0B)/w^0 \cdot w^0 = 0C - w^0 0B$.

Now drop the zero-interest-rate (zero-rate-of-profit) assumption. After all, sharing out between landowners and capitalists determines the system's dynamic. Furthermore, we must account for the capital accumulated when the system becomes stationary—how could capital be accumulated if the only savers, the capitalists, never had net income?

'Capitalists' include farmers renting land from landowners and hiring peasants.

The essential result, a stationary state imposed by the land constraint, is unaffected by the switch in stipulations: specify a rate of interest (equal to the rate of profit here), i^0, at which *entrepreneurs* forgo additional accumulation and lapse into 'landowner' behaviour, spending all of their incomes. Of course, the length 0B would have to be adjusted. At a positive interest rate, farmers would pull in their intensive margins of cultivation. Fewer than 0B labourers would work the land in the stationary state. The corn-surplus available for feeding industrial workers would be less.

The note which follows this section shows how machine rents and commodity prices behave as the inevitable, perhaps affluent, stationary state is approached. Valuing outputs at constant prices, Fig. 3 crudely

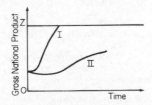

Fig. 3   Classical Dynamics

suggests classical dynamics. If landowner shares lag behind *entrepreneur* shares over the major span of development history, more consumption will be productive. Relatively more corn will be used to feed workers fabricating machinery or tilling the soil. Curve I will describe economic history and not Curve II, drawn up for a case in which landowners' shares are persistently higher.

Only if the land restraint is removed, can the upper limit, 0Z, be broken through. If food can be obtained at fixed terms of trade from abroad in exchange for 'our' manufactures, the land restraint will have been removed. The economy's possibilities for food production then can at least be represented by its production function for manufactures and variable inputs in indirect food production will enjoy constant returns to scale.

Define K_t as the stock of homogeneous capital in the tth period, a predetermined amount. K_{t1} is capital employed on the fixed aggregate lump of land. The price of manufactured goods, measured in corn, is p. Other corn-values include i, the hire-price of a machine, and

R, total rental proceeds of landowners. The equilibrium of the classical system in the tth period is determined through equations (2) to (5) in the variables p, i, R, and K_{t1}:

$$w^0(K_t - K_{t1}) + i(K_t - K_{t1}) = p(K_t - K_{t1}) \tag{2}$$

$$w^0 K_{t1} + i K_{t1} + R = f(K_{t1}) \tag{3}$$

$$i K_t + R = p(K_t - K_{t1}) \tag{4}$$

$$w^0 K_t = f(K_{t1}) \tag{5}$$

In both sectors one labourer associates with one machine. Total employment depends on total accumulation, K_t. Nor is there a wages fund problem. Current output feeds the workers. Labour supply is infinitely elastic at w^0. Since the number of labourers in the manufacturing sector is equal to the number of machines employed there, the manufacturing sector's wage bill is $w^0(K_t - K_{t1})$.

Competition assures that wages and machine rents exactly absorb total revenues—hence equation (2). Equation (3) requires that total corn production, defined on the number of labour-capital doses in agriculture (K_{t1}) and denoted $f(K_{t1})$, be shared amongst claimants (before consumption of course) so that nothing remains after wages, machine rents and land rents are paid. The left-hand side of equation (4) defines total demand for manufactures, measured in corn. The right-hand side of equation (4) defines the value of manufactures (at p), since $K_t - K_{t1}$ units are produced. Equation (5) requires that the wage bill equals the supply of corn. Workers, the only corn eaters, consume all of their incomes.

Taking total differentials of equations (2) to (5)

$$(K_t - K_{t1})\,di + (K_t - K_{t1})\,dp - (w^0 + i - p)\ dK_{t1} + 0\ dR = (w^0 + i - p)\,dK_t \tag{6}$$

$$K_{t1} \qquad di + 0 \qquad dp + (w^0 + i - f')\,dK_{t1} + 1\ dR = 0 \qquad dK_t \tag{7}$$

$$K_t \qquad di + (K_t - K_{t1})\,dp + p \qquad dK_{t1} + 1\ dR = (p - i) \qquad dK_t \tag{8}$$

$$0 \qquad di + 0 \qquad dp + f' \qquad dK_{t1} + 0\ dR = w^0 \qquad dK_t \tag{9}$$

The left-hand determinant's value is $\Delta = -f'[(K_t - K_{t1})^2 + (K_t - 1)(K_t - K_{t1})] < 0$. Note that

$$di/dK_t = (K_t - K_{t1})[(i - p) - (w + f')]/\Delta = \begin{vmatrix} (w^0 + i + p) & K_t - K_{t1} & -(w^0 + i - p) & 0 \\ 0 & 0 & (w^0 + i - f') & 1 \\ (p - i) & K_{t1} - K_t & p & 1 \\ w^0 & 0 & f' & 0 \end{vmatrix} \div \Delta \tag{10}$$

The numerator will be positive if $f'(1 - p + i) > (1 - p + i)$, i.e. if $f' > 1$ in the solution. The marginal productivity of a dose of labour-capital must exceed unity. This condition is easily met: e.g., $w^0 > 1$ assures that $f' > 1$ in equilibrium. If the inequality condition is met, the hire-price of machinery must fall as capital accumulates. The rate of profit can be defined as i/p, the ratio of the hire-price (rent) of capital to the price of a unit of capital. By equation (2), $p = w + i$, the rate of profit is $i/(i + w)$ and

$$d[i(i + w)^{-1}]/di = w^0/(i + w^0)^2$$

The rate of profit falls as i falls and, if the inequality-condition is met, i *does* fall as accumulation increases. Q.E.D.

3. MARXIAN SHARDS

In Marxian economics the concept of the limitational land factor is eschewed. The logical consequences are profound—more profound than Marx realized. But somehow the olio comprised of Ricardian and Marxian thought, admixed with marginalism, has led to modern macroeconomics, indelibly associated with Keynes.

§ 2

We define Marxian technology: the one and only good is produced by labour-*cum*-capital—one unit of labour per period, working with one machine, produces one unit of final product per period. Next we stipulate that workers consume all of their incomes whilst capitalists plough back all of their profits into their businesses. ('Accumulate, accumulate! That is Moses and the prophets.')

It would follow, from what has been said thus far, that, if the *rate of exploitation*, roughly the proportion of profits (non-wage) income to wage income were high, investment would be correspondingly high, as would be the rate of growth of employment in industry and labour-income: employment and accumulation are rigidly linked up by the Marxian production function. In other words, since the fundamental Marxian model poses no problem of *effective demand*, in this model the level of employment depends only on the level of capital accumulation, given the technique(s) of production built into that capital. Indeed this Marxian system could carry on indefinitely at an arbitrarily high rate of exploitation, i.e. low rate of consumption. If profits were 80 per cent of national income, so would be investment expenditure. For a unitary capital-output ratio, the rate of accumulation would be 80 per cent per annum!

§ 3[1]

Of course, Marx could not be comfortable with a model which was at best Stalinist and at worst portrayed how capitalism could chug on unperturbedly at arbitrarily high rates of exploitation. It would not have been natural for Marx as a classical economist to accept such a verdict:

> 'It was a generally accepted tenet in the orthodox economics of Marx's day that there is a long run tendency for the rate of profit on capital to fall. Marx accepted this view and set himself to account for the phenomenon of falling profits. His explanation does not turn upon the difficulty of realizing surplus value—the problem, as we now say, of a deficiency of effective demand—but is intended to be valid even when that problem does not arise.
> 'He based his explanation upon the rising organic composition of capital [to be taken as capital per man employed]....'[2]

If the rate of profit were surely to fall secularly due to increasing capital per employee—at least tacitly suggesting development of a clog on accumulation—the rate of exploitation would have to be constant (or falling) unless in some sense the *marginal productivity of capital* were falling. The proof is easier if we note that the rate of profit can be defined as

$$\frac{\text{profit}}{\text{circulating capital} + \text{fixed capital}} \simeq \frac{\text{profit}}{\text{wages} + \text{fixed capital}}$$

$$= \frac{\Pi}{K_1 + K_2}$$

always neglecting the matter of effective demand until ¶2.3 §§4.

It is assumed that the circulating capital consists of wage goods and the unit-interval is defined, so that the wage bill for that interval is equal to the amount of wage goods that must be kept in stock.

It becomes obvious that if the rate of exploitation (here Π/K_1) and marginal productivity of capital (best thought of here as Π/K_2) each were constant, the rate of profit would be constant. Also that the rate of profit would fall if Π/K_2 were to fall over time, the rate of exploitation remaining constant. Nor can we neglect the case which completes the taxonomy, an increasing rate of exploitation more than offset by falling marginal productivity of capital.

Alas, so to derive a falling rate of profit is to do violence to Marxian logic (as did K. Marx himself):

1) so long as the marginal productivity of capital is positive, increasing accumulation will lead to increased output per employee. So if the real-wage rate does not increase, the share of labour would secularly fall—*and* the Marxian wage-theory *does* call for a constant or falling real-wage rate and hence for a secularly increasing rate of exploitation.

2) 'An attempt might be made ... to rescue Marx from his inconsistency by arguing that, in a given state of knowledge, the marginal productivity of capital must be assumed to fall very sharply beyond a certain point. On that assumption, accumulation will lead sooner or later to a falling rate of profit, even when real wages are constant. But it is very un-natural to assume given knowledge in a dynamic system, and, certainly, that assumption is alien to Marx's method, for, in his scheme, an increase in the ratio of capital to labour can only occur as a result of ... a change in technical knowledge. ... A theory of falling profits based on the falling marginal productivity of capital would be something quite different from Marx's theory'.[3]

Recall also that we showed in ¶2.2 §§2 (especially in the note at the end of that section) that it was the limitational land-factor that set up the falling rate of profit in Ricardo's theory. Marx specifically eschewed this concept! In the case of the falling rate of profit Marx's classical instinct was betrayed by his deviationism.

We conclude then that, so long as the matter of effective demand is ignored, Marxian logic, requiring as it does an increasing rate of exploitation and no worse than constant *marginal productivity of capital*, calls for secularly increasing rates of profit.

§ 4[4]

The *bête noire* for Marx then was *effective demand*. As Mrs. Robinson shows, he came close to the heart of the matter from time to time, especially in his theory of industrial crisis, but all in all:

> '[t]he theory of the falling rate of profit is a red herring across the trail, and prevented Marx from running the theory of effective demand to earth.'[5]

The discords were to be resolved by the Liberal, Keynes, many years later.

Briefly limning the factors required for conversion of the Marxian model into a modern model of income and employment, whilst noting that both are in the *bootstrap* family, *entrepreneurs* (and others once the theory of consumption is enlarged) must be given *options* for the use of their savings and the allocation of their resources: physical investment, cash hoarding, bonds, etc.

If capital markets are highly imperfect, the decision to save can perforce be a decision to make a physical investment. For example, a farmer who is unable to buy financial instruments necessarily would channel his savings into a new silo, land clearing, etc., always excluding cash hoarding.

Thus Keynes! Once financial assets are introduced, the requirement for moving economic equilibrium, that is, that if ρ^* is to be an equilibrium rate of growth, the rate of profit generated at ρ^* must induce accumulation at the rate ρ^*, no longer can be fulfilled automatically. A number of the central themes of modern economics, being in a way the logical extension of Marx's pother over the falling rate of profit in its macro-guise, burst out at this point of the argument, including:

1) the dependence of the level of aggregate demand on the rate of economic growth (cf. Part IV);
2) the extent to which a capitalist system can grow as rapidly as *entrepreneurs* wish it to grow. Although, by the same token, if *entrepreneur* animal spirits should flag, their profits will fall along with the rate of growth, leading to still more depressed spirits, etc. (cf. Part IV);
3) the relationship between distribution of income and economic growth, possibly the most characteristic Ricardian–Marxian theme (at least when the theory of value—the labour theory of value—is put aside).

Perhaps the seminal article for contemporary discussion is Nicholas Kaldor, 'Alternative Theories of Distribution', *Review of Economic Studies*, Vol. 23, No. 2, 1955–1956. A brilliant critique and extension of Kaldor's system was presented by Luigi Pasinetti in the *Review of Economic Studies*, Nov. 1962. Mrs. Robinson's work, cited in ¶2.3, is also highly valuable in this connexion.

It should be noted that the relationship between distribution and accumulation also is significant in a stream of literature entirely different from that of ¶2.3, namely the 'forced saving' theme associated with the Swedish school and the late Sir Dennis Robertson (noting that I am using 'forced saving' entirely for evocative purposes, *not* as a word of art). See D. H. Robertson, *Banking Policy and the Price Level* (London: Staples Press Ltd.; 1949) and Sir Dennis Robertson, *Essays in Money and Interest* (London: Collins; 1966). A good introduction to the Swedish school approach is W. J. Baumol (with Ralph Turvey), *Economic Dynamics* (New York: The Macmillan Co.; 1951), Chap. 8. An exceptionally able 'Swedish' statement is Erik Lindahl, *Studies in the Theory of Money and Capital* (London: George Allen & Unwin; 1939). Note Lindahl's correct analysis of 'forced saving', cf. especially pp. 155 and 173.

4. A SIMPLE NEO-CLASSICAL MODEL

The central *motif* is 'general-equilibrium as determined by the interaction of endowments, techniques, and tastes'. The institutional setting is a private ownership economy, although Chapter 11 shows that it need not be. The actors are guided by prices and, indeed, producers are assumed simply to be maximizing wealth or profits or some other value-weighted sum. The governing technique of analysis is comparative statics. It answers such queries as 'how would clothing prices relative to food prices be affected by improvements in house-building technology?' Neo-classicism focuses on prices. Prices are parameters for individual traders *and* endogenous variables to be determined in general-equilibrium. Prices are weights in calculations of individual wealth and income *and* emerge from dual solutions to primal social problems of efficient use of resources.

If the decision-unit's own labour is an important input in production, as typically is true for a family farm, the theory of the firm and that of consumer choice cannot be partitioned. Queries such as 'should I take a longer siesta or produce enough for another bowl of rice' cannot then be ignored. On the other hand, the consumer-preferences of the president of Gigantic Corporation can be neglected and Gigantic shareholders typically spend no time on company affairs. Not that tastes and preferences can be altogether neglected even in the Gigantic case, especially if risk is introduced. Tastes and preferences are introduced into the producers' sector in the Gigantic case through the share market: contending managements planning for more profitable programmes at the same level of risk ideally would outbid others.

In modern economics, most production decisions are taken by firms, not household-firms. To the extent that preference analysis impinges upon the theory of the firm, that disembodied being is dealt its own utility function, which ignores consumption. The firm does not consume commodities for pleasure. Ideally the firm's utility function can be made to collapse into a value-of-shares-maximization criterion.

§ 2

A simple model reveals much. There are to be two factors, labour and capital. Each capacity is 100 units. Each factor is zero-elastic in supply: 100 units of each can be obtained at any non-negative price. There are two final products, food and clothing. Technologies are rigid: 1 unit of labour associates with 2 units of capital to obtain 1 unit of (capital-intensive) food per period; 2 units of labour associate with 1 unit of capital to obtain 1 unit of (labour-intensive) clothing per period.

Technologies and endowments interact. Compare Fig. 4. The feasible region is 0APB; the feasible frontier is APB. Only at P, the vertex, are both constraints, AF and EB, binding; one or the other factor is redundant at any feasible point other than P.

No point belonging to segments AP or PB is categorically 'inferior' to any other: something must be sacrificed if any point belonging to APB is superseded. *Choice* must be made between the technologically efficient points belonging to APB. Chapter 3 formally analyses household-choice and Chapter 10 social-choice.

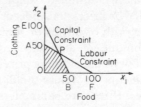

Fig. 4   Endowments and Technology

We pause for two observations, one on 'holism', the other on the rôle of prices in neo-classical economic theory.

Karl Popper has punctured 'holistic' theories attributing more or less literally organic properties to the state.

'Holism' ascribes to the whole, France, organic properties of Frenchmen: an 'holistic' view sees France as growing, decaying, waxing, waning, falling ill, etc.[6]

The abstract object, United States of America, is incorporeal, inanimate. It neither likes nor dislikes. It was not born. It does not live. It will not die. Tastes and preferences can be attributed to Americans but not to America. Perhaps this is unfortunate. The model, as stated, could, upon specification of American preferences, be manipulated to discover the most preferred point belonging to APB. But a long, circuitous route, not completed until the end of Chapter 10, must be taken in order properly to treat simultaneously the preferences of individuals comprising a society.

Intuition suggests that household preferences should give rise to demand functions or correspondences for commodities, functions defined on prices. Prices define the terms on which commodities can be substituted for each other. Profit-maximizing firms, forced by limited market power to be price takers, can be expected to choose productions which maximize price-weighted sums defining differences between receipts and costs.

Amongst other things, prices define the terms of trade between labour and objects of consumption.

In general, each household owns a variety of productive resources. In a capitalist system, relative-price changes affect wealth-distribution as well as market rates of substitution between commodities. Thus, if changed tastes cause the price of food to increase relative to the price of clothing, owners of productive agents specialized to food tend to gain at the expense of owners of productive agents specialized to clothing: capitalists benefit at the expense of labourers. Why? Initial excess demand for food and initial excess supply of clothing lead to higher food- and lower clothing-prices: clothing producers plan to release labour in greater proportion to capital than food producers plan to employ. Equilibrium requires that capital-rents rise relative to wage rates, inducing adoption of more labour saving techniques. How might the distributive and allocative roles of pricing be divorced? One device would be re-distribution through tax-subsidy policies. Again, an idealized socialist system might make subventions to households which bear no relation to shadow prices of factor services. Cf. Chapter 11 *infra*.

§3

Consider a *competitive market*, an abstract concept. *Inter alia* producers take as given their output- and input-prices.

Some commodities used in the production of commodities might be fabricated within the firm. Still in a competitive economy such commodities, if traded at all, will be perfectly elastic in demand or supply for any seller or buyer in the open market: prices will be parameters for all concerned.

The text's model cannot determine the size-distribution of producers.

Competitive firms, seeking to maximize their values, will try to expand marginally-profitable and contract unprofitable processes. The result in the system of ¶2.4§§2 is that average costs of production will equal prices in equilibrium. If price exceeds cost, factor prices will be bid up. If cost exceeds price, the item will be dropped.

Turn again to Fig. 4. Stipulate the existence of Point Q, belonging to APB, at which there can exist general competitive equilibrium so that at prices $(\bar{p}_1, \bar{p}_2)$ planned demands *and* supplies are described by Q. Surprisingly concrete inferences can be drawn if prices are *normalized* on a *numéraire*'s price. Specifically, define the price of food, p_1, as 1: food is the *numéraire* good. All other prices are to be normalized on p_1: if 2 units of clothing exchange for 1 unit of food, $p_2 = 0.5$.

Unit distance must be defined in any scheme of measurement. Consider measurement of heat, weight, height, etc.

The argument leads to equations (11) and (12):

$$w_1 + 2w_2 = 1 \qquad\qquad (11)$$

$$2w_1 + w_2 = p_2 \qquad\qquad (12)$$

Competition assures that in equilibrium prices will be equal to costs of production.

Marginal and average costs are identical for individual producers in this model.

What if Q belongs to AP, not P? Capital will be redundant. Competition amongst capitalists—i.e. everyone—will assure that rent of capital, w_2, will fall to zero so that $\bar{w}_1 = 1$ and $\bar{p}_2 = 2$. (Equilibrium values always are barred: the equilibrium value of p_r is denoted $\bar{p}_r$.)

What if Q belongs to BP, not P? Labour will be redundant. Competition amongst labourers—in general everybody—will assure that the wage rate, w_1, will fall to zero so that $\bar{w}_2 = 0{\cdot}5$ and $\bar{p}_2 = 0{\cdot}5$.

In this way upper and lower limits for equilibrium values of w_1, w_2, and p_2 have been established: $\bar{w}_1$ cannot exceed 1 and $\bar{w}_2$ cannot exceed 0·5, whilst either, but not both, might be zero; $\bar{p}_2$ ranges between 0·5 and 2.

What if Q is at P? Both constraints then bind; neither factor is redundant. Equilibrium values for w_1, w_2, and p_2 will range between 0 and 1; 0 and 0·5; and 0·5 and 2 respectively.

As more techniques and commodities are introduced, including commodities produced exclusively by one or another factor, redundancy possibilities in equilibrium fade away. The feasible frontier becomes smoother. Tangent planes to the surface can be defined for more and more price ratios.

Sensitivities of demands to relative prices, elasticities of substitution in demand, will determine the specific equilibrium values. Above all there is the interdependence of endowments, techniques, and tastes. The Golden Fleece of classical price theory is unattainable: relative prices cannot be explained invariantly against demand.

§4

Considering the simple model's algebra, equations (13) to (16) of **S1** state clearance conditions for the food, clothing, labour, and capital markets while equations (17) and (18) reflect profit-maximizing behaviour of competitive producers. Satisfaction of **S1** defines general-equilibrium.

$D^1(p_2, w_1, w_2)$ defines demand for food on p_2, w_1, and w_2 for example. D^1 is a functional operator, *not* a variable of the system. y_1^s and y_2^s are supplies of food and clothing. Equations (15) and (16) define capacity constraints.

$$D^1(p_2, w_1, w_2) = y_1^s \tag{13}$$

$$D^2(p_2, w_1, w_2) = y_2^s \tag{14}$$

$$y_1^s + 2y_2^s = 100 \tag{15}$$

S1

$$2y_1^s + y_2^s = 100 \tag{16}$$

$$w_1 + 2w_2 = 1 \tag{17}$$

$$2w_1 + w_2 = p_2 \tag{18}$$

§5

There are six equations in the five unknowns p_2, w_1, w_2, y_1^s, and y_2^s, but it can be proved that one of equations (13) to (16) is redundant. The crux is equation (19):

$$w_1 \tilde{y}_1^s + w_2 \tilde{y}_2^s + (y_1^s + p_2 y_2^s - w_1 \tilde{y}_1^d - w_2 \tilde{y}_2^d) = y_1^d + p_2 y_2^d \tag{19}$$

The planned supply of the jth factor is denoted $\tilde{y}_j^s$ and that of the ith output, y_i^s. The planned demand for the ith output is denoted y_i^d. Underlying equation (19) is the assumption that planned expenditures are equated with planned incomes, that *budget constraints* are exactly observed. Hence the left-hand side of equation (19) defines the nominal value of aggregate demand. It defines planned incomes for any constellation of prices. The planned income from sales of the services of the jth factor is $w_j \tilde{y}_j^s$, planned profits, $\mathbf{p} \cdot \mathbf{y}^s - \mathbf{w} \cdot \tilde{\mathbf{y}}^d$. (Planned receipts of firms are $\mathbf{p} \cdot \mathbf{y}^s$ and planned disbursements by firms are $\mathbf{w} \cdot \tilde{\mathbf{y}}^d$.) Therefore the right- and left-hand sides of equation (19) define the same thing: aggregate demand expressed in 'money'. *Upon postulation of budget constraint*, equation (19) becomes an identity.

Walras's Law is implicit in equation (19). This can be seen at once simply by rearranging terms:

$$w_1(\tilde{y}_1^s - \tilde{y}_1^d) + w_2(\tilde{y}_2^s - \tilde{y}_2^d) + p_2(y_2^s - y_2^d) = y_1^d - y_1^s \tag{20}$$

That is,

$$-\sum_1^{n-1} E_i = E_n, \qquad \sum^n E_i = 0 \tag{21}$$

where E_i is an excess (*planned*) demand. In words, *Walras's Law* asserts that in a system under budget constraint, the nominal excess demand for the nth commodity, E_n, is equal to the sum of nominal excess supplies of the other $n-1$ commodities in absolute value and is opposite in sign. We may put the Law as follows: in a 'competitive' system under budget constraint, values of excess demands are *linearly dependent* so that at least one excess-demand equation is always redundant.

Our model of a simple economy can be manipulated to demonstrate Walras's Law in yet another way. Thus consider a special problem: show that excess demand for food must be zero if the other markets are equilibrated. Agreed the answer is obvious from equation (20), but consider this more elaborate demonstration which may have a certain didactic value. First restate the special problem: it is to be shown that satisfaction of equations (14) to (18) assures satisfaction of equation (13). Then note that satisfaction of equations (17) and (18) assures that profits will be zero, that unit costs will be equated with prices, so that:

$$y_1^s + p_2 y_2^s - w_1 \tilde{y}_1^d - w_2 \tilde{y}_2^d = 0 \tag{22}$$

Next note that satisfaction of equations (15) and (16) assures that $\tilde{y}_j^d = \tilde{y}_j^s$, so that equation (19) can be rewritten:

$$w_1 \tilde{y}_1^d + w_2 \tilde{y}_2^d = y_1^d + p_2 y_2^d \tag{23}$$

Since satisfaction of equations (17) and (18) implies equation (22) there follows:

$$y_1^s + p_2 y_2^s = y_1^d + p_2 y_2^d \tag{24}$$

However, satisfaction of equation (14), assures that $y_2^d = y_2^s$. Hence:

$$y_1^s = y_1^d \quad (!) \tag{25}$$

§6

S2, a more-elegant form of S1, distils neo-classical theory:

$$f^2(p_2, w_1, w_2; \tilde{y}_1^0, \tilde{y}_2^0) = 0 \tag{26}$$

$$f^3(p_2, w_1, w_2; \tilde{y}_1^0, \tilde{y}_2^0) = 0 \qquad \textbf{S2} \tag{27}$$

$$f^4(p_2, w_1, w_2; \tilde{y}_1^0, \tilde{y}_2^0) = 0 \tag{28}$$

Functions f^i determine excess demand for clothing, labour and capital. Upon solving **S2** for $(\bar{p}_2, \bar{w}_1, \bar{w}_2)$, totally differentiate **S2** around the solution point:

$$f_{p2}^i \, dp_2 + f_{w_1}^i \, dw_1 + f_{w_2}^i \, dw_2 = -f_{\tilde{y}_1}^i \, d\tilde{y}_1 - f_{\tilde{y}_2}^i \, d\tilde{y}_2 \qquad i = 2, 3, 4 \tag{29}$$

Comparative-statics operations, the very stuff of neo-classical value theory, now can be performed. The matrix of the coefficients of the left-hand side of equations (29) is denoted (f_j^i) and its determinant Δ. The cofactors of the first column of (f_j^i) are Δ_{21}, Δ_{31}, and Δ_{41}. A change in the supply of capital, *ceteris paribus*, affects the equilibrium price of clothing as in equation (30).

$$d\bar{p}_2/d\tilde{y}_2^0 = -(\Sigma f_{\tilde{y}_2}^i \Delta_{i1})/\Delta \qquad i = 2, 3, 4 \tag{30}$$

§7

Empty spaces must be filled in, but the outlines of neo-classical economic theory are clear. Corroborative material mostly consists of variations on the theme:

'general equilibrium as determined by interaction of endowments, techniques and tastes.'

1. Cf. Joan Robinson, *An Essay on Marxian Economics* (London: Macmillan & Co.; 1949), Chap. 5. Also Paul M. Sweezy, *The Theory of Capitalist Development* (New York: Oxford University Press; 1942).
2. Joan Robinson, *An Essay on Marxian Economics* (London: Macmillan & Co.; 1949), p. 35.
3. Joan Robinson, *An Essay on Marxian Economics* (London: Macmillan & Co.; 1949), pp. 37–38.
4. Cf. Joan Robinson, *An Essay on Marxian Economics* (London: Macmillan & Co.; 1949), Chap. 6. Also her introduction to Rosa Luxemburg, *The Accumulation of Capital* (London: Routledge & Kegan Paul; 1951), pp. 13–28. Also Joan Robinson, *The Accumulation of Capital* (London: Macmillan & Co.; 1956), esp. Book 2 and her *Essays in the Theory of Economic Growth* (London: Macmillan & Co.; 1962), esp. pp. 17–21 and Part II.
5. Joan Robinson, *An Essay in Marxian Economics* (London: Macmillan & Co.; 1949), p. 51.
6. Karl Popper, *The Poverty of Historicism* (London: Routledge & Kegan Paul; 1957).

PART II

Some Microeconomic Theory

CHAPTER 3

Consumer Choice

1. INTRODUCTION TO PART II

Part II elaborates the neo-classical theory of ¶4 and then sets up a microeconomic basis for Keynesian theory as well. *Optimization* by households and firms under constraint is the *pièce de résistance* of each of its six chapters. Part II lays behaviourist foundations for Part III which shows how interaction of atomistic economic decision-units, each maximizing an objective function—perhaps a value-weighted sum—leads to certain laws of motion including the special case of general competitive equilibrium. As Chapter 11 shows, these decision-units need not own the resources they manage for the theory of general competitive equilibrium to be relevant. Chapter 11 shows how socialist economics can be approached neo-classically.

Not all of Part II leads up to neo-classical general-equilibrium theory. Only theory about firms and households trading under purely-competitive conditions does so. However, Chapters 6 to 8, dealing with imperfect competition, monopoly and oligopoly, are important for modern income theory about firms and households typically unable to sell or buy all they would like to at going prices. Modern income theory can be interpreted so as to preserve a sense of general-equilibrium.

2. INTRODUCTION TO CHAPTER 3

The bulk of Chapter 3 deals with perfectly knowledgeable consumers governed by specified axioms and under non-stochastic constraints. (Decision-making under uncertainty is treated only laconically in ¶3.6 and ¶3.7.) Fortunately, Chapter 3 can easily be generalized and extended. Once the 'standard theory of ordinal utility' is ingested, most of conventional theory becomes accessible: the theory of the firm, theorems about optimal growth configurations, welfare economics, all can be grasped.

53

54

3. THE AXIOMATIC APPROACH TO CONSUMER CHOICE THEORY

Assumptions about preferences necessary for later proofs of the existence of general competitive equilibrium are now to be set out.[1] Very little cross-reference is necessary between ¶3.3 and ¶3.4:

1) ¶3.4 postulates existence of continuous utility functions possessing continuous first- and second-order partial derivatives whilst ¶3.3 does not require that utility functions exist;

Strictly the 'continuous first- and second-order partial derivative' requirement is all that is needed. But 'this function would be of little interest if it were not continuous'.[2] Compare ¶3.3 §§4.

2) ¶3.4 tacitly adopts strong-convexity assumptions.

The strong-convexity assumption requires that, if bundles x_j^1 and x_j^2 are indifferent for the jth consumer, the bundle

$$tx_j^2 + (1-t)x_j^1$$

will be preferred to either, t being a positive fraction.[2]

§2

The primal concepts of a formal choice theory yielding consumer equilibrium and continuous individual demand functions (a luxury) and consistent with requirements for existence of general-equilibrium are consumption sets, preferences, and wealth constraints.

§3

The consumer's consumption plan concerns inputs (food for example) represented by positive numbers and outputs (labour for example) represented by negative numbers. Not all consumption plans (consumptions) which a consumer might contemplate are technologically possible:

'the decision for an individual to have during the next year as a sole input one pound of rice and as output 1000 hours of some type of labour could not be carried out.'[3]

Nor could one plan to work more than 24 hours a day. The set of all technologically possible consumptions for the jth consumer is to be called his consumption set, X_j. Among other things X_j is convex and connected. No two points in X_j can be joined by a straight line not contained in X_j (crudely, convexity); X_j is made up of one piece (crudely, connectedness).

X_j also is closed and has a lower bound. As for closure, cf. footnote, p. 55. Lower boundedness simply requires that there exist a point x each of whose coordinates is less than any point in X_j. Surely this is plausible: consumptions cannot be less than zero; there are physiological limits on outputs. Upper-boundedness requires that a set not have points arbitrarily far from the origin and that the set be contained within some closed cube.

§4

The consumer contemplates X_j according to his *preferences*. It is assumed that, as between any two bundles x_j^1 and x_j^2, the consumer either prefers one or the other or is indifferent (the *axiom of selection*). The *j*th consumer's preferences are to be transitive: if he prefers x_j^1 to x_j^2 and x_j^2 to x_j^3, he prefers x_j^1 to x_j^3. The *j*th consumer cannot become satiated. No matter which consumption in X_j is contemplated, there always is another consumption, also in X_j, which he prefers.[4] In this way:

> 'the consumption set X_j is partitioned into indifference classes. Is it possible to associate with each class a real number in such a way that, if a class is preferred to another, the number of the first is greater than the number of the second? In other words, given a set completely preordered by preferences, does there exist an increasing... real-valued function on that set? Such a set is called a *utility function*....'[5]

Debreu proves that existence of a *continuous* utility function is assured if, so to speak, the *j*th consumer's preferences are smooth.

Begin with *closedness*. To say that X_j is closed is to say that X_j contains all of its accumulation points. Cf. T. Apostol, *Mathematical Analysis* (Reading, Mass.: Addison-Wesley Pub. Co.; 1957), pp. 43–44: '... z is called an accumulation point of **S**, provided that every neighbourhood of **z** [**z** need not be in **S**] contains at least one point of **S** distinct from **z**.' [T. Apostol (1957), p. 43.] How can **z** not be in **S**? Consider a tiny hole in **S**. Thus closedness and continuity.

[k] In general a function f is continuous at the point x^0 if '$x^q \to x^0$, $y^0 = f(x^0)$, $y^q = f(x^q)$' implies '$y^q \to y^0$'. That is, as x^q approaches x^0, y^q approaches y^0, y^q and y^0 being defined on x^q and x^0 by f.

Debreu shows[5] that, if one assumes that for any point x_j in X_j the set of points in X_j at least as desired as x_j and the set comprised of points in X_j at most as desired as x_j both are closed in X_j, then existence of a continuous utility function can be proved.

There must be made an important convexity assumption about preferences, albeit not as strong as that of the note at the end of ¶3.3 §1. Roughly speaking, if x_j^2 is preferred to x_j^1, then a weighted average of x_j^2 and x_j^1 will be preferred to x_j^1, the weights being positive fractions t and $(1-t)$.

M. Richter elegantly develops the *Representability Problem* in M. Richter, 'Revealed Preference Theory,' *Econometrica*, Vol. 34, No. 3 (July 1966), pp. 635–645. (Cf. his bibliography, pp. 644–645.) The Representability Problem is a more-rigorous evolvement of the *Integrability Problem* [cf. R. G. D. Allen, *Mathematical Analysis for Economists* (London: Macmillan & Co. Ltd.; 1938), pp. 440–442 and R. G. D. Allen, *Mathematical Economics* (London: Macmillan & Co. Ltd.; 1956), pp. 669–670], noting that Richter essentially disproves Allen's concluding dictum.

There are in fact *two* representability problems: '(1) given a demand function, can we tell whether it could be induced by a utility function...; (2) given a demand function, can we tell whether it could be induced by a preference relation?' (Richter (1966), p. 635). Richter solves both problems. As for the first, he establishes a theorem together with a corollary (admittedly not the strongest possible) for a consumer of ¶3.3: if the set of all bundles chosen for some budget is convex and the set h(**B**) is closed, then the consumer is representable by a utility function. The set h(**B**) 'may be thought of as the set of most desired bundles available under budget B'. (Richter (1966), p. 635.)

Perhaps the most interesting feature of Richter's analysis is that 'in fact, with these new methods one can show that "almost" every rational competitive consumer is representable'. [Richter (1966), p. 641.] ' A consumer h is *rational*... if there exists a binary relation G ("at least as good as") on **X** [a set of bundles] which is total, strongly reflexive, and transitive on **X**....' [Richter (1966), p. 636.] The reflexive law of logic is a = a. [Cf. G. Birkhoff and S. MacClane, *A Survey of Modern Algebra* (New York: The Macmillan Co.; 1953), rev. ed., p. 3.]

Finally we note the following interesting remark: 'the interest of representability lies in the fact that, when faced with difficult problems in economic theory, economists often assume they can replace consumer preferences by numerical representations or utility functions. The question then arises: How much does this assumption limit the resulting economic theory?... Since a representable consumer acts as though he were maximizing a numerical function subject to budget constraints, representability is a necessary and sufficient condition for applicability of utility theory to consumer theory.' [Richter (1966), p. 636.] So we see why it is especially interesting to find that the answer to Richter's question is, 'not much'.

§5

Total expenditure is to be constrained by wealth. The consumer's problem is to achieve the most preferred point in X_j which is consistent with his wealth constraint.

Commonly, loosely, called his budget constraint. More precisely, a bundle is to be selected from the set of feasible bundles in X_j not less preferred than any other feasible bundle which can be purchased.

We focus on derivation of a demand correspondence between the *j*th consumer's wealth and the prices facing him and his optimal consumption plan. If the consumption set X_j is compact as well as convex, then, subject only to a quite trivial exception, the demand correspondence from the set of price-wealth pairs to that of optimal feasible-consumptions will be continuous. This is necessarily unique under the strong-convexity assumption of the note at the end of 3 §1. This result turns out to be important.

A compact set is closed and bounded. Boundedness and closedness are defined on pp. 54–55.

The correspondence is between $(\mathbf{p}, w_j)$ and $\bar{x}_j$, where w_j is the *j*th consumer's wealth.

§6

The utility function is not important in formal analysis. The argument simply focuses on properties of correspondences between price-wealth constellations and equilibrium consumptions as mediated through a consumption set (a commodity space) and various general properties of preferences. The theory turns on measurable objects: prices and commodities.

¶3.3 and Debreu's book ignore interdependence of utilities. Your rates of consumption of oranges, automobile services, etc., have no effect on my preferences which, accordingly, are defined on *my* consumptions only. This assumption cruelly wounds preference analysis as a guide to welfare economics.

4. ORDINAL UTILITY

¶3.3 shaped a rigorous theory especially equipped to lead into an axiomatic approach to general-equilibrium. ¶3.4, concerned with properties of choices by households with unlimited appetites and limited budgets, is looser. The theme is choosing at margins, the melody being carried by the differential calculus. Since the calculus requires highly restrictive stipulations, ¶3.5 becomes interesting: the method of *revealed preference* poses thought-experiments based on less drastic restrictions on preference and shucks off the heavy burden of the utility function.

§2

'Utility function' was defined in ¶3.3. The *utility analysis of choice*, the matter of ¶3.4, begins with certain problems in coordinate transformations.

An *ordinal* measure ranks bundles only as 'most preferred', 'next most preferred',..., 'least preferred'. Ordinal measures are unique only up to monotonic transformations; *cardinal* measures are unique up to choice of origin and unit distance.

Consider this example. The jth consumer (household) contemplates bundles $x_j^1, x_j^2, \ldots$. He prefers x_j^1 to x_j^2 and prefers x_j^2 to x_j^3. Column (2) of Fig. 1 is a correct ordinal ranking. So is Column (3). Indeed so would be any other column in which the ordering was unchanged. Any monotone of Column (2) tells the same ordinal story. The gaps between entries of Columns (2) and (3) tell different *cardinal* stories.

Again referring to Fig. 1, let us compare Columns (3) and (4). These are substantively identical, even cardinally. Columns (3) and (4) appear to be different only because of a tacit shift in origin. Now consult Fig. 2: its new scale is constructed without changing the positions of the objects being measured. It is less obvious that Columns (3) and (5) of Fig. 1 tell the same story, but Fig. 3 shows that they do. Once again the points stay put. Only the descriptive numbers are changed and then only because of a change in the definition of unit distance. Perhaps, upon reflexion, the result should have been obvious: any system of measurement arbitrarily determines unit length, but ratios of measured distances are invariant against the stipulation of unit distance, given the origin.

(1) BUNDLE	(2) UTILITY[a]	(3) UTILITY[b]	(4) UTILITY[c]	(5) UTILITY[d]
x_j^1	100	100	91	10
x_j^2	70	20	11	2
x_j^3	2	10	1	1

Fig. 1   Ordinal Rankings

	x_j^3	x_j^2	x_j^1
0 1	9 10	20	100
	0 1	11	91

Fig. 2   Shift in Origin

	x_j^3	x_j^2	x_j^1
0	10	20	100
0	1	2	10

Fig. 3   Change in Definition of Unit Distance

It will be shown that the weaker, ordinal, stipulation about the measurability of utility suffices here.

Mathematical physics has been more deeply concerned about invariance against coordinate transformations and has successfully deployed the *tensor calculus* in that connexion. 'To grasp a condition of the world as completely as it is in our power to grasp it, we must have in our minds a symbol which comprehends at the same time its influence on the results of all possible operations. Or, what comes to the same thing, we must contemplate its measures according to all possible measure codes.... A tensor expresses simultaneously the whole group of measure numbers associated with any world condition.' A. S. Eddington, *The Mathematical Theory of Relativity* (Cambridge: The Cambridge University Press; 1924), 2nd ed., p. 3.

Let us proceed fairly systematically, hopefully developing the simplest notions of the tensor calculus. We shall not meaningfully penetrate economic theory with the tensor calculus but perhaps will lay a foundation. Also note that excellent introductions to the subject include J. L. Synge and A. Schild, *Tensor Calculus* (Toronto: University of Toronto Press; 1949), and G. Y. Rainich, *Mathematics of Relativity* (New York: John Wiley & Sons Inc.; 1950).

Transformation of coordinates $\mathbf{x}$ into $\mathbf{x}'$ is, let us say, accomplished by $\mathbf{x}' = f(\mathbf{x})$ so that, to a linear approximation, $d\mathbf{x}_j' = (\partial \mathbf{x}_{ji}'/\partial \mathbf{x}_i) d\mathbf{x}_i$. Then the quantities comprise a *contravariant vector*. In 4-space a contravariant vector can be written:

$$dx_\mu' = \sum_{\alpha=1}^{4} (\partial x_\mu'/\partial x_\alpha) dx_\alpha \qquad \mu = 1, 2, 3, 4 \tag{1}$$

Of course, α and μ are coordinate systems: we are switching from system α to system μ. A *covariant vector* in 4-space is a set of four quantities transformed by

$$dx'_\mu = \sum_{\alpha=1}^{4} (\partial x_\alpha/\partial x'_\mu)\, dx_\alpha \qquad \mu = 1, 2, 3, 4 \tag{2}$$

Covariant vectors appeal less to the intuition than do contravariants.

In fact our vectors have been *tensors* of the first rank. Consider now the transformation

$$x'_\mu = f^\mu(x_1, x_2, x_3, x_4) \qquad \mu = 1, 2, 3, 4 \tag{3}$$

associated with the 4×4 matrix (containing, of course, 16 elements)

$$(\partial x'_{\mu\alpha}/\partial x_\alpha) \qquad \alpha', \mu = 1, 2, 3, 4 \tag{4}$$

and, implicitly, also the 4×4 matrix

$$(\partial x_{\alpha\mu}/\partial x'_\mu)$$

A set of quantities (Υ^{mn}) (here 16) are said to be components of a *contravariant tensor* of the second order if they transform according to the equation

$$\Upsilon'^{rs} = \Upsilon^{mn}(\partial x'^r/\partial x^m)(\partial x'^s/\partial x^n) \qquad r, s, m, n = 1, \dots, 4 \tag{5}$$

The definition of a *covariant tensor* is close to the surface:

$$\Upsilon'_{rs} = \Upsilon_{mn}(\partial x^m/\partial x'^r)(\partial x^n/\partial x'^s) \tag{6}$$

§3

Utility is not satisfaction, nor is it a psychic concept. Utility is merely a style of index numbers ranking preferences. But the utilitarian or Benthamite stream of thought did (does?) regard utility as a measure of pleasure. Juxtaposing this error with cardinality, interpersonal comparison, and diminishing marginal utility of income, august economists have made baseless arguments for egalitarianism. (Cf. note at the end of this section.) We shall show, however, that rigorous demand theory, associating consumption plans or observed market behaviour with price-wealth constellations, can be based on ordinal utility or on *no* utility. Even if 'utility' is retained, the central propositions of demand theory can be derived assuming interpersonal incomparability and are invariant against increasing or decreasing marginal utility of income.

The 'old' welfare economists thought of 'national utility' rather as one thinks of national income. For them utilities could be added. The origin and unit distance being defined, utilities of different persons could be compared and added up. Thus cardinalism and interpersonal comparisons. Furthermore, the 'old' welfare economists felt intuitively that as wealth or income grew utility increments fell. Thus diminishing marginal utility of income. Next two jokers were inserted into the deck:

1) all 'persons' (it never was clear how families ought to be treated) were to be alike as pleasure machines;

2) interdependence was to be neglected so that possibilities of your pain giving me pleasure or of my enjoyment of my house depending on yours were to be neglected.

The fruit, when placed within a naïve statical model was egalitarianism: so long as wealth was unevenly distributed, 'national utility' could be increased by taxing the rich in favour of the poor.

Remove one of the jokers. Assume that persons are not alike as pleasure machines: (some) archbishops should be called upon to subsidize playboys! 'We are not amused.'

Chapter 10 examines a 'new' welfare economics, based on ordinal utility or none at all and evoked by the term 'Pareto optimality'.

After the Italian economist and sociologist Vilfredo Pareto, author of *Manuel d'Économie Politique.*

Once again we will return an unfavourable verdict, arguing that economic theory should not become tied to consensual theories of the state.

There are deeper objections to basing intertemporal policies (are there any other?) on utility. 'I' today am different from 'me' tomorrow. Today's events will make me unpredictably different tomorrow. Professor Popper has shown that one cannot predict effects of future discoveries. Cf. K. Popper, *The Poverty of Historicism* (London: Routledge & Kegan Paul; 1960), 2nd ed.

Benthamism ('the greatest good of the greatest number'), rooted in Hobbesian possessive individualism, lives on even in sophisticated modern utility-orientated approaches to social choice. [For a most useful discussion of 'possessive individualism', see C. B. Macpherson, *The Political Theory of Possessive Individualism: Hobbes to Locke* (Oxford: The Clarendon Press; 1962).] Still the nexus, the state, cannot be necessarily an additive combination of individuals, recalling again how hard it is to deal with families. Nor is this to embrace 'holist' fallacy. Stopping far short of Fichte, the state's logical, as against organic, substance can be said not to be apprehensible through opinion polls. The General Will, Rousseau's slack variable, cannot disguise the Government's responsibility for unborn persons, minors and the 'me' of tomorrow. Nor is Revelation to be dismissed, although Thomist proofs of the existence of God might not be accepted. Who is to say that, *a priori*, Kings are not elect of God?

Cf. Professor Pigou, a writer whom I much admire nonetheless: 'We must not hesitate, therefore, to conclude that, so long as the dividend as a whole is not diminished, any increase, within wide limits, in the real income enjoyed by the poorer classes, at the expense of an equal decrease in that enjoyed by the richer classes, is practically certain to involve an addition to economic welfare.' [A. C. Pigou, *The Economics of Welfare*[5] (London: Macmillan; 1950), 4th ed., p. 96.] (For Pigou, the *national dividend*, an objective concept, was to be counterpointed with *economic welfare*, an admittedly 'elastic' concept.) Of course, to assert that economic theory cannot justify egalitarianism *a priori* is not to say that egalitarianism cannot be justified (as perhaps it might by Revelation).

§ 4

Utility theory now is to be tied to demand theory. Happily a two-commodity model can develop the important themes of the utility analysis of choice: equation of internal- with external-rates of substitution: the

rôle of convexity: substitution- and income-effects, comprising price
effects. Consider Fig. 4: AB, the price- or budget-line, is the frontier of the
feasible region 0AB: purchases cannot exceed \$200. Commodity 1 and
Commodity 2 can be substituted in the market at the rate of two units of
Commodity 1 for one unit of Commodity 2: $p_1 = \$1$; $p_2 = \$2$.

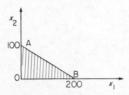

Fig. 4   The *j*th Consumer's Budget Constraint

X_j, defined as in ¶3.3, here is the positive quadrant of Fig. 4. Only inputs are being considered.

The accounting unit, the money of account, is to be the dollar.[6]

Next a continuous ordinal utility function is defined on the rates of
consumption x_1 and x_2: $U = U(x_1, x_2)$. Consider the indifference classes
of the function U obtained by sorting out horizontal cross-cuts in the
3-space comprised of points referred to x_1, x_2 and U. The strong-convexity
assumptions of ¶3.4 yield up the indifference map of Fig. 5 (imposed on
Fig. 4): the subjective (internal) rate of substitution between Commodity 1
and Commodity 2 diminishes as x_1 increases relative to x_2.

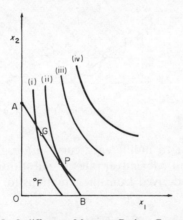

Fig. 5   Indifference Map *cum* Budget Constraint

Postulation of a continuous utility function $(U_1, U_2 > 0)$ assures symmetry and reflexness. Now, comparing Fig. 6, non-satiety assures that $U_D > U_C$ whilst symmetry of preferences implies $U_C = U_E$ and $U_D = U_E$, so that symmetry, and also reflexness, lead to $U_D = U_C$. Ergo $U_D > U_C$ *and* $U_C = U_D$ *if* indifference curves could intersect! So postulation of a continuous utility function (in conjunction with non-satiety) precludes intersection of indifference curves.

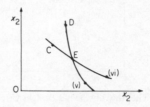

Fig. 6   Transitivity and All That

Utility is to be maximized subject to budget constraint. Obviously $\bar{x}$ will be on AB: there always is a point belonging to AB, for example, G, which is preferred over any feasible point, for example F, not belonging to AB. Under our convexity and non-intersection assumptions, the optimality of P is intuitively obvious. Any indifference class at a higher level of utility is altogether outside of the feasible region.

Where thoroughgoing convexity is not required, the correct statement is that at a solution such as P the indifference curve must be convex to the origin. Otherwise a small movement from P would lead to higher utility or, alternatively, the utility level achieved at P could be achieved with less expenditure. The diagram makes this clear.

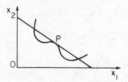

Fig. 7   Concavity at P

Line AB is tangent to indifference curve (ii) at P: the external and internal (objective and subjective) rates of substitution are equal at P.

This result can be derived from the equations for indifference curves and price-lines:

$$dU = 0 = U_1 \, dx_1 + U_2 \, dx_2 \qquad (7)$$

In words, 'as one moves along an indifference curve', total utility is constant. Hence equation (7) holds in the limit for small variations in x_1 and x_2, where the partial derivative U_1 is the rate at which utility changes with x_1 at $(\bar{x}_1, \bar{x}_2)$, x_2 held constant. Equation (8) follows from equation (7):

$$-dx_1/dx_2 = U_2/U_1 \tag{8}$$

Note that dx_1/dx_2 must be negative so long as both consumptions have positive marginal utility, i.e. so long as the partial derivatives are positive. Equation (9) describes a price-line:

$$p_1 x_1 + p_2 x_2 = k \tag{9}$$

Differentiate equation (9) with respect to x_1 and x_2, obtaining equation (10) or (11).

$$p_1 \, dx_1 + p_2 \, dx_2 = 0 \tag{10}$$

$$-dx_1/dx_2 = p_2/p_1 \tag{11}$$

The slopes of the indifference curve and the price-line are equal in equilibrium: $-U_1/U_2 = -p_1/p_2$. The price-line is tangent to the indifference curve containing P at P: the marginal utilities are proportional to the prices.

Turn to comparative statics. Fig. 8 concerns consumer response to a reduction in p_1, money-income and p_2 held constant.

Strictly we are concerned with *replacement sets*, 'the price of Commodity i' from which p_1 and p_2 are drawn. Strictly, p_1 symbolizes a particular value, a drawing from its replacement set, and *not* the replacement set itself, i.e. 'price of Commodity 1'.

The new budget line is AC. Equilibrium consumption of Commodity 1 increases by TZ whilst that of Commodity 2 decreases by LM: equilibrium occurs at R instead of P. The change in planned consumption of Commodity 1 incident to a change in its price is an *own-price effect*.

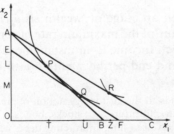

Fig. 8   Components of Price Effects

A thought-experiment permits a price effect to be broken down into two components, substitution- and income-effects, leading to one of the signal demonstrations in traditional economic theory. Upon a change in p_1, the consumer's income is to be adjusted (here reduced) so that the equilibrium utility-level is unchanged. The budget-line EF reflects such a *compensated* price change, leading to the price-effect TU.

TU is a *substitution-effect* of a price change. TU must be positive for $\Delta p_1 < 0$ and negative for $\Delta p_1 > 0$: the convexity of the set of consumptions preferred to P requires that Q be to the right of P if the budget-line is flattened.

POINT. The substitution effect of a positive (negative) own-price change is unambiguously negative (positive).

Cross-relationships, i.e. effects of changes in the price of one commodity on demand for another, are considered in ¶3.4 §§8.

UZ is an *income-effect* of a price change, that part of the price effect, TZ, unaccounted for by a relative-price change, by the substitution effect. UZ reflects the influence of a change in the equilibrium level of utility. The income effect is ambiguous: a commodity might be *superior* or *inferior* for the jth consumer. Demand for superior goods increases with income whilst that for inferior goods decreases as income is conceived to increase, *ceteris paribus*. An inferior good might be a *Giffen Good*: the own-price effect might be perverse.

Cf. ¶3.4 §§6. The amount of 'money' freed or the initial deficit induced by a price change will depend on how much expenditure the commodity absorbs in the initial plan. Thus a Giffen Good is an inferior good which initially is important enough in the consumption plan for the income effect to swamp out the substitution effect.

Note that a commodity need not be uniquely superior or inferior for a consumer. Thus my demand for hamburger might increase with income over a certain range and then decrease as modest affluence gives way to *entrecôte-bordelais* riches. Also note that it can be impossible to set up empirical counterparts to the text's thought-experiments. The text defines hypothetical plans being made at an instant in time whilst data collected from the 'real' world either will be collected over a fairly long time span or for different persons now.

§5

We pause to tighten up usage of 'wealth *vis à vis* income'. Income is best defined as the value of the maximum rate of consumption permitting wealth to remain intact. Income is an instantaneous flow rate.[7] (In most of Chapter 3 initial and end-period wealth are to be zero.) What is the jth consumer's wealth?

'[Wealth] corresponds to the customary notion of present value of everything (real estate, cars, furniture, ..., stocks, bonds, ...) the jth consumer owns, adding debts owed to him, subtracting debts he owes, ... each item being properly discounted.'[8]

Perhaps the definition should be recast to emphasize that the *j*th consumer owns *himself*, a source of future receipts from labour service.

One's wealth can be immense and one's income negative: a paralytic's sole assets could be a stock of valuable paintings, declining in price. A man without wealth could have a large income: perhaps a boxing champion.

Finally, cash inflow and income are not the same. A man may enjoy unrealized capital gains whilst not earning a salary, receiving dividends, etc., still he may earn more income than another who enjoys substantial cash inflow from non-appreciating property.

The present value of receipts R_1 and R_2, accruing one and two years from now, is $\rho_1 R_1 + \rho_2 R_2$ where $\rho_i = 1/(1+r_i)$, r_i being the appropriate discount rate. Since \$1 invested now would accumulate to \$$(1+r_1)$ in a year, a rational purchaser would pay no more than \$$1/(1+r_1)$ for the right to receive \$1 one year from now: the *present value* of the claim is \$$1/(1+r_1)$. In an idealized world, but one excluding involuntary servitude so that one cannot sell *himself*, the text's definition of wealth becomes

$$W_{Nj} + \sum_{}^{i} \rho_i R_{ij}$$

where W_{Nj} is the market value of the *j*th consumer's non-human wealth and R_{ij} is the *i*th element in the *j*th consumer's time-series of receipts from sales of his labour services.

Note that here, as virtually everywhere in this book, taxation-effects are neglected.

§6

Turning to *the algebra of consumer choice*, the problem is to maximize utility subject to a budget constraint: $U = U(\mathbf{x})$ is to be maximized subject to $\mathbf{p} \cdot \mathbf{x} = Y$, $U(\mathbf{x})$ having continuous first- and second-order partial derivatives.

In order to lighten notation subscripts are dropped when meaning is not thereby obscured. Note that the analysis above concerns *one* consumer.

($U(\mathbf{x})$ also is to be continuous, although this property is not analytically necessary for what follows.) We are to form the Lagrange function $U(\mathbf{x}) - \lambda(\mathbf{p} \cdot \mathbf{x} - Y)$. The Lagrange multiplier, λ, is an unknown and can be interpreted as the marginal utility of income. Partial differentiation of the Lagrange function with respect to $x_1, x_2, \ldots, x_n$ and λ leads to **S1**:

$$U_i - \lambda p_i = 0 \qquad i = 1, 2, \ldots, n \tag{12}$$

S1

$$\mathbf{p} \cdot \mathbf{x} = Y \quad \text{or} \quad \sum_{}^{n} p_i x_i = Y \tag{13}$$

S1 is to be solved for $\bar{\mathbf{x}}$, $\bar{\lambda}$. When utility is maximized, $U_r/U_s = p_r/p_s = \lambda > 0$. So the solution is invariant against a *k*-fold increase in all prices and in income: standard demand functions of the form $\mathbf{x} = \mathbf{f}(\mathbf{p}, Y)$ are zero-order homogeneous in $\mathbf{p}$ and Y.

The economic interpretation of $\bar{\lambda}$ as the marginal utility of income is now to be demonstrated. Define the marginal utility of income as dU/dY, noting that $dU = \Sigma U_i \, dx_i$. Budget constraint requires $dY = \Sigma p_i \, dx_i$. In equilibrium $U_i = \lambda p_i$. Hence

$$dU/dY = \lambda \Sigma p_i \, dx_i / \Sigma p_i \, dx_i = \bar{\lambda}$$

Equilibrium values of λ can often be interpreted as marginal values of constraint relaxations. Cf. Chapter 5.

§7

S1 states only the first-order conditions for a relative extremum. The second-order condition requires that the constrained second differential of the utility function be negative. If utility is to be maximized, permissible variations in consumption from $\bar{x}$ must lead to lower utility levels. Recall the definition of $d^2(y)$ where $y = f(x_1, x_2)$:

$$\begin{aligned}
d^2 y &= d(f_1 \, dx_1 + f_2 \, dx_2) \\
&= (f_{11} \, dx_1 + f_{21} \, dx_2) \, dx_1 + (f_{12} \, dx_1 + f_{22} \, dx_2) \, dx_2 \qquad (14) \\
&= f_{11} \, dx_1^2 + 2f_{12} \, dx_1 \, dx_2 + f_{22} \, dx_2^2
\end{aligned}$$

$f_{rs} = f_{sr}$ by Young's theorem.

Building up from a function of two variables, the second differential of a utility function with n independent variables is seen to be a quadratic form:

$$d^2 U = (dx)' A (dx) \quad \text{or} \quad d^2 U = \sum\sum U_{rs} \, dx_r \, dx_s \qquad (15)$$

A is an $n \times n$ matrix of second-order partial derivatives, the first row being $(U_{11}, U_{21}, \ldots, U_{n1})$. The alternative form of equation (15) is built up by forming the vector:

$$\begin{aligned}
(U_{11} \, dx_1 + U_{12} \, dx_2 + \ldots + U_{1n} \, dx_n) \, dx_1 \\
\cdots\cdots\cdots\cdots\cdots\cdots\cdots\cdots\cdots\cdots\cdots\cdots\cdots\cdots\cdots\cdots \qquad (16) \\
(U_{n1} \, dx_1 + U_{n2} \, dx_2 + \ldots + U_{nn} \, dx_n) \, dx_n
\end{aligned}$$

each row being of the form $\left(\displaystyle\sum_{s=1}^{n} U_{rs} \, dx_s \right) dx_r$, and then adding up the rows.

The economic interpretation of U_{rs} is the rate at which the marginal utility of the consumption of the rth commodity changes with x_s. For 'true' substitutes, $U_{rs} = U_{rs} < 0$ and for 'true' complements $U_{rs} = U_{rs} > 0$.

In general there will exist a set of consumption vectors x^*, associated with a set of vectors λ^*, which are relatively optimal (i.e. which lead to relative constrained maxima) and which accordingly satisfy the text's first- and second-order conditions.

Amongst vectors x^* are vectors $\bar{x}$ achieving a global (constrained) maximization. The text discusses $\bar{x}$, assumed for simplicity to be unique, and its appurtenant $\bar{\lambda}$. Vectors for which all 'inputs' are not positive and 'outputs' negative are excluded. (Labour services are negative consumptions.) Chapter 5 and its notes take up the relation between Lagrange-multiplier theory and activity analysis, specifically in connexion with Kuhn–Tucker theory.

Inequality- and non-negativity-constraints are neglected until Chapter 5 with the exception of ¶4.2. In fact, however, Lagrange-multiplier theory can be extended to inequality constraints and can develop optima at which some constraints are inactive and/or some activities nil. But such extensions are apt to be computationally infeasible. Cf. G. Hadley, *Nonlinear and Dynamic Programming* (Reading, Mass.: Addison-Wesley Pub. Co.; 1964), pp. 69–72.

The second-order condition for our consumer problem keys on our Lagrangian formulation. The Lagrange function, z, is $U(x) - \lambda(\mathbf{p} \cdot \mathbf{x} - Y)$. The first-order partial derivatives of the Lagrange function are:

$$\partial z/\partial x_i = U_i + \lambda p_i \tag{17}$$

$$\partial z/\partial \lambda = Y - \mathbf{p} \cdot \mathbf{x} \tag{18}$$

The second-order partial derivatives are:

$$\partial^2 z/\partial x_i \, \partial x_j = U_{ij} \qquad \partial^2 z/\partial x_i \, \partial \lambda = p_i \tag{19}$$

$$\partial^2 z/\partial \lambda \, \partial x_i = p_i \qquad \partial^2 z/\partial \lambda^2 = 0 \tag{20}$$

The second-order condition is that the quadratic form:

$$\boldsymbol{\delta}' \begin{bmatrix} \partial^2 z/\partial \lambda^2 & & \partial^2 z/\partial \lambda \, \partial x_i \\ & \partial^2 z/\partial x_i \, \partial x_j & \\ \partial^2 z/\partial x_i \partial \lambda & & \end{bmatrix} \boldsymbol{\delta} \tag{21}$$

be negative definite.

Now let us reformulate the matrix just above in terms of the consumer problem:

$$\begin{bmatrix} 0 & & p \\ & U_{ij} & \\ p & & \end{bmatrix} \tag{22}$$

The second-order condition requires that the bordered Hessians (Hessians being determinants of matrices composed of second-order partial derivatives) must obey the alternation of signs of expressions:

$$\begin{vmatrix} 0 & p_1 & p_2 \\ p_1 & U_{11} & U_{12} \\ p_2 & U_{12} & U_{22} \end{vmatrix} > 0; \qquad \begin{vmatrix} 0 & p_1 & p_2 & p_3 \\ p_1 & U_{11} & U_{12} & U_{13} \\ p_2 & U_{12} & U_{22} & U_{23} \\ p_3 & U_{13} & U_{23} & U_{33} \end{vmatrix} < 0; \dots \tag{23}$$

Adjacent determinants, formed by cutting out the outer row and column as we 'move to the left', differ in sign. As Professor Allen shows, the second-order condition also can be written:

$$\sum\sum (\Delta_{rs}/\Delta)\delta_r\delta_s < 0 \tag{24}$$

The second-order condition essentially requires that the set of consumptions preferred to $\bar{\mathbf{x}}$ be convex in the neighbourhood of $\bar{\mathbf{x}}$.[9]

where Δ is the determinant of the matrix of expression (22), Δ_{rs} is the cofactor of the element U_{rs} and where the δs can take any value not all zero. The vector $\boldsymbol{\delta}$ can be interpreted as a vector of price changes, $\mathrm{d}\mathbf{p}$: inequality (24) is built up from addition of the rows of expression (25):

$$[(\Delta_{11}/\Delta)\,\mathrm{d}p_1 + \ldots + (\Delta_{1n}/\Delta)\,\mathrm{d}p_n]\,\mathrm{d}p_1$$
$$\cdots\cdots\cdots\cdots\cdots\cdots\cdots\cdots\cdots\cdots\cdots\cdots\cdots \tag{25}$$
$$[(\Delta_{1n}/\Delta)\,\mathrm{d}p_1 + \ldots + (\Delta_{nn}/\Delta)\,\mathrm{d}p_n]\,\mathrm{d}p_n$$

The sum must be negative. Obviously, then, if $\mathrm{d}p_1 \neq 0$, whilst $\mathrm{d}p_2 = \mathrm{d}p_3 = \ldots = \mathrm{d}p_n = 0$, inequality (24) requires, since $(\mathrm{d}p_1)^2$ is positive, that:

$$\Delta_{11}/\Delta < 0 \tag{26}$$

Inequality (26) is highly important. It is at the heart of the proof of the sign of the substitution effect.

§8

Comparative statics are developed by differentiating the first-order conditions (12) and (13), obtaining system **S2**:

$$0 + p_1\,\mathrm{d}\bar{x}_1 + \ldots + p_n\,\mathrm{d}\bar{x}_n = -\bar{x}_1\,\mathrm{d}p_1 - \bar{x}_2\,\mathrm{d}p_2 - \ldots - \bar{x}_n\,\mathrm{d}p_n + \mathrm{d}Y$$
$$p_1(-\mathrm{d}\bar{\lambda}) + U_{11}\,\mathrm{d}\bar{x}_1 + \ldots + U_{1n}\,\mathrm{d}\bar{x}_n = \bar{\lambda}\,\mathrm{d}p_1$$
$$\cdots\cdots\cdots\cdots\cdots\cdots\cdots\cdots\cdots\cdots\cdots\cdots\cdots\cdots\cdots \text{ S2} \tag{27}$$
$$p_n(-\mathrm{d}\bar{\lambda}) + U_{1n}\,\mathrm{d}\bar{x}_1 + \ldots + U_{nn}\,\mathrm{d}\bar{x}_n = \bar{\lambda}\,\mathrm{d}p_n$$

The comparative statics of the text hold up only to the extent that its linear approximations are acceptable. Of course, the text's comparative statics generally pertain only to neighbourhoods of equilibria, depending as they do on limit theorems.

Observe that the matrix of coefficients of the left-hand side of **S2** is identical with the matrix of expression (22): the determinant of the matrix of 'left-hand-side' coefficients of **S2** is Δ.

Three expressions, derived from **S2**, are especially interesting:

$$\mathrm{d}\bar{x}_r/\mathrm{d}p_r = -\bar{x}_r\Delta_{0r}/\Delta + \bar{\lambda}\Delta_{rr}/\Delta \tag{28}$$

$$\mathrm{d}\bar{x}_r/\mathrm{d}p_s = -\bar{x}_s\Delta_{0s}/\Delta + \bar{\lambda}\Delta_{sr}/\Delta \tag{29}$$

$$\mathrm{d}\bar{x}_r/\mathrm{d}Y = \Delta_{0r}/\Delta \tag{30}$$

Only one parameter shifts in each instance: p_r in equation (28); p_s in equation (29); Y in equation (30). (The matrix's first row is labelled 'zero'.)

In equations (28) and (29) the price-effect has two terms and $\bar{x}_r\,dp_r$ units of 'money' are absorbed (released) by a price increase (decrease) in the case of equation (28). The original consumption, $\bar{x}$, then costs $\bar{x}_r\,dp_r$ units more (less). But equation (30) shows that the effect on consumption of the rth commodity of a reduction in income of $\bar{x}_r\,dp_r$ units is $-(\Delta_{rr}/\Delta)\bar{x}_r\,dp_r$: the first of the right-hand terms of equation (28) can be construed as the income effect of an own-price change. In interpreting the expression $\bar{\lambda}\Delta_{rr}/\Delta$ consider simultaneous changes in two parameters, specifically p_r and Y which is to change by $\bar{x}_r\,dp_r$ units. Equation (31) follows:

$$d\bar{x}_r = (-\bar{x}_r\Delta_{0r}/\Delta + \bar{\lambda}\Delta_{rr}/\Delta + \bar{x}_r\Delta_{0r}/\Delta)\,dp_r = (\bar{\lambda}\Delta_{rr}/\Delta)\,dp_r \qquad (31)$$

Hence $(\bar{\lambda}\Delta_{rr}/\Delta)\,dp_r$ is to be interpreted as the effect on equilibrium consumption by the jth consumer of the rth commodity of a *compensated* change in its price. It is the *substitution-effect* of a price change and is *approximately* equal to the effect of a price change accompanied by an income change such that maximized utility would be unchanged. Similarly, $(\bar{\lambda}\Delta_{sr}/\Delta)\,dp_s$ is a substitution-effect measuring the change in the equilibrium consumption of the rth commodity occasioned by a change in p_s accompanied by an income-change of $\bar{x}_s\,dp_s$ units. If Δ_{sr}/Δ is positive, the rth and sth commodities are substitutes; if Δ_{sr}/Δ is negative, the commodities are complements, always for the jth consumer.

Mnemonic examples would be butter and eleomargarine (substitutes) and phonograph-records and phonograph-needles (complements), but, rigorously, nuts and tennis racquets might be substitutional or complementary pairs.

POINT. In the traditional model of consumer choice, the price effect is broken down into a substitution- and an income-effect. The substitution-effect approximately explains that part of the variation of equilibrium consumption caused by changes in relative prices, utility being held constant.

The Slutsky compensation is inaccurate. The consumer is overcompensated. If he is given $\bar{x}_r\,dp_r$ more units of 'money' when p_r increases by dp_r, he can continue to purchase $\bar{x}$ if he wishes to do so. However, he will not wish to maintain $\bar{x}$: $\bar{x}$ will not be optimal relative to new relative prices. Thus a consumer compensated by $\bar{x}_r\,d\mathbf{p}_r$ will achieve a higher utility level as a result of the experiment.

Dr. Mosak has proved that the error in the Slutsky compensation is of the second order of smalls, decreasing more rapidly than the other arguments as the differentials of prices and/or income approach their (zero) limiting values. We are reminded, *en passant*, that the differential expressions for the text's dependent variables are approximations of exact changes: they are first differentials. This is to say that the text deals with a linear approximation to the utility (hyper)surface in the neighbourhood of the initial equilibrium, $\bar{x}$.

§ 9

Rules can now be accumulated about signs of price-, income- and substitution-effects. The procedure brings the second-order condition into play and invokes a *correspondence principle*: inferences about signs of comparative-statics relationships are drawn from the stipulation that the second-order condition is satisfied.

Sometimes the second-order condition is called a stability condition. The consumer is to obey the rule: upon achieving a feasible-consumption $\mathbf{x}^*$ try the adjacent ground, moving to the highest feasible neighbouring ground unless all feasible neighbouring ground is lower, in which case, stay put. If the second-order condition holds, a consumer obeying the rule always will reestablish $\bar{\mathbf{x}}$ even if mini-shoved away from it: $\bar{\mathbf{x}}$ then is a stable equilibrium. The correspondence principle, owing to Professor Samuelson, concerns inferences about otherwise ambiguous comparative statics flowing from postulation of dynamic stability.

The following inferences, amongst others can be accumulated for the comparative statics of **S2** from the first- and second-order conditions:

1) the ratio $d\bar{x}_r/dp_r$ $(dp_i = 0, i \neq r)$ is unambiguously negative for a compensated price change;

As we have defined the substitution effect, proposition 1) asserts that the substitution effect of a (negative) positive price change is (positive) negative.

2) at least one pair of commodities must be substitutes;
3) a group of commodities whose prices always maintain the same proportions with one another can be treated as a single commodity.

Proposition 1) easily is proved. It has been shown that Δ_{rr}/Δ must be negative and that $\lambda > 0$ if the first- and second-order conditions are to be satisfied. Ergo, $\lambda\Delta_{rr}/\Delta < 0$. The substitution effect of an own-price change is defined by the equation $d\bar{x}_r = \lambda\Delta_{rr}/\Delta\, dp_r$. Q.E.D.

The second-order condition sheds no light on the sign of the income effect. For a commodity to be a *Giffen Good*, i.e. for $d\bar{x}_r/dp_r > 0$, the following inequality must hold:

$$|\bar{x}_r\Delta_{0r}/\Delta| > |\lambda\Delta_{rr}/\Delta|$$

The absolute value of the income effect (where, of course, $d\bar{x}_r/dY < 0$) must exceed that of the substitution-effect. This cannot be true unless $\bar{x}_r$ is large: a *Giffen Good* must be an inferior good which is important in the initial budget.

Proposition 2) follows from equation (33):

$$\sum\sum X_{rs}\, \delta_r\, \delta_s < 0 \tag{32}$$

$$\sum_s X_{rs}\, \delta_s = 0 \tag{33}$$

The notation is switched. The substitution-effect component $\lambda\Delta_{sr}/\Delta$ is written X_{rs}.

The symmetry of the underlying matrices of cross-partial derivatives (Hessian matrices) assures that $X_{sr} = X_{rs}$.

Equation (33) can be proved to hold independently of the stability condition.

By definition

$$\sum_s X_{rs}p_s = (\bar{\lambda}/\Delta) \sum_s \Delta_{rs}p_s$$

Now examine the first row of the underlying $(n+1) \times (n+1)$ matrix of expression (22): $(0, p_1, p_2, \ldots, p_n)$. The first row of the matrix is to be cross-multiplied with the cofactors of the $(r+1)$st row. A basic theorem of the algebra of determinants requires that the inner product be zero. Hence

$$\sum_s X_{rs}p_s = 0$$

Q.E.D.

Recalling the slight restrictions on the vector $\boldsymbol{\delta}$, substitute $\mathbf{p}$ for $\boldsymbol{\delta}$. Recall that $X_{rr} < 0$. Referring now to equation (33), the fact that $\mathbf{X}_{rr} < 0$ requires that:

$$\sum_{s \neq r} X_{rs}p_s = -X_{rr}p_r > 0 \tag{34}$$

There must be at least one commodity, not commodity r, such that an increase in its price, accompanied by a compensating change in income, causes an increase in the equilibrium rate of consumption of commodity r.

Proposition 3) is harder to prove. For one thing, groups of goods can be lumped together only as values: leeks and oranges cannot sensibly be added up. Equation (35) shows how the *value* of purchases of the sth commodity, $\bar{v}_s$, is affected by a change in the price of the rth commodity:

$$d\bar{v}_s/dp_r = p_s(-\bar{x}_r\Delta_{0r}/\Delta + \bar{\lambda}\Delta_{rs}/\Delta) \tag{35}$$

Now define $d\mathbf{p}$ as a price change in the proportion dp_r/p_r. Equation (36) follows:

$$d\bar{v}_s/dp = p_s(-\bar{v}_r\Delta_{0r}/\Delta + p_r\bar{\lambda}\Delta_{rs}/\Delta) \tag{36}$$

Compare equation (37):

$$d\bar{v}_s/dp = -\bar{v}_r(\partial\bar{v}_s/\partial Y) + p_rp_sX_{rs} \tag{37}$$

Consider a change in the price of each of commodities $1, 2, \ldots, m$ such that: $dp_1/p_1 = dp_2/p_2 = \ldots = dp_m/p_m = dp$, whilst $dp_{m+1} = dp_{m+2} = \ldots = dp_n = 0$, and write $\bar{v} = \sum \bar{v}_r$. The effect on the value of demand for any of the first m commodities selected arbitrarily, say for commodity 1, is:

$$dv_1/dp = -\sum_{r=1}^m \bar{v}_r(\partial v_1/\partial Y) + \sum_{r=1}^m p_rp_1X_{r1} \tag{38}$$

Summing over the m relations of the form of equation (38), i.e. adding up the values of changes in consumption of commodities $1, 2, \ldots, m$,

$$d\bar{v}/dp = -\bar{v}(\partial v/\partial Y) + \sum_{}^{m}\sum_{}^{m} p_r p_s X_{rs} \tag{39}$$

Inequality (40) follows:

$$\sum_{}^{m}\sum_{}^{m} p_r p_s X_{rs} < 0 \tag{40}$$

Specifically, inequality (40) follows from inequality (32): the vector δ is $(p_1, \ldots, p_m, 0, 0, \ldots, 0)$.

The price-, income- and substitution-effects derived for the aggregate of commodities $1, 2, \ldots, m$ are of precisely the same form as effects derived for equilibrium consumption of a single commodity:

> '... if the prices of a group of goods change in the same proportion, that group of goods behaves just as if it were a single commodity.'[10]

§ 10

The basic algebra of consumer choice is concluded by showing that results obtained for a utility function $U(\mathbf{x})$ are invariant against replacement of U by $\Phi(U)$, provided that Φ is a monotone of U, i.e., $\Phi'(U) > 0$. Since $\partial\Phi(U)/\partial x_r = \Phi'(U) \cdot U_r$ and $\partial\Phi(U)/\partial x_s = \Phi'(U) \cdot U_s$, the first-order conditions are indeed invariant against the transformation. The second differential of $\Phi(U)$ is:

$$d^2\Phi = \Phi'' dU^2 + \Phi' d^2U = (\sum U_r dx_r)^2\Phi'' + \Phi' \sum\sum U_{rs} dx_q dx_s$$
$$= \sum\sum \Phi''U_r U_s dx_r dx_s + \sum\sum \Phi'U_{rs} dx_r dx_s \tag{41}$$

The element of the $(s+1)$st column and the $(r+1)$st row of the determinant bordered by $(0, p_1, \ldots, p_n)$ is $\Phi'U_{rs} + \Phi''U_r U_s$. It is to be shown that the value of this determinant, Δ^*, and of its minors and cofactors differ from corresponding values of Δ and its minors and cofactors only by a positive factor $[\Phi'(U)]^{n-1}$ so that all statements made thus far about second-order conditions, price-effects, etc., continue to hold up unqualifiedly.

The own-price effect was $(-\bar{x}_r\Delta_{0r}/\Delta) + (\lambda\Delta_{rr}/\Delta) dp_r$.

In equilibrium, $p_r = \Phi'U_r/\bar{\lambda}$ so that Δ^* can be written:

$$\Delta^* = \begin{vmatrix} 0 & \Phi'U_r/\bar{\lambda} \\ & \Phi'U_{rs} + \Phi''U_r U_s \\ \Phi'U_r/\bar{\lambda} & \end{vmatrix} \tag{42}$$

where $\Phi'U_r/\bar{\lambda}$ is an n-vector (to be interpreted as a row- or column-vector as circumstances make obvious) and the 'inner matrix's' first element is $\Phi' U_{11} + \Phi'' U_1^2$. Multiply the first row and first column by $\bar{\lambda}/\Phi'$:

$$\Delta^* = (\Phi'/\bar{\lambda})^2 \begin{vmatrix} 0 & U_r \\ & \Phi' U_{rs} + \Phi'' U_r U_s \\ U_r & \end{vmatrix} \tag{43}$$

Subtract $\Phi'' U_r$ times the sth element of the first row from the corresponding element of each of the other rows. The value of the determinant is not changed:

$$\Delta^* = (\Phi/\bar{\lambda})^2 \begin{vmatrix} 0 & U_r \\ & \Phi' U_{rs} \\ U_r & \end{vmatrix} \tag{44}$$

Substitute $\bar{\lambda} p_r/\Phi'$ for U_r, and multiply the first row and first column above by $\Phi'/\bar{\lambda}$

$$\Delta^* = \begin{vmatrix} 0 & p \\ & \Phi' U_{rs} \\ p & \end{vmatrix} \tag{45}$$

Multiply the first column by Φ':

$$\Delta^* = (1/\Phi') \begin{vmatrix} 0 & p \\ & \Phi U_{rs} \\ \Phi' p & \end{vmatrix} \tag{46}$$

Divide all rows but the first by Φ':

$$\Delta^* = (\Phi')^{n-1} \begin{vmatrix} 0 & p \\ & U_{rs} \\ p & \end{vmatrix} \tag{47}$$

Q.E.D.!

§11

Two important extensions of the algebra of consumer choice are to be made:

1) multiple constraints (¶3.4 §§11);
2) the labour-leisure choice (¶3.4 §§12).

Multiple constraint is common in life: the consumer typically can shop only for a few hours and cannot stock more than certain numbers of pounds of various foods in his freezer, the capacity of which cannot be expanded for some days. (Recall the definition of $\mathbf{X}_j$ in ¶3.3.) What is worse practical work almost always requires that constraints be inequalities.

Consider this problem. An American college professor, working in Europe in 1968, is to be paid in blocked funds—funds not convertible into United States dollars. However, he continues to have some dollar income. Furthermore some of his dependents and property interests remain in America. (The analysis is useful for the case of firms with foreign branches.)

There are to be $2n$ commodities. x_r, $r = 1, 2, \ldots, n$, is a consumption in America; x_s, $s = 1, 2, \ldots, n$, is a consumption in England. The n-vector of United States consumptions is denoted $\mathbf{x}^*$ and that of English consumptions $\mathbf{x}^{**}$. The household is to maximize $U(\mathbf{x}^*, \mathbf{x}^{**})$ subject to $\mathbf{p}^* \cdot \mathbf{x}^* = Y^*$ and $\mathbf{p}^{**} \cdot \mathbf{x}^{**} = Y^{**}$, all values being expressed in a common accounting unit.

Form the Lagrange function

$$U(\mathbf{x}^*, \mathbf{x}^{**}) - \lambda_1(\mathbf{p}^* \cdot \mathbf{x}^* - Y^*) - \lambda_2(\mathbf{p}^{**} \cdot \mathbf{x}^{**} - Y^{**})$$

The first-order conditions are:

$$U_r - \lambda_1 p_r = 0 \qquad r = 1, 2, \ldots, n \tag{48}$$

$$U_s - \lambda_2 p_s = 0 \qquad s = 1, 2, \ldots, n \tag{49}$$

$$\sum^n p_r x_r = Y^* \tag{50}$$

$$\sum^n p_s x_s = Y^{**} \tag{51}$$

The $2n+2$ equations are to determine $\bar{\mathbf{x}}^*$, $\bar{\mathbf{x}}^{**}$, $\bar{\lambda}_1$, and $\bar{\lambda}_2$. Note that:

$$\bar{\lambda}_1 = U_r/p_r \qquad r = 1, 2, \ldots, n \tag{52}$$

$$\bar{\lambda}_2 = U_s/p_s \qquad s = 1, 2, \ldots, n \tag{53}$$

Hence in equilibrium:

$$\bar{\lambda}_1/\bar{\lambda}_2 = (p_r/p_s)(U_r/U_s) \tag{54}$$

What is the economic interpretation of $\bar{\lambda}_i$? The marginal utility of income derived from the ith country?

Define dU:

$$dU = \sum U_r\, dx_r + \sum U_s\, dx_s \tag{55}$$

Specify that $dY^{**} = 0$ so that

$$0 = \sum p_s \, dx_s = (1/\bar{\lambda}_2) \sum U_s \, dx_s \tag{56}$$

Thus

$$\sum U_s \, dx_s = 0 \tag{57}$$

Obtaining the differential of the first budget constraint,

$$dY^* = \sum p_r \, dx_r = (1/\bar{\lambda}) \sum U_r \, dx_r \tag{58}$$

Equation (59) follows:

$$dU/dY^*_{(dY^{**} = 0)} = \sum U_r \, dx_r/(1/\bar{\lambda}_1) \sum U_r \, dx_r = \bar{\lambda}_1 \tag{59}$$

Indeed, $\bar{\lambda}_i$ *is* to be construed as the marginal utility of income derived from the ith country. Accordingly if $\bar{\lambda}_1/\bar{\lambda}_2$ were 1, whilst the market rate of exchange were \$2.40/£1, the professor would use a *shadow rate* very different from the objective rate. The problem has been defined to prevent the professor from making international exchanges: departure of subjective- from objective-rates of substitution has been without operational significance. Correcting this omission, assume that, having arrived at the solution $(\bar{x}^*, \bar{x}^{**})$, associated with $(\bar{\lambda}_1, \bar{\lambda}_2)_2$ under the initial stipulations, it becomes possible to transfer income. Then rationally he would forgo a chance to earn 18s. if the necessary research required him to buy a book in America costing \$1!

§ 12

Analysis of labour-leisure choices turns up material linking up the theories of the household and the firm. Such analysis verges upon the theory of finance: share-holding links households and firms.

Modern economic theory of competitive equilibrium divorces consumption- from production-decisions. Ideally, the consumer simply makes a consumption plan. Labour-services enter into the plan as elements of the consumption vector x_j. True, hours-worked affect income, *but* the household makes this decision as a seller of labour services and *not* as a producer.

The text glides over an important point: in the neo-classical theory of Chapter 3 households *choose* their incomes; in Keynesian theory, households are constrained by possible inability to find outlets for their labour. Cf. Chapters 9 and 12.

The only thing produced by the household ideally is utility. The household of the theory considers wages of management but never effects of household decisions on net-worths of firms. Modern theory deems a household operating a family farm as a consumer selling labour to itself *qua* producer:

> 'in the study of production, when one abstracts from legal forms of organization (corporations, sole proprietorships, partnerships, . . .) and types of activity . . . one obtains the concept of a *producer*, i.e. of an economic agent whose rôle is to choose (and carry out) a production plan,'

> 'Interlocking directorships pose problems like those resulting from comingling utility theory and the theory of the firm: a shareholder in Companies A, B, C, . . . becomes interested in a weighted average of A, B, C, . . . shares, an interest which can be in conflict with that of any one firm.'[11]

The producers simply are to maximize the net values of their plans.

Utility theory, then, is divorced from the theory of the firm. The theoretical firm simply maximizes a value-weighted sum on its set of feasible-outputs. However, households and firms *are* linked up by the mechanics of general-equilibrium in at least two ways: the influence of 'demand' on prices as explained in Part I; the forces determining securities prices. In pure theory all firms are treated as corporations (limited companies) issuing share capital. The shares are owned by households. In the simplest case, abstracting from uncertainty, households bid for the shares of firms. In consequence managements maximizing discounted values of production plans, and hence share values, will tend to replace managements committed to other plans. Thus is the rôle of the take-over bid.

So it is 'modern' households, maximizing preference preorderings defined on consumption sets, merely offer labour services to firms who form production plans to maximize their share values.

'Modern' theory is intuitively plausible for giant firms. Theories about General Motors' behaviour doubtless can neglect the labour-leisure tastes of General Motors' president. Executive tastes enter through error terms in econometric counterparts to the theory.

As it happens, General Motors presidents seldom have cherished leisure.

However, the theory is implausible for the family farm, nor does it work well for one who simply prefers to work for himself, not charging himself (*qua* producer) his market wage rate. Accordingly, a special theory is called for. The special theory incidentally sheds light on backward-bending supply curves of labour (i.e., on negative associations between wage rates and supplies of labour services in specified ranges): will 'natives' wish to work less if the price of rice, measured in labour, falls?

Again the model is interpreted for only one period. Dropping subsequently the subscript j, the 'consumption' $\mathbf{x}_j$ (the subscript j is immediately to be dropped) is comprised of the $n-1$ 'outputs', $x_1, x_2, \ldots, x_{n-1}$ and the (labour) input, x_n. The farmer's income is derived entirely from sales of a single crop, y, not entering into his consumption set. Its price is denoted p_y. He produces the crop by combining m hired inputs, $\tilde{\mathbf{y}}$, purchased at prices $\mathbf{w}$, with his own labour. His budget constraint requires that:

$$\sum_{i=1}^{n-1} p_i x_i = p_y y - \sum_{j=1}^{m} w_j \tilde{y}_j \tag{60}$$

The production function is:

$$z = \Phi(\tilde{\mathbf{y}}, x_n) \tag{61}$$

The problem is to maximize $U = U(\mathbf{x})$ subject to equations (60) and (61). Form the Lagrange function:

$$V = U(\mathbf{x}) - \lambda_1 \left(\sum^{n-1} p_i x_i - p_y y + \sum w_j \tilde{y}_j \right) - \lambda_2(y - \Phi) \tag{62}$$

The first-order conditions are obtained by partially differentiating the Lagrange function with respect to each of the variables, including the λs, and setting the partial derivatives equal to zero:

$$U_i - \lambda_1 p_i = 0 \qquad i = 1, 2, \ldots, n-1 \tag{63}$$

$$U_n + \lambda_2 \Phi_n = 0 \tag{64}$$

$$\lambda_1 p_2 - \lambda_2 = 0 \tag{65}$$

$$-\lambda_1 w_j + \lambda_2 \Phi_j = 0 \qquad j = 1, 2, \ldots, m \tag{66}$$

$$\sum^{n-1} p_i x_i = p_y y - \sum w_j \tilde{y}_j \tag{67}$$

$$y = \Phi(x_n, \tilde{y}) \tag{68}$$

The first-order conditions are assumed to determine $\bar{\mathbf{x}}, \bar{\tilde{\mathbf{y}}}, \bar{y}$, and $\bar{\lambda}$.

Manipulation of equations (63) to (68) is revealing. Witness equation (69):

$$-U_n/U_i = p_2 \Phi_n/p_i \qquad i \neq n \tag{69}$$

Assume that the marginal utility of labour is negative, that labour incurs *dis*utility. Then $-U_n/U_i$ is positive and equation (69) requires that the rate at which the farmer's disutility from working is substituted for utility from consumption of the ith commodity—a subjective rate—be equal to the objective (market) rate of exchange between his labour and x_i, noting that Φ_i is the marginal productivity of the farmer's labour so that $p_y \Phi_n$ is the value of the marginal product of the farmer's labour. (Strictly, the marginal product is $\Phi_n \, dx_n$.)

If the second-order condition is met so that the preference and production functions are convex in the neighbourhood of $(\bar{\mathbf{x}}, \bar{\mathbf{y}})$, the substitution-effect of a reduction in p_y would cause the farmer to work less and, on the whole, to hire fewer inputs, i.e. to reduce y.

The first-order conditions include $w_r/\Phi_r = w_s/\Phi_s = p_y$. If $\Phi_{ss} < 0$ and $\Phi_{sn} = 0$, then the decrease in w_j/Φ_j necessary to maintain the equalities consequent to $dp_y < 0$ will be achieved only if $d\tilde{y}_j < 0$.

Compare Chapter 4 for a rigorous demonstration that output must fall if p_y falls—if *entrepreneur* labour can be neglected or if 'leisure' is not superior for the *entrepreneur*.

However, if, so to speak, leisure is strongly superior, if the farmer tends 'substantially' to reduce his labour inputs as p_y increases, he might wish to work longer hours if p_y were to fall.

'Leisure' is a crude expression. 'Leisure' is not amongst $\mathbf{x}$. Instead $U(\mathbf{x})$ reflects effects of working longer or shorter hours on utility associated with a consumption $\mathbf{x}$.

What are the consequences of such a price-effect? The first differential of output is defined by equation (70):

$$\mathrm{d}y = \sum_{j=1}^{m} \Phi_j \, \mathrm{d}\tilde{y}_j + \Phi_n \, \mathrm{d}x_n \tag{70}$$

By assumption $\mathrm{d}x_n > 0$. It follows from the first-order condition that:

$$w_r = \Phi_r p_y \tag{71}$$

that inputs of factors technologically substitutional with the farmer's labour will be cut back ($\Phi_{rn} < 0$ in such cases) whilst inputs complementary with his labour could increase if Φ_{sn} were sufficiently positive. Obviously the farmer would fire some hired hands. Finally, if the farmer's labour, valued at $\Phi_n p_y$, were a small proportion of the value of total inputs in the initial equilibrium, y surely would fall. Consider the limiting case in which $x_n \to 0$, the case of Chapter 4, a case which is more and more appropriate for modern agriculture.

The special theory, then, includes at least the following prerequisites for planned production to increase because of a decline in the price of *the* final product: 'leisure' must be strongly superior; *entrepreneur* labour must be 'important' (and predominantly technologically complementary with other factors); it must be physically possible for the producer effectively to work harder. (What if he already were going flat out during planting and harvesting?) A fanciful illustration of the remote possibility $d\bar{y}/dp_y < 0$ would find $dp_y < 0$ causing the farmer to dismiss the hired hands, withdraw his children from school, equip them with tractors (the tractors might be rented), and work the fields with his children under floodlights.

The theory of the *n*-product farm is tougher. The special theory's implications then become more diffuse. Cf. Chapter 4.

The text neglects effects on demand for commodity *y* of reduced farm income. If the commodity were consumed by farmers and were strongly superior, then $dp_y < 0$ might indeed lead to $d\bar{y} > 0$, defining $\bar{y}_j$ as the planned excess supply of the *j*th farmer.

§ 13

¶3.4 §§13, unlike ¶3.4 §§11 and 12, does not add dimensions to the utility analysis of consumer choice. It merely takes up *extended time horizons* which, as it happens, can be considered without additional analytics. This is not surprising. Recall the definition of a commodity of Chapter 1.

The discussion of ¶3.4 §§13 makes it possible to place a controversial subject, *the economics of conscription*, in a new perspective. Thus the matter of ¶3.4 §§14, et seq. concluding ¶3.4.

Let us pursue a neo-classical, as against Keynesian (consumption function) line of attack : the *j*th consumer is to be constrained only by the prices of the commodities he buys and sells, including his labour, his endowments, and his skills. The *j*th consumer faces perfectly elastic demand for his supplies in the problem of ¶3.4 §§13.

The *j*th consumer is restricted to consumption plans obeying inequality (72).

$$\int_0^\tau h(t)e^{-rt}\,dt \le \int_0^\tau g(t)e^{-rt}\,dt \tag{72}$$

where date zero is 'now' and date τ is the end of his planning horizon. The receipt stream is $g(t)$, *r* is *the* discount rate, and $h(t)$ defines the 'money' outflow associated with the 'real' 'hyper' consumption stream, $f(t)$. The stream $g(t)$ is restricted to a feasible set determined by the subject's endowments and capabilities and the prices of the commodities, including factor services, which he sells.

The new consumer-choice problem is on all fours with the old, as will become clear in the discussion in Chapter 10 of the optimization principle of Pontryagin. In particular, price-effects are generated by changes in functions $\phi(t)$, where :

$$p_i = \phi^i(t) \tag{73}$$

noting that *p* includes factor prices. Events such as confiscation of one's assets at date zero or imprisonment for 6 months at date *h* affect decisions made at dates zero or *h* on consumptions at date *n*. Roughly speaking, if the composite consumption for each date is superior, then the misfortunes will lead to more-negative consumptions later. If 'leisure' is superior, the subject will take less of it—at least if the misfortunes were not to impair his working ability (as *death* surely would do).

§ 14

Economic theory suggests that national wealth might be greater if honours graduates, research assistants, and others are drafted for military service instead of common labourers. It suggests that, to the extent that conscription is used, national income might be stimulated by onerous terms of compulsory service. Our reasoning turns on 'the conscript's life-cycle adjustment to military service'.

Consider first Conscript Alpha, whose professional training is to be interrupted for two years. Contrast him with Conscript Gamma, a labourer for whom military pay and benefits are economically identical with his preferred civilian alternative. Then reflect on a polar case. Alpha's estate plan is to be invariant against military service. Indeed Alpha insists upon an invariant present value of lifetime earnings. In other words, Alpha, upon discharge from military service, will become a highly charged economic particle determined, quite fortuitously, to restore to the stream of national income the inroads made by military service. Any value which might be placed by social accountants on military expenditures is disregarded.

Perhaps Alpha will accelerate his remaining education and training, work more days than he would have worked after his discharge up to normal retirement age, and then retire later. For Alpha social and private ends are harmonized.

Doubtless Alpha would regret being conscripted, and perhaps a money-measure might be attached to his regret. Surely if compensation schemes like the substitutions of the American civil war are put aside, the fact that O. Warbucks II is willing to pay £10,000 to avoid military service, whilst R. Crachitt offers but 30 bob to avoid the same service, in a war which both may oppose, can justify Warbuck's exemption and Cratchitt's conscription only in a horrible society.

Not so for Gamma. He would be no less slothful after his discharge. (Of course, if forced to soldier without pay, Gamma might try, upon discharge, to work harder in order to replenish his exhausted savings.)

POINT. The more a conscript regards himself as exploited, the greater is his incentive—given the feasible responses available to him—to add to national wealth upon being discharged. Alternatively, the 'exploited' conscript is likely to adopt a social criterion whilst the mercenary soldier, albeit no more selfish, adopts a socially dissonant criterion.

An enlisted man, Soldier Omega, for whom the army offers a superior economic opportunity will, upon quitting the army, be, if anything, above the target he would have set if denied military opportunity, and thus will have an incentive to act 'antisocially'—to slack more and save less.

§ 15

Defence manpower demands directly affect sources of manpower flows. Effects of defence withdrawals of stocks from the labour mass on the measured national income—it is best to centre on civilian-product components—and on wealth depend on the equivalent to induced changes in monetary velocity. Will service streams of the n manpower classes not in the military build up offset the loss of the services of the m classes in the military at date t?

It is useful to dichotomize adjustments to defence manpower demands:

a) adjustments directly related to prospective or past military service, reflected, for example, in micropropensities to save;
b) adjustments only indirectly related to military manpower demands.

¶3.4 §§14 has shown that a) adjustments may be larger and more conducive to national wealth, the greater the apparent private sacrifice has been. At least quite orthodox preference orderings, leading up to modern theories of life-cycle consumption behaviour, are consistent with the conclusion of ¶3.4 §§14. However b) adjustments are either neutral for conscription versus voluntary enlistment (when rooted in 'market imperfection' arguments) or tend to favour a volunteer army to the extent that it is harder to substitute for higher skills.

b) adjustments can be further divided into effects of:

1) relative-price changes in idealized competitive markets;
2) market imperfections.

As for b)1) adjustments, if appropriate elasticities of substitution are high enough, older workers, endowed with certain conscripts' skills (and perhaps once conscripts themselves) can easily be induced to postpone retirement, or the m classes of civilian labour can be induced to work more overtime hours, etc. The b) 1) *rationale* is well known in economics. Adverse effects of parametric changes always are overstated if effects of potential price changes are neglected and, similarly, effects of price changes are 'underrated' unless induced substitutions are accounted for.

Turning to b) 2) adjustments, perhaps conscription of mathematicians would cause more overtime to become available to programmers anxious to work more, but discouraged by the costs of searching for high-overtime employers under tranquil pre-conscription conditions. Older specialist workers, unable to slash their supply prices due to cousins of minimum-wage legislation, might happily postpone retirements. Of course, if the total volume of civilian employment were substantially below the 'full employment' level, military manpower recruitment would affect the distribution of welfare rather than national income.

b) adjustments produce a mixed bag. The more elastic is the economy and the lower is the negative correlation between elasticities of substitution and skill levels, the stronger is the case for conscription under a national-income criterion. If conditions were such that b) 1) adjustments were not impeded by conscription, it could be argued that conscription leads to *increased* national income. b) adjustments, here totally effective, would be augmented by a) adjustments, reflecting 'microsacrifices'.

§ 16

Finally we ponder on implications of the analysis for expensive policies of national grandeur or even aggression and then on certain 'phoenix' phenomena such as the rise of postwar Germany and Japan.

Putting aside the conscription versus voluntary recruitment issue, the life-cycle consumption theory *cum* capital theory of ¶3.4 §§13–15 suggests that the effects of governmental profligacy or of disaster on the economic power even of states without *dirigiste* economies are less than one-period analysis asserts. This conjecture surely is not discouraged by historical episodes of the sort just mentioned. Furthermore, it is consistent with admittedly recondite invariance theorems about asset accumulation of the sort developed by Clower and Burstein.[12] In other words, the professional advice of modern economic theorists well may encourage rulers, thus more confident of the survival properties of the state's economy, to push vast, dangerous schemes. True these schemes may be abhorrent to economists, traditionally devoted to bourgeois-liberal consensus. History has many cunning passages and contrived corridors.

5.   REVEALED-PREFERENCE

¶3.5 hastily sketches Professor Samuelson's theory of revealed-preference, important *here* only because of its close relationship with ¶3.3 and its extension. Revealed-preference theory deals with certain correspondences between prices and consumptions which ideally could be established experimentally, so that demand correspondences could be defined independently of the cumbersome and largely non-operational calculus of utility theory. Preferences of consumers adhering to specified axioms, and revealed by their conduct, could be a basis for prediction of consumer behaviour.

Revealed-preference theory hinges on two basic assumptions:

1) consumer preferences are 'convex enough' for consumption x^n never to be revealed to be preferred to x^1, if it is revealed that $x^1 > x^2$, $x^2 > x^3, \ldots, x^{n-1} > x^n$, i.e. x^1 is preferred to x^2, etc.:

2) and this is really a version of 1) above, if $\mathbf{x}^1$ is revealed to be preferred to $\mathbf{x}^2$, $\mathbf{x}^2$ cannot be revealed to be preferred to $\mathbf{x}^1$. Since $\mathbf{x}^1$ is revealed to be preferred to $\mathbf{x}^2$ when $\mathbf{x}^1$ is purchased when $\mathbf{x}^2$ is cheaper, $\mathbf{x}^2$ will not be purchased when $\mathbf{x}^1$ is cheaper.

§2

Most of the theorems of ¶3.4 can be proved through revealed-preference. Consider the sign of the substitution-effect. Assume that the consumer is indifferent between $\mathbf{x}^1$ and $\mathbf{x}^2$, but purchases $\mathbf{x}^1$ at prices $\mathbf{p}^*$. Recalling that $\mathbf{x}^1$ and $\mathbf{x}^2$ are vectors, there follows inequality (74):

$$\mathbf{p}^* \cdot \mathbf{x}^1 \leq \mathbf{p}^* \cdot \mathbf{x}^2 \tag{74}$$

However, $\mathbf{x}^2$ is purchased at $\mathbf{p}^{**}$. Hence:

$$\mathbf{p}^{**} \cdot \mathbf{x}^2 \leq \mathbf{p}^{**} \cdot \mathbf{x}^1 \tag{75}$$

Inequalities (76) and (77) follow from inequalities (74) and (75):

$$\mathbf{p}^* \cdot \mathbf{x}^1 - \mathbf{p}^* \cdot \mathbf{x}^2 = \mathbf{p}^*(\mathbf{x}^1 - \mathbf{x}^2) = -\mathbf{p}^*(\mathbf{x}^2 - \mathbf{x}^1) \leq 0 \tag{76}$$

$$\mathbf{p}^{**} \cdot \mathbf{x}^2 - \mathbf{p}^{**} \cdot \mathbf{x}^1 = \mathbf{p}^{**}(\mathbf{x}^2 - \mathbf{x}^1) \leq 0 \tag{77}$$

Add together inequalities (76) and (77):

$$-\mathbf{p}^*(\mathbf{x}^2 - \mathbf{x}^1) + \mathbf{p}^{**}(\mathbf{x}^2 - \mathbf{x}^1) = (\mathbf{p}^{**} - \mathbf{p}^*)(\mathbf{x}^2 - \mathbf{x}^1) \leq 0 \tag{78}$$

That is to say, for indifferent consumptions $\mathbf{x}^2$ and $\mathbf{x}^1$, the vector product $(\mathbf{dp}) \cdot (\mathbf{dx})$ is negative. Specifically consider $dp_1 \neq 0, dp_2 = dp_3 = \ldots = dp_n = 0$: all elements of $\mathbf{p}^*$ and $\mathbf{p}^{**}$ are to be equal except for the first. Inequality (79) follows:

$$(\mathbf{p}_1^{**} - \mathbf{p}_1^*)(\mathbf{x}_1^2 - \mathbf{x}_1^1) \leq 0 \tag{79}$$

If $d\mathbf{p}_1 > 0$, consumption of commodity 1 must either fall or stay the same: if $d\mathbf{p}_1 < 0$, consumption of commodity 1 must either increase or stay the same, restricting choice, of course, to commodity bundles which are indifferent for the jth consumer.

6. VON NEUMANN–MORGENSTERN UTILITY

If decision makers, for example consumers, adhere to certain axioms, their preferences can be described by utility functions which are unique up to choice of origin and unit distance, although interpersonal comparison remains impossible. The basic theorems are developed in J. von Neumann and O. Morgenstern's great book, *Theory of Games and Economic Behaviour*.

Von Neumann–Morgenstern (N–M) utility analysis is applicable to a number of fields including the theories of oligopoly and diplomatic and military strategy. The fundamental N–M tool, the theory of convex sets, links N–M utility analysis, activity analysis (including the Kuhn–Tucker theory of Chapter 5), the theory of the existence and optimality of competitive equilibrium, and optimal-growth theory.

¶3.6 is to:

1) state the underlying axioms, §§2;
2) develop a simple N–M utility function, §§3;
3) apply N–M utility to insurance and gambling by households, §§4;
4) apply N–M theory to strategy, §§5.

§2

Von Neumann and Morgenstern[13] develop five basic axioms. Behaviour of consumers adhering to these axioms can be ordered by an N–M utility function.

1) COMPLETENESS. As between any two outcomes, the decision maker either prefers one or the other or is indifferent between them. Furthermore, preferences are transitive: $A > B, B > C$, implies $A > C$.

2) CONTINUITY. 'If w is preferred to u, and an even more preferable v is also given, then the combination of u [with probability α] with a chance of $1 - \alpha$ of v will not affect w's preferability to it if this chance $[1 - \alpha]$ is small enough.'[14]

The N–M probabilities are subjective and are not to be associated with limiting proportions characterizing random-sampling processes.

3) INDEPENDENCE. If outcomes A and B are indifferent ($A = B$), as are C and D ($C = D$), then a lottery ticket offering A or C is indifferent with one offering B or D regardless of the probability, α, that the first ticket will yield A and the second B. I.e., the ticket $(A_{\mathrm{pr}\,\alpha}, C_{\mathrm{pr}(1-\alpha)})$ is indifferent with the ticket $(B_{\mathrm{pr}\,\alpha}, D_{\mathrm{pr}(1-\alpha)})$, regardless of the value taken by the positive fraction α.

4) UNEQUAL PROBABILITY. Other things the same, the ticket offering the better odds on a favourable outcome is preferred.

5) COMPOUND PROBABILITY. 'It is irrelevant whether a combination of two constituents is obtained in two successive steps: first the probabilities $\alpha, 1 - \alpha$, then the probabilities $\beta, 1 - \beta$; or in one operation, the probabilities $\gamma, 1 - \gamma$, where $\gamma = \alpha\beta$.'[14]

I.e., a horseplayer is indifferent between receiving a parimutuel ticket for the 8th race on which his chance of a \$2 pay-off is 0·2 and a 'double' on the 6th *and* 7th races, the odds being 1:2 and 2:5 (the probabilities being 0·5 and 0·4 of course).

§3

The five axioms lead up to the crucial equation (80):

$$U_b = \alpha U_a + (1-\alpha)U_c \tag{80}$$

α being a probability to be determined. A and C are defined outcomes to be assigned positive real numbers U_a and U_c. Imbedded in the axioms is the assumption that the expected utility of a lottery ticket is $\alpha U_a + (1-\alpha)U_c$. Accordingly, if $\alpha = \hat{\alpha}$ and U_b is the utility of a non-stochastic outcome B and if inequality (81) holds, the decision maker will opt for the lottery ticket.

$$U_b < \hat{\alpha}U_a + (1-\hat{\alpha})U_c \tag{81}$$

N–M men are indifferent towards risk. For them a bird in hand is worth two in the bush only if the probability of catching the latter is as little as 0·5.

Event *B* is preferred to *A*. Referring back to equation (80), arbitrarily specify U_a as 0 and U_b as 1:

$$1 = \alpha(0) + (1-\alpha)U_c \tag{82}$$

The subject is to specify the level of α, α^*, which leaves him indifferent between the certain outcome *B* and the lottery ticket offering probability α^* of *A* and probability $(1-\alpha^*)$ of *C*. What if $\alpha^* = 0·9$? Then, $U_c = 10$. The operations uniquely define U_c upon choice of origin ($U_a = 0$) and unit distance ($U_b - U_a = 1-0 = 1$). Similarly unique results can be obtained for outcomes *D, E, ...*

Since the operations cannot yield up positive numbers for outcomes less preferred than *A*, *A* must be the least-preferred of outcomes under consideration. To that extent, choice of origin is not arbitrary, but only to that extent.

§4

Consider Fig. 9:

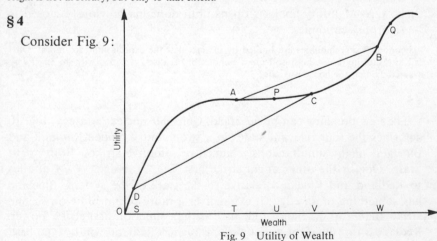

Fig. 9 Utility of Wealth

The curve plots an *N–M* utility function defined on a household's wealth. The curve increases at a decreasing rate up to the inflexion point *P* at which it increases at an increasing rate up to the inflexion point *Q*. The *N–M* utilities of lottery tickets with coupons providing for wealth 0T or 0W will be represented by points belonging to the chord *AB*, depending on the value of α.

$\hat{U} = \alpha U_b + (1-\alpha)U_a$: $dU/d\alpha = U_b - U_a$. That is expected utility increases at the constant rate $U_b - U_a$ as α increases. The locus of utilities of the lottery tickets has the end points $B\,(\alpha = 1)$ and $A\,(\alpha = 0)$. The locus is a straight line since the segment TW can be interpreted as representing continuous variation in α over the range (0, 1), and $d\hat{U}/d\alpha$ is constant.

The expected utility of a ticket is a linear combination of U_a and U_b. The expected utilities exceed the utilities of the mathematical expectation of wealth implicit in '*AB*' lottery tickets. Similarly, the expected utilities of lottery tickets offering 0V or 0S are *less* than the utilities of their mathematical (wealth) expectations.

Next consider a household with wealth 0V facing probability α that its house will burn down leaving it with wealth 0S. It clearly would be willing to pay an insurance premium UV, leaving it with certain wealth 0U rather than accept Nature's lottery ticket leading to the mathematical expectation 0U. What if the household is offered an Irish Sweepstakes ticket costing \$VT, paying \$VW and having a mathematical expectation of \$0U? Purchase of the ticket will reduce the household's expected wealth, but, still, it will gamble. Prospects of wealth OW, perhaps leading to a new social level, are so exciting that unfair odds become attractive.

¶3.6 §§4, based on work by Professors Friedman and Savage, shows:

1) how simultaneous gambling and insuring are sensible within an *N–M* framework; and
2) how *N–M* utility analysis opens unto domains previously closed to rigorous economics.

Econometric possibilities are limited by the fact that the expectations are moral. Do I fail to insure my house because I am a gambler or because I wrestled with an angel who assured me that the house was safe?

§5

The new domains can be far afield. Consider nuclear strategy. Fig. 10 describes the four relevant states in a two-country model. Redland and Blueland might simultaneously launch pre-emptive strikes. Both might 'wait'. One or the other might strike first. Fig. 11 assigns *N–M* utilities to Redland and Blueland relative to the state of the system. Blueland has something of an edge: it can deliver a more brutal blow on second strike than can Redland and, indeed, has superior first-strike power. Redland's threshold for a first strike is higher. Redland will not 'go first'

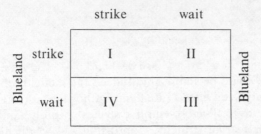

Fig. 10   States of the Redland–Blueland System

unless it assigns a higher probability to being hit first than is true vice versa. This becomes clear through inequalities (83) and (84) defining critical probabilities α and β:

$$20 > \alpha(0) + (1-\alpha)100 \tag{83}$$

$$60 > \beta(30) + (1-\beta)100 \tag{84}$$

Country	State			
	I	II	III	IV
Redland	0	0	100	20
Blueland	40	60	100	30

Fig. 11   Utilities Relative to States

$\alpha^* = 0\cdot80$: $\beta^* = 0\cdot57$. An N–M Redland will strike if it assigns a probability to Blueland's going first in excess of $0\cdot80$ whilst Blueland will strike first if it assigns a probability in excess of $0\cdot57$ to Redland's striking.

An N–M Blueland, knowing that Redland's threshold is high, will be more ready to go to the brink of war than will be an N–M Redland.

Assume that a substantial part of Blue missile strength has been at 'soft' bases highly vulnerable to a Red first strike. If such Blue bases were 'hardened', the pay-off matrix would change significantly. The crux would be greater Blue capacity to withstand a pre-emptive strike against its bases and the consequent reduction in pay-off to Red for going first. The Blue reprisal will be more terrible. Compare Fig. 12:

Country	State			
	I	II	III	IV
Redland	0	0	100	10
Blueland	40	60	100	35

Fig. 12   Revised Utilities Relative to States

Inequalities (85) and (86) follow:

$$10 > \alpha(0) + (1 - \alpha)100 \tag{85}$$

$$60 > \beta(35) + (1 - \beta)100 \tag{86}$$

The revised values for α^* and β^* are 0·90 and 0·62. The Blue 'hardening' strategy clearly would be stabilizing. Indeed the model probably under-estimates its stabilizing effects: Redland authorities are likely to assign lower probabilities to Blue pre-emptive strikes once Blueland has shifted towards a second-strike strategy. Contrast Fig. 12 with the results of exclusive reliance by Blue on 'soft' bases, bases so soft that Blue could not retaliate at all if hit first, but where Blue's first-strike could annihilate Redland.

7. UNCERTAINTY

There are at least two ways in which a plan can go wrong or, conversely, lead to pleasant surprise. Nature might change its mind: a flood occurs. A planner's execution might be faulty: his hammer hits his finger. ¶3.7 belonging, after all, to a largely deterministic book, mostly is concerned with events exogenous to the decision maker—events such as floods.

¶3.7 §§2 explores an informal example concerning a firm. ¶3.7 §§3 concerns households and firms. This should not be disturbing: the argu-ment has been modulating towards the new key of Chapter 4 at least since ¶3.4 §§12. The rather formal treatment of ¶3.7 §§3 has a benign and important by-product: it shows how, in its full generality, ¶3.3 encom-passes future markets and decisions on consumptions and productions over extended time horizons; how the analysis of ¶3.3 could have been interpreted in terms of the indefinite future. What is more, ¶3.3 encom-passes assets, stocks. Compare G. Debreu:

> '... the full generality of the concept of commodity... should always be kept in mind. By focusing attention on changes of dates one obtains *as a particular case* of the general theory of commodities... a theory of saving, investment, capital, and interest. Similarly, by focusing attention on changes of locations one obtains, *as another particular case* of the same general theory, a theory of location, transportation, international trade, and exchange.'[15]

§2

Cf. ¶6.2 §§10 *infra.*

The management of Aleph Company Ltd. at date 0 contemplates a research programme leading, they think, to the probability distribution of Fig. 13.

A more-rigorous analysis would specify the (subjective) confidence intervals as well, and would consider more than the first-moments of probability distributions.

The market value of Aleph shares at date 0 is 0A. The expected value of the shares at date 1, if the programme is undertaken, is 0B, but, if the programme fails, Aleph shares will become virtually worthless. Perhaps a fully-knowledgeable share market would be much less sensitive to the programme's results; perhaps a heavily funded management could retain control even if the programme fails. The Aleph management, not having command of enough funds to wage a battle for control, adopts a *lexicographic* ordering. All is subordinated to a single criterion, re-appointment at date 1, in turn keyed to the price of Aleph shares. Nor would the programme necessarily be undertaken by a sole proprietor: his decision would depend on utilities assigned to various outcomes, moral expectations and attitudes towards risk.

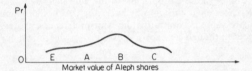

Fig. 13   Probability Distribution for Value of Aleph Shares at Date 1

L'affaire Aleph may be placed in an $N-M$ context, noting that the ¶3.7 §§2 problem is truly stochastic, whilst in ¶3.6 *hypothetical* behaviour in risky situations merely permitted construction of a utility function ranking *non-stochastic* events. The management's $N-M$ utility function rates 're-election' as 100 and 'rejection' as 0. For simplicity assume that there are only two possible events, election and rejection. Share value at date 1 of 0E or less will lead to certain rejection; the range EA associates with a probability of 0·75 of re-election; AB with 0·80; BC with 0·90; any result better than 0C with certain re-election. Finally assume that the probability-density function leads to equation (87):

$$U = 0{\cdot}3(0) + (0{\cdot}1)(0{\cdot}75)(100) + (0{\cdot}1)(0{\cdot}8)(100)$$
$$+ (0{\cdot}48)(0{\cdot}90)(100) + (0{\cdot}02)(100) = 60{\cdot}7 \qquad (87)$$

Equation (87) implies that $\Pr(S \leq 0E) = 0{\cdot}30$; $\Pr(0C < S \leq 0A) = 0{\cdot}10$; $\Pr(0A < S \leq 0B) = 0{\cdot}10$; $\Pr(0B < S \leq 0C) = 0{\cdot}48$; $\Pr(0C < S) = 0{\cdot}02$. Of course, S = share-value at date 1.

If certain share-value would be 0A in the null case, expected utility would be 75: the programme would be rejected although its expected returns exceed opportunity costs.

In a non-stochastic world with perfect markets, shareholders, viewing the firm simply as a money-spinner, would force managements always to maximize share-values. This strategy would maximize present values of shareholders' consumption plans (including estate-values). Management-strategy in an uncertain world may be more complex. Market value no longer necessarily reflects the 'truth'. If I, now in control, am right and 'they' are wrong, and if I can ride out the storm, I may be able to bring out a new product, serenely buying in Aleph shares from a sceptical market, awaiting the Aleph bubble, likely to occur, I think, in a few years upon my judgement being vindicated. Indeed I might initially make short sales of Aleph shares.

The influence of 'riskiness' of company programmes on share values in a stochastic world is not as simple as usually is suggested. After all, stock-market investors choose their portfolios from menus including the securities of *all* companies. It would be surprising if the Market were to encourage managements to black out knowledge of the whole field of (uncertain) choice (cf. The note in ¶6.2 §§9). In other (very approximate) words, the stock-market investor should be exploiting the Law of Large Numbers so that, even if he has risk aversion, he should be urging more-aggressive policies on each of his managements than if he were invested only in one company. This point becomes glaringly obvious for a unit-trust (mutual fund). Surely 'riskiness and securities-prices' should be empirically investigated along these lines.

Thus insertion of stochastic features into the analysis directly links up preferences and productions in the case of the sole proprietor. In the pure theory of joint-stock companies (corporations) preferences enter through the back door. Although managements are concerned only with share-value maximization, investor-preferences, expressed in the Bourse, affect securities-prices (although perhaps not as much as one might think). Cf. ¶6.2 §§10.

§3

¶3.7 §§3 crudely sketches Debreu's analysis.[16]

The theory of ¶3.3 easily may be extended to accommodate extended planning horizons and commodities for future production or delivery. Prices being determined in today's dealings can include prices of futures (e.g. No. 2 Red Winter Wheat available in Chicago at date t). A model, conforming to models of competitive general-equilibrium under certainty in its shape and implications, can be built up around an elaborate system of futures pricing.

Assume that uncertainty is generated by Nature calling 'heads' or 'tails'. In an agricultural economy 'heads' may mean rainfall $\geq k$ inches and 'tails' rainfall $< k$ inches. The theory accommodates an indefinitely large, albeit finite, number of such events. Traders during period 0 make plans in terms of the 2^t environmental sequences which could generate the state of the system at date t.

There is no uncertainty about the current period.

Futures trading in the revised system is in commodities defined not only as 'No. 2 Red Winter Wheat available in Chicago at date t', but also relative to events. Amongst the commodities is 'No. 2 Red Winter Wheat available in Chicago at date 1 in the event that heads have been called at date 1'.

As in the simpler model, producers attempt to maximize present values of production plans. Financial markets are excluded: interest rates are implicit in prices of commodities of different dating. However, a production plan concerns commodities defined relative to events: if a producer must deliver 100 units of butter at date 1, he would at date 0 sell 100 units of butter for date 1 delivery in the event heads *and* 100 units in the event tails. It follows that a purchase at date 0 of 100 units of butter for date 1 delivery *in any event* involves purchase of *both* of the commodities.

The consumer similarly arranges his purchases relative to events. His wealth constraint (intertemporal budget constraint) is determined by his share-holdings in the firms and by his labour sales. His plan must accommodate to alternative sequences of states of Nature. These affect his potential labour income(s).

The weakest convexity assumption about preferences implies risk aversion. (The weakest convexity assumption is, if x^2 is preferred to x^1, $tx^2 + (1-t)x^1$ also will be preferred to x^1.)[17]

There is to be no speculation about price behaviour. The current *tâtonnement* is to determine all future prices. However, in more complicated models there would have to be a fresh *tâtonnement* each period, as a date hitherto excluded from the time horizon became eligible.

> 'The formal identity of this theory of uncertainty with the theory of certainty developed earlier allows one to apply here all the results established [earlier].'[18]

Amongst these results is proof of the existence of an equilibrium for a theoretical competitive private ownership economy.

Uncertainty leads to criteria which are more complicated than mere value-weighted sums: outcomes cannot then be evaluated by scalars, only by n-dimensional numbers.

8. STOCK-FLOW GOODS

Almost any physical object is durable to some extent. Durables which can be currently produced are stock-flow goods. Both their stocks and their flow-rates of output are important. Stocks do not have time-dimensionality; flows can be interpreted only as time-derivatives.

Introduction of stock-flow goods does not affect consumption theory, but consumption activities must be meticulously defined in order to avoid serious confusion. For example, the consumption activity, drinking milk, is categorically different from the activity, holding milk in one's ice box for later consumption. Amongst other things, one uses an ice box in the latter activity, immediately suggesting (correctly) that the two implicit consumptions bear different prices.

§2

The central idea of 'stock-flow' can be developed through a simple model treating a stock-flow good, such as freight cars, and completing the transition to Chapter 4.

Freight cars are to be hired out by source holders who make a market for used cars and acquire new cars from manufacturers. Old and new cars, sources of freight service, are measured in standard efficiency units: a new car gets a higher rating than does an old car. Carriers rent equipment from source holders and provide shipping services for firms and households.

System **S3** is to determine market equilibrium, i.e. equalities of supplies and demands, at date t:

$$s_t = \Phi(p_t) \tag{88}$$

$$d_t = I_t + kS_t \tag{89}$$

$$I_t = \lambda(D_t - S_t) \tag{90}$$

$$D_t = \Psi(p_t, r_t, i_t^0) \qquad \mathbf{S3} \tag{91}$$

$$S_t = S_0 + \int_{-\infty}^{t} I(\theta) \tag{92}$$

$$s_t = d_t \tag{93}$$

$$r_t = f(S_t, \beta) \tag{94}$$

Ideally **S3** generates a *recursive* process from market-clearance to market-clearance, once initial conditions have been defined, determining its variables $s_t, d_t, I_t, D_t, S_t, p_t$, and r_t.

The glossary of symbols is:

s_t = flow rate of supply of sources
p_t = price of sources
d_t = flow rate of demand for sources
I_t = flow rate of investment demand
kS_t = replacement demand, determined by the depreciation rate, k, and the stock of sources at t, S_t
D_t = optimal stock at date t as seen by source-holders
λ = scalar converting excess demand for a stock (here $D_t - S_t$) into a flow (here I_t)

For $\lambda = 1$ and $D_t - S_t = 20$, investment demand is at the rate of 20 units per period, say per biennium. If flows were to be measured as annual rates, λ would be defined as $\frac{1}{2}$.

r_t = rent commanded by sources at date t

i_t^0 = a discount rate determined outside the model and hence exogenous
to it

β = a vector of final-demand parameters, also exogenous to the model

$\Phi(p_t)$ determines s_t. $\Psi(p_t, r_t, i_t^0)$ determines D_t. $f(S_t, \beta)$ determines the rent of a standard freight-car at date t. Satisfaction of equations (93) and (94) respectively assure clearance of the new-source and rental markets.

System **S4** describes a stationary full-equilibrium solution:

$$S_t = \Phi(p_t) \tag{95}$$

$$d_t = kS_t \tag{96}$$

$$S_t = \Psi(p_t, r_t, i_t^0) \qquad \textbf{S4} \tag{97}$$

$$d_t = s_t \tag{98}$$

$$r_t = f(S_t, \beta) \tag{99}$$

The subscript, t, can be dropped in a stationary economy. In full equilibrium, $S_t = \bar{S}$: 'potential' and actual stocks are equal. Furthermore, in full equilibrium close linkage exists between $\bar{r}$ and $\bar{p}$, given k and i^0: returns from holding freight cars will, at the margin, yield rate of return i^0. Otherwise the stock of freight cars would be growing or decaying.

REFERENCES

1. Cf. G. Debreu, *Theory of Value* (New York: John Wiley & Sons; 1959), Chap. 4.
2. G. Debreu, *Theory of Value* (New York: John Wiley & Sons; 1959), p. 56.
3. G. Debreu, *Theory of Value* (New York: John Wiley & Sons; 1959), p. 51.
4. G. Debreu, *Theory of Value* (New York: John Wiley & Sons; 1959), p. 55.
5. G. Debreu, *Theory of Value* (New York: John Wiley & Sons; 1959), pp. 55–56.
6. Cf. M. L. Burstein, *Money* (Cambridge, Mass.: Schenkman Publishing Co. Inc.; 1963), Chap. I.
7. Cf. J. R. Hicks, *Value and Capital* (Oxford: The Clarendon Press; 1946), 2nd ed., Chap. 14.
8. G. Debreu, *Theory of Value* (New York: John Wiley & Sons; 1959), p. 62.
9. R. G. D. Allen, *Mathematical Economics* (London: Macmillan & Co. Ltd.; 1964), 2nd ed., p. 660.
10. J. R. Hicks, *Value and Capital* (Oxford: The Clarendon Press; 1946), 2nd ed., p. 313. Professor Hicks invented the theorem.
11. G. Debreu, *Theory of Value* (New York: John Wiley & Sons; 1959), p. 37.
12. Cf. R. W. Clower and M. L. Burstein, 'On the Invariance of Demand for Cash and Other Assets,' *Review of Economic Studies*, 1960.
13. J. von Neumann and O. Morgenstern, *Theory of Games and Economic Behaviour* (Princeton: Princeton University Press; 1944), pp. 26–29.
14. J. von Neumann and O. Morgenstern, *Theory of Games and Economic Behaviour* (Princeton: Princeton University Press; 1944), p. 27.
15. G. Debreu, *Theory of Value* (New York: John Wiley & Sons; 1959), p. 32.
16. G. Debreu, *Theory of Value* (New York: John Wiley & Sons; 1959), Chap. 7.
17. Cf. G. Debreu, *Theory of Value* (New York: John Wiley & Sons; 1959), p. 101.
18. G. Debreu, *Theory of Value* (New York: John Wiley & Sons; 1959), p. 102.

CHAPTER 4

Theory of the Competitive Firm;
Marginalism and After

1. INTRODUCTION

There never has been a competitive firm in the sense of this chapter.

The concept 'industry' largely is eschewed in favour of the n-product firm. Purely- and perfectly-competitive are used synonomously in Chapter 4. Cf. Chapter 6.

The qth competitive firm of the theory maximizes an inner product $\mathbf{p} \cdot \mathbf{y}_q$ on a set $\mathbf{Y}_q$ of feasible-outputs, inputs being assigned negative numbers. ($\mathbf{Y}_q$ includes outputs for future dates and $\mathbf{p}$ includes their prices.) Above all, prices are parameters for the competitive firm of the theory. Such a firm always acts as if it can sell all it chooses to offer at $\mathbf{p}$. In market equilibrium it can do just that.

Once interpreted in terms of measured variables subject to random disturbances, the theory of the competitive producer has explained much data. Recall ¶1.5 §§2: prices established in a general competitive equilibrium can, under certain circumstances, be interpreted as Lagrange multipliers in a maximization of a criterion defined on socially feasible outputs. Responses of optimizing competitive firms and households to prices can lead in general-equilibrium to proportions between marginal utilities and marginal costs, etc., corresponding perfectly with requirements of the technocratic welfare-maximization problem. Partly for these reasons, the theory of competitive equilibrium, abstract as it is, has attracted theorists of both capitalist and socialist economies.

Needless to say, the theory of the competitive producer, together with that of the 'competitive' household, are the skeleton of standard economic theory.

§2

What is a firm (producer) in the pure theory of a competitive economy?

All resources are to be owned by the households. Services of productive resources are purchased by producers from households.

PRELIMINARY DEFINITION. A producer is a production set on which profits are being maximized.

The theory is about intensities of production and consumption activities, considered in space and in time. Although the expressions 'firm' and 'producer' are used interchangeably, they carry different connotations: 'firm' connotes 'ownership of or by'; 'producer' connotes 'action by'. So the preliminary definition must be reconsidered. Indeed we project a corollary to it.

COROLLARY TO THE PRELIMINARY DEFINITION. The qth firm is defined by a vector $\boldsymbol{\theta}_q$ identifying the proportions in which households share in its profits.

$$\left(\sum_j \theta_{qj} = 1 \right)$$

The definition of a producer-firm is completed: a production set on which profits are being maximized (hence a producer), the profits to be shared according to the vector $\boldsymbol{\theta}_q$ (hence a firm).

Profit, the value of the qth production plan, need not be zero in the theory of competitive equilibrium. (Cf. note, p. 206, Chapter 9.) However, a *deus ex machina* of initial endowments must be deployed in order to loosen the grip of imputation of proceeds to underlying resources entirely owned by households.

In conventional models of isolated competitive industries, non-zero profits arise in market equilibrium from imputation of economic rents to firms conceived to own specialized resources.

2. THE AXIOMATIC APPROACH TO THE THEORY OF PRODUCTION UNDER COMPETITION

Once again there is to be set out a theory, that of production, which has special relevance for the proof of the existence and other properties of general competitive equilibrium.

§2

The central notions are producer, production plan, the set of production plans and profit maximization.

§3

The feasible-productions open to the qth producer are denoted $\mathbf{Y}_q$. $\mathbf{y}_q$, belonging to $\mathbf{Y}_q$, is the qth producer's production plan. As in the consumption problem of ¶3.3, outputs are represented by positive and inputs by negative numbers. Assumptions on production sets include:

(1) $\mathbf{Y}_q$ and $\mathbf{Y}$, the set of productions feasible for the economy, are closed,

leading to continuity, 'i.e. let $\mathbf{y}_q^*$ be a sequence of productions; if all the $\mathbf{y}_q^*$ are possible for the qth producer, and if $\mathbf{y}_q^* \to \mathbf{y}_q^0$, then $\mathbf{y}_q^0$ is possible for the qth producer.'[1]

2) It is possible for all $\mathbf{y}_q$, and hence for $\mathbf{y} = \Sigma \mathbf{y}_q$, to be zero. This is called *the possibility of inaction*.

3) Free production is impossible. Outputs cannot be achieved without inputs.

4) *Irreversibility*. 'The productive process cannot be reversed, since, in particular, production takes time and commodities are dated.'[2]

5) *Additivity*. If productions $\mathbf{y}_q^1$ and $\mathbf{y}_q^2$ are possible, so is $\mathbf{y}_q^1 + \mathbf{y}_q^2$.

6) $\mathbf{Y}$ is a convex. If $\mathbf{y}^1$ and $\mathbf{y}^2$ are possible, so is $t\mathbf{y}^1 + (1-t)\mathbf{y}^2$, $(0 \le t \le t)$. Assumption 6) rules out increasing returns: if inputs are increased in proportion k_1, outputs will not increase in proportion $k_2 > k_1$.

7) No *firm* enjoys increasing returns to scale. (Assumption 6) does *not* require that $\mathbf{Y}_q$ be convex.)

8) If a total production, $\mathbf{y}$, has all its inputs zero, it is possible. This is an assumption of *free disposal*. (Of course, $\mathbf{y}$ is conditioned by assumption 3) above.)

The firms are completely vertically integrated: no transactions take place between producers as such. Any inputs used by producers are acquired from households, if not acquired 'internally'. So intermediate commodities can be ignored: each commodity of the theory may enter the commodity space of the consumer.

§4

The profit of the qth producer is defined as $\mathbf{p} \cdot \mathbf{y}_q$ and total profit is $\mathbf{p} \cdot \mathbf{y}$. The producer maximizes his profit relative to prices $\mathbf{p}$ and is, of course, a price-taker. The producer chooses his most profitable feasible output.

In the theory, a shareholder working for his firm is a hired hand. The market value of shareholders' services is charged against each firm's profit.

Thus is the qth *supply correspondence* associating production plans with prices. The supply correspondence permits profit functions to be defined relative to prices. This, together with the additivity and possibility-of-inaction assumptions, permits definition of an aggregate production vector $\mathbf{y}$ maximizing aggregate profits relative to $\mathbf{p}$ (i.e., aggregate planned profits).

A correspondence is a more-general concept than is a function. A supply function would associate a unique $\mathbf{y}_q$ with $\mathbf{p}$, whilst a correspondence associates a set of outputs by the qth producer with $\mathbf{p}$. Existence of general-equilibrium depends only on existence of supply- and demand-correspondences.

§5

The analysis leads to a simple demonstration, due to Professor Samuelson, of the unambiguously non-negative effect of an increase in own-price on own-rates of planned output. (Inputs are negative outputs.) The qth producer's optimal production relative to $\mathbf{p}^*$ is $\mathbf{y}_q^*$, whilst $\mathbf{y}_q^{**}$ is optimal relative to $\mathbf{p}^{**}$. By definition of optimality:

$$\mathbf{p}^*\mathbf{y}_q^{**} \leq \mathbf{p}^*\mathbf{y}_q^* \tag{1}$$

i.e.:

$$\mathbf{p}^* \cdot \Delta\mathbf{y}_q \leq 0, \qquad -\mathbf{p}^* \cdot \Delta\mathbf{y}_q \geq 0 \tag{2}$$

By the same token:

$$\mathbf{p}^{**} \cdot \mathbf{y}_q^{**} \geq \mathbf{p}^{**} \cdot \mathbf{y}_q^* \tag{3}$$

i.e.:

$$\mathbf{p}^{**} \cdot \Delta\mathbf{y}_q \geq 0 \tag{4}$$

So

$$\Delta\mathbf{p} \cdot \Delta\mathbf{y}_q \geq 0 \tag{5}$$

For $\Delta p_1 \neq 0, \Delta p_i = 0, i \neq 1$,

$$\Delta p_1 \cdot \Delta y_{q1} \geq 0 \tag{6}$$

'Δ' indicates that the relationship holds for 'large' changes in price.

If p_1 were the price of a factor, equation (6) states that the qth producer either would cut back or leave unchanged his optimal utilization of factor 1 if $\Delta p_1 > 0$. The additivity assumption leads to inequality (7):

$$\Delta p_{q1} \cdot \Delta y_1 \geq 0 \tag{7}$$

Recall Assumption 5) *supra*.

The substitution-effect of an own-price change is unambiguous in a production problem. ¶4.3 arrives at this result in a more cumbersome manner.

3. THE MARGINALIST THEORY OF THE COMPETITIVE FIRM

The theory of the competitive firm is a special case of the theory of the conjecturally independent firm. 'Does the firm take prices of products and factors which it does not quote as data?' 'Yes' in Chapters 4 and 7 and, for the most part, in Chapter 6. The only important distinction we make between *monopolists* and *competitors* is that, whilst *all* prices are data for the latter, the former quotes prices for produced or purchased products. The purely-competitive firm, operating in perfectly-competitive markets, is constrained as a marketer only by prices. The monopolist quotes prices and is constrained by limits on sales possibilities at such prices.

Chapter 6, 'Imperfect Competition', takes up problems of firms in *n* seller markets which lack significant power but where important frictions and uncertainties exist.

Modern income theory is projected more easily from monopoly theory than from models of pure competition.

§2

Inputs are to be represented by negative and outputs by positive numbers: the *q*th competitive firm considers producing vector $\mathbf{y}_q$ comprised of inputs and outputs. Only one-period cases are considered until ¶4 §§9.

Let us drop the subscript *q*. The criterion is maximization of the inner-product $\mathbf{p} \cdot \mathbf{y}$. The firm is considered to have contracted in advance for some resources. Indeed the contracts are so deeply imbedded in the problem that **y** includes only variable inputs. Only variable inputs remain objects of the firm's decision. Only the resource limitations implicit in the predetermined contractual arrangements constrain the size of the firm's operations. Once these contracts are specified, the firm's size will come to be determined by product- and factor-prices interacting with technology in the course of profit maximization.

The constraint on maximization of $\mathbf{p} \cdot \mathbf{y}$ is the firm's *production function*. It is assumed that the production function is continuous and possesses continuous first- and second-order partial derivatives. It can be written explicitly as in equation (8):

$$y_r = F(\mathbf{y}') \qquad y_r \notin \mathbf{y}' \tag{8}$$

The implicit form of the production function is:

$$f(\mathbf{y}) = 0 \tag{9}$$

If y_r concerns an output, equation (8) defines the maximum production of the *r*th commodity on required levels of other outputs and on the variable inputs. If y_r concerns an input, equation (8) defines the minimum (algebraically maximum) amount of the *r*th commodity required for $\mathbf{y}'$ being at least as great algebraically as its specification.

If a firm purchases steel beams and vends them to a customer, a production activity is thus defined. Another production activity might find the firm fabricating the beams in its factories.

As it happens, a programming problem underlies $f(\mathbf{y})$. It will be specified in Chapter 5.

§3

The objective, then, is to maximize $\mathbf{p} \cdot \mathbf{y}$ subject to the production function:

$$\max \mathbf{p} \cdot \mathbf{y} \qquad \text{st } f(\mathbf{y}) = 0 \tag{10}$$

Form the Lagrange function:

$$V = \mathbf{p} \cdot \mathbf{y} - \lambda f(\mathbf{y}) \tag{11}$$

Partially differentiate the Lagrange function with respect to $y_1, y_2, \ldots, y_n$, and λ, setting the partial derivatives equal to zero:

$$p_i - \lambda f_i = 0 \tag{12}$$
$$\mathbf{S1}$$
$$f(\mathbf{y}) = 0 \tag{13}$$

Solve **S1** for $(\bar{\mathbf{y}}, \bar{\lambda})$. The first-order conditions are of the form:

$$f_r/f_s = p_r/p_s \tag{14}$$

It is important to prove that $\bar{\lambda} > 0$. Defining the production function explicitly as $y_1 = F(y_2, \ldots, y_n)$, form the Lagrange function $\mathbf{p} \cdot \mathbf{y} - \lambda(y_1 - F)$. One of the first-order conditions is $p_1 - \lambda = 0$. Hence $\bar{\lambda} > 0$, since p_1 is positive. It appears to be impossible to establish the result in this way if the production function cannot be written explicitly, but compare note preceding ¶3.4.

Figure 1 usefully interprets the first-order conditions, but first the hth price line is defined:

$$p_r y_r + p_s y_s = c_h \tag{15}$$

For two outputs, c_h is a level of revenue from productions (y_r, y_s), the vector $\mathbf{y}''$, *not* including (y_r, y_s), having been specified. For two inputs, c_h is a level of expenditure on inputs (y_r, y_s) for specified $\mathbf{y}''$. For output y_r and input y_s the reference line is defined by **angle** θ of Fig. 1 implying the ratio p_r/p_s: equilibrium cannot occur except at a point such as p^3 at which the internal rate of substitution is equal to $\tan \theta$ in absolute value.

In each instance, p_r/p_s defines a market rate of substitution, the rate at which one (positive or negative) output can be substituted for another at a given level of revenue, expenditure, or net revenue. Compare equation (16):

$$p_r \, dy_r + p_s \, dy_s = 0 \qquad -dy_s/dy_r = p_r/p_s \tag{16}$$

Fig. 1 implies three classes of subsidiary maximization problems. Each of the curves describes pairs (y_r, y_s) consistent with $\mathbf{y}''$. In each such pair (y_r^*, y_s^*), y_r is algebraically maximized, given y_s^*, and vice versa, always relative to the problem's constraints.

Optimization in each instance occurs at a point at which the internal rate of substitution equals the market rate. This becomes clear if the production function is differentiated with respect to arguments r and s:

$$f_r \, dy_r + f_s \, dy_s = 0 \qquad -dy_s/dy_r = f_r/f_s \qquad (17)$$

In words: 'At each of points P the price line is tangent to the *sub production function*.'

The curvatures reflect the second-order condition: rates of substitution between commodities r and s must diminish in equilibrium, i.e., the internal rate of substitution of commodity s for commodity r must decrease as y_r is to increase, *ceteris paribus*. Note that the convexity requirement of ¶4.2 pertains only to the aggregate set Y. ¶4.3 needs stronger assumptions about production sets than does ¶4.2.

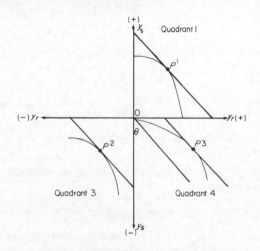

Fig. 1   Graphic First-order Conditions

Thus consider P^1: in equilibrium, the rate at which outputs can be substituted for each other in production (f_r/f_s) should be equal to the rate at which they can be substituted in the market: if $p_r = kp_s$, it pays to substitute the rth for the sth commodity (or *vice versa*) until, at the margin, k units of the sth must be sacrificed to obtain an additional unit of the rth commodity. Consider P^2: in equilibrium, the rate at which inputs can be substituted for each other in production (f_r/f_s) should be equal to their market rate of substitution. If $p_r = kp_s$, it pays to substitute one for the other until one more unit of the rth would offset subtraction of k units of the sth input.

The first-order conditions strictly apply only in the limit. The text's description is heuristic.

The analysis of Fig. 1 subsumes the so-called marginal-productivity theory of distribution. Assume that $y_1, \ldots, y_m$ are outputs whilst $y_{m+1}, \ldots, y_n$ are inputs. Consider using (absolutely) more of input $m+1$ whilst $dy_{m+2} = \ldots = dy_n = 0$. The optimal allocation of dy_{m+1} accords with equation (18):

$$(p_1 f_{m+1})/f_1 = \ldots = (p_m f_{m+1})/f_m = p_{m+1} \tag{18}$$

How is f_{m+1}/f_i $(i = 1, 2, \ldots, m)$ to be interpreted? Consider equation (19):

$$f_i \, dy_i = -f_{m+1} \, dy_{m+1}, \qquad |dy_i/dy_{m+1}| = f_{m+1}/f_i \qquad i = 1, 2, \ldots, m \tag{19}$$

Equation (19) defines the rate at which the ith output changes with the $(m+1)$st input, all other outputs and inputs held fixed: f_{m+1}/f_i can be defined as the *marginal productivity* of the $(m+1)$st factor in the production of the ith output. Denote f_{m+1}/f_i as $MPP_{i,m+1}$. Equation (18) then can be written:

$$(MPP_{i,m+1})p_i = p_{m+1} \tag{20}$$

In words: 'In competitive equilibrium the value of the *marginal product* of the sth factor in the production of the rth output, VMP_{rs}, is equal to the sth factor price.'

The equilibrium conditions of equation (20) govern comparative-statics analysis of effects of changes in input- or output-prices on planned inputs or outputs. Inevitably, the second-order condition must first be developed.

§4[3]

The second-order condition for the producer problem is derived in just the same way as that for the consumer problem. The Lagrange function, $\mathbf{p} \cdot \mathbf{y} - \lambda f$, leads up to the quadratic form:

$$\boldsymbol{\delta}' \begin{bmatrix} \partial^2 z/\partial \lambda^2 & & \partial^2 z/\partial \lambda \, \partial y_i \\ & \partial^2 z/\partial y_i \, \partial y_j & \\ \partial^2 z/\partial y_i \, \partial \lambda & & \end{bmatrix} \boldsymbol{\delta} \tag{21}$$

The analogue to expression (3.22) is:

$$\begin{bmatrix} 0 & & -f_i \\ & -\lambda f_{ij} & \\ -f_i & & \end{bmatrix} \tag{22}$$

Let us divide all rows by $(-1/\bar{\lambda})$:

$$
\begin{bmatrix}
0 & & f_i/\bar{\lambda} \\
 & f_{ij} & \\
f_i/\bar{\lambda} & &
\end{bmatrix}
\tag{23}
$$

The second-order condition requires that all of the determinants of inequalities (24) be negative (so that the quadratic form is positive definite).

$$
\begin{vmatrix}
0 & f_1 & f_2 \\
f_1 & f_{11} & f_{12} \\
f_2 & f_{12} & f_{22}
\end{vmatrix} < 0; \quad
\begin{vmatrix}
0 & f_1 & f_2 & f_3 \\
f_1 & f_{11} & f_{12} & f_{13} \\
f_2 & f_{12} & f_{22} & f_{23} \\
f_3 & f_{13} & f_{23} & f_{33}
\end{vmatrix} < 0; \dots
$$

$$
\begin{vmatrix}
0 & \dots\dots f_n \\
\vdots & f_{ij} \\
f_n &
\end{vmatrix} < 0
\tag{24}
$$

§5

Comparative statics are developed by differentiating the first-order conditions comprising **S1**:

$$
0 + f_1 \, d\bar{y}_1 + \dots + f_n \, d\bar{y}_n = 0
$$

$$
(f_1/\bar{\lambda}) \, d\bar{\lambda} + f_{11} \, d\bar{y}_1 + \dots + f_{1n} \, d\bar{y}_n = dp_1/\bar{\lambda} \qquad \textbf{S2} \quad (25)
$$

$$
\dots\dots\dots\dots\dots\dots\dots\dots\dots\dots\dots\dots\dots\dots\dots\dots
$$

$$
(f_n/\bar{\lambda}) \, d\bar{\lambda} + f_{1n} \, d\bar{y}_1 + \dots + f_{nn} \, d\bar{y}_n = dp_n/\bar{\lambda}
$$

The matrix of coefficients of the left-hand side of **S2** is identical with matrix (23) except that the first row is not multiplied by $(1/\bar{\lambda})$. Corresponding determinants will have the same sign: the determinant of **S2**, for example, will be negative.

As in Chapter 3, we denote the first row of **S2** as row zero so that its cofactors are Δ_{0s}.

We next note that, analogously to inequality (3.24), the second-order condition for the producer problem can be written:

$$
\sum\sum (\Delta_{rs}/\Delta)\delta_r\delta_s > 0
\tag{26}
$$

For $\delta = d\mathbf{p}$, $dp_r \neq 0$, $dp_s = 0$ $(r \neq s)$,

$$
(\Delta_{rr}/\Delta)(dp_r)^2 > 0 \quad \therefore \ (\Delta_{rr}/\Delta) > 0
\tag{27}
$$

Own-price and cross-effects are written:

$$d\bar{y}_r/dp_r = \Delta_{rr}/\bar{\lambda}\Delta > 0 \tag{28}$$

$$d\bar{y}_r/dp_s = \Delta_{sr}/\bar{\lambda}\Delta \tag{29}$$

The positiveness of $\bar{\lambda}$ assures that, if a product price increases, *ceteris paribus*, the competitive firm will plan to produce more of that product and that an increase in a factor price, again *ceteris paribus*, causes a competitive firm to plan to use less of that factor. This, the statement of equation (28), follows then from inequality (27). (Recall that for a factor, y_r is negative.)

Equations (26) to (29) also show that in the traditional theory of the firm the price effect consists only of a substitution-effect. There is no income-effect. Why? The constraint does not contain prices.

Properties of cross-effects, effects of changes in p_r on planned outputs of commodity 1 or intake of commodity s, are farther from the surface. Examine equation (30) derived, together with inequality (32), precisely as were expressions (3.32) and (3.33). (Again we move freely between δ, **p**, and d**p**.)

$$\sum_s Y_{rs}\delta_s = 0 \tag{30}$$

It has been established that $Y_{rr} > 0$. Hence,

$$\sum_s{}' Y_{rs}\delta_s < 0 \tag{31}$$

($\sum'$ indicates that the summation is only for $r \neq s$.)

Inequality (31) establishes that there must be at least one instance in which an increased factor-price leads to increased use of another factor or to a reduced output and that an increased output-price leads to decreased production of at least one other output or to increased use of at least one factor. Also that the total value of substitutions must exceed that of 'complementations'.

Inequality (32) leads to the 'group-of-goods' theorem of ¶3.4 §§9. It suffices here merely to note that for $dp_1 \neq 0, dp_2 = dp_3 = \ldots = dp_n = 0$, if indeed such a theorem holds, then commodities $2, \ldots, n$ can be treated as a group. However, at least one pair must be substitutes. Here there is only one pair: Q.E.D.

$$\sum\sum Y_{rs}\delta_r\delta_s > 0 \tag{32}$$

§6

¶4.3 §§5 leads to a supply function relating $\bar{y}_q$ to **p**. Since production functions are stipulated to be independent until ¶4.3 §§11, aggregate supply functions also are implied. ¶4.3 §§7 traditionally analyses relationships between marginal costs of competitive firms and prices, leading to discussion in ¶4.3 §§8 of rent and increasing-, decreasing- or constant-cost production under incompletely- and fully-adjusted conditions. ¶4.3 §§9 takes up the *long run* and the *short run* explaining that, ironically, passage of time is irrelevant to the theory. ¶4.3 §§10 embellishes the structure thrown up by ¶4.3 §§1–5, explicitly studying production over n periods. ¶4.3 §§11 concerns externalities, ways in which the rth production function can be affected by y_s.

§7

Marginal Cost and Price

The definition of incremental cost of a small increase in output y_1 holding constant $y_2, \ldots, y_m$, varying inputs $y_{m+1}, \ldots, y_n$, is built up through equations (33) and (34):

$$\mathrm{d}y_1 = (1/-f_1) \sum_{m+1}^{n} f_i \, \mathrm{d}y_i \tag{33}$$

$$\mathrm{d}C = - \sum_{m+1}^{n} p_i \, \mathrm{d}y_i \tag{34}$$

Consulting equation (36), the appropriate cost-increment is defined by equation (35):

$$\mathrm{d}C = p_1[(-1/f_1)\Sigma f_i \, \mathrm{d}y_i] \tag{35}$$

In equilibrium $f_i/f_1 = p_i/p_1$. That is:

$$p_i = (f_i p_1)/f_i, \tag{36}$$

permitting equation (34) to be written as equation (35), but the right-hand side of equation (35) is nothing other than $\mathrm{d}y_1$ as defined in equation (33): in the competitive firm's equilibrium:

$$\mathrm{d}C/\mathrm{d}y_1 = p_1 \qquad (\mathrm{d}y_2 = \mathrm{d}y_3 = \ldots = \mathrm{d}y_m = 0) \tag{37}$$

The rate at which total cost changes with output is equal to price in competitive equilibrium.

If p_1 can be associated with each consumer's marginal valuation of commodity 1 and its marginal cost with the value of incremental resources (valued at opportunity cost), marginal-cost pricing has obvious importance for welfare economics. (For simplicity, assume that each consumer uses commodity 1.)

§ 8

Rent, etc.

The programming analysis of Chapter 5 will be especially fruitful in relating prices and outputs to rents earned by or attributed to productive agents fixed in supply. But the model of ¶4.3 brings out an important characteristic of rents (hire-prices): there is a sense in which rents of agents fixed in supply are price-determined rather than price-determining. True, the lessee of a unique store site correctly treats the hire-price as a cost. Indeed it is a social opportunity cost: in a fully adjusted economy, the site rent charged to the rth firm will be no less than the bid made by the sth firm. On the other hand, since supplies of specified sites are perfectly price-inelastic, their hire prices will be *determined* by final-product prices— by 'demand'. Prices of such sites as assets will be determined only by hire-prices and discount factors. The assets are not reproducible.

Cast the variables into logarithms. The elasticity of the relationship then is the slope of $f(\pi)$ where the log of the dependent variable, χ, is function f of the log of the independent variable π. Recall that d log $y = y/\mathrm{d}y$. Hence d log y/d log $p = (\mathrm{d}y/\mathrm{d}p)(p/y) = \eta, \sigma,$ (η and σ being demand and supply elasticities). Elasticities permit sensitivity-measures to be invariant against choice of scale.

If a factor is perfectly elastic in supply with respect to its price, the supply relation can be plotted as a flat line (p being measured on the ordinate): $\sigma = \infty$.

By way of contrast, consider a factor which is perfectly elastic in supply at $100. If perpetuities yielded 10 per cent per annum, its full equilibrium perpetual rental, in a world of certainty, would be $10 per annum.

In full equilibrium, the stock will be constant. Replacements in full equilibrium will be bought in at $100. If rents were below $10 per annum, stocks would be decaying.

Note that this factor's hire-price can be determined without reference to final-product prices or 'demand', except in so far as interest rates and costs of production are being determined in the economy's general equilibrium. The factor's rôle in final-product markets is *price determining*. And, of course, the 'elastically-supplied factor's asset-price, $100, is determined by its cost of production alone, subject to the irrefragable interdependence of all prices in the economy's general-equilibrium.

Next consider a case in which two firms contemplate production of identical vectors $\mathbf{y}^*$. Firm Aleph controls a unique productive asset, not in $\mathbf{y}^*$, perhaps an indivisible piece of land or a contract with a talented production manager. Firm Beth, like all other firms under consideration, does not utilize any specialized resources. Hence, in equilibrium, Firm . Beth will earn zero profits at $\bar{\mathbf{p}}$: competition would assure that, as long as Beth were earning positive profits—above and beyond interest and depreciation charges—there would be entry into activities yielding the components of $\mathbf{y}^*$.

In so far as shareholders work for the company or own physical capital used by the company, the company is charged the market-rental. Profits are calculated so as to impute market values to all employed resources. It is the residual, after such imputations, which is to be zero.

Indeed all non-Aleph firms must earn zero profits in a fully-adjusted economy. Ignoring tiny Aleph, $\bar{\mathbf{p}}$ must emerge at which the vector $\bar{\mathbf{y}}(=\sum_q \mathbf{y}^*)$ will correspond exactly with commodity demands and factor supplies at $\bar{\mathbf{p}}$ and $\bar{\mathbf{p}} \cdot \mathbf{y} = 0$.

By assumption $\mathbf{p} \cdot \mathbf{y}^*_{\text{Aleph}} > 0$, noting that the vector $\mathbf{y}^*_{\text{Aleph}}$ excludes Aleph's utilization of the services of its unique asset. Two possibilities are to be considered:

1) Aleph owns the unique asset outright;
2) Aleph hires the asset through competitive bidding.

Under 1) Aleph's shares will have positive worth whilst a poltergeist Beth, in a world of certainty, will have no net worth. Aleph, under 1), is a *super-marginal competitive firm*. Under 2), Aleph's potential *economic rent* (return above opportunity cost of utilized resources) is appropriated by the source-owner.

Capital gains might have been rung up by Aleph's founders, depending on what they paid for their 'exclusive' asset, but Aleph's profitability would neither make Aleph shares more appealing than Beth shares at equilibrium share prices nor encourage Beth-like firms to challenge Aleph.

Relationships between competitive models and efficient use of economic resources abound. Economists concerned with resource allocation are anxious to render their criteria insensitive to forms of ownership. In cases 1) *and* 2) the economist *and*, as it happens, a profit-maximizing Aleph, will impute to the cost of Aleph's activities the opportunity cost of the specialized resource operated by Aleph, viz. the highest rent offered by another firm. If Aleph does not make a paper loss when subject to such an imputation, one can conclude—if rigid requirements of universal competitiveness in a tranquil, stationary environment are met—that the value of the national 'dividend' could not be increased by wrenching the specialized resource from Aleph's control.

The zero-profit criterion for competitive equilibrium (taking up the 'Beth' case) sometimes is thought incorrectly to require that competitive firms produce under constant returns to scale. For a correct analysis see P. A. Samuelson, *Foundations of Economic Analysis* (Cambridge, Mass.: Harvard University Press; 1947), Chap. IV.

The constant-returns case is interesting and doctrinally important however. If there are constant returns to scale, an increase of all inputs in proportion k is accompanied by a k-fold increase in all outputs: if $\mathbf{y}^*$ satisfies $f(\mathbf{y}^*) = 0$, so will $k\mathbf{y}^*$: $f(\mathbf{y}^*) = f(k\mathbf{y}^*)$: the function f is zero-order homogeneous in y. It follows from Euler's theorem that $\sum f_i y_i = 0$. In equilibrium $\lambda f_i = p_i$: $f_i = p_i/\lambda$. Therefore, Euler's theorem requires that $(1/\lambda)\sum p_i y_i = 0$, that $\sum p_i y_i = 0$. *Firms in competitive equilibrium experiencing constant returns to scale must. earn zero profits.*

Since a competitive firm producing under constant returns to scale can *in posse* expand its productions indefinitely without increasing its unit costs, the second-order condition breaks down. Indeed, in this context, perhaps one should say that the stability condition breaks down. In any event, the analysis of Chapter 4 does not suffice to determine the scale of a competitive firm experiencing constant returns to scale and hence to outlay.

§9

The Long Run

In the *long run* the qth firm can fully adjust inputs $y_{m+1,q}, \ldots, y_{nq}$. Adjustment possibilities are imperfect in the *short run*, but beware of injecting ideas of temporal sequence into this statical analysis.

By definition, fully-adjusted possibilities are at least as favourable as incompletely-adjusted possibilities: *status quo ante* is always available. Hence, *long run* costs never exceed *short run* costs and can be less, and *long run* supply elasticities must be at least as great as *short run* supply elasticities.

Next consult Fig. 2. Newly established prices, expected to prevail forever, lead to an AB unit shift in the optimal steady-state utilization of the sth factor. How should the shift be worked out over time? The answer partly depends on interest rates: the higher are interest rates, *ceteris paribus*, the less is the present value of deferred receipts. Accordingly, if outlays must be made now and if a larger outlay is necessary to achieve *path ξ* than *path ε* than *path υ*, ξ will be chosen, (again *ceteris paribus*), at 'very low' interest rates and υ at 'very high' interest rates, although there exists, in general, an interest rate structure for which ε is optimal.

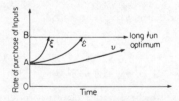

Fig. 2   Temporal Adjustment

POINT. The fact that a *long run* cost curve reflects full adjustment to a hypothetical steady-state production, whilst a *short run* cost curve reflects incomplete adjustment, neither means that the firm necessarily is moving towards a *long run* (and hence steady-state) position (it might be planning to grow), nor that *in theory* time is required to shift to a *long run* position.

Similar arguments can be made about *short run* and *long run* elasticities of demand. A once-and-for-all change in p_r, *ceteris paribus*, will lead to sequential changes in consumption. Such sequences can be rigorously analysed if the model is defined over an extended time horizon.

Indeed the underlying statical theory does not contemplate 'time'. In conventional economic theory, *short run–long run* analysis, being thoroughly statical, does not play out over time.

§ 10

Time

After limning a general model of the intertemporal planning of a competitive firm, we consider specific problems of costs and outputs.

Commodities of different date are to be different commodities. *Location* continues to be neglected. Futures-trading is precluded. Spot prices at future dates are parameters. Indebtedness can be discharged only when delivery is made.

¶4.3 §§10, unlike ¶4.2, requires discount factors. The present value of \$1 to be received three periods from now being \$$1/(1 + r_1)(1 + r_2)(1 + r_3)$, we denote $(1/(1 + r_t))$ as ρ^t. The firm is to maximize:

$$\rho^1 \mathbf{p}^1 \cdot \mathbf{y} + \rho^1 \rho^2 \mathbf{p}^2 \cdot \mathbf{y}^2 + \dots + \rho^1 \rho^2 \dots \rho^T \mathbf{p}^T \cdot \mathbf{y}^T \qquad (38)$$

subject to:

$$f(\mathbf{y}^1, \mathbf{y}^2, \dots, \mathbf{y}^T) = 0. \qquad (39)$$

Current-dated commodities are not to be discounted: $\rho° = 1$. For the sake of simplicity, $\mathbf{y}°$ is predetermined. So $\rho°$ and $\mathbf{y}°$ can be dropped above. Finally, the subscript q also is dropped.

The first-order conditions are given in **S3**:

$$
\begin{array}{lll}
1) & \rho^1 p_i^1 - \lambda f_{y_i} = 0 & \\
\dots\dots\dots\dots\dots\dots\dots\dots\dots & i = 1, 2, \dots, m & \textbf{S3} \quad (40) \\
T) & \rho^1 \dots \rho^T p_i^T - \lambda f_{y_i^T} = 0 &
\end{array}
$$

Amongst other things, the first-order conditions imply that

$$f_{y_i^T}/f_{y_i^1} = \frac{\rho^1 \dots \rho^T p_1^T}{\rho^1 p_1^1} \qquad (41)$$

In words, the discounted prices of commodities, identical except for dating, must be proportionate to the rate at which they can be substituted in intertemporal production.

Consider a firm possessed of enough of a unique, indispensable and irreplaceable input to make 100 units of commodity 1. How should it plot its productions and sales over time? Equation (41) offers important clues.

¶4.3 §§10 is batting practice for ¶10.6–¶10.8.

Now consider the ways in which a change in the vector $(p^1, p^2, \ldots, p^T)$ can affect the over-all production plan.

And, since ¶4.3 §§10 is only batting practice, its presentation of the comparative statics of intertemporal production is non-rigorous.

It becomes difficult to revert back to a 'one-period' mode of analysis. In particular, if the single planning period is so large that interactions of today's productive activities with tomorrow's events are swallowed up, most of the practical problems of production planning will have been assumed away *ab initio*. Logically, however, the one- and T-period cases are on all fours, and the one-period analysis *is* a useful exercise. Finally, note that the analysis of ¶4.2 is intertemporally sophisticated.

Assume that the firm was fully adjusted to initial **p**, **p***, and was in fact in a steady state, producing $\mathbf{y}^{*1} = \mathbf{y}^{*2} = \ldots = \mathbf{y}^{*T}$.

For various good reasons, think of T as a very large number.

Now **p**** is to become operative. Assume that, in due course, a new steady-state (**y****) will become established. Meanwhile, input–output constellations must be shaped relative to interest rates as well as prices, as indeed is **y****. Furthermore, technological advantages of bulk-purchase must be set off against disadvantages of massive, abrupt changes. In the upshot there will come to be at each date a set of capacities to be worked with variable inputs, but these capacity sets are objects of choice at $t = 0$, the temporal origin. In this way there is determined an optimum relative to initial conditions.

The *optimal* arrangement of steady state production will not be practically important in a growing, changing economy. That is one reason why the theory of the steady growth of competitive economies has interested some theorists. Envisage steady percentage growth of all endowments. The number of firms might also steadily expand or initial firms might grow at a steady rate as they ingest the steadily-growing underlying capacities. In either case, in this abstruse model, all aggregate inputs and outputs come to expand at the same steady rate. A powerful model of this type, that of J. von Neumann, is treated in ¶10.8 infra. The competitive counterpart of the von Neumann model is simply an interpretation of the dual-problem.

Practical production problems concerning lengths of production runs, batch sizes, whiskey- or beer-ageing, etc., can be cast up in the empirical counterpart to the model of ¶4.3 §§10.

A firm is assigned the task of delivering three assembled airplanes at the end of period 2, this being period 0. Feasible production-sequences include $(3, 0, 0)$, $(1, 1, 1)$, and $(0, 0, 3)$. The firm must contract for very large doses of machine-hours of certain equipment specialized to its productions, if it is to obtain such equipment at all.

Lumpiness and indivisibility make their début! These dark sisters play an important role in Chapter 6.

It considers, then, the saving in machine rent possible in the $(3, 0, 0)$ sequence as against the steady gain in productivity as workers gain experience in a $(1, 1, 1)$ sequence, or the effects of building up forces for the $(0, 0, 3)$ sequence, accompanied by interruption of production in periods 0 and 1.

The second sequence might lead to costs $(10, 8, 10)$ (in millions of dollars); the first might require a period 0 outlay of \$27 million. For $r_1 = r_2 = 0\cdot10$, the present value of *sequence two* costs would be less than \$26 million. *Sequence two* would become preferred.

The output yielded by a plane stored this period is a new commodity, a plane aged one period. The cost of obtaining the new commodity is controlled by interest rates. The new commodity's productive rôle is to yield a marketable plane later. Obvious analogies include beer or whiskey production.

Assume that the firm's only assets are non-negotiable service contracts. Then in the first sequence the three planes are immediately to be sold to the firm's source-holding *alter ego* for the present value of the contract price. It is often useful to postulate shadow transactions within firms.

§ 11

Externalities

Three cases involving external effects of one firm's actions on others are to be taken up:

1) water pollution;
2) education;
3) aircraft engineers.

Cases 1) and 2) concern *technical* economies and diseconomies; case 3) concerns a *pecuniary* diseconomy. In 1) and 2) the qth firm's actions affect others' technological possibilities for transformation of inputs into outputs. In 3) its actions affect prices paid by others for inputs.

An analogous case finds a firm increasing its outputs, thereby reducing the market price received by other producers. Sometimes when businessmen get the hang of this point they end up in gaol.

The full reach of ¶4.3 §§11 is achieved only in Chapter 10. Suffice it to say now that:

a) it is socially desirable for decisions to reflect 1) and 2) but not 3);
b) the market mechanism of an idealized competitive economy ignores external pecuniary effects, but also might ignore external technical effects.

1) *Water pollution.* If an upstream paper mill dumps noxious effluvia into a stream, downstream producers (including consumers 'producing' utility) would be injured. Properly, downstream production functions should include a variable y^{m+1}, the output of the upstream firm.

Assume that each of the m downstream firms produces one product: the same product, with the same two inputs. Equation (42) displays the production function of the qth downstream producer:

$$y_1^q = f^q(y_2^q, y_3^q : y^{m+1}) \qquad q = 1, 2, \ldots, m \tag{42}$$

At the margin:

$$dy_1^q/dy_1^{m+1} = \partial f^q/\partial y^{m+1} < 0 \qquad dy_2^q = dy_3^q = 0 \tag{43}$$

2) *Education.*

The text takes up technocratic progress and measurable inputs and outputs. An economically tangential case would concern the humanities. Broad liberal education might be necessary for successful representative government, but none would find it financially profitable to contribute to liberal education and only the contributions of a very few would have perceptible effects.

We here introduce the dynamics of technical progress whilst setting out a case in which market prices do not properly reflect social productivity.

A typical explicit production function at date t, dropping superscript q, is to be:

$$y_{1t} = f(y_{2t}, \ldots, y_{nt}; \varepsilon_t) \tag{44}$$

where:

$$\varepsilon_t = \Phi(\mathbf{u}(t)), \tag{45}$$

ε being a shift operator governing technical progress, itself depending on controls $\mathbf{u}$, defined on time. Controls include expenditures on higher education, hours of quality radio programming, etc., so that $\mathbf{u}(t)$ is a vector of time paths of controls. Next we associate each vector-function $\mathbf{u}^*(t)$ with a path of expenditure $\psi^*(t)$.

Focusing on education, consider a private, competitive, 'for-profit' educational system. The emergent path $\psi^{**}(t)$ doubtless would not reflect fully production functions $\mathbf{f}$. Why? It is impossible to prevent an industrialist from utilizing new techniques without paying the education industry, just as it is impossible for investors to appropriate all of the fruits of their expenditures without some sort of social intervention. Nor is it clear that feasible interventions could be formidable. For example, what sense would it make for students to sign articles promising to turn over to their university the fruits of any innovation they might make which reflects their training? Tuition charges are not likely to come to

112 *Economic Theory*

reflect meaningful pay-off possibilities even in an ugly philistine-orientated educational system. So $\psi(t)$ would tend to lie below its optimal path (in whatever sense we may employ this locution) to the extent that social-exceed private-returns—to the extent that positive effects of educational expenditures on transformation-possibilities over time are not fully reflected in market prices.

3) *Aircraft engineers.* Assume that each class Aleph aircraft builder must employ 10 class Alpha engineers, but that he cannot gain by hiring more than ten, if labour-hoarding strategies are disregarded. Then total demand for Alphas by Alephs will be $10z$ where z is the number of Alephs. Assume that the supply function for Alphas can be written:

$$S = bw - a \tag{46}$$

Hence:

$$\bar{w} = (10z + a)/b \tag{47}$$

and

$$d\bar{w}/dz = 10/b > 0 \tag{48}$$

Additional Aleph entrants impose pecuniary diseconomies on existing firms. Wage-bills are forced up. This is not a social diseconomy. Technological terms of trade between inputs and outputs are not affected. Indeed additional entry is socially desirable if the value of the entrants' net produce exceeds opportunity costs of production, taking into account what then would be the higher social value of Alpha-engineer services.

There are a number of qualifications, one being labelled 'second best'. Cf. Chapter 10 *infra*.

1. G. Debreu, *Theory of Value* (New York: John Wiley & Sons; 1959), p. 39.
2. G. Debreu, *Theory of Value* (New York: John Wiley & Sons; 1959), p. 40.
3. Cf. J. R. Hicks, *Value and Capital* (Oxford: The Clarendon Press; 1946), 2nd ed., p. 320; P. A. Samuelson, *Foundations of Economic Analysis* (Cambridge, Mass.: Harvard University Press; 1947), p. 62, and J. Henderson and R. Quandt, *Microeconomic Theory* (New York: McGraw-Hill Book Co. Inc.; 1958), Appendix A.

CHAPTER 5

Theory of the Competitive Firm:
Programming

1. INTRODUCTION

The central topic continues to be maximization of criteria subject to constraint.

The traditional techniques of Chapter 4 are not altogether satisfactory for at least these reasons. We wish to do more than describe the hull of the set of feasible-productions. Why not show how alternative data lead up to specific alternative ways of doing things and to specific alternative intensities of activity-operation? Secondly, traditional treatments are confined to equality constraints. Not only are inequality constraints interesting; often to require equality constraints is to bound the solution away from its optimal feasible value or, perhaps, to make the problem insoluble. Thirdly, continuing decisions on investment, based on comparison of market prices with internal resource valuations, are not made explicit traditionally, nor is the fact that resources necessarily are temporarily fixed in supply to the firm. Fourthly, classical calculus cannot link up theories of the competitive firm and of production with the theory of general-equilibrium. Finally, classical mathematical methods cannot formally deal with concavities or with holes and other discontinuities in production surfaces, nor with lumpinesses such as minimum lot-sizes. It is desirable to offer explicit topological interpretations of these.

Cf. the note preceding ¶3.4 §§7. Classical mathematical methods, properly extended, are often computationally infeasible rather than theoretically inadequate for the problems taken up in this book.

Programming, included in *activity analysis*, goes far to rectify these shortcomings, sometimes iteratively. However, Chapter 5 takes up only abstract models. Only in Chapter 6 is the pertinence of activity analysis for messy practical problems suggested.

2. KUHN–TUCKER THEORY AND THE THEORY OF THE FIRM[1]

R. Dorfman, P. Samuelson and R. Solow, *Linear Programming and Economic Analysis* (1958) often is denoted *DOSSO* in what follows.

The objective of the qth firm is to maximize a revenue function defined on activity levels $\mathbf{x}$ subject to inequality constraints. An activity is a way of doing things. Each activity yields outputs and absorbs inputs. In general the rates at which outputs are yielded or inputs absorbed are not independent of activity levels. Activities, in general, are not linear. Revenues associated with activities are net. Expenditures on inputs not restricted in maximum supply to the firm are subtracted from receipts. Only in the competitive case are prices evaluating activities independent of the levels at which activities are being operated. Only in the competitive case can levels of inputs and outputs be assumed not to affect prices.

The level or *intensity* of a non-linear activity must refer to (be normalized on) the level of one of its inputs or outputs. For example, the level of an activity yielding oranges and lemons and employing land and labour might be defined by the number of oranges yielded. The intensity of a linear activity is easily defined: the sth activity can be described by coefficients a_{is} determined up to a factor of proportionality, i.e. up to $a_{2s}/a_{1s}, \ldots, a_{ns}/a_{1s}$. Arbitrarily select an admissible vector $(a_{1s}, \ldots, a_{ns})^*$ and stipulate that it is to correspond with operation of the sth activity at unit intensity. Do this for all s. Then drop the asterisk, lightening the notation.[2]

The level of a non-linear activity, even of a competitive producer, affects the activity's net revenue: inputs might increase relative to outputs at higher intensities of operation.

Each activity absorbs resources fixed in supply to the firm over the decision period: floor-space, shelf-space, machine-time.

§ 2[3]

The central mathematical assumptions for Kuhn–Tucker theory are that the set of feasible input–output combinations be convex and that the described functions be continuous and differentiable. The seminal Kuhn–Tucker article[4] was confined to constraints of the form of inequalities (2), as we shall be. Furthermore, the revenue function of equation (1) is to be concave (as it would be if linear) and functions $\mathbf{g}(\mathbf{x})$ are to be convex.

§ 3

The objective function to be maximized, here a revenue function, is:

$$R = f(\mathbf{x}) \qquad \text{i.e. } R = f(x_1, \ldots, x_n) \tag{1}$$

The function f is defined on $\mathbf{x}$. The expression $f(\mathbf{x})$ masks a sub-programming problem: the revenue of an activity depends on prices charged for its output. If outputs $y_1^*, y_2^*, \ldots y_h^*$ are associated with activity levels $\mathbf{x}^*$, then $p_1, p_2, \ldots, p_h$ are to be chosen to maximize $\mathbf{p} \cdot \mathbf{y}^{**}$, outputs which are destroyed rather than sold comprising the vector $(\mathbf{y}^* - \mathbf{y}^{**})$. Each activity vector thus associates with total revenue R^*.

The constraints are of the form:

$$\mathbf{g}(\mathbf{x}) \le \mathbf{b} \tag{2}$$

$$\mathbf{x} \ge \mathbf{0} \tag{3}$$

where the rth inequality, $g^r(\mathbf{x}) \le b^r$, requires that total absorption of the rth capacity, defined by $g^r(\mathbf{x})$, shall not exceed the amount available.

Consider a linear case with two activities and two capacity constraints and where x_1, operated at unit level, absorbs $1 \cdot 5$ units of the first capacity and 2 of the second, whilst x_2, so operated, absorbs 2 units of the first and $0 \cdot 75$ of the second capacity. The inequalities defining the capacity constraints then are written $1 \cdot 5 x_1 + 2 x_2 \le b_1$ and $2 x_1 + 0 \cdot 75 x_2 \le b_2$.

There are m constraints; $\mathbf{b}$ is an m-vector. Sometimes it is useful to write inequalities (2) implicitly:

$$\mathbf{h}(\mathbf{x}) \le \mathbf{0} \tag{4}$$

§ 4

There are four fundamental theorems, developed by Kuhn and Tucker, about the pure-mathematical counterpart to the *mathematical* problem, $\max f(\mathbf{x})$ st $\mathbf{h}(\mathbf{x}) \le \mathbf{0}$, given the stipulations of ¶5.2 §§2. The theorems are to be stated before economic interpretations are offered, emphasizing that economic theory merely associates abstract mathematical entities with economic data-series.

If $\bar{\mathbf{x}}$ maximizes $f(\mathbf{x})$, subject to $\mathbf{x} \ge \mathbf{0}$ and to $\mathbf{h}(\mathbf{x}) \le \mathbf{0}$, then, of course:

1)

$$\mathbf{h}(\bar{\mathbf{x}}) \le \mathbf{0} \tag{5}$$

Furthermore, there exists a vector $\bar{\lambda}$ such that:

2) if

$$h^r(\bar{\mathbf{x}}) < 0, \quad \text{then} \quad \bar{\lambda}_r = 0 \cdot \tag{6}$$

and:
3)

$$f_i - \sum_{j=1}^{m} \bar{\lambda}_j h_i \le 0 \qquad i = 1, 2, \ldots, n \tag{7}$$

where f_i is the partial derivative $\partial f / \partial x_i$ and h_i is the partial derivative $\partial h / \partial x_i$.

Since $\mathbf{h(x)} = \mathbf{g(x)} - \mathbf{b}$, $\partial \mathbf{h}/\partial \mathbf{x} = \partial \mathbf{g}/\partial \mathbf{x}$, where $\mathbf{b}$ is a vector of constants, economically interpreted as capacities as it happens.

Furthermore:
4) if

$$f_s - \sum^m \bar{\lambda}_j h_s < 0, \quad \text{then} \quad \bar{x}_s = 0 \tag{8}$$

Inequalities (5) to (8) hold if $\mathbf{\bar{x}}$ maximizes $f(\mathbf{x})$. What if a specified vector $\mathbf{x}^*$ obeys the constraints and there can be found a vector $\boldsymbol{\lambda}^*$ satisfying inequalities (5) to (8) for $\mathbf{x} = \mathbf{x}^*$? Does it follow that $\mathbf{x}^*$ maximizes $f(\mathbf{x})$? The answer is yes.

What is the economic interpretation of $\bar{\lambda}_r$? Each λ is associated with a constraint: there is a pre-ordering between the m-vectors $\bar{\boldsymbol{\lambda}}$ and $\mathbf{b}$. $\bar{\lambda}_r$ is to be interpreted as the marginal-profitability effect of the rth capacity constraint, as the rate at which the value of the programme increases with the rth capacity at $\mathbf{\bar{x}}$.

§5

Can the λ's be interpreted as Lagrange multipliers? Yes. In the solution, the Lagrange multipliers, one for each constraint, are identical with corresponding $\partial \bar{R}/\partial \mathbf{b}$ elements and the multipliers satisfy inequalities (5) to (8), the Kuhn–Tucker conditions. Thus, the interpretation of Lagrange multipliers is as *shadow prices* of capacity-constraints.

Exercise. Reinterpret the ¶3.4 consumer-choice problem in the language of ¶5.2, once again identifying the marginal utility of income with λ.

The fact is that the classical Lagrange problem, $\max f(\mathbf{x}) \text{ st } \mathbf{g(x)} = \mathbf{b}$, is a special case of the Kuhn–Tucker problem (not itself the most general problem of this class) $\max f(\mathbf{x}) \text{ st } \mathbf{g}^1(\mathbf{x}) \leq \mathbf{b}, \mathbf{g}^2(\mathbf{x}) = \mathbf{b}, \mathbf{x} \geq \mathbf{0}$.[5]

Pursuing generalized Lagrange-multiplier theory, we analyse the statement: if the primal problem is feasible it will have the same solution value as its dual problem and $(\mathbf{\bar{x}}, \bar{\boldsymbol{\lambda}})$ will define a saddle point of the associated Lagrange function. The dual problem is to minimize the Lagrange function:

$$f(\mathbf{x}) - \lambda_1(g^1(\mathbf{x}) - b_1) - \ldots - \lambda_m(g^m(\mathbf{x}) - b_m) = F(\mathbf{x}, \boldsymbol{\lambda}) \tag{9}$$

subject to inequalities (10) and (11):   **S1**

$$f_i - \lambda_1 g_i^1 - \ldots - \lambda_m g_i^m \leq 0 \qquad i = 1, 2, \ldots, n \tag{10}$$

$$\lambda \geq 0 \tag{11}$$

The primal problem is constrained by:

$$\mathbf{g}(\mathbf{x}) \leq \mathbf{b} \tag{12}$$

$$\mathbf{x} \geq \mathbf{0} \tag{13}$$

Restricting vectors $\mathbf{x}$ to $\mathbf{x} \in \chi$, where χ is the set of activity levels obeying inequalities (12) and (13), postulate that $\bar{\mathbf{x}}$ yields a relative maximum of f. If $\bar{\mathbf{x}}$ is substituted into expressions (10), there exists $\bar{\lambda}$ such that expressions (10) are satisfied *as equalities* and $F(\mathbf{x}, \lambda)$ is maximized relative to $\bar{\lambda}$, and is equal to $f(\bar{\mathbf{x}})$, at $(\bar{\mathbf{x}}, \bar{\lambda})$ in the neighbourhood of $(\bar{\mathbf{x}}, \bar{\lambda})$. Furthermore, in the neighbourhood of $(\bar{\mathbf{x}}, \bar{\lambda})$, $F(\mathbf{x}, \lambda)$ is minimized relative to $\bar{\mathbf{x}}$ at $(\bar{\mathbf{x}}, \bar{\lambda})$. That is:

$$\max_{\mathbf{x}} F(\mathbf{x}, \bar{\lambda}) = \min_{\lambda} F(\bar{\mathbf{x}}, \lambda) = F(\bar{\mathbf{x}}, \bar{\lambda}), \quad \text{or} \tag{14}$$

$$F(\mathbf{x}, \bar{\lambda}) \leq F(\bar{\mathbf{x}}, \bar{\lambda}) \leq F(\bar{\mathbf{x}}, \lambda) \tag{15}$$

The Lagrange function has a saddle point at $(\bar{\mathbf{x}}, \bar{\lambda})$ *and* achieves a constrained minimum at $(\bar{\mathbf{x}}, \bar{\lambda})$.

A global extremum is a particular example of a relative extremum.

For specification of necessary properties of objective and constraining functions for a relative extremum to be a global extremum, cf. G. Hadley, *Nonlinear and Dynamic Programming* (Addison-Wesley Publishing Co. Inc.: Reading, Mass.; 1964), pp. 185–194.

Indeed, the stipulations of ¶5.2 §§2 are contrived so that an extremum does exist *and* that any extremum *is* a global extremum.

So dualism, a mathematical notion, has singular economic interest: Lagrange multipliers can be interpreted as constraint values. Compare competitive equilibrium as maximization of net revenues *cum* minimization of imputed resource values. Expressions (10) clamour for recognition as criteria for valuing resources, in order to assure efficient production by profit-maximizing producers.

§6

Returning to mundane work, it is to be *proved* that in the solution the values of the Lagrange multipliers are identical with corresponding values of $\partial \bar{R}/\partial b$ and that the multipliers satisfy inequalities (5) to (8).

The appropriate Lagrange function is that of equation (9) and the first-order conditions are given in **S1**, comprised of expressions (10) to (13). Only equalities are being considered. Indeed a deception is being practised: somehow the non-binding constraints at $\bar{\mathbf{x}}$ have been divined. Thus, if initially there were Q potential capacity constraints, and if potential constraints $(m+1), \ldots, Q$ are non-binding at $\bar{\mathbf{x}}$, the Lagrange function could have been written:

$$f(\mathbf{x}) - \sum_{}^{m} \lambda_j(g^j(\mathbf{x}) - b_j) - \sum_{m+1}^{Q} \lambda_j(g^j(\mathbf{x}) - b_j) \tag{16}$$

with $\lambda_{m+1} = \lambda_{m+2} = \ldots = \lambda_Q = 0$.

POINT. If the rth constraint is non-binding in solution, $\bar{\lambda}_r = 0$, a fundamental proposition of Lagrange-multiplier theory.[6]

Differentiate equations $\mathbf{g}(\mathbf{x}) = \mathbf{b}$ with respect to $\mathbf{x}$ and $\mathbf{b}$:

$$\begin{aligned} g_1^1 \, dx_1 + \ldots + g_n^1 \, dx_n &= db_1 \\ \cdots\cdots\cdots\cdots\cdots\cdots\cdots\cdots\cdots\cdots\cdots \\ g_1^m \, dx_1 + \ldots + g_n^m \, dx_n &= db_m \end{aligned} \qquad \textbf{S2} \quad (17)$$

Bearing in mind that **db** is a vector of arbitrary increments, **S2** is comprised of m equations in the n unknowns **dx**. Next rewrite the remaining equations in **S1**:

$$\begin{aligned} g_1^1 \lambda_1 + \ldots + g_1^m \lambda_m &= f_1 \\ \cdots\cdots\cdots\cdots\cdots\cdots\cdots\cdots\cdots \\ g_n^1 \lambda_1 + \ldots + g_n^m \lambda_m &= f_n \end{aligned} \qquad \textbf{S3} \quad (18)$$

S3 is comprised of n linear equations in m unknowns. **S2**+**S3** contains $n+m$ linear equations in $n+m$ unknowns, recalling that the partial derivatives are evaluated at $\bar{\mathbf{x}}$.

Form the system **S4** with determinant Δ of rank $(n+m)$:

$$\begin{vmatrix} g_1^1 \, dx_1 + \ldots + g_n^1 \, dx_n & = db_1 \\ \cdots\cdots\cdots\cdots\cdots\cdots\cdots & \quad 0 \\ g_1^m \, dx_1 + \ldots + g_n^m \, dx_n & = db_m \\ & g_1^1 \lambda_1 + \ldots + g_1^m \lambda_m = f_1 \\ \quad 0 & \cdots\cdots\cdots\cdots\cdots\cdots\cdots\cdots \\ & g_n^1 \lambda_1 + \ldots + g_n^m \lambda_m = f_n \end{vmatrix} \qquad \textbf{S4} \quad (19)$$

In the usual cofactor notation:

$$\partial \bar{x}_s / \partial b_r = \Delta_{rs} / \Delta \tag{20}$$

but:

$$d\bar{R} = f_1 \, d\bar{x}_1 + \ldots + f_n \, d\bar{x}_n \tag{21}$$

Accordingly:

$$d\bar{R}/db_r = \sum_{i=1}^{n} f_i \Delta_{ri} / \Delta \tag{22}$$

Next, an expression is to be obtained for $\bar{\lambda}_r$. Repeat **S3**. Repeat **S2**, but take **db** $= 0$:

$$g_1^1 \, dx_1 + \ldots + g_n^1 \, dx_n = 0$$
$$\cdots\cdots\cdots\cdots\cdots\cdots \qquad\qquad \textbf{S5} \quad (23)$$
$$g_1^m \, dx_1 + \ldots + g_n^m \, dx_n = 0$$

Arrange system **S6**:

$$
\begin{vmatrix}
g_1^1\lambda_1 + \ldots + g_1^m\lambda_m & & & = f_1 \\
\cdots\cdots\cdots\cdots\cdots & & 0 & \\
g_n^1\lambda_1 + \ldots + g_n^m\lambda_m & & & = f_n \\
& g_1^1 \, dx_1 + \ldots + g_1^1 \, dx_n = 0 & & \\
& \cdots\cdots\cdots\cdots\cdots\cdots & & \\
0 & g_1^m \, dx_1 + \ldots + g_n^m \, dx_n = 0 &
\end{vmatrix}
\qquad \textbf{S6} \quad (24)
$$

Schematically arranged, the left-hand sides of systems **S4** and **S6** are:

$$
\begin{vmatrix} m.n & 0 \\ 0 & n.m \end{vmatrix} \ \textbf{S4} \qquad
\begin{vmatrix} n.m & 0 \\ 0 & m.n \end{vmatrix} \ \textbf{S6} \qquad (25)
$$

Since the determinant of a matrix is equal to that of its transpose, the determinant of **S6**, the transpose of **S4**, is Δ. Equation (26) determines $\bar{\lambda}_r$:

$$\sum_{i}^{n} f_i \Delta_{ir}/\Delta = \bar{\lambda}_r = d\bar{R}/db_r \qquad (26)$$

The cofactors Δ_{ir} and Δ_{ri} are equal: the corresponding minors are based on transposed matrices and $r+i = i+r$.

The movements $d\bar{x}_s = (\Delta_{rs}/\Delta)\,db_r$ are optimal to a linear approximation, and for these reasons. The programme has been reduced to a linear programme in the neighbourhood of $\bar{x}$. Movements $d\bar{x}_s$ satisfy both the primal and dual constraints of the associated linear programme ('find dx such that …'), but a feasible solution to the primal problem which satisfies the dual constraints as equalities (i.e. a feasible zero-profit solution) is *optimal*. It follows that $dR = \sum_i (f_i \Delta_{ri}/\Delta)\,db_r$ is a *maximized* revenue effect of a capacity change (to a linear approximation).

Since Kuhn–Tucker λ's *are* Lagrange multipliers, the multipliers just obtained should satisfy the Kuhn–Tucker conditions (inequalities 6 to 8). Inequality (6) surely will be satisfied: the Lagrange multiplier for a non-binding constraint is zero. Inequalities (7) merely are the first-order conditions of the Lagrange problem. As for inequality (8), if $\bar{x}_s > 0$, the first-order condition $f_r - \sum_{}^{m} \lambda_j h_s^j = 0$ is met. If the first-order condition were *not* met, $\bar{x}_s > 0$ could not appear in the solution. Thus is shown the linkage between Kuhn–Tucker/Lagrange-multiplier theory and price-imputation to capacity constraints.[7]

§ 7

Inequalities (5) to (8) now can be translated into the language of economics:

1) Only productions which do not exceed capacity constraints are to be contemplated.
2) If in the solution a capacity constraint does not bind, rational calculation treats the resource as a free good.
3) If resources (capacities) are valued at shadow prices equal to their marginal-revenue products, no activity will earn more than a zero-profit, and the imputed value of the resources will equal the maximized value of the firm's productions.

Shadow prices are used because these are prices assigned internally to commodities not to be traded during the decision period.

(4) If an activity cannot earn as much as the imputed value of absorbed resources, it will not be operated.

As (3), based on inequality (7), makes clear, in the solution, the rate at which an activity contributes to revenue is equal to the rate at which it absorbs properly-valued capacity-values. However, it is possible that:

'in certain razor's edge cases, where an active constraint becomes inactive for an infinitesimal change in b_j in a certain direction, it may be necessary to interpret $\partial \bar{R}/\partial b_j$ as a one-sided derivative.'[8]

This qualification applies to **S2–S6** and **S8–S9**. The analysis of ¶5.2 §§5 requires that differentials be small enough for the active-constraint set to be unchanged and breaks down at the razor's edge.

Of course, a constraint-value will be more likely suddenly to fall off, say to zero, if inputs can be adjusted only in sizable lumps within a handful of processes, as might be true in the real world (cf. Chapter 6). Indeed the frequency of razor's edge cases in the real world appears to explain much behaviour that would be inexplicable in a 'smooth' context—witness brain drains, automation-effects, and insensitivities of labour-demands to wage-rate variation, all considered in Chapter 6.

§ 8

The fact that capacities have thus far been treated as fixed does *not* mean that programming excludes theory of choice of constraint-levels. To the contrary, comparison of shadow prices with market prices, comparison of internal with external valuations, governs decisions on capacity levels and, hence, on $\dot{b}$ and $\dot{x}$. Thus, if a firm were to value $\bar{\lambda}_r$ at \$10 and the market rental were \$8, it would, *ceteris paribus*, begin to increase its utilization of the rth service, or, if the market rental were \$12, it would begin to phase out the service from its operations.

POINT. The programming approach to the theory of the firm masks a theory of investment behind a *short run* façade—and it is operational: engineering data, plugged into an intertemporal programming apparatus, yield up quantified sequences of *optimal* inputs and outputs.

The text defines a criterion for optimal investment programmes, one which is strictly applicable only for a given activity space relative to convex input–output opportunity-sets. Only directional criteria are defined. The full problem is to maximize a present-value criterion defined on capacities defined on time, e.g., $PV = F(\alpha, \beta, \gamma, \ldots)$ where $\alpha, \beta, \gamma, \ldots$ are parameters of expressions such as $b_{rt} = f'(t)$. If prices of outputs and inputs are assumed to be constant over time, and if costs of capacity-change are invariant against the way in which capacities are changed (all at once, gradually, etc.), and if convexity requirements are met, a non-linear investment programme can be defined:

$$\max \Phi(\alpha, \beta, \gamma, \ldots) \text{ st } R_t = f(\mathbf{x}_t), \qquad \mathbf{h}(\mathbf{x}_t, \mathbf{b}_t) = 0 \tag{27}$$

The text works on the fringe of this problem. Upon penetrating its core, one encounters a sub-problem: choice of the activity space and the capacity categories.

Under no circumstances will the $(n+1)$ dimensional surface—profits being a function of the n activity intensities—be linear. True, expansion at fixed intensity- and capacity-ratios would lead to a constant rate of profit, but non-proportional expansion of capacities would not realize constant returns even in the linear case. Consider what happens when the capacity with the largest growth rate becomes redundant.

3. LINEAR PROGRAMMING AND THE THEORY OF THE FIRM

Linear programming is a special case of the problem of ¶5.2, one in which all input-output-revenue relationships can be described by such expressions as $ax + b = 0$. Linear programming is highly plastic. In its operational-analysis guise it leads to concrete solutions of business problems. As microeconomic theory, it ingests opportunity-cost and economic rent. It pierces the optimality properties of competitive general-equilibrium.

§2

The shibboleth of our economics-orientated statement of linear programming is *duality*.

The objective is to maximize $\mathbf{r} \cdot \mathbf{x}$ st $\mathbf{Ax} \leq \mathbf{b}$, $\mathbf{x} \geq 0$, $\mathbf{A}$ being an *activity matrix* and $\mathbf{x}$ and $\mathbf{b}$, column vectors. Let us detail the constraints:

$$a_{11}x_1 + a_{12}x_2 + \ldots + a_{1n}x_n \leq b_1$$
$$\cdots\cdots\cdots\cdots\cdots\cdots\cdots\cdots\cdots\cdots\cdots\cdots \qquad \text{S7} \quad (28)$$
$$a_{m1}x_1 + a_{m2}x_2 + \ldots + a_{mn}x_n \leq b_m$$

The coefficient a_{rs} is the amount of the rth capacity absorbed by the sth activity operated at unit level. a_{rs} occupies the rth row and sth column of **A**.

If $\bar{x}$ is a solution relative to $(\mathbf{r}, \mathbf{b})$, then $k\bar{x}$ is a solution relative to $(\mathbf{r}, k\mathbf{b})$. Linear production features constant returns to scale.

The crucial properties of linear programming are best developed through simultaneous consideration of the *primal* problem just expressed and its *dual*. First we must state a useful theorem, noting that a feasible programme is a vector $\mathbf{x}^*$ obeying the problem's constraints:

> 'If in any problem there is any optimal feasible programme, there is an optimal feasible programme which involves no more than m activities at non-zero levels, where m is the number of restrictions to which the solution must conform.'[9]

Problems of intertemporality are avoided until Chapter 10. For now, today's actions are stipulated to have no effect on tomorrow's options.

The theorem asserts that a firm which is properly described by a linear-programming model never need operate more activities than it has capacity constraints, and follows naturally from another theorem asserting that an m-space can be spanned by m basic vectors, i.e., that any point in such a space can be achieved by properly weighting the m basic vectors.

§3

Dualism in Linear Programming

Linear programming falls out as a special case of Lagrange Multiplier/Kuhn–Tucker theory. Cf. G. Hadley, *Nonlinear and Dynamic Programming* (Addison-Wesley Publishing Co. Inc.: Reading, Mass.; 1964), pp. 202–205. In a linear programme $f(\mathbf{x})$ is of the form $\mathbf{r} \cdot \mathbf{x}$ and the constraints, $\mathbf{Ax} \leq \mathbf{b}$. The Lagrange function is written

$$F(\mathbf{x}, \lambda) = \mathbf{r} \cdot \mathbf{x} + \lambda_1 \left(b_1 - \sum^n a_{1i} x_i \right) + \ldots + \lambda_m \left(b_m - \sum^n a_{mi} x_i \right)$$

The dual problem is to minimize F, subject to

$$\Sigma \lambda_j a_{j1} \geq r_1$$
$$\ldots\ldots\ldots\ldots$$
$$\Sigma \lambda_j a_{jn} \geq r_n$$

Hadley shows that the value of the dual's solution is exactly equal to the minimized valued of $\lambda \cdot \mathbf{b}$, constrained as above.

There is a deep connexion between linear programming and game theory, which when explored casts the dualistic properties of linear programming into high relief. Consider a two-person zero-sum game: your winnings are my losses. Existence of a solution requires, *inter alia*, that my maximum losses incident to your optimal response to my actions are equal to my minimum losses incident to my optimal response to your actions. Our problems are each other's duals. Existence of a solution to the game depends upon existence of a saddle point of a relevant function.

Put aside economics. Simply define the dual of the primal problem:

$$\max \mathbf{r} \cdot \mathbf{x} \text{ st } \mathbf{Ax} \leq \mathbf{b}, \qquad \mathbf{x} \geq 0 \tag{29}$$

The dual problem is:

$$\min \lambda \cdot \mathbf{b} \text{ st } \mathbf{A}'\lambda \geq \mathbf{r}, \qquad \lambda \geq 0 \tag{30}$$

or, in less compact notation:

$$\min \lambda_1 b_1 + \lambda_2 b_2 + \ldots + \lambda_m b_m \tag{31}$$

s.t.

$$\lambda_j \geq 0 \qquad j = 1, \ldots, m \tag{32}$$

$$\lambda_1 a_{11} + \lambda_2 a_{21} + \ldots + \lambda_m a_{m1} \geq r_1$$
$$\cdots\cdots\cdots\cdots\cdots\cdots\cdots\cdots\cdots\cdots \qquad \mathbf{S8} \quad (33)$$
$$\lambda_1 a_{1n} + \lambda_2 a_{2n} + \ldots + \lambda_m a_{mn} \geq r_n$$

The matrix of coefficients a_{rs} in **S8** is the transpose of that of **S7**.
Employ these definitions:

1) a feasible programme (problem) is one for which there exists a feasible vector;
2) a feasible vector satisfies the constraints of the programme;
3) a feasible vector is an optimal vector if it maximizes or minimizes the programme as called for;
4) the value of the optimal vector is the value of the programme.

The fundamental and familiar mathematical results are:[10]

1) if both a programme and its dual are feasible, then both have optimal vectors and their values are the same. If either programme is not feasible, neither has an optimal vector;
2) if $\mathbf{x}^*$ and λ^* are to be optimal vectors for $\mathbf{Ax} \leq \mathbf{b}$ and $\mathbf{A}'\lambda \geq \mathbf{r}$ (where $\mathbf{x} \geq \mathbf{0}, \lambda \geq \mathbf{0}$), then $x_s^* = 0$ if

$$\sum_{j=1}^{m} \lambda_j a_{js} > r_s$$

3) similarly,

$$\lambda_r^* = 0 \quad \text{if} \quad \sum_{i=1}^{n} a_{ri} x_i^* < b_r$$

The theorems assert that, if $\mathbf{x}^*$ is optimal relative to $\mathbf{r}$, then the value of the firm's activities, $\mathbf{r} \cdot \mathbf{x}^*$, is equal to the imputed value of the firm's resources, but that, otherwise, the imputed value of the firm's resources will exceed the value of its activities. Alternatively, the theorems assert that net profitability of processes operated in 'equilibrium' is zero whilst net profitability of excluded processes would be negative. Also that a resource which is redundant in the solution of a firm's programme is assigned a zero shadow price.

It has been established that the maximum value of a primal programme is equal to the minimum value of its dual. In Chapter 5 primal problems always call for maximization. In the language of economics, only if a firm operates optimally will it be able to earn zero imputed profits. At activity intensities $x \neq \bar{x}$ it will make imputed losses. Its total revenues will be less than at $\bar{x}$ and its total imputed costs more than at $\bar{x}$.

Again the standard theory of the competitive firm threatens to surface. In competitive equilibrium a price mechanism operates as an invisible hand guiding the profit-maximizing firm towards least-cost production.

§4

At the risk of repetition, a marginal-revenue-product interpretation can be offered for values associated with the constraints of the linear problem. Recall the theorem of ¶5.3 §§2: no more than m activities comprise a solution vector if there are m capacity constraints. Only equalities need be considered in ¶5.3 §§4. If an inequality holds for a dual constraint, the corresponding activity is not operated.

Assume that the firm's optimal programme will be an m-vector $(\bar{x}_1, \ldots, \bar{x}_m)$ or, alternatively, an n-vector $(\bar{x}_1, \ldots, \bar{x}_m, 0, \ldots 0)$. Thus, all of the capacity constraints will bind (will be active) at $\bar{x}$.

Consider the vital 'real world' problem, introduction of new activities and capacities. Thus a firm would want to change its activities space if it had excess capacities which lumpinesses did not allow to be reduced (cf. Chapter 6). An interesting example might be the inauguration in 1966 by Barclay's Bank, a huge British clearing bank, of a credit-card service, allegedly partly to take up slack in computer utilizations.

The tableaux equivalent to **S4** and **S6** are **S9** and **S10**. Again the determinants and corresponding cofactors of the two systems are equal.

$$
\begin{vmatrix}
a_{11}\,dx_1 + \ldots + a_{1m}\,dx_m & & = db_1 \\
\cdots\cdots\cdots\cdots\cdots\cdots & 0 & \\
a_{m1}\,dx_1 + \ldots + a_{mm}\,dx_m & & = db_m \\
& a_{11}\lambda_1 + \ldots + a_{m1}\lambda_m = r_1 & \\
0 & \cdots\cdots\cdots\cdots\cdots\cdots & \\
& a_{1m}\lambda_1 + \ldots + a_{mm}\lambda_m = r_m &
\end{vmatrix}
\quad \text{S9} \quad (34)
$$

Again denote the determinant of the system as Δ and the cofactor of the element occupying the rth row and sth column as Δ_{rs}. Equations (35) and (36) follow:

$$\partial\bar{x}_s/\partial b_r = \Delta_{rs}/\Delta \qquad db_i = 0, \quad i \neq r \tag{35}$$

$$\partial\bar{V}/\partial b_r = \sum_{i=1}^{m} r_i \Delta_{ri}/\Delta \tag{36}$$

Next **S10** is written:

$$\left|\begin{array}{l} a_{11}\lambda_1 + \ldots + a_{m1}\lambda_m \qquad\qquad\qquad\qquad\qquad = r_1 \\ \cdots\cdots\cdots\cdots\cdots\cdots \qquad\qquad 0 \\ a_{1m}\lambda_1 + \ldots + a_{mm}\lambda_m \qquad\qquad\qquad\qquad = r_m \\ \qquad\qquad a_{11}\,\mathrm{d}x_1 + \ldots + a_{1m}\,\mathrm{d}x_m = \mathrm{d}b_1 \\ \qquad 0 \qquad\quad \cdots\cdots\cdots\cdots\cdots\cdots\cdots\cdots \\ \qquad\qquad a_{m1}\,\mathrm{d}x_1 + \ldots + a_{mm}\,\mathrm{d}x_m = \mathrm{d}b_m \end{array}\right| \quad \textbf{S10} \ (37)$$

and:

$$\bar\lambda_r = \sum_s r_s \Delta_{sr}/\Delta = \mathrm{d}\bar V/\mathrm{d}b_r \tag{38}$$

Consider $\partial\lambda_Q/\partial b_r$. The analysis pertains to effects on prices of small changes in factor endowments, including population movements.

$$\partial\lambda_Q/\partial b_r = \Sigma r_i(\partial^2 x_i/\partial b_i \partial b_r) \tag{39}$$

The text offers no clue about the necessary calculations. Expressions such as $\partial\bar x_s/\partial b_r$ in equation (35) merely are gradients based on the general form of Taylor's expansion, set out below for two-variables.

In life, programmes often approximate production possibilities through a series of linear functions so that the resulting surface is piecewise-linear and resulting errors often fall well within tolerable limits.

Finally, recall from the note following ¶5.2 §§8 that the function $V = \Psi(\mathbf{b})$ is *not* linear in **b** although it is first-order homogeneous in **b**.

There follows a Taylor's Expansion for a two-variable case:

$$f(\bar x + h) = f(\bar x) + f'(\bar x)h + \frac{f''(\bar x)h^2}{2!} + \ldots + \frac{f^n(\bar x)h^n}{n!}$$

§5

We now consider implications flowing from the assumptions that the economy's firms operate linear activities in competition and that excess-demands are zero at $\bar{\mathbf{r}}$.

Of course, in a true general-equilibrium analysis the existence of general-equilibrium must be proved, taking account of *demand* correspondences (cf. Chapter 9).

§6

First, the value of aggregate output is being maximized relative to $\mathbf{r} = \bar{\mathbf{r}}$. This result easily is proved. The individual firm is maximizing $\mathbf{r}_q \cdot \mathbf{x}_q$ subject to $\mathbf{A}_q\mathbf{x}_q \leq \mathbf{b}_q$. By definition of an equilibrium, demands are equal to available supplies of all marketable resources values at positive prices.—The size of the qth firm at date t is restricted by $\mathbf{b}_q(t)$.—If it were possible for any firm to increase its profits by operating any or all of its activities at different levels, given its capacities, it would bid for or offer *marketed* inputs used in such activities and there would result excess demand or supply for various commodities. (Observe that activity levels are not rates of output of commodities.) The postulation that all excess demands are zero, then, is equivalent to one that no firm can increase the total value of its activities. Since external effects are excluded, if $r_q \cdot x_q$ has been maximized for all q (subject to $A_q x_q \leq b_q, x_q \geq 0$), $\Sigma r_q \cdot x_q$ has been maximized (subject to $Ax \leq b, x \geq 0$).

§7

There is a dualistic, market-orientated approach to the 'value' properties of a competitively-organized linear economy. Assume that each firm hires all of its resources in open markets: yesterday's contracts determine today's capacities. In a stationary competitive equilibrium, no firm can profit from changing the collection of resources it is hiring. In this equilibrium the value of each activity equals the total rent collected by source-owners. Otherwise *entrepreneurs* would wish to change activity levels and resource-hire contracts.

Each firm in a stationary competitive equilibrium maximizes $r_q \cdot x_q - v_q \cdot b_q$. Imputed- and market-values of resource constraints are equal: $\bar{\lambda}_q = v_q$. So each profit-maximizing producer, striving for minimum-cost production, minimizes the total value of economic resources under his control consistent with the market-imposed constraint that activities shall not show positive profits, whilst each achieves maximum—zero—profits relative to *his* data.

At date t, the competitive producer, precommitted as he is with respect to resources under hire, simply tries to maximize $r \cdot x_q$ over the set of feasible activity levels.

Alternatively, in stationary competitive equilibrium:

$$r \cdot x^* = v^* \cdot b \tag{40}$$

x^* being a vector of equilibrium activity intensities. Observing that the notional aggregate objective is to maximize $r \cdot x - v \cdot b$, the notional aggregate programme is subject to the constraints:

$$Ax \leq b \tag{41}$$

$$A'v \geq r \tag{42}$$

$$x \geq 0, \qquad v \geq 0 \tag{43}$$

For the excluded activity, the $(m+1)$st,

$$\sum^m v_i a_{im+1} > r_{m+1}$$

For the included mth activity,

$$\sum v_i a_{im} = r_m$$

The theorems of ¶5.3 assure that (x^*, v^*) maximizes $r \cdot x - v \cdot b$: the maximized value of the primal problem ($\max r \cdot x$ relative to r) is equal to the minimized value of its dual ($\min v \cdot b$ relative to b); $v \cdot b$ achieves a minimum at v^*, subject to the dual constraints.

The text above does *not* show that a competitive equilibrium is socially optimal. Cf. ¶5.3 §§9–10.

§8

Following D. Gale,[11] we find that:

1) 'if there is a competitive equilibrium ... then this equilibrium forces all firms to behave as though they all belonged to a single unit whose purpose was to maximize the gross value of output;'[12] and
2) 'if the total gross income of the economy is bounded above then there exists a competitive equilibrium.'[13]

This 'competitive equilibrium' is special: it is defined without regard for consumer preferences; the outputs are assumed to satisfy the households if, indeed, they must be satisfied. Furthermore the maximization property of this equilibrium defined by 1) is only pseudo-efficient (cf. ¶5.3 §§9–10).

Specifically, a competitive equilibrium is defined as a set of prices and activities consistent with:

1) each firm obeying its capacity constraints;
2) demands and supplies for intermediate commodities (making their début!) being equal;

Intermediate commodities are not to be objects of consumption.

3) profit maximization;
4) redundancy (inactivity of constraints) implying corresponding zero rents.

Symbolically, a competitive equilibrium requires

$$\max(r_q \cdot x_q - (G_q x_q)' \Pi_q) \quad \text{for all } q \tag{44}$$

In general r_q is of lower rank than r: each firm engages in different activities. In ¶5.3 §§8 *et seq.* no market-price interpretation is offered for values associated with vectors b_q. These never are more than imputed valuations.

$$B_q x_q \leq b_q \qquad \text{for all } q \tag{45}$$

$$\sum_{q=1}^{Q} G_q x_q \leq \sigma \tag{46}$$

$\mathbf{B}_q$ is the matrix (γ_{rs}). In extended form,

$$\gamma_{11}x_{1q} + \gamma_{12}x_{2q} + \ldots + \gamma_{1n}x_{nq} \leq b_{1q}$$
$$\cdots\cdots\cdots\cdots\cdots\cdots\cdots\cdots\cdots\cdots\cdots\cdots\cdots\cdots \qquad (47)$$
$$\gamma_{m1}x_{1q} + \gamma_{m2}x_{2q} + \ldots + \gamma_{mn}x_{nq} \leq b_{mq}$$

Absorption of the non-marketable capacity 1 by activity 1 operated at unit level is given by γ_{11}.

$\mathbf{G}_q$ is a matrix indicating how the qth firm's activities absorb intermediate commodities fixed in aggregate supply according to a vector $\boldsymbol{\sigma}$. Absorption of intermediate commodities is distinguished from that of capacities $\mathbf{b}_q$ rather narrowly: whilst both non-marketable- and intermediate-commodity capacities are rigidly fixed in the aggregate, intermediate-, in contrast with non-marketable commodities can be variably allocated amongst producers. $\boldsymbol{\Pi}$ is the price vector corresponding to $\boldsymbol{\sigma}$.

Theorem 1) asserts that, at competitive equilibrium prices underlying $\bar{\mathbf{r}}$, the gross value of output is maximized. By definition of a competitive equilibrium:

$$\bar{\mathbf{r}} \cdot \bar{\mathbf{x}}_q - (\mathbf{G}_q \bar{\mathbf{x}}_q)'\bar{\boldsymbol{\Pi}} \geq \mathbf{r} \cdot \mathbf{x}_q^* - (\mathbf{G}_q \mathbf{x}_q^*)'\bar{\boldsymbol{\Pi}} \qquad (48)$$

where $(\bar{\mathbf{x}}_q)$ is a set of equilibrium vectors and $(\mathbf{x}_q^*)$ a set of feasible vectors. Competitive equilibrium 'value' vectors are $\bar{\mathbf{r}}$ and $\bar{\boldsymbol{\Pi}}$. (Throughout the rest of the argument of ¶5.3 §§8, the vectors pertinent to activities of the qth firm are augmented by appropriate zeros so that the ranks of vectors $\mathbf{x}$ and $\mathbf{x}_q$, for example, are equal.) Hence:

$$\Sigma\bar{\mathbf{r}} \cdot \bar{\mathbf{x}}_q - \Sigma\bar{\mathbf{r}} \cdot \mathbf{x}_q^* \geq \Sigma(\mathbf{G}_q\bar{\mathbf{x}}_q)'\bar{\boldsymbol{\Pi}} - \Sigma(\mathbf{G}_q\mathbf{x}_q^*)'\bar{\boldsymbol{\Pi}} \qquad (49)$$

It follows from inequality (46) that:

$$\Sigma\boldsymbol{\Pi}'\mathbf{G}_q\mathbf{x}_q^* \leq \boldsymbol{\Pi}'\boldsymbol{\sigma} \qquad (50)$$

Now, since in a competitive equilibrium redundant capacities are free:

$$\Sigma(\mathbf{G}_q\bar{\mathbf{x}}_q)'\bar{\boldsymbol{\Pi}} = \bar{\boldsymbol{\Pi}}'\boldsymbol{\sigma} \qquad (51)$$

Thus the right-hand side of inequality (49) cannot be negative. Then:

$$\sum\bar{\mathbf{r}} \cdot \bar{\mathbf{x}}_q \geq \Sigma\bar{\mathbf{r}} \cdot \mathbf{x}_q^* \qquad (52)$$

Theorem 2) can now be made more precise: if the total gross income of the economy is bounded from above relative to a non-negative (and non-null) vector $\mathbf{r}^*$, then there exists a competitive equilibrium $(\mathbf{r}^*, \bar{\mathbf{x}})$, which is to say that $\mathbf{r}^*$ belongs to the set $(\bar{\mathbf{r}})$.

The proof proceeds via the problem max $\Sigma\mathbf{x}_q \cdot \mathbf{r}^*$ subject to inequalities (45) and (46). The problem's bounds assure that there exists a set of vectors ($\bar{\mathbf{x}}_q$) solving the problem. So the problem's dual also is feasible: there exist vectors $\bar{\mathbf{v}}_q$ and $\bar{\Pi}$ minimizing $\Pi \cdot \sigma + \Sigma \mathbf{v}_q \cdot \mathbf{b}_q$ subject to:

$$(\mathbf{G}_q)'\Pi_q + (\mathbf{B}_q)'\mathbf{v}_q \geq \mathbf{r}_q^* \quad \text{for all } q \tag{53}$$

Hence:

$$\Sigma \bar{\mathbf{v}}_q \cdot \mathbf{b}_q + \bar{\Pi} \cdot \sigma = \Sigma \mathbf{r}_q^* \cdot \bar{\mathbf{x}}_q \tag{54}$$

It remains to show that ($\bar{\mathbf{x}}_q$), $\bar{\Pi}$ yield a competitive equilibrium. Since the vectors $\bar{\mathbf{x}}_q$ clearly are feasible, it only remains to show that they are optimal relative to $\mathbf{r}^*$. The basic duality theorem asserts that vectors $\bar{\mathbf{x}}_q$ will be optimal if:

$$\bar{\mathbf{v}}_q \cdot \mathbf{b}_q = \mathbf{r}_q^* \cdot \bar{\mathbf{x}}_q - (\mathbf{G}_q)'\bar{\Pi}_q \quad \text{for all } q \tag{55}$$

also that:

$$\bar{\mathbf{v}}_q \cdot \mathbf{b}_q + (\mathbf{G}_q)'\bar{\Pi} \geq \mathbf{r}_q^* \cdot \mathbf{x}_q^* \quad \text{for all } q \tag{56}$$

ie.:

$$0 \leq \Sigma \bar{\mathbf{v}}_q \cdot \mathbf{b}_q + \Sigma(\mathbf{G}_q \mathbf{x}_q^*)'\bar{\Pi} - \Sigma \mathbf{r}_q^* \cdot \mathbf{x}_q^* \tag{57}$$

It follows from inequality (54) that for $\mathbf{x}^* = \bar{\mathbf{x}}$, inequality (57) reduces to

$$0 = 0 \tag{58}$$

recalling that, in a competitive equilibrium redundant capacities are free.

'But the right-hand side of (57) is the sum of non-negative terms. . . . Therefore each such term is zero, which gives the desired equation (55).'[14]

§9

In an economy with linear, and hence *convex*, production possibilities competitive equilibria are *technocratically* efficient. (Consumption is being neglected.)

Assume that the set $\mathbf{Y}$, comprised of n-dimensional real numbers, is convex. Consider the non-negative vector $\mathbf{p}^*$. There exists a real number M such that $\mathbf{p}^* \cdot \mathbf{y} \leq M$, $\mathbf{y} \in \mathbf{Y}$, and for $\mathbf{y}^*$ such that $\mathbf{p}^* \cdot \mathbf{y}^* = M$, it is known that $\mathbf{y}^*$ is on the frontier of $\mathbf{Y}$.

Now interpret $\mathbf{Y}$ as a set of (positive and negative) outputs possible for a 'linear' production sector. It follows at once that a competitive equilibrium is efficient: it maximizes $\mathbf{p}^* \cdot \mathbf{y}$ on $\mathbf{Y}$. Indeed M = 0. In this way we establish linkage between the value-orientated criterion of ¶5.3 §§8 and the technocratic criterion of ¶5.3 §§9.

The underlying theorem also establishes that for any efficient vector $\mathbf{y}^{**}$ there exists a competitive equilibrium at $\mathbf{p}^{**}$ maximizing $\mathbf{p} \cdot \mathbf{y}^{**}$.

§ 10

There is perhaps a deeper argument establishing the theorem of ¶5.3 §§9. Consider $\mathbf{p}^*$, an n-vector in $\mathbf{R}^n$, i.e. an n-dimensional real number. Next consider points $\mathbf{y}^*, \mathbf{y}^* \in \mathbf{R}^n$, for which $\mathbf{p}^* \cdot \mathbf{y}^* = c$, a scalar, where $\mathbf{p}^* \cdot \mathbf{y}^* \leq c$. Vectors $\mathbf{y}^*$ comprise the set $\mathbf{H}$. Now consider any two vectors belonging to $\mathbf{H}$, $\mathbf{y}^{*1}$ and $\mathbf{y}^{*2}$:

$$\mathbf{p}^* \cdot (\mathbf{y}^{*2} - \mathbf{y}^{*1}) = 0 \qquad (59)$$

$\mathbf{p}^*$ is the *normal* to $\mathbf{H}$. $\mathbf{p}^*$ and $\mathbf{H}$ are *orthogonal*.

Next consider an aspect of a fundamental theorem due to Minkowski: a convex subset $\mathbf{H}$ has a *positive* normal if and only if each point belonging to $\mathbf{H}$ is *not* in the interior of $\mathbf{Y}$ (where $\mathbf{H} \in \mathbf{Y}$), the set from which vectors $\mathbf{y}$ are drawn, i.e. if and only if $\mathbf{H}$ belongs to the *convex hull* of $\mathbf{Y}$.

Turning to economics, interpret $\mathbf{p}^*$ as a non-negative price vector and $\mathbf{H}$ as a set of feasible (positive and negative) outputs.

Disposal costs are nil. Hence no element of $\mathbf{p}^*$ can be negative.

Recall the complexities in defining production possibilities in a system in which inputs can enter into household preference functions. 'Labour' is an example: it makes little sense to define the production possibilities of a non-slave economy via fixed labour capacities.

Finally the available potential labour supplies in the real world become determined rather as in a closed Leontief system. Thus ¶5.3 §§10 shows only that whatever labour is used is used efficiently.

Obviously $\mathbf{H}$ is an efficient set: comparing any vector $\mathbf{y} \in \mathbf{Y}$ with $\mathbf{y}^{*1} \in \mathbf{H}$, $\mathbf{H} \in \mathbf{Y}$:

$$\mathbf{p}^* \cdot (\mathbf{y} - \mathbf{y}^{*1}) \leq 0 \qquad (60)$$

Inequality (60) follows from the definition of a normal: the equality sign holds for $\mathbf{y} \in \mathbf{H}$; otherwise the inequality sign holds.

Do competitive equilibrium outputs in a 'linear' economy belong to $\mathbf{H}$? Yes. Profit-maximizing behaviour assures that competitive equilibrium outputs satisfy the equation:

$$\mathbf{p}^* \cdot \mathbf{y} = 0 \qquad (61)$$

whilst, for non-equilibrium outputs:

$$\mathbf{p}^* \cdot \mathbf{y} < 0 \qquad (62)$$

$\mathbf{p}^*$ is a positive normal to $\mathbf{H}$, so competitive equilibrium outputs (i.e. outputs in a competitive equilibrium relative to $\mathbf{p}^*$) are efficient.

More-complex production possibilities are considered in Chapter 10. The style of analysis is rather the same, however. It transpires that competitive equilibria are efficient under the more general conditions as well and that any efficient set of outputs can be a competitive equilibrium.

Again it can be proved that any set of efficient outputs, any **y** belonging to the convex hull of **Y**, belongs to the set **H**** associating with the non-negative vector **p****. That is to say, any set of efficient outputs can be a competitive equilibrium.

REFERENCES

1. Cf. R. Dorfman, P. Samuelson, and R. Solow, *Linear Programming and Economic Analysis* (New York: McGraw-Hill Book Co.; 1958), pp. 198–201, hereafter referred to as *DOSSO*. Also, G. Hadley, *Nonlinear and Dynamic Programming* (Reading, Mass.: Addison-Wesley Publishing Co. Inc.; 1964), Chap. 6.
2. Cf. D. Gale, *The Theory of Linear Economic Models* (New York: McGraw-Hill Book Co.; 1960), p. 6.
3. Cf. G. Hadley, *Nonlinear and Dynamic Programming* (Reading, Mass.: Addison-Wesley Publishing Co. Inc.; 1964), Chap. 6 and S. Karlin, *Mathematical Methods and Theory of Games in Programming and Economics*, Vol. 1 (Reading, Mass.: Addison-Wesley Publishing Co. Inc.; 1959), Chap. 7.
4. H. Kuhn and A. Tucker, 'Nonlinear Programming,' *Proceedings of the Second Berkeley Symposium*, J. Neyman, ed. (Berkeley and Los Angeles: University of California Press; 1951), pp. 481–492.
5. See esp. G. Hadley, *Nonlinear and Dynamic Programming* (Reading, Mass.: Addison-Wesley Publishing Co. Inc.; 1964), Chaps. 3 and 6.
6. G. Hadley, *Nonlinear and Dynamic Programming* (Reading, Mass.: Addison-Wesley Publishing Co. Inc.; 1964), pp. 69–72.
7. G. Hadley, *Nonlinear and Dynamic Programming* (Reading, Mass.: Addison-Wesley Publishing Co. Inc.; 1964), Chap. 6.
8. G. Hadley, *Nonlinear and Dynamic Programming* (Reading, Mass.: Addison-Wesley Publishing Co. Inc.; 1964), p. 192 (with notational changes).
9. *DOSSO*, p. 162 (with a slight change in notation).
10. For proofs: D. Gale, *The Theory of Linear Economic Models* (New York: McGraw-Hill Book Co.; 1960), Chap. 3.
11. D. Gale, *The Theory of Linear Economic Models* (New York: McGraw-Hill Book Co.; 1960), Chap. 3, pp. 90–93.
12. D. Gale, *The Theory of Linear Economic Models* (New York: McGraw-Hill Book Co.; 1960), p. 90
13. D. Gale, *The Theory of Linear Economic Models* (New York: McGraw-Hill Book Co.; 1960), p. 91.
14. D. Gale, *The Theory of Linear Economic Models* (New York: McGraw-Hill Book Co.; 1960), p. 92.

ERRATUM. Mr. Lewis has shown me that the proofs, pp. 118–119, 124–125 are wrong. Correct proofs follow from systems $\mathbf{A}(\mathbf{dx}) = \mathbf{db}$ and $\mathbf{A}'\lambda = \mathbf{r}$. So $\lambda = (\mathbf{A}')^{-1}\mathbf{r}$ and $\mathbf{dx} = \mathbf{A}^{-1}(\mathbf{db})$ and $dV = \mathbf{r}'(\mathbf{A}^{-1}(\mathbf{db}))$. Thus $dV(db_r)^{-1} = db_r^{-1}\mathbf{r}'(\mathbf{A}^{-1}(\mathbf{db})) = \lambda_r$ for $\mathbf{db} = (0, \ldots, 0, db_r, 0, \ldots, 0)$!

CHAPTER 6

Imperfect Competition

Imperfect Competition

[It exists], 'when, because of peculiar conditions of the market or advantages held by certain buyers or sellers, prices can be abnormally influenced by one or more traders.... Monopolistic or semi-monopolistic advantages held by certain traders also create imperfect competition.'[1]

Pure Competition

'In the literature of economics, this market situation—where each seller is faced with a horizontal demand curve for his output—has been given [the] name "pure competition". This name, unfortunately, is misleading, since this market situation is neither more nor less competitive than many others.'[2]

1. INTRODUCTION

It is not easy to separate the materials of Chapters 6 and 7: in both the firm solves for a price policy; prices are not data. However, Chapters 6 and 7 are distinct from Chapter 8: the former ignore *conjectural interdependence*. Reactions of other firms are not explicitly analysed.[3]

There are at least two significant differences between the concrete substances of Chapters 6 and 7:

1) Firms in Chapter 6 are price-quoters because economic frictions segregate the market into miniscule enclaves, whilst in Chapter 7 firms have general market power.
2) It follows from 1) that strategies of many firms, including sweet-shops and chemists, flow from subjective probability distributions of feasible sales, thus leading into Part IV, *Macrodynamics*. Chapter 6 deliberately leads into Part IV whilst Chapter 7 is strictly microeconomic.

Cf. ¶1.5 §§5 and Part IV. Seminal remarks in this connexion are in M. Kalecki, *Theory of Economic Dynamics* (London: George Allen & Unwin; 1954), pp. 91–95.

And, rather paradoxically, so is R. Triffin, *Monopolistic Competition and General Equilibrium Theory* (Cambridge, Mass.: Harvard University Press; 1940). Professor Triffin was not at the time concerned with macroeconomic theory. Indeed his preference was for extreme disaggregation.

Chapter 6, close to flesh and blood as it is, is diffuse. Apart from dispersion caused by 'frictions' and from tugs from macroeconomic theory, there are at least two other centrifugal forces:

1) the firms of Chapter 6 are not simply stipulated to be maximizing share-values relative to objective data. Indeed the leeway brought about by friction-created economic enclaves (let alone the brute strength of the 'monopolies' of Chapter 7) requires that 'sociological' or 'behaviouristic' theories of the firm be considered (cf. ¶6.2 §§10);
2) rather tenuously, the relaxations of stipulations of Chapter 6 permit richer understanding of a number of social problems, including *brain drain*, optimal unemployment, and automation (cf. ¶6.3).

§ 2

It was urged in ¶1.5 §§5 that modern macroeconomic theory could be much simplified if *all* traders could be deemed price-quoters, necessarily responding to subjective views of sales (purchases) possibilities. Perhaps gadfly-like, we argued that by thus suppressing the very concept of equilibrium we could avoid perplexities of disequilibrium analysis.

The facet of the analysis of Chapter 6 which permits a simpler macroeconomic theory also leads to a more satisfying model of the representative firm. It is not clear that even the idealized farmer takes prices strictly as parameters. Perhaps the most persistent problem of, say, a tiny petrol-station proprietor concerns sales possibilities at prices he quotes.

All of this is accomplished through elaboration of the rôle of *friction*.

§ 3[4]

Chapter 6's frictions transform the general-field theory of Chapters 4 and 5 into analyses of disjoint fields. The cost of this disconnectedness is unbearable if a general-equilibrium interpretation is sought, but slight if one wishes merely to tie up special classes of events, say mergers or, in future, product lines to be added or dropped by whom.

Before entering into the concrete work of the chapter (¶6.1 §§4 et seq.), we pause to consider how its mode of analysis demolishes part of the central mass of Chapters 4 and 5—the objective meaning of the concept, value-of-marginal-product (let alone *marginal-revenue-product*). It thus prepares the ground for Keynesian economics as well as for ¶6.3.

The analogy to Keynesian economics is completed simply by observing that 'marginal efficiency of capital' is a value concept and surely must be subjective for the Keynesian producer. I prefer to make this statement without qualification. You might prefer to restrict it to an *ex ante* sense, a restriction that would not affect my argument here. Cf. M. L. Burstein, 'Review of G. Horwich, *Money, Capital, and Prices*,' *Journal of Political Economy*, April 1966, pp. 217–219, where I argued emphatically against the use of the objective notion, 'marginal productivity of capital', in income theory.

Recall from ¶4.3 §§7 that in the orthodox theory of price, value-of-marginal-product or *marginal-revenue-product* at date *t* are objective notions. *Inter alia*, the underlying demand functions are completely and objectively specified.

> Needless to say, the individual trader in a purely-competitive market need have no knowledge of demand or supply functions.
>
> Note that 'value of marginal product at date *t*' becomes a subjective notion if the *tâtonnement* under study does not specify p_t and/or we do not specify that this *tâtonnement* is once-and-for-all.

However, if the underlying functions are merely subjective probability-density functions, the normative implications of *value product* disintegrate.

> It will suffice to confine oneself to demand conditions in future, although I should prefer not to restrict the argument in this way: 1) what does 'now' ever really mean in an empirically orientated economic theory?; 2) uncertainty considerations appear to be important in any theoretically-meaningful discussion of current trading. Cf. R. W. Clower, 'On the Theory of *n*-Seller Markets,' unpublished (!)

In other words, if producer-behaviour is to be governed by producer-opinion about demand conditions instead of by price parameters or demand functions, then, to predict that 'marginal revenue will equal marginal cost' is to make an empty statement. At the least, 'marginal revenue' has now been defined as 'that number which is equal to the number assigned to marginal cost in the mind of the producer': 'When I use a word', said Humpty Dumpty, a neo-classical economist, 'it means just what I choose it to mean—neither more nor less.'

At least three important implications are to be drawn from the transformation of *value product* and *marginal-revenue-product* into subjective notions:

1) '...[a] cohesive Keynesian income theory [requires] a value-orientated rather than a physical notion of marginal efficiency of capital. At date *t* a Keynesian firm is offered a limited menu of investment opportunity under...constant returns to scale.'[5] (Cf. Part IV *infra*.)
2) *Opinions* about possibilities for sales expansion become so important that the theory indifferently accommodates stagnant economies featuring high rates of profit (their capitalists having low animal spirits) and rapidly-growing economies with low rates of profit (*their* capitalists being ardent). Pursuing the same line of argument, capitalists and others of Country North might profit greatly from immigration from South. The immigrants might be satisfied with low wages whilst high profit rates might do little to influence labour-demand (centring on 'labour widening'). The upshot again will depend on sales-possibilities views.[6]

3) From a welfare-optimality standpoint, there is little reason to distinguish between observable states of competition and monopoly. Neither can achieve Pareto-Optimality, since producers in both are governed by the feasible-sales region of ¶6.2 §§5, a subjective notion leading to all-round monopoly pricing. (Cf. Chapter 10.)

§4

What are the frictions?

1) Demand functions are discontinuous. For example, demand for the jth firm's outputs is likely to be fairly elastic over some ranges and highly inelastic over others.

2) One must incur costs in order to change one's price quotations. One must incur costs in order to find out what are the prices one faces, leading to 3).[7]

3) Information can be obtained only at a cost. A seller, disappointed with his sales, cannot ascertain what has gone wrong, except at a cost. Sellers might judge that it would cost too much to acquire the information necessary to make price lists reflect demand fluctuations, regular or irregular. Thus Odeon cinema tickets might cost 50¢ from 9.00 a.m. to 7.00 p.m. and $1 from 7.01 p.m. to midnight. Finally, buyers, rather than incur the costs necessary to find out what are price quotations at this very moment, are willing to pay insurance premiums by foregoing unknown cut-rate prices in favour of published price schedules.

Information-cost theory enlarges the analysis of advertising. There is obvious social benefit from supply of information about existence of new commodities, Ajax's desire to dispose of its rotting fishes, today's Postillon menu, etc. There is private reward if *nos informations* carry widely and penetrate deeply. In the rough equilibrium of 'real worldly' competitive markets revenues beyond direct expenses cover advertising expenditures amongst others.

Image-making advertising is not considered. It is agreed that much of the psychic content of modern life is provided by phantasies provoked by advertising to viewers huddled around idiot boxes. Are they worse off for it? Are you?

4) Markets for future commodities frequently do not exist and, when they do, offer incomplete listings and involve heavy transactions costs.

5) Traders often are capital rationed; traders often cannot fine-tune their borrowings; the distribution of borrowings might not be well correlated with the distribution of notions of marginal efficiencies of capital, which are necessarily subjective, let alone *ex post* efficiencies.

6) Consumers and producers are not all at one location, but, once commodities are locationally specified, commodity-categories splinter off into numerous subcategories. The vendor of alpha corn flakes at location A must take account of the competing commodity, alpha corn flakes at location B (often selling at a different price).

7) Households and other buyers must consider the costs, monetary and otherwise, of purchasing commodities in various combinations at various times at various locations. Resulting cost functions tend to be lumpy: once one has driven one's car to town and parked it, much expense is invariant against the number of shops visited on that trip. Since 'shopping cost' functions vary from household to household, a vector $\mathbf{p}^*$ for commodities f.o.b. shopping centre in fact reflects vectors $\mathbf{p}^{*1}, \mathbf{p}^{*2}, \ldots, \mathbf{p}^{*R}$ ($\mathbf{p}^{*r}$ being prices for commodities *delivered* to the rth household).

8) Buyers must consider the lumpy costs of storing and maintaining purchases.

9) Productive processes usually cannot be accurately described by continuous functions: feasible-output surfaces have holes and bumps. So to speak, production possibilities are often sporadic and jerky.

10) The cost of information and uncertainty and ignorance, together with sometimes-unachievable economies of size, make the condition of entry more tenuous than in a 'continuous' world. This leads up to making the takeover bid less formidable than it would be in an idealized world (but cf. ¶6.2 §§10).

2. MODELS OF FIRMS IN IMPERFECT COMPETITION

¶6.2 sets up a model which takes account of the frictions in ¶6.1 §§4 and which becomes the basis for ¶6.3's discussion of topics in social policy.

§ 2

The thrust of ¶6.1 §§4 was that 'real world' frictions make markets discrete. Typically, trading groups comprise a small number of buyers and sellers, each centring on the moves and countermoves of the relatively few firms comprising his rivals and natural customers or suppliers. In ¶6.2 it is assumed that each firm can calculate how demands for its products associate with pricing policies. It is tacitly stipulated that a firm maximizing profits relative to these demand conditions is to ignore possibilities of strategies for *joint*-profit maximization or of strategies which might lure rivals into traps containing business death or which might warn others not to trespass upon 'our' vital interests.

§ 3

The basic model of ¶6.2 is more realistic than the models of Chapters 4 and 5, but it is statical: the model cannot be put into motion upon being supplied with initial conditions. Still a few time derivatives can be remarked.

1) If Firm Aleph is earning supernormal net revenues overall, not explained by the imputed rents of non-reproducible agents under its control (e.g. a site or the unique talents of its general manager), it soon is likely to feel pressure. Perhaps others will try to duplicate Aleph methods *in toto*. It is more likely that other firms will think harder about undertaking one or more Aleph activities. Indeed its success is likely to be the main reason why it even occurs to others to do things the Aleph way.

2) If Firm Beth is earning subnormal net revenues overall, whilst correctly imputing the charges of what might be inferior basic resources, it is likely to think seriously about going out of business altogether or of dropping some of its activities (imputed values of Beth hired inputs will tend to be less than market values). Beth executives and shareholders will tend to be earning imputed rents which are less than their external evaluators.

2) is more subtle than the counterpart argument that activities earning negative profits, when resources are valued at shadow prices, should be dropped.

3) and 4), 4) being the converse of 3). Suppose that Firm Gimmel finds that activity alpha contributes exceptionally to the value of the Gimmel programme, say, in terms of a ratio, the numerator being the contribution of alpha to the Gimmel programme and the denominator the gross proceeds of the activity. Then it must expect others to attempt activity alpha *à la* 1) above.

The contribution of activity alpha is measured simply by comparing the value of the present programme with one from which alpha is excluded. In the short run, the appropriate alternative would be the initial activity space *sans* alpha. In a longer run, appropriate activities may be drawn from other activity spaces.

§4

As in Chapter 5, all of the models of Chapter 6 treat production as an instantaneous process, thus avoiding complexities bound up in shift-work. However shift-work can be encompassed by simple programming models. Group the decision-period, the day, into N intervals, ignoring in the non-dynamic model interdependence of activities belonging to different groups. Each activity now is to be identified by the interval $(1, 2, \ldots, N)$ within which it occurs. Capacity restrictions must be similarly identified: a minute of machine-time of a given class might be valued at $100 at 10 a.m. and at $1 at 10 p.m. Lumpiness might crop up: in order to increase capacity $1_{10 a.m.}$, capacity $2_{10 p.m.}$ might have to be increased one-for-one.

Imperfect competition is developed through a series of sub-models.

The theme of ¶6.2 §§5 is the *feasible-sales* region which, together with effects of *lumpiness in capacity-variation*, explains much business behaviour.

¶6.2 §§6, an excursion from the main line of argument, concerns *selection of activity spaces*, whilst ¶6.2 §§7, in connexion with 'lumpiness', concerns '*survivor tests*'.

¶6.2 §§8 takes up *time-profiles* of demand in conjunction with frictions.

¶6.2 §§9 shows how, in life, firms must accommodate to *uncertainty*, and usually must pay a price for uncertainty. For example, excess supply or demand can be expected to occur quite frequently in basically tranquil markets.

The work of ¶6.2 §§5 intersects with *integer programming*. Cf. William J. Baumol, *Economic Theory and Operations Analysis* (Englewood Cliffs, N.J.: Prentice-Hall Inc.; 1961), Chap. 7, and, *en passant*, study his Chap. 6 ('Nonlinear Programming') as well. Cf. also A. Charnes and W. W. Cooper, *Management Models and Industrial Applications of Linear Programming* (New York: John Wiley & Sons Inc.; 1961), Vol. 1, pp. 204–207, and George B. Dantzig, *Linear Programming and Extensions* (Princeton: Princeton University Press; 1963), Chap. 26. Note that the text above is concerned only with situations in which *capacities b* can only be discontinuously altered, inevitably putting special stress on the problem of one-sided derivatives (cf. ¶5.7 §§7). Integer linear programming proper is concerned with the requirement that one or more of solution values $\bar{x}$ of a programme be integers. While posing important computational problems and having valuable practical uses, integer-programming theory is nested within the framework of Chapter 5.

§5

The representative firm is to operate two activities, each perhaps involving many inputs and outputs. (Nor are *coq-au-vin* service and *coupe-St.-Jacques* service the same activity.) Pricing policies are described by the scalar k. Only two pricing policies are considered: Policy A, underlying Fig. 1, prices right up to the brink: for $k > k^A$, demand becomes $(0, 0)$. Policy B, underlying Fig. 2, stares into the abyss which is the dual of that for A: for $k < k^B$, net revenues are negative (i.e., the cost of the fowl, wine, natural gas, etc., exceeds the revenue of the activity in question). But net revenues are positive for $k = k^B$.

Upon introducing promotion policies, the *feasible-sales regions*, the shaded areas of Figs. 1 and 2, become defined. Of course, a firm might not choose to achieve its potential sales: witness the prestige that can be conferred by queues.

Lines AB and CD of Figs. 1 and 2 refer to capacity-constraint 1. The capacity can be installed only in lumps: if reduced from the level reflected

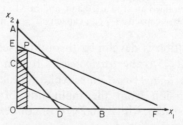

Fig. 1   An Imperfectly-competitive Firm, Revenues **r**'.

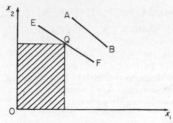

Fig. 2   An Imperfectly-competitive Firm, Revenues r^2.

by AB, it must become that reflected by CD. Line EF describes capacity-constraint 2 which also can be changed only in discrete jerks. Capacity 1 might be floor space. Capacity 2 might be the number of castings which a particular machine can produce during the period.

Standby-capacity is neglected. A certain steel might be yielded both by activity r and activity s. Activity s, using obsolete plant, is packed in mothballs now and is not operating. If the price of steel should increase, or the feasible-sales region become enlarged, activity s might again become profitable and its plant would be reactivated.

N.B. Activities which are in *any* way different from each other must be treated as different activities.

Optimization occurs at points P and Q of Figs. 1 and 2.

Fig. 2 having served its purpose, discussion will now be confined to Fig. 1, noting that the programme solved by P is characterized by *lumpiness* and *discontinuity*.

Elaborating the lumpiness-discontinuity theme, capacity 1 is and is not redundant: it has no scarcity value, but if its level were reduced (necessarily discontinuously), profits would fall. Capacity 2 verges on redundancy: no gain would be realized from relaxing it despite the fact that the second constraint is active at P. 'Verging upon redundancy' characterizes 'lumpy' situations, in which sales cannot be increased without new price-promotion policies, and pours cold water on marginal-productivity theories of factor pricing in complex situations.

It has been established that perfectly-competitive firms in equilibrium would pay factors *values of marginal products*. But, as soon as firms face demands of less than perfect elasticity, the *values of marginal products* criterion breaks down. Thus in the text above, a firm might pay \$1 an hour to labourers, each of whom would impose an hourly loss of \$100 if he departed, if the initial position is on the frontier of the feasible-sales region. There might be nothing to be gained by hiring more labourers, an example of discontinuity in $\partial V/\partial b_r$.

The analysis suggests that 'decreasing costs' will crop up frequently in life. Once the financial milk necessary to achieve constraint AB has been spilt, unit overhead costs decline as outputs increase up to the point at which AB binds. To appeal to the intuition by comparing incommensurates, if the size of the market were small relative to the discrete lumps of capacities, firms would be hard pressed to achieve full capacity-utilizations. Quasi-redundancies would be common.

Our feasible-sales regions perhaps are best interpreted through the *kinky-oligopoly demand* analysis of ¶8.2 §§3 : a perfectly-elastic demand segment links up with a perfectly-inelastic segment (   ). Trade dries up completely if the firm attempts to charge more than p_i^*, but retaliatory opposition strategies will assure that price-cutting below p^* will not gain trade and indeed could cause the region to bend back on itself. (p^* will vary from firm to firm, reflecting locational factors, ambience, etc.) Indeed the upshot perhaps is best expressed by a 'point demand curve' defining the optimal feasible price (p^*) and the maximum feasible-sales level.

The profitability of a lateral shift in the demand 'kink' is obvious if lumpiness has led to initially decreasing unit costs together with, say, constant marginal costs—or perhaps marginal cost simply is below price. A more complex case would find the firm in constant-cost production with average (including capital) cost equal to price. In the 'real world' of increasing costs of gearing (leverage), an increase in the firm's feasible size is apt to permit a change in (financial) structure, allowing the firm's shares to achieve a higher price-earnings ratio. Alternatively, the capitalization factor applied to the firm's shares at its initial scale will become higher and the firm will be able profitably to become more geared in the course of expansion, so that each share carries more indebtedness—levers a larger mass—in the new and more favourable financial equilibrium.

§6

Taking up selection of activity spaces, considerable ingenuity is often necessary if new activities are to be matched up with idle capacities. Account must be taken of the firm's borrowing power, the complementary qualities of new and extant products and the advantages of new activities which do not require erection of new lumpy capacities, not completely absorbable by the new optimum activity mix. For example, a grocer should not add typewriter ribbons to his product line unless he also plans to supply a full line of office matériel.

§7

Implications of the theory of imperfect competition for survival prospects of small speciality firms make up a mixed bag.

The text surely implies that 'survivor tests' should be highly disaggregated, that statistical evidence based on comparisons of dollar-volumes with costs per dollar of output of broad classes are not likely to be worth much. Cf. George J. Stigler, 'The Economies of Scale', *Jour. of Law. and Econ.* (1958), and J. Johnston, *Statistical Cost Analysis* (New York: McGraw-Hill Book Co.; 1960), pp. 166–168.

Large firms able simultaneously to offer standard and special services without unprofitably increasing direct costs or capacities may charge little more than out-of-pocket costs for speciality lines, relying on their ability to fit specialities into vacant nooks and crannies of production surfaces. To this extent, frictions impede speciality firms. However, if frictions permit Ogre Ltd. to enjoy permanent supernormal returns from commodity S, Ogre might choose to price S high enough for speciality houses to huddle under its umbrella, achieving moderate profitability.

Lumpinesses and indivisibilities inherent in, say, computerized operations, might discourage large companies from considering many specialized activities, a facet boding well for speciality houses producing luxury goods in affluent, buoyant economies. Examples might include watches, pottery, or dresses, some produced by machines working to computerized programmes, others by hand. If Ogre were mostly engaged in mechanized production, it would probably prove unprofitable to set up cottage-industry branches. It could not avoid contradictions in promoting competing mechanically- and hand-hewn products unless it carefully segregated the two branches, perhaps considerably increasing its accounting costs.

So it is that tiny firms are able to be highly profitable: spatially- and technically-induced isolation, together with strong customer loyalty, sometimes build up secure, if miniscule, enclaves.

There is a rough tendency for outside entry into activities now earning supernormal profits. 'Rough' because lumpiness and discontinuity can give small firms in remote places monopoly power, and 'remoteness' need not be spatial.

How might profits be abnormal? Calculate values of optimal intertemporal programmes for activity spaces including and excluding the rth activity. If the increment to the value of the firm's shares incident to inclusion of the rth activity is 'high', others are likely to want to 'have a go'. In the continuous case, an adjusted programme finds imputed and market values of employed resources to be equal, so that the firm's present value can be imputed entirely to its management contracts, good will, sites, etc., valuing these at market.

§8

It becomes important to identify demands by the time at which they occur. Consider a restaurant or hotel. At least two frictions crop up:

1) even under fully-adjusted conditions, some capacities must remain rigid over regularly recurring demand cycles. Few capacities—surely not the skilled-labour force—can be subjected to rheostat-like control;
2) frictions described in ¶6.1 make it impossible for the firm to employ a complex pricing policy reflecting cyclical and other variations in demand.

Vertically-integrated enterprises sometimes can overcome frictions inherent in the sociology of the open market. Thus, managers and supervisors of integrated companies might be furnished with elaborate 'shadow' price schedules for the tth day each morning whereas a firm attempting such pricing in an open market soon would be hammered. Cf. Chapter 11 for related problems in non-private ownership economies.[8]

A rational firm, then, often must select a programme under which capacities will be idle at times during the day whilst, at other times, queues will form up. Pricing often must be simple: only such rough-hewn adjustments as characteristically cheaper dinners than comparable luncheons in financial districts might be possible. Again, consider lower week-end rates at commercial hotels.

Note how frictions can break up 'the' market into semi-isolated pockets, in which there interact quite small numbers of buyers and sellers, each inevitably taking account of responses of his fellows to his pricing and promotion policies *à la* Chapter 8. Accordingly, it is dangerous to define markets broadly or to assume that a firm's behaviour is per force explicable by the theory of the competitive firm, just because it is small.

Considering another aspect of cyclical demand interacting with frictions, restaurant or hotel promotions might emphasize off-peak facilities. On the other hand, if promotion leads to better off-peak business, it is also likely to lead to longer queues and more refusals to serve during rush hours. Should not peak-hour prices simultaneously be raised, partly to make off-peak buying more attractive, partly to cash in better on peak demand and to avoid ill will generated by queueing (at least outside of England!)? However, ill will often burgeons when a specialist seller obviously maximizes profits: an expensive restaurant might arouse suspicion if it offers a cheap luncheon. Discontinuities in demand, reminiscent of the kinky-oligopoly-demand case of Chapter 8, might lead to a drastic falling off of custom for a now-popular restaurant if it substantially raises its prices.

Queueing is consistent with an equilibrium state. After all, a ticket purchased after a 30-second wait and one purchased after a 30-minute wait are different objects. The market might decree that labour is too valuable to be used to reduce queueing time, that the journey-*cum*-30-second-wait-for-ticketing costs too much to be worth producing. Alternatively, a firm might wish to acquire more labour in order to offer services with less queueing.

Again it is necessary to make fine commodity-discriminations: one difference between *coq au vin* dispensed in a *bistro* and that at a three-star restaurant is that at the former one is likely to have to wait for a table but will be served exigently once seated, whilst at the premier restaurant seating will be immediate and service leisurely.

Price-changes annoy speciality clients, and others. Accordingly, since 'speciality' price changes are apt to be infrequent, they tend to be substantial. However, keep in mind the costs of making price changes. Finally note that one purpose of promotion policy might be to lengthen the peak period itself. Smoothing of demand can permit substantial economies.

We[9] turn to a more-formal discussion of 'peak-load theory' from the standpoint of production and investment—rather than pricing—policy. Business life is to depend on being able to satisfy peak demand at prices which cannot be raised without demand disintegrating (the firm faces a point demand curve). Standing proxy for demand are power requirements, which can be supplied either by nuclear equipment with heavy capital and low operating costs or conventional low capital and high operating cost equipment. Off-peak requirements are at the rate of B kilowatts per minute for b minutes, peak requirements at the rate of

A kws. per minute for a minutes. Defining nuclear and conventional capacities as x_1 and x_2:

$$x_1 + x_2 \geq A \qquad (1)$$

$$x_1 + x_2 \geq B \qquad (2)$$

Indeed inequality (1) can be written as an equality in a non-stochastic universe. Why then keep more than *peak* capacity requirements? Capital cost is a function of the capacities:

$$\chi = g_1 x_1 + g_2 x_2 \qquad (3)$$

and, of course $g_1 > g_2$. Peak-production costs, recalling that *all* capacity is to be used during the peak period, are:

$$c^1 = a(c_1 x_1 + c_2 x_2) \qquad (4)$$

Off-peak production costs are:

$$c^2 = b(c_1 u_1 + c_2 u_2) \qquad (5)$$

noting that off-peak outputs u will be less than capacities x.

In a steady state the problem is:

$$\min(g_1 + ac_1)x_1 + (g_2 + ac_2)x_2 + b(c_1 u_1 + c_2 u_2) \qquad (6)$$

st

$$x_1 \geq 0 \qquad (7)$$

$$x_2 \geq 0 \qquad (8)$$

$$0 \leq u_1 < x_1 \qquad (9)$$

$$0 \leq u_2 \leq x_2 \qquad (10)$$

$$x_1 + x_2 = A \qquad (11)$$

$$u_1 + u_2 = B \qquad (12)$$

The constraints can be simplified. We know that any nuclear equipment at hand will be used in preference to conventional equipment, so that inequality (9) can be rewritten as:

$$u_1 = x_1 \qquad (13)$$

and, of course, holds for $x_1 = 0$. After further substitution, the constraints finally can be written:

$$x_1 \geq 0 \qquad (7)$$

$$A - x_1 \geq 0 \qquad (14)$$

$$x_1 = u_1 \qquad (13)$$

$$B \geq u_1 \qquad (15)$$

$$A - B \geq x_1 - u_1, \text{ i.e. since } x_1 = u_1 \text{ (by equation 13)}, A \geq B \qquad (16)$$

Correspondingly, the objective function can be rewritten:

$$\min[g_1 - g_2 + a(c_1 - c_2)]x_1 + b(c_1 - c_2)u_1 + k \qquad (17)$$

Fig. 3 graphs the constraints:

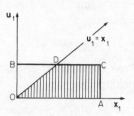

Fig. 3   The Constraints of the Peak-demand Problem.

Now consider the iso-cost curves:

$$C^0 = [\quad]x_1 + b(c_1 - c_2)u_1 + k \qquad (18)$$

An especially interesting case finds the common slope, du_1/dx_1, to be positive but less than 45°, leading to the optimum D at which the firm maintains in equilibrium nuclear plant with capacity B and meets incremental peak requirements with conventional equipment.

§9

Consider Fig. 4. (Of course, demand-changes will not affect all outputs of an activity in the same way. This is assumed for the sake of simplicity.) Region 1 is in some sense an expected region equivalent to a mean of a continuous conditional probability distribution. Region 2 is like a point in an upper tail two standard deviations from the mean, whilst Region 3 is like a corresponding point in the lower tail.

Firm Aleph, with a lot of productive capacity relative to the demand specifications, heavily profits if Region 2 should hold and is clobbered if

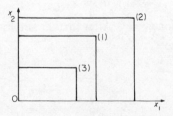

Fig. 4   Imperfect Competition: Stochastic Demands Relative to $\mathbf{r}^1$ at Moment t.

Region 3 should apply. Aleph's conjugate, Beth, with small productive capacity, profits less under (2) and is hurt less under (3).

Thus, if demand can be described only in the terms of probabilism, it would be a very lucky firm which can look back and find that it has done as well as perfect foresight would have permitted. Consider how costs (or expected costs) of uncertainty come about. ¶6.1 shows that prices must be chosen ahead of time: costs of price changes and technocratic lags require precommitment. Now a risk-averting firm, having consulted the pay-off matrix associating profits with possible states of nature and assigned probabilities to the states, might decide to play for safety, charging lower prices than would maximize expected profits in order to insure against the catastrophe of its immense fixed plant standing idle. Again, it might become content with less capacity. The directors wince when they have to turn away customers, but do not fret about how to find cash to meet heavy fixed charges if there is a slump.

¶6.2 §§9 has implication for promotion- as well as price-policy: a firm might seek to change its conditional-probability distribution of feasible-sales regions in order to reduce the riskiness of its operations. It might diversify its activities. It might hope to increase demand for its outputs with the intention often of turning away buyers, in order to have better odds against the wolf ever appearing at its door. It might try to exchange expected demand which is high, but fragile, for expected demand which is lower, but more stolid.

G. Dantzig shows with characteristic lucidity how some programming models can be adapted to uncertainty.

Following Dantzig, consider the problem of minimizing variance for fixed expected cost. We are to be in the shoes of a portfolio manager buying shares x. Assume that p_j is independent of x_j (our rate of purchase) and that σ^2 of p_j is known, as is σ_{jk} between p_j and p_k. And $\sigma_{jk} = \sigma_j \sigma_k \rho_{jk}$, ρ_{jk} being a correlation coefficient. $\sigma^2_{(x_j \cdot p_j)} = x_j^2 \sigma_j^2$. $\sigma_{(x_j \cdot p_j)(x_k \cdot p_k)} = x_j x_k \sigma_{jk}$. It follows that the variance (V) of expected-cost (E) is

$$V = \sum_{j=1}^{n} \sum_{k=1}^{n} x_j x_k \sigma_{jk}$$

If prices are independent so that $\rho_{jk} = 0$,

$$V = x_1^2 \sigma_1^2 + \ldots + x_n^2 \sigma_n^2$$

If $\rho_{jk} = 1$

$$\sqrt{V} = \Sigma x_i \sigma_i$$

The problem is to minimize V for $E = E^*$, i.e. to find a collection of securities of expected cost E^* for which variance is minimized. The special cases and the general case can be solved by known procedures.[10]

Finally, an interesting aspect of the *law of large numbers* comes into play. The more varied are the sources of demand, whether variegation arises from many types of consumers for one product or from offer of many products, the less need be the expected costs of uncertainty. The less will be the relative dispersions of conditional-probability distributions from their means. So, save for frictions, large companies, especially large conglomerated companies, are able at the same level of risk, to come closer to maximization of expected values than are small firms. (Implying that *N–M* utility is not controlling. Where *N–M* utility does control, risk-attitudes are unaffected by the *law of large numbers*.) In a frictionless world of risk-aversion (and hence not of *N–M* utility) larger firms would tend to have lower unit costs of production. To the extent that *frictionless* competition governed, so prices would be forced below levels at which smaller firms could operate without taking unacceptable risks.

More precisely, the larger firm would adopt processes permitting it to earn normal profits at $p^* < p^{**}$, p^* and p^{**} permitting normal returns on invested capital to large and small firms respectively. Less precisely, valuing outputs at stated prices, minimum cost per dollar's worth of output would tend to be less for larger firms. Then small firms could come under severe pressure when larger firms are operating short of levels permitting minimum unit cost.

An excellent general reference for Chapter 6 is Edward Chamberlin, *The Theory of Monopolistic Competition* (Cambridge, Mass.: Harvard University Press; 1938).

Under imperfect competition, lower unit-costs of larger-volume firms are quite consistent with survival of smaller-volume, higher-cost, less-profitable firms selling the same commodity at the same price. An example is petrol stations. Nor need such a situation be inconsistent with a rough general equilibrium: *subjective* marginal rates of return govern investment decisions. The highly profitable Gigantic Fuel Co. might be content with its present size and have no desire to bid capital away from the upthrusting, albeit struggling, Alyosha Energy Corporation.

An interesting example of uncertainty in economics concerns 'optimal unemployment'. A cost of uncertainty becomes defined: unemployment is necessary for maximization of expected national income.

Considering a static model of production, production is defined on employment (more precisely, the number of labour contracts, N and on vacancies, V. A railroad's output depends upon the number of labour contracts *and* on unfilled slots: perhaps the engine drivers did not show up today. Thus equation (19):

$$x = \phi(N, V) \tag{19}$$

Output is to be an annual rate and V the average daily number of vacancies. We note that vacancies pertain to labour requirements of on-going processes and not to *ex ante* production plans.

What determines V? An attractive model would resemble one concerning molecular collisions in the dynamical theory of gases. Physical concepts such as: number of molecules per cm^3, number and frequency of collisions, heat, pressure, etc., would be given economic interpretations such as: number of unemployed, rate per day at which vacancies are filled, intensity of search, cost of search, etc. (not necessarily in corresponding order). Empirical research would seek out the appropriate thermodynamical problem (choice of counterpart gas, etc.). Cf. Sir James Jeans, *The Dynamical Theory of Gases* (New York: Dover Publications, Inc.; 1954), 4th ed., originally published by Cambridge University Press. I am indebted to Dr. J. M. Woollen and to Mr. K. Shimizu in this connexion.

Modulating away from the dyamical theory of gases, the proportion of vacancies at date 0 filled by date h is to be a function of the number of unemployed and the number of vacancies: the number of random collisions of unemployed and employers seeking to fill vacancies over this interval will depend on these variables (noting that our model is over-aggregated—that each unemployed worker is not suited for each vacancy). If potential full employment is N^*, then unemployment is $(N^* - N)$: N can stand proxy for the unemployment variable, as it does in equation (20):

$$V = \theta(N) \tag{20}$$

In statics the problem is to maximize ϕ subject to θ. Forming the appropriate Lagrange function and setting partial derivatives equal to zero, the first-order condition is:

$$\phi_N = \theta_N \phi_V \tag{21}$$

If output is to be maximized, the marginal productivity of employed labour should be equal to:

(rate at which average vacancies $\times$ (marginal dis-productivity of
increases with N) vacancies)

In dynamics (perhaps, better, 'in meta-statics'), following the 'Pontryagin theory' of ¶7.5 §§4, the problem is to maximize the integral:

$$J = \int f[N(t), V(t)]\,dt \tag{22}$$

subject to:

$$\dot{V} = g(N, V), \tag{23}$$

the Hamiltonian being $f + \psi g$ and $\bar{\psi}_t$, having the interpretation as the marginal valuation of the stock of vacancies at date t. The canonical equations are:

$$\dot{V} = g(N, V) \tag{23}$$

and

$$\dot{\psi} = -f_V - \psi g_V, \tag{24}$$

the *control* being the number of labour contracts, N, so that

$$\partial H/\partial N = f_N + \psi g_N = 0 \tag{25}$$

is necessary for dynamic optimality; equation (25) must hold for all t. (Recall that a functional such as f is in fact a function of an indefinitely large number of variables, namely all values taken by N and V over the interval of integration.)

It is clear from equation (25) that equation (21) falls out as a special case of the intertemporal analysis. Finally we observe that $\dot{V}$ has an obvious 'collision-rate' counterpart.

§ 10

Cf. ¶3.7 §§2.

A sampling of the massive literature of behaviourist producer theory includes William J. Baumol, *Business Behaviour, Value and Growth* (New York: Macmillan; 1959), esp. Part I and Chaps. 9 and 10; R. Cyert and J. March, *A Behavioural Theory of the Firm* (Englewood Cliffs, N.J.: Prentice-Hall; 1963); P. J. McGuire, *Theories of Business Behaviour* (Englewood Cliffs, N.J.; Prentice-Hall; 1964); O. E. Williamson, 'Hierarchical Control and Optimum Firm Size', *Journal of Political Economy*, April 1967, pp. 123–138.

¶6.2 §§10, completing our discussion of the mechanics of imperfect competition, is concerned with interaction of *behaviourist* or sociological theories of the firm with the theory of finance. The analysis is prefaced by a dictum: it seems to me that behaviourist writers neglect the theory of finance, together with growing shareholder power, and that their conclusions are biased as a result. This growth in shareholder power stems in part from arbitrage effects of the developing art of the takeover bid and in part from the sophistication and raw size of the rapidly growing, thoroughly unsentimental, unit trust (mutual fund) industry. Our dictum leads up to a test of conflicting hypotheses, but the demonstrated feebleness of economic hypotheses to explain much of microdata makes unlikely a conclusive test of significance.

It is easy to explain why 'behaviourism' is not taken up before Chapter 6. After all Chapters 4 and 5 define a producer as a production set on which profits are being maximized. Cf. ¶4.1 §§2. Thus the theory of the purely-competitive producer. In Chapters 6 to 8, more varied producer behaviour is at least conceivable for a number of reasons:

1) the economic enclaves of Chapter 6 and the naked power of the firms of Chapters 7 and 8 *per se* permit producers (firms) some leeway, e.g.
   a) profits beyond survival requirements can be used to finance *Kultur*, or,
   b) as a reservoir supporting what might be marginally-unprofitable sales maximization designs
   IF
   either *the* managers or the manager-facet (the Dr. Jekyll facet?) of the manager–shareholder personality can prevail over a share-value-maximization principle;

   Recalling Adam Smith, it is not clear that we should favour management mandarins who direct resources in directions which titillate them.

2) the argument of ¶4.7 §§2, buttressed by ¶¶6.1 and 6.2, suggests that the cost of information, the inadequacies of information, the costs of replacing management, etc., contribute to a degree of managerial independence, certainly if the shareholders become content with eccentric criteria.

§ 11

Having conceded that behaviourist theories of the firm cannot be discarded *ab initio*, we next propose to limn a domain in which such approaches promise to be useful *a priori*. Finally, we shall outline a financially-orientated theory of the firm, one allotting a simple criterion to producers, shoving complexities into stock market theory.

§ 12

'Behaviourism' is a promising approach to at least three situations, one encompassed by *orthodox* statics, another by *orthodox* friction, the third, more or less, by *disequilibrium-analysis*.

1) The managing-director of Beth Co. Ltd., a toy manufacturer, is peculiarly attuned to childish fancies, and is also an ardent admirer of the music of François Poulenc. He may, within obvious limits of exploitation, have Beth set up a Poulenc foundation which will make massive disbursements subsidizing Poulenc performances, Poulenc sweatshirts, etc. Mr. X may choose thus to exploit his rent of ability.

2) Even if X cannot earn a rent of ability it is probable that in the rough-hewed equilibrium of the 'real world', X could divert Beth profits to 'Poulenc' ends. After all, *normal returns* is a vague notion in an uncertain world. A takeover bid is not likely to ensue because Beth earns 8% instead of 9% on its capital (on account of X's Poulenc activities). Nor is the (admittedly ordinary) X-management likely to be replaced by Beth shareholders—at least not by my ilk. Perhaps the Dreyfus Fund would be less amused.

3) Once we specify that day to day economic life is largely in *disequilibrium* relative to the equilibrium state of our model, we become interested in adjustment processes. In *this* connexion it is highly important to know who gets on the telephone first. Characteristics of information-exchange, the organization of decision-making, etc., all become fuel for explanations of the dynamics of *disequilibrium*. Cf. Chapter 7, appendix.

Perhaps 3) can lead to détente between *orthodox* and *revisionist* theorists of the firm. Adjustment-dynamics cannot get off the ground without behaviourist orientation. Surely *revisionists* regret their stress on normal states.

§13

Financial policies such as dividend-pay-out or leverage (gearing) are not to be studied in this book. Attention here is confined to commodity spaces and price spaces.

¶6.2 §§13 begins from the implications of the share-value maximization criterion of ¶4.2. Can this criterion be fitted into a satisfactory theory of the firm under the stipulations of Chapters 6 to 8?

The elegant simplicity of a theory rooted in instantaneous share-value maximization is attractive. Conceding that the *price-theory* complexities of Chapters 6 to 8 would be undimmed, nevertheless we would be happy to shove all the 'bumf'—say risk-taking attitudes affecting choices of product-line promotions or between conciliation and business war—into the theory of the stock market. We would like permit managements simply to contemplate $f(\mathbf{x})$: ($f(\mathbf{x})$ determines share-value). This being so we could be indifferent to preference theory, at least if the process of finding $\bar{\mathbf{x}}$ is costless, as it is not except under *tâtonnement*.

'At least if...*tâtonnement*.' Chilling words, not only sapping the *instantaneous*-share-value criterion, but also comprising a wedge for 'ownership versus control'. (Cf. note at the end of ¶3.7 §§2.) Why is the instantaneous-share-value criterion sapped? Because only an absurd stipulation can keep it wholly intact: takeover bids must be so omnipotent that control of Company Gimmel would switch over any time its management (perhaps faithfully obeying controlling shareholders) was not in a régime maximizing the value of Gimmel shares *now*. Otherwise:

1) 'Poulenc' strategies could be pursued at least for some time; and
2) even a strictly wealth-maximizing controlling group would look beyond today's share market.

Glossing 2) a strategy which the market esteems lightly today may send shares sky high next month. Surely Mr. Clore can be held at bay for a month? For a year?

Agreed, we have not established an airtight 'financially orientated' theory of the firm, but ¶6.2 §§13 does lead into paths of economic theory more congenial to the economist than are the psycho-sociological directions of behaviourist statics.

3. IMPERFECT COMPETITION THEORY AND SOCIAL POLICY

Two problems are considered:

1) emigration and immigration of factors of production, specifically *brain drains* of professional people and influxes of labourers;
2) technological change leading to greater capital intensity, i.e. automation.

In each case the typical discontinuity of such partial derivatives as $\partial V/\partial b_r$ is important. Indeed, in so far as discontinuities result from properties of 'feasible-sales regions', Keynesian economics loom up.

§2
Factor Movements: *Brain Drain*

Perhaps economics ignores the most obvious reason to regret emigration of scientists, middle-level managers and others: thus are lost the very persons who supply the society's potential for innovation, upthrust, and commitment. However, statics is the natural domain of economic thought.

Under smooth statical stipulations, if factors are receiving their value products, a small exodus leads roughly to a stand-off in the sense that incomes per head of the stay-at-homes are scarcely affected. If the *r*th market rental is $\partial V/\partial b_{r_q}$ for all q, national income will—under our stipulations—fall by about

$$\sum_{q=1}^{M} \sum_{r=1}^{R} \frac{\partial V}{\partial b_{rq}}$$

for a small emigration of M persons within factor-classes $1, \dots, R$— approximately the total income which they had received. If the adding up stipulation $\Sigma f_i y_i = x$, holds, subtraction of a unit of the ith factor still need not leave *per capita* income of the rest unchanged. Of course, *large scale* emigration could have significantly adverse effects on average income *per capita* for the same reason that a massive cutback in water supply could paralyse a country in which water is at present virtually a free good.

We recall Adam Smith's diamond-water paradox.

Incomes of substitutional factors may become higher as a result of emigration even though national income per head falls.

This result also holds for linear production, although ordinary techniques cannot derive expressions like $\partial^2 V/\partial b_1 \partial b_2$ for linear models. The general argument easily is clinched: if the rth constraint were reduced, leading to abandonment of the sth activity, and if the qth capacity were used exclusively in the sth activity, the qth constraint would become worthless.

The text illuminates civil-defence economics. It is misleading, if not dangerous, to analyse consequences of hypothetical nuclear exchanges by slicing boloney from a Cobb–Douglas production function. What if New York's water supply were eliminated? Marginal analysis is worthless in such a case.

Factors can easily verge on redundancy under the non-smooth stipulations of imperfect competition. The services of a chemical engineer to an oil refinery might have an imputed value of \$100,000 per year. A second engineer at that station might be valuable only as a stand-by capacitor. It follows that prevailing salaries of engineers may be substantially less than \$100,000, depending on demand and supply. If emigration were to tighten active constraints, wages of stay-at-home engineers might substantially increase. So apparently the aggregate loss of value product may substantially exceed the earnings of the departed engineers.

Stock-flow analysis moderates estimates of *brain drain* costs. Thus assume that engineering schools are to be built up so that there is achieved a specified time-path of stocks of engineering talent. The greater is *brain drain*, measured as a flow, the greater must be annual expenditure on engineering training (the effect being similar to prolongation of training-periods). If the incremental social cost of operating engineering schools at levels high enough to offset the drain is \$Z per year, it can be said that the drain costs \$Z per year, perhaps of a lower order of magnitude than the apparent criterion's cost.

Additional mitigation is suggested by the 'Keynesian' analysis of ¶6.2 §§3, page 154 (putting aside the fact that we may ignore substitution possibilities, thus overstating hypothetical losses): if the resources pumped into engineering training, including the opportunity costs of the trainees, are underemployed, in the Keynesian sense of that word, the $Z figure exaggerates the cost of the drain. Indeed 'Keynesian' reasoning points out an especially important qualification to apparent *brain drain* losses: if the rate of growth of demand for alpha-technicians in Country A is 10,000 per year and if, say, 5000 of the 15,000 alpha-technicians finishing training in A emigrate each year, it is obvious that A is not suffering from an alpha drain *per se*. (A similar result can be extracted from neo-classical theory, although, characteristically, it is much harder to apply it to ongoing events. Some sort of moving general-equilibrium in Country A may simultaneously require 10,000 more alphas per year in A *and* emigration of another 5000.)

Brain drains of professors, doctors, and others whose salaries might be fixed by the state, have consequences which must be costed in imputed rather than official prices as a general rule. At these fixed salaries, supplies of qualified persons might fall short of demands whilst imputed values of their services exceed the fixed salary levels.

The text emphasizes the close links between imperfect competition theory and Keynesian economics (cf. ¶6.2 §§3 last sub-paras). Again we are reminded that the counterpart to the wage indeterminacy of ¶6.3 §§2 is profit indeterminacy. We recall that, for Keynes, investment by firms flows from moral expectations of profitabilities of actions valued in money of account and is importantly influenced by expectations of future 'feasible-sales regions'. Accordingly, very high average rates of profit can be associated, we recall, with flaccid *entrepreneur* animal spirits. A low-wage, high-profit economy might be stagnant indeed. Entrepreneurs, however sleek and fat might not wish to expand their operations.

§3

Factor Movements: Immigration

Southern European immigrants have promoted the North's postwar affluence. The explanation lays open the economics of discrimination under the rubric 'theory of non-competing groups'. One implication is chilling: often developed economies capable of substantial sustained rates of capital accumulation are well advised to permit massive influxes of immigrant labourers, if the immigrants are then forbidden to compete outside selected employments, perhaps distasteful to the *übermenschen*. Nor is the implication different for groups of indigenous disfavoured persons: negroes in some white societies; untouchables and others.

Perhaps relevant Swiss activities absorb three inputs: alpha labour-service; beta labour-service; gamma machine-time. If immigrant workers from the south of Italy were to do beta work and if their supply were highly elastic at some 'low' wage rate, it easily is shown that Swiss *per capita* income could be higher than if the Swiss had to provide alpha *and* beta labourers—certainly if there is enough capital to engage Swiss as alpha operatives only. Say that 30 alphas and 10 betas, together with 20 gamma machines, working for one year, can produce 100 units of output. If alphas and betas belonged to competing (Swiss) groups of equal skill, per annum output per head would be 2·5 units, stipulating that Swiss workers own the capital in their household guises. If Italians could be brought in at a wage rate of 1 unit per annum, and if 40 gamma machines could be accumulated, total output would be 200. Annual output per Swiss worker, after the Italians were paid off, would be 6 units.

Again, assume that two linear activities, each absorbing the same amount of machine-time, can be operated. Activity 1, already described, can be represented as $(0·3, 0·1, 0·2, 1)$, the elements being alpha labour, beta labour, gamma machinery, and final output. Activity 2 correspondingly is $(0·5, 0, 0·2, 1)$. Activity 2 does not employ beta labour. An economy operating only activity 2 and controlling 20 gamma machines, together with 50 native labourers, could produce 100 units of final output: Swiss income per head must be less if Swiss preferences precluded performing beta work and if immigration is forbidden. Indeed, if the native labour supply could not be further increased, machine-time might even come to be a redundant capacity.

We might set up a Cobb–Douglas aggregate production function:

$$y = A(z_1^\alpha \cdot z_2^\beta \cdot z_3^\gamma) \tag{26}$$

Aggregate output, y, is a function of inputs z, perhaps 'capital', native labour, and imported labour. The exponents are positive fractions. Next consider equations (27) to (29):

$$\partial y/\partial z_2 = \beta A z_1^\alpha z_2^{\beta-1} z_3^\gamma \tag{27}$$

$$\partial^2 y/\partial z_2\, \partial z_3 = \gamma\beta A z_1^\alpha z_2^{\beta-1} z_3^{\gamma-1} > 0 \tag{28}$$

$$\partial^2 y/\partial z_2^2 = (\beta-1)A z_1^\alpha z_2^{\beta-1} z_3^\gamma < 0 \tag{29}$$

y/z_j is the marginal productivity of the jth factor. Assume that machine rents and wage rates are equal to marginal productivities, an assumption facilitated by the stipulation that $\alpha+\beta+\gamma = 1$. Equation (29) shows that a given group's wage rates will fall if the group is augmented, but equation (28) shows that wage rates of native workers increase with the size of the non-competing group (z_3) comprised of immigrants or negroes. It is in the native interest for the 'outside' groups to be large and locked in.

Equations (26) to (29) also show why capitalists tend to be in favour of integration. Assume that $\partial y/\partial z_2 > \partial y/\partial z_3$. If qualified immigrants were allowed to take on natives' jobs, the effect on the marginal productivity of capital would be like that of an increase in the total labour force—positive. Thus, if native and immigrant workers were in fact identical, total rentals of capitalists could not be maximized unless all labourers had the same marginal productivity in equilibrium.

Finally, the Cobb–Douglas analysis illuminates *brain drain* economics. The complementary properties of factors causes a decrease in the amount of the rth factor to lead to lower marginal productivity of the sth factor in neo-classical equilibrium. Thus emigration of some engineers, while perhaps leading to higher incomes for, say, 20 thousand fellow engineers, would lead to lower incomes for, say, 2 million others. Nor is this point vitiated if the 20 thousand engineers gain more than the 2 million others lose, as would be true around a stable equilibrium at which profits are being maximized (requiring that the second differential of profit should be negative in each case). In democratic politics 2 million outweighs 20 thousand.

Substantial labour flows can occur from A to B even if wage rates are observed to be always the same at both locations. If, for example, B's economy is growing faster than A's, labour must flow from A to B in order to keep wages the same. Note also that higher wages in B 'in isolation' might reflect greater B-preference for labour-intensive goods instead of greater capital accumulation in B. Finally, if B wages *are* higher than A wages, and if labour-capacities typically verge on redundancy in both places, it is possible that B wages will soon be observed to fall without unemployment, effective demand or prices substantially changing in either country and without A wages rising for that matter. The threat of importation of A workers might suffice to induce B workers to accept wage cuts. However, the second-round effect might be a wage cut in A: A unions might come to fear that B goods, now produced at lower labour-cost, will be dumped in A.

Next note that analysis of real foreign investment is on all fours with that of immigration of human capital: the usual result is for domestic factors in the receiving country to become engaged in higher-yield activities. However two additional points should be made.

1) In the 'real world' the comparative rates of return under consideration are cast up by moral expectations by firms working against 'feasible-sales regions'. Real-capital flows become sensitive to realized and anticipated growth experience.

2) Important complementary properties cannot be captured within the compasses of given activity and commodity spaces, since, within a specified space, effects of availability of new techniques and new commodities cannot be interpreted. Prototype real international investment finds imported physical capital associating on terms at least as favourable to native factors as those previously available. True, if supplies of complements to imported capital are not perfectly elastic—emergent from the bush for example—returns per unit of *native* capital will be lower because of loss of complements to the new enterprises. However, continuing in this neo-classical vein, the value of product foregone by *native* firms necessarily is less than the value of incremental factor payments by the *immigrant* capitalists. *Native* capitalists would stay in the bidding so long as the value of 'lost' factors (the analysis need not be marginal) fell short of the cost of retaining such factors, a cost which will be pecuniarily understated to the extent that average-factor-cost, instead of higher marginal-factor-cost is used in calculations.

Effects of real foreign investment are more obviously favourable to the receiving country under 'Keynesian' stipulations. Mounting accelerator effects can lead to significant take-off as 'feasible-sales region' forecasts become more sanguine.

§4

Automation

Consider effects of increased availability or attractiveness of capital-intensive processes on industrial employment and wage rates, together with these observations and stipulations.

1) Processes are to be regarded as vertically integrated: all stages of fabrication from raw materials to final vending are encompassed within each activity. After all, a final-assembly process might use $1 million worth of machinery watched by one worker, the machinery might have a life of one year and might itself be produced with 100 man–years of

labour, together with miniscule non-labour inputs. The *integrated* process would be labour intensive.

2) Elaborating and refining 1), the labour inputs pertinent to an integrated process are those required for servicing and keeping intact non-human sources of productive services as well as direct labour *and* should be distinguished from labour inputs required for *initial* construction. For example, an oil pipeline might require huge labour inputs in its construction whilst requiring no labour for maintenance and servicing. The pipeline construction activity is labour-intensive; the pipeline operation activity uses no labour. Hence in an idealized *proche-Orient* oil sheikdom, employment would depend upon the economy's rate of growth, in turn governing pipeline expansion. Such is the first example here of an *accelerator principle* linking a variable y, not with x, but with $\dot{x}$, x's time derivative.

3) It is useful to define a number of highly labour-intensive activities (i.e. labour-intensive relative to *scarce* resources employed) including 'subsistence' activities in the non-cash sector. Massage is a labour-intensive 'cash' activity in many places. Grubbing for tubers with sticks in unenclosed commons is a subsistence activity. Once such activities become imbedded in the model, the central long run problem of economic policy is seen to be sustaining rapid enough accumulation of capital (including human skills) to permit a desired fraction of a growing potential labour force to be employed in activities with high yields per worker employed, yields increasing with technological advance. If all goes well, operated labour-intensive activities will have high-value yields also; handcrafts concocting delicacies for affluent *bourgeoisie* will thrive. However, surges in know-how could lead to miserably low wages in unorganized craft activities and to substantial numbers of workers actually returning to the bush. Meanwhile a relatively few factory workers would earn high incomes under shelter of exclusive unionism. On the whole, things have gone well in the West for several centuries.

Traditionally, the labour- or capital-intensity of a productive process has been measured by angle θ of Fig. 5.

Analogous directions can be defined in n space.
The production function is to be homogeneous; the rate of substitution between two factors is to depend only on the ratio y_r/y_s, where y_j is the amount employed of the jth factor.

Similarly, technological change traditionally has been called capital-saving, labour-saving, or neutral as the radius vector of Fig. 5, passing through the equilibrium point of the new isoquant, is to be rotated towards the ordinate, towards the (capital) abscissa, or not at all—factor-product prices held fixed. Recall how effects on equilibrium prices and outputs of changes in parameters controlling technical knowledge are neo-classically analysed in terms of partial gradients in the neighbourhood of an initial solution-point, the upshot being determined by relative values of elasticities of substitution, factor supplies and product demands.

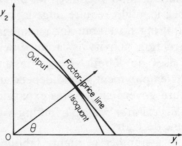

Fig. 5   Technique Defined by Labour-capital Ratios Relative to a Homogeneous
Production Function.

'Automation' also can be analysed via Joan Robinson's *Accumulation of Capital.*

Prof. Robinson's approach is highly 'discontinuous' and accordingly tends to exaggerate the impact of technological change, unlike 'smoother' traditionally neo-classical analysis.[11]

Fig. 6 describes three techniques to be considered by a representative firm in a system aggregated up to 'labour, capital and output', neglecting depreciation. 'The' rate of interest is 10%. Values are calculated on the basis of specified wages and prices.

	Technique 1	Technique 2	Technique 3
Value of annual output	$100	$100	$10,000
Wage bill	80	40	1
Value of capital employed	100	500	50,000
Capital costs	10	50	5,000
Annual costs	90	90	5,001
Rate of profit	10%	10%	$\simeq 50\%$

Fig. 6   Profitabilities of Alternative Techniques (each depicted at unit level).

Assume that, at the outset, only techniques 1 and 2 are available. The firm will be indifferent between the techniques under certainty.

Risk-avoiders in the 'real world' might opt for technique 1, whilst risk-preferrers would be attracted by the gearing opportunities of technique 2.

Now technique 3 becomes available. Technique 3 can only be operated on a large scale and requires erection of a massive plant to be manned by a Ph.D. seated before a Rube Goldberg console. Provided that frictions do not preclude communication between locations (requiring decentralized production), *entrepreneurs* would wish to operate technique 3 at initial wages, prices, and interest rates.

The new technique's profitability is exaggerated by the system's level of aggregation. In life, when it becomes possible to produce a commodity much more cheaply, its price plummets, at least in reasonably competitive markets.

Not even a 49% fall in real wages would make technique 1, let alone the more capital-intensive technique 2, as profitable as technique 3.

Assume that prices of final goods and of 'machinery' stay fixed, thus introducing a Ricardo-like assumption of equal profitability between sectors. To the extent that 'machinery' prices are to fall, the text's argument is buttressed.

This scenario conjures up drastic, perhaps unbearable, shocks to the social-economic system. Strongly regressive income–wealth redistribution is foretold. Drastic shifts in location and occupations of the labour force are portended. Once the implicit accelerator effects of massive investment expenditures reversed their course as reconstruction of the economy's plant and equipment became completed, substantial unemployment could be anticipated. Subsequently the bulk of the labour force would settle into what might become its new functions: weeding plutocratic gardens, handcrafting artifacts, catering banquets whilst garbed in antique costumes, etc.

More precisely, average wage rates would come to depend on the accumulation of capital. Consider a case in which no labour is employed in manufacturing. Then the real income of the capitalists simply is the value of manufactured product, manufactures being *numéraire* throughout. Then assume that workers neither consume each others' services nor save: aggregate real income of workers is measured by their consumption of manufactures. If capitalists consume only the services of workers (assumed to operate without meaningful capitals *à la* a Robinsonian version of a traditional Marshallian firm) the terms of trade between workers and capitalists can be measured by the physical volume of manufactures as against that of workers' services. The greater is the accumulation of capital, and hence output of manufactures, the higher is the average real-wage rate.

Less simply, consider capitalists and workers (to be deployed entirely outside manufacturing and who indeed can be stipulated to be self-employed non-capitalists). Each will have positive propensities to consume manufactures and services conditioned by prices and incomes. In consequence, equilibrium real-wage rates will emerge from the interaction of accumulation, population, and 'cross tastes', including elasticities of substitution in consumption. If accumulation is low, worker-population high, capitalist preferences for services low (Keynes's Widow's Cruse!), and worker preferences for manufactures high—then real-incomes of workers in equilibrium can be abysmally low.

A two-country model of 'real' international trade is precisely *à propos*. This is not a coincidence: *international* trade is logically indistinguishable from trade between *any* separable decision units.

158 *Economic Theory*

History repeatedly has refuted apocalyptical forebodings about effects of technological progress. Instead the masses have been released from onerous chores within low yield activities and absorbed into high-yield activities permitting remarkably higher wage rates at quite steady rates of profit. Higher wages have been accompanied by notable improvements in factory conditions. The motif has been steady accumulation of non-human capital and improvement of human skills, accompanied by smooth transition in the nature of economic activities.

REFERENCES

1. Cf. H. Sloan and A. Zurcher, *A Dictionary of Economics* (New York: Barnes & Noble; 1961), 4th ed., rev. 1963, p. 163.
2. A. Alchian and W. Allen, *University Economics* (Belmont, Cal.: Wadsworth Pub. Co.; 1967), 2nd ed., p. 106 (fn. 1).
3. Cf. G. Stigler, *Five Lectures on Economic Problems* (London: Longmans & Co.; 1949), 'Monopolistic Competition in Retrospect,' pp. 12–24.
4. A. Alchian and W. Allen, *University Economics* (Belmont, Cal.: Wadsworth Pub. Co.; 1967), 2nd ed., Chaps. 8, 17, 18 and 21.
5. M. L. Burstein, 'Review of G. Horwich, *Money, Capital, and Prices, Journal of Political Economy*, April 1966, p. 218, fn. 4b.
6. See also Charles P. Kindleberger, *Europe's Postwar Growth: The Rôle of Labour Supply* (Cambridge, Mass: Harvard University Press; 1967).
7. A. Alchian and W. Allen, *University Economics* (Belmont, Cal.: Wadsworth Pub. Co.; 1967), Chap, 8, p. 104.
8. M. Burstein and coworkers, *Econometric Studies in Trucking* (Dubuque, Iowa: Wm. C. Brown & Co.; 1965), pp. 106–137.
9. The remainder of ¶6.2 §§8 is but a slightly-modified version of Pierre Massé, *Optimal Investment Decisions* (Englewood Cliffs, N.J.: Prentice-Hall, Inc.; 1962), pp. 150–154.
10. G. Dantzig, *Linear Programming and Extensions* (Princeton: Princeton University Press; 1963), Chap. 25, pp. 499–513, fn. 5a. Cf. also Harry M. Markowitz, *Portfolio Selection* (New York: John Wiley & Sons Inc.; 1959) and A. Charnes and W. W. Cooper, *Management Models and Industrial Applications of Linear Programming* (New York: John Wiley & Sons Inc.; 1961) Vol. I.
11. N. J. Robinson, *Accumulation of Capital* (London: Macmillan & Co. Ltd.; 1956), esp. Chap. 10.

CHAPTER 7

Monopoly

1. INTRODUCTION

The statical theory of monopoly is but a particular instance of Kuhn–Tucker theory. Formally, pure monopoly is distinguishable from pure competition simply because non-linearities in the revenue function, $f(\mathbf{x})$, of a monopolist can arise from properties of demand functions whilst prices are data for the competitive producer. Less formally, the study of monopoly theory arouses interest in price policies.

After ¶7.2's discussion of the statical theory of monopoly, we move on to special problems of price policy, ¶7.3 applies the statical theory to price discrimination and tied sales. ¶7.4 introduces intertemporal planning, emphasizing effects of 'this year's' outputs on 'next year's' costs of production or demands. Then ¶7.5, PROFITS AND ENTRY, develops more general problems of intertemporal price policy through the classical calculus of variations and the Pontryagin Maximum Principle, thus verging upon important new developments in the theory of intertemporal optimization.

Chapter 7, unlike Chapter 8, does not consider *conjectural interdependence*. In Chapter 7, reactions of other firms, whilst perhaps being embedded in, say, the demand functions calculated by 'our' firm, are not explicitly analysed. In Chapter 8, reaction functions are in the core of the analysis. In a sense conjectural problems underlie the demand functions of Chapter 7 in the way that programming problems underlie the production functions of Chapter 4.

2. PURE THEORY OF MONOPOLY: STATICS

We explore the revenue function $f(\mathbf{x})$. In ¶5.2 $f(\mathbf{x})$ was non-linear because total net revenue did not show a constant return to the scale of activity levels, but prices were data. ¶7.2 establishes another basis for non-linearity: here *optimal* final-product prices can be defined only relative to activity levels.

159

Is the tranquil monopolistic environment, the sometimes-violent world of small-numbers oligopoly, or the impersonal milieu of imperfect competition the most likely to favour technical progress?

A monopsonist quotes prices on one or more of his inputs. A monopolist-monopsonist-competitor quotes some prices of outputs and inputs and takes others.

§2

Analysis of a Monopolist's Revenue Function

An activity vector $\mathbf{x}^*$ can be associated with an output vector $\mathbf{y}^*$. The revenue-maximization subproblem is to choose $\mathbf{p}^*$ to maximize $\mathbf{p}^* \cdot \mathbf{y}^{**}$, $\mathbf{y}^{**} \leq \mathbf{y}^*$ being a sales vector. Amongst the activities are obtaining of intermediate products from other firms and selling these, perhaps without transformation, to one's own customers. The distinction between $\mathbf{y}^*$ and $\mathbf{y}^{**}$ is important: revenues might be greater if some outputs are destroyed. This is a common problem in the theory of joint production: 'industry' marginal revenue from mutton might be negative whilst that of sheep-gland extract, produced in fixed proportions with mutton, might be very high. Of course, the 'disposal problem' becomes less important as the monopolist can contemplate more activities, each yielding up outputs in different proportions. Disposal of the rth output is inconceivable in the competitive case so long as:

$$(\text{selling cost})_r - p_r < (\text{disposal cost})_r$$

That is:

$$p_r > (\text{selling cost})_r - (\text{disposal cost})_r$$

§3

Having shown how $f(\mathbf{x})$ is derived in the monopoly case, ¶5.2 can be incorporated into Chapter 7 by reference, completing the pure theory of monopoly.

§4

Consider cost-imputation from the standpoints of activity analysis and accountancy. In programming, constraint values are *not* independent of the activities spaces $\mathbf{X}_q$: the value of the rth constraint, say oven space, is affected by the choice to include or exclude bread production from the field of choice and will reflect the level at which such an activity is to be operated. In accountancy the total of overhead cost to be charged to the activities is invariant to the field of choice and the activity levels. Alternatively, a programmer calculates values of capacities fixed for a decision period whilst an accountant allocates a stipulated volume of 'fixed cost' amongst activities. The programmer treats the 'overhead' as an unknown to be determined. The accountant treats 'overhead' as predetermined.

As it happens, the accountant's problem, as traditionally formulated, is irrelevant for rational calculation.

3. APPLICATIONS: PRICE DISCRIMINATION

The price discriminator might seek merely to exploit existing differences between spatially-, temporally-, psychologically-, or income-differentiable segments of his markets (thus passive discrimination); or seek to hit upon an optimal mix of promotions, model-lines, branding, and pricing with the idea of *changing* attitudes (thus active discrimination). A profit-maximizing discriminator will use both tactics. Happily the underlying theory is the same.

The work of ¶7.3 is as follows:

1) indicate why the subject belongs to monopoly theory;
2) analyse passive price discrimination for cases in which each buyer is quoted a single price (similarly for discriminating monopsony);
3) analyse passive discrimination featuring multipart tariffs for individual buyers, noting that the imbedded possibility of perfect discrimination is important in welfare economics;
4) analyse 'active' price discrimination.

§2

Segmentation and Monopoly

Under purely competitive conditions, cost differentials correspond with price differentials in equilibrium. Otherwise possibilities for profitable arbitrage would be immediately and massively exploited. Of course, meaningful market power, while necessary for discrimination, is not sufficient. General Motors, in contrast with a skilled brain surgeon, might be unable to achieve many passive discriminations.

More meticulous commodity specification digests the 'cost differentials' of the text so that any objects ordered by a generating vector in the space R^n bear the same price.

§3

Discrimination between Groups: Non-temporal segmentation

The objective is to maximize revenue from outputs $\mathbf{y}^*$ associated with activity levels $\mathbf{x}^*$, assuming, for simplicity, that all outputs are to be marketed. Assume that the monopolist deals with Q groups, each insensitive to what others are paying, and that he produces N commodities:

$$
\begin{aligned}
y_{i1} &= f^{i1}(p_i) & i = 1, 2, \ldots, Q \\
&\cdots\cdots\cdots\cdots \\
y_{iN} &= f^{iN}(p_i) & i = 1, 2, \ldots, Q
\end{aligned}
\tag{1}
$$

The maximum amount of commodity 1 which can be sold to the ith group is defined by function f^{i1}. The N-vector of prices charged to the ith group is represented by $\mathbf{p}_i$. The firm's objective, *once $\mathbf{x}^*$ is specified*, is to choose $\mathbf{p}$ to maximize:

$$R = \sum_{i=1}^{Q} \sum_{j=1}^{N} p_{ij} y_{ij} \tag{2}$$

carefully defining prices to be net of selling cost. Equations (1) and (3) comprise the constraints on the maximization of R:

$$\sum^{Q} y_{i1} = y_1^*$$
$$\cdots\cdots\cdots\cdots \tag{3}$$
$$\sum^{Q} y_{iN} = y_N^*$$

For simplicity, equations (3) are equalities: possibilities for deliberately inducing queues are put aside.

After some straightforward substitutions, the constraints can be written:

$$\sum_{i=1}^{Q} f^{i1}(p_i) = y_1^*$$
$$\cdots\cdots\cdots\cdots\cdots \tag{4}$$
$$\sum_{i=1}^{Q} f^{iN}(p_i) = y_N^*$$

Upon forming the appropriate Lagrange function, the first-order conditions can be written:

$$f^{1j} + \sum_{j}^{N} \lambda_j (\partial f^{1j}/\partial p_{1j}) = 0 \qquad j = 1, 2, \ldots, N$$
$$\cdots\cdots\cdots\cdots\cdots\cdots$$
$$f^{Qj} + \sum_{j}^{N} \lambda_j (\partial f^{Qj}/\partial p_{Qj}) = 0 \qquad j = 1, 2, \ldots, N \tag{5}$$
$$\sum_{i=1}^{Q} f^{ij} = y_j^* \qquad j = 1, 2, \ldots, N$$

The first-order conditions require that the 'marginal profitabilities' be zero: it must be impossible to increase total revenue by shifting sales from one segment to another. Only implausible coincidence would find $p_{1r} = p_{2r} = \ldots = p_{Qr}$. In general each group will be charged a different price.

Consider a special case. A one-product firm's costs are $C = C(y_1 + y_2)$, the demand laws being $y_1 = F(p_1)$, $y_2 = g(p_2)$. The objective is maximization of $p_1 y_1 + p_2 y_2 - C$, i.e.,

$$y_1 F^{-1}(y_1) + y_2 g^{-1}(y_2) - C(y_1 + y_2)$$

F^{-1} and g^{-1} being inverse functions. The first order conditions are:

$$y_1 F^{-1}{}'(y_1) + F^{-1}(y_1) = C'$$
$$y_2 g^{-1}{}'(y_2) + g^{-1}(y_2) = C'$$

That is to say in equilibrium $MR_1 = MR_2 = MC$.

The marginal revenues can be written $MR_j = p_j(1 + 1/\eta)$ where η_j is the point elasticity of demand, $d \log y_j / d \log p_j$. $\bar{p}_1 = \bar{p}_2$ only if $\bar{\eta}_1 = \bar{\eta}_2$. The equilibrium prices can in general be identical only if the demand laws are log-linear and have identical slope coefficients when written in logs.

There are many examples of passive price discriminations between groups in everyday life: 'dumping' in international trade; medical, legal, and other professional fees; simultaneous editions of hard- and paper-covered books; etc.

§4

Discrimination within Groups: Temporal Segmentation; Perfect Discrimination

A group, a set of identical demand elements, could be an individual consumer. Commodities must be carefully specified. Services rendered at different times *are* different. Even if only one demand function is to be formulated for the whole market at each moment, a different function would be appropriate at each moment. Transporters, electricity suppliers, cinema operators and others would rarely keep their prices unchanged from hour to hour. The temporal segments are also linked: buyers can virtually substitute purchases made at 9 a.m. for purchases made at 2 p.m.; suppliers can trade off a.m. for p.m. sales.

Fig. 1 can become a basis for almost any of the ¶7.3 §§4 discriminations.

The demand curve, as drawn up, permits the consumer's utility level to increase as lower prices are specified. The proposed price changes are not income-compensated. It follows that definite integrals taken 'under' such curves overstate maximum amounts which can be extracted from buyers confronted with all-or-none offers. Little is thus sacrificed didactically and there *does* exist a pseudo-quantitative measure, owing to Prof. Hotelling, which avoids the error built into Fig. 1.

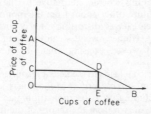

Fig. 1   Mr. Green's Daily Demand for Coffee.

$OAB is an approximate measure of the amount which Mr. Green could be forced to pay each day for the right to drink 'free' coffee. If the marginal cost of coffee, f.o.b. Green, were $OC, the firm could maximize its profits from Green by charging him approximately $ACD for the right to buy coffee at price $OC.

A simple thought-experiment verifies the areas. Ask Mr. Green what he is prepared to pay for the right to drink *one* cup of coffee a day. *Then*, given the agreement already reached on the first cup, ask him what he is prepared to pay for the right to drink a second cup, etc. Subject only to the *caveats* of the note above Mr. Green could be fully exploited. And he would pay a different price for each cup of coffee bought.

The analysis illuminates the economics of quantity discounts and peak-load versus off-peak pricing of electricity and coach seats through its theme of discrimination bottomed on elasticity of demand. However, non-discriminatory, but differential, pricing emerges from competition, reflecting imputed zero rents for redundant capacities. Thus, ideally, purely competitive road haulage tariffs would sink to out-of-pocket cost levels whenever redundancy developed.

This refers to redundancy which cannot be corrected by shifting capacities to new locations.

Possibly, price discrimination will permit an activity to be undertaken which otherwise would not be operated in the long run. Thus assume that activity 1, the only activity permitting the River *Eau* to be bridged, would yield a maximum annual revenue above operating expenses of $10,000 under non-discriminatory pricing, whilst interest, depreciation, and other capital charges are $15,000 per annum. Perhaps discrimination would permit the activity to yield annual net revenues of $20,000 (i.e. net of operating expenses), but beware of drawing policy implications. Other activities yielding indiscriminately priced outputs could become underrated as outlets for scarce resources if discrimination were permitted for *Pont de l'Eau* charges. Welfare-optimal pricing would be keyed on low or nil tariffs whenever capacity was not strained and on high tariffs when overcrowding loomed, subject to ethics of distribution.

Criteria for social and private optimality can be very different. Consider a lone impoverished pedestrian desperately needing to cross a bridge at a time when profit maximization calls for a toll of $100 although the bridge is not crowded. He will turn back and descend the stair.

The rational monopolist would wish either to practise perfect discrimination or to combine marginal cost pricing with auxiliary devices. He would thus maximize what the engineer Dupuit called the total benefit from production of the commodity, all to be siphoned off by the monopolist. A siphoning scheme alternative to the text's lump-sum taxation device might force buyers to acquire other goods from the monopolist at surcharged rates. Chapter 10 makes clear that such excises, distorting rates of transformation in production and consumption, are inefficient, Higher revenues can be obtained without forcing buyers into less-preferred positions. However, excising might be the most profitable *feasible* strategy.

Thus elementary monopoly pricing leads to inefficient resource allocation which, amongst other things, reduces potential monopoly profit. Monopolists are encouraged to develop more complicated strategies, including price discrimination, tied sales, and vertical integration. The strands of analysis are drawn from the theory of the firm, the theory of taxation and welfare economics. Cf. the appendix to Chapter 7.

§ 5

Active Price Discrimination

Modern marketing is as concerned to influence as to adapt to buyers' preferences. Glancing behind the ambiguous façade of Madison Avenue, will not a rational firm with market power, confronted with constraints on forced segmentation of its markets, often try to induce buyers voluntarily to spin off into separate groups? Broadly speaking, the device is the *model line*. Thus a cigarette company might promote some brands with films showing he-men of the Old West trussing calves and others with pictures of effete scions of ducal houses swathed in Liberty silk. Indeed voluntary segregation amongst potential buyers of cigarettes, toiletries, clothing, etc., often is so great that members of one group would be ashamed to be seen using brands preferred by another.

4. INTERTEMPORAL PLANNING: ALUMINIUM AND AUTOMOBILE EXAMPLES

A monopolist should take account of effects of present actions on future costs and demands even if outside entry can be neglected.

§ 2

An Aluminium Case

Scrap aluminium is used in the production of virgin aluminium. *Ceteris paribus*, then, the greater is aluminium output this period, the lower will be the costs of production next period.

§ 3

An Automobile Case

Just as the aluminium case abstracted from temporal interdependence of demand, the automobile case abstracts from temporal interdependence of costs. Used cars are competitive with new cars. *Ceteris paribus*, then, the greater is automobile output this period, the less will be the demand for new cars next period; the lower will be used-car prices.

§ 4

The aluminium and automobile cases are encompassed by the criterion:

$$\max f(y_1) + F(y_1, y_2)/(1+i) - c(y_1) - C(y_1, y_2)/(1+i) \qquad (6)$$

A partial-equilibrium approach is followed. A first step towards a general-equilibrium approach would be to set up explicit excess-demand functions for used cars and/or scrap metals of appropriate datings.

Current revenue is a function of current output: $R_1 = f(y_1)$. Period 2 revenue depends on period 2 output *and* on period 1 output, given still earlier outputs. Identical reasoning bottoms the cost functions. Since the firm's present value is to be maximized, revenues and outlays must be dated and discounted. The first-order conditions are:

$$f' + F_1/(1+i) = c' + C_1/(1+i) \tag{7}$$

$$F_2 = C_2 \tag{8}$$

Equation (7) requires that the discounted sum of marginal revenue effects should be equal to that of marginal cost effects.

The aluminium case finds equation (7) rewritten as:

$$f' = c' + C_1/(1+i) \tag{9}$$

Since $C_1 < 0$, the adjusted analysis suggests that production should be greater in period 1 (or, more generally, in the plan's earlier periods) than would be called for by one-period analysis.

The automobile case finds equation (7) rewritten as:

$$f' + F_1/(1+i) = c' \tag{10}$$

Since $F_1 < 0$, less output is called for in period 1.

Cost savings for $t > T$ are ignored. Only a few remarks can be made here about plans with rolling horizons. The text's criterion strictly applies only when the future beyond the end of the planning horizon is totally blacked out. It is tempting to peep behind the curtain, especially in the case of stochastic decision models.

This leads to another observation: it would be eccentric for a firm not to use an error-learning process, otherwise it would woodenly persist in conduct which statistical theory suggests has little likelihood of being correct. As soon as this is recognized, simple maximization of expected present value or at least deterministic planning goes by the board. Finally, to the extent that a firm's management cannot lock up a decisive percentage of the firm's shares, its objective becomes maximization of share value. If it does not maximize share value, takeover bidders might come into control. The extent to which present value and maximized share value criteria are alike depends on the influence of risk, uncertainty, and variegation of share market opinion. The two criteria are identical only under full information and perfect certainty.

5. INTERTEMPORAL ANALYSIS: PROFITS AND ENTRY

Perhaps Firm Aleph today is able to behave like a monopolist in the sense of Chapter 7. How might others be deterred from horning in? One strategem centres on pricing policies. It might pay Aleph in the long run to charge lower prices than would maximize current profits. Aleph's profits might then be a less attractive lure to potential entrants and perhaps then it could blanket enough of the market to close out otherwise virgin territories.

§ 2

¶7.5 concerns decisions of great practical importance: choices leading to optimal *time-paths* of productions, consumptions, prices, etc. *Practical importance*? It is difficult to conceive of a decision in Life which is not about *time-paths*. Only in textbooks do *entrepreneurs* decide on actions for *this* moment. True we have established theories for consumers and producers general enough to encompass *time*. Until now concrete procedures, like the classical calculus of variations methods of ¶7.5 §§3 and the Pontryagin methods of ¶7.5 §§4, have not emerged. *Optimal time-paths*? It was established in Chapter 4 that 'real world' producers think in present value terms either directly or indirectly under a maximization of share value criterion. Surely *consumers* consider the future! So the connexion between 'micro' optimality and intertemporal choice theory is obvious. It will be established in Chapter 10 that Pareto-optimum theory flows naturally from the generalized models of producers and consumers of Chapters 3 and 4. Still one of the natural extensions of the techniques of ¶7.5 §§3 and 4, that to *social* optimality, is perhaps unsound. Thus some are inclined to define *collective* utility functions as integrals over intertemporal outcomes and then state as a collective problem the maximization of such an integral. This procedure is not inherently invidious, but we must understand that such holistic devices are divorced from traditionally atomistic welfare economics (emphatically including the theory of Pareto-optimatility). A person and a society are metaphysically incommensurate objects. This said, I am quick to agree that the calculus of variations and its extensions have promise for improved 'social engineering'. Thus alternative objective functions might be defined on Gross National Product and a general price index over time. Evaluations of alternative policies would be sensitive to the weighting of the objective functions. Any of us, deciding upon weights according to his preferences, could then evaluate alternative policies much more precisely than before. (Is the added precision factitious?)

These themes, digressive here, but ineluctable, are to be picked up in Chapter 10.

§ 3[1]

The monopolist's objective is to maximize a definite integral defining total profit, neglecting discounting for simplicity:

$$V = \int_{t_0}^{t_1} \{p_t y_t - \Phi(y_t)\} \, dt \qquad (11)$$

where p_t and y_t, price and output at date t, are defined by equations (12) and (13):

$$p_t = f(t) \tag{12}$$

$$y_t = F(t) \tag{13}$$

Functions f and F are to be chosen so as to maximize the integral, noting that $\Phi(y_t)$ defines the rate at which the cumulant of cost is increasing at $t = t^*$.

At the outset, p_{t_1} is fixed at $p_{t_1}^*$. Once the initial price, $p_{t_0}^*$, is specified, the end points $(p_{t_0}^*, p_{t_1}^*)$ are thus fixed and a classical analysis can proceed. The demand law is:

$$y_t = g(p_t, \dot{p}_t) \tag{14}$$

Now Euler's equation can be brought into play:

$$py - \Phi(y) = \dot{p}(p - d\Phi/dy)(\partial y/\partial \dot{p}) + \text{constant} \tag{16}$$

Consider a problem calling for maximization of a definite integral defined on the continuous variable p where p is to be defined on time. Fixed end-points for p are to be stipulated. Euler's equation states a necessary condition for such maximization, determining $f(t)$ under certain further conditions. Amongst these conditions is the requirement that the function being integrated, cf. equation (11), be defined on p and $\dot{p}$. Thus equation (11) can be written:

$$V = \int_{t_0}^{t_1} \Psi(t, p, \dot{p})\, dt \tag{15}$$

Euler's equation is:

$$\partial\Psi/\partial p = d(\partial\Psi/\partial\dot{p})/dt$$

In the text's problem, Ψ defines an instantaneous rate of profit-generation.

Recalling that $y_t = g(p_t, \dot{p}_t)$, equation (16) is a first-order differential equation in p and is not necessarily linear. Upon integrating equation (16), the criterion becomes maximized relative to $p_{t_1} = p_{t_1}^*$. The complete solution requires that p_{t_1} be chosen so that a global maximum is achieved.

§4

I am indebted to Dr. John Williamson in connexion with this text, but he is entirely free from responsibility for any errors present there.

¶7.5 §§4 in fact makes a transition to Chapter 8: it takes up for the first time in the book explicit analysis of other firms' reactions to 'our' policies.[2]

Our Pontryagin theory discussion flows from an 'entry' problem. Very simply, a monopolist's net revenue at date t is to be a function of the price he charges and of the degree ('stock') of entry which has occurred. Putting aside discounting, the monopolist, Aleph is to maximize J over the interval $t_0 \rightarrow t_1$ where:

$$\dot{J} = f(x, u) \tag{17}$$

$$J = \int_{t_0}^{t_1} f(x(t), u(t))\, dt \tag{18}$$

subject to:

$$\dot{x} = g(x, u) \tag{19}$$

The function $u^*(t)$ describes a particular path for the *control*—price—over the decision period. $x^*(t)$ is a particular path for 'degree of entry'. The value of the integral, J, is defined on these functions of time and obviously depends on choice of *control-path*. (The function f describes the rate of change of a cumulant, of course, and has a net-revenue interpretation.) The problem boils down to selection of the optimal feasible *control-path*, $\bar{u}(t)$, the rate of change in the stock of entry being determined by equation (19).

The Pontryagin Maximum Principle calls for a procedure which extends the Lagrangian methods already explored. We form the *Hamiltonian* $f + \psi g$ and then write the *Hamilton canonical equations*:

$$\dot{x} = \partial H / \partial \psi \tag{20}$$

i.e.

$$\dot{x} = g \tag{21}$$

$$\dot{\psi} = -\partial H / \partial x \tag{22}$$

i.e.

$$\dot{\psi} = -f_x - \psi g_x \tag{23}$$

These equations must hold at all times along optimal paths. Furthermore, the Principle asserts that, if $\bar{u}(t)$ is indeed an optimal control, then the Hamiltonian attains its maximum at all times relative to the set of feasible controls. So we obtain the necessary condition:

$$\partial H / \partial u = 0 \tag{24}$$

i.e.

$$f_u + \psi g_u = 0 \tag{25}$$

We pause for some highly plausible specifications about signs of partial derivatives: 1), $f_x < 0$; 2), $g_x < 0$; 3), $f_u > 0$; 4), $g_u > 0$.

1) asserts that: *ceteris paribus*, the higher the degree of entry, the less profitable will be Aleph's operations;
2) that: *ceteris paribus*, the rate of increase of entry will be less, the greater is entry now;
3) that: a higher price will increase instantaneous net-revenue;
4) that: entry is encouraged by higher prices.

So:
$$\psi = -(f_u/g_u) < 0 \tag{26}$$

The shadow price associated with the stock of entry, this being the economic interpretation of ψ, is negative when an optimal control is being deployed. Turning back to equation (23) the rate of change of this negative shadow price at any instant is ambiguous along an optimal *control-path*; that is to say, the necessary conditions for optimization are ambiguous unless concrete functions are supplied. Now it is intuitively appealing to suggest that the departure of u_t from the instantaneous net-revenue-maximizing price is, in absolute terms, an increasing function of ψ (whilst being a decreasing function of the algebraic value of ψ) and that $\dot\psi < 0$, for $\psi < 0$, implies that Aleph's optimal strategy finds him using less and less of his power to extract monopoly rent *now*. However, the ambiguity about $\dot\psi$ prevents us from cashing in on this intuition, thus reminding us that for most practical purposes mathematical economics must be numerate to be useful.

These crumbs of Pontryagin theory whet one's appetite for inter-temporal welfare economics. What other kind of welfare economics can really be interesting?

CHAPTER 7—APPENDIX: VERTICAL INTEGRATION AND EFFICIENT PRICING IN THE THEORIES OF COMPETITION AND MONOPOLY

1. INTRODUCTION

Section 2 deals with a competitive structure of industry. Making an obvious extension of activity analysis and recalling some basic theory of economic dynamics, it shows how pressures for vertical integration arise under competition. Section 3 concerns an oligopolist environment. Its coda takes up the intersection of vertical integration theory with American antitrust law. Section 4 comes to centre on a recondite problem: extension of monopoly through vertical integration by 'bottleneck monopolists'.

2. VERTICAL MERGER AND RESOURCE ALLOCATION UNDER COMPETITIVE CONDITIONS

Even purely-competitive markets would not lead to efficient resource use in the most idealized economy, if only the stipulation of *tâtonnement* were abandoned.

Stipulate that competitive equilibrium is optimal. But today or to-morrow or the day after tomorrow prevailing prices will not be equi-librium prices. I have considered elsewhere a 'real world' case, private motor carriage.[3] It appears that even in an hypothetically unregulated motor carriage industry, tariffs would correspond badly with efficient prices most of the time. This suggests that shippers may be encouraged to operate private carriage in order to realize profits from managing resources, whilst unhampered by market static.

Prof. Alchian shows that competitive norms eventually could be achieved by ignorant firms snuffling about in an uncertain environment simply by trial and error and by imitation of lucky colleagues. Obviously this does not lead to continuous efficiency.[4]

§2

A proof is possible, at least for a case neglecting information-cost theory. Consider a competitive industry with an integrated sector, I, and an unintegrated sector, U, each using the same technology and engaged in the same activities. Assume that existing and potential firms have identical U-shaped average cost curves. A representative I-firm can deal with 'true' cost data: 'sociology' does not impinge upon intrafirm transfers within a rational firm. A representative U-firm will respond to factitious data, data not corresponding to 'true' data except when the complex is in full equilibrium.

We wish to show that on the average I-firms will achieve higher realized rates of return than will U-firms, and to show that U-firms, responding to distorted signals, will, over any interval for which demand and supply are unbalanced earn lower profits.

Conceding that in full equilibrium costs of production as seen by either set of firms will be the same, consider the case of a temporarily overbuilt industry. Perhaps there has been a decline in demand. Assume that many inputs used by the industry are produced with specialized equipment and do not have alternative uses. If these input prices fall sluggishly and erratically, U-firms will face 'inflated' input prices and will produce less at prevailing final-product prices than they should.

Adherence to fake cost curves might lead to higher industry profits. Competitive industries produce more than profit-maximizing industry output in equilibrium.

Over an excess-supply interval the collective income statement for I will be better than for U. Finally consider an industry which is temporarily underbuilt. Perhaps demand has increased. I-firms, spurred on by product-price increases and higher shadow rents, will pump hard and rapidly accomplish appropriate investment outlays, whilst U-firms will face shortages of intermediate goods (inputs) whose supplies must respond to erratic price changes. U-firms will not be able to increase their outputs as rapidly as they want to or as rapidly as integrated channels would permit.

U-firms, then, have an incentive to integrate, perhaps through merger, in order to realize the fruits of efficient pricing.

§ 3

Consider a linear-programming formulation. The firm's criterion is maximization of $\mathbf{r} \cdot \mathbf{x}$, noting that costs of 'outside' resource rentals are to be deducted from gross revenues in computing $\mathbf{r}$. The dual problem is to minimize $\lambda \cdot \mathbf{b}$ subject to $A'\lambda \geq \mathbf{r}$. Also $\mathbf{r} \cdot \mathbf{x}(\max) = \lambda \cdot \mathbf{b}(\min)$. In their solutions, *U*-firms will be governed by the equalities $A'w^* = \mathbf{r}$ instead of by $A'\overline{\lambda} = \mathbf{r}$, where w^* refers to rents determined in open markets and λ solves the *integrated* dual problem. Hence *U*-firms will employ a non-optimal programme except in full equilibrium when, ideally, the competitive market processes solve the dual and, hence, the primal problem or problems.

$\mathbf{r} \cdot \overline{\mathbf{x}} = \overline{\lambda} \cdot \mathbf{b}$ is known to be a maximum: *integrated* profits are known to be maximized in the solution of the *integrated* programme relative to $\mathbf{r}$. *U*-firms, obeying false dual constraints, will not be able to achieve the optimal state outside full competitive industry equilibrium.

3. BENIGN AND PRE-EMPTIVE MERGERS UNDER OLIGOPOLY

If a supplier acquires an actual or potential customer, a vertical merger, it is likely that the acquired outlet will favour the acquiring firm. Still foreclosure effects might be miniscule and incidental. The merger might be *benign*. On the other hand, a vertical merger which has deliberate and/or substantial foreclosure effects is *pre-emptive*. (Here we consider only pre-emptive mergers which are both deliberate and substantially preclusive.) The burden of Section 3 is that vertical mergers, whether *benign* or *pre-emptive*, tend to lead to lower final-product prices, especially if *conglomerate merger* can be accomplished easily.

§ 2

Categories 1) to 6) of *benign* vertical merger, described hereunder, can be put aside.

1) TAX-MOTIVATED MERGERS. Undistributed profits taxes and death duties can control, keeping in mind that going-concern assets often are not liquid.
2) MERGERS BASED ON UNACHIEVED SIZE-ECONOMIES. A downstream manufacturer might wish to produce additional products in order to absorb idle machine time.
3) QUALITY CONTROL. A firm might wish to maintain its own quality control, especially when its purchases have been interlaced with others on upstream assembly lines.

4) ASSURANCE OF REGULAR SUPPLY-FLOWS. This case can be especially important when rigidities lead to 'shortages' during booms. Cf. Section 2 and case 8) in the text.

5) AVOIDANCE OF RATE REGULATION. 'If I can sell myself a key input at an inflated price, I shall have established a basis for a higher maximum tariff, at least if officials are rather naive.' (But 6) infra is probably a better explanation of such cases.)

6) AVOIDANCE OF EFFECTS OF IMPERFECT COMPETITION AT OTHER LEVELS. If one of Beth's inputs customarily is priced above competitive levels, Beth might profitably produce it itself. Cf. United States versus Yellow Cab. Co., 332 U.S. 218 (1947).

Simply to state categories 7) to 10) is to show that such vertical mergers, at worst logical applications of presumptively legal upstream power, do not rely on foreclosure.

7) INDIRECT PRICE DISCRIMINATION. Perhaps Dogpatch can be penetrated if costs of production can be cut. Perhaps Aleph produces key inputs for products which might be sold in Dogpatch. However, Aleph does not wish to perturb its (intermediate) level by practising selective price-cutting and must avoid Robinson–Patman trouble. Hence Aleph, the upstream firm, might enter into the final-product market, charging its outlets shadow prices for inputs based on actual upstream cost, perhaps not tampering with published input prices.

8) AVOIDANCE OF CLUMSY OPEN-MARKET PRICING. The competitive analogue has been thoroughly developed in Section 2.

9) ASSURANCE OF COMPETITION DOWNSTREAM. In the many situations in which downstream competition benefits upstream firms, the latter might set up firms below in order to make downstream markets more competitive and in order to make downstream firms behave more like their agents.

10) AVOIDANCE OF INTERNECINE STRIFE DOWNSTREAM. In contrast with 9), the upstream oligopolist, Gimmel, might conclude that complications of timing of film runs, cinema-ticket pricing, appropriate distribution of advertising expenditures between locations and media, etc., require control of downstream resources if profits are to be maximized. The argument does not pivot on foreclosure of rival film producers. Indeed it holds even if Gimmel has irrevocably monopolized film production.

Case 10) might explain the famous Paramount case. Cf. Paramount Famous Lasky Corporation versus United States, 282 U.S. 30 (1930).

First- and second-run cinemas do not sell the same product even when exhibiting the same film.

Bottleneck cases are treated as *non-benign* whether or not *pre-emptive* elements are important. Bottleneck power is so formidable that it almost certainly will be treated as an inherently dangerous object in the courts.

§ 3

Pre-emptive vertical mergers concern foreclosure. In each *pre-emptive* instance, rivals' opportunities are restricted and such restriction is at the heart of the matter. In no instance can price-effects of *pre-emptive* mergers be categorically described as 'favourable' or 'unfavourable', but the weight of evidence yielded by thought experiment suggests that final-product prices will tend to be lower as a result even of *pre-emptive* vertical mergers. In each instance conglomeration possibilities increase the likelihood of a vertical merger leading to lower final-product prices.

1) THE QUIET LIFE. Imagine that each of a fairly large number of producers of an input used exclusively by Industry A acquires an A firm. Concentration of industrial power hardly would be affected, but acquiring firms, ensconced within protected channels, could relax rather more. Looming conglomerated ogres might prevent torpor however.

2) RAISING THE ANTE. If a blade monopolist could corner the existing handle market, would-be entrants would have to put up larger stakes. Handle-production could not be contemplated unless the producer were prepared to make blades. The counter theme again appears: restrictive positions based on mere size—positions arising out of imperfections of capital markets—cannot be sustained against powerful conglomerate firms.

It is tacitly assumed, of course, that entry into the blade business is *possible*.

3) EXPANSION OF THE ACQUIRING FIRM'S MARKET SHARE. The courts stress 3): if Aleph buys out a downstream firm it can assure itself of the acquired firm's custom. However, the result well could be lower prices of intermediate and final products, depending on the response of 'excluded' upstream producers. If anxious to maintain their sales or market-shares, they would be tempted to cut prices, or such acquisitions might break up a tacit status quo: dog-eat-dog tactics might be revived. True, such strengthening of the acquiring firm might cause upstream rivals to toss in their hands and become followers and higher market prices might result. Again potential action by aggressive conglomerates countervails.

Turning to *downstream* effects, the extent to which market penetrations of acquired firms might increase would largely be governed by their ability to charge lower prices. Assume, for example, that the acquiring firm comes to price its products to its acquisition at marginal cost whilst maintaining its open-market quotations. Assume that, as a result, the acquired firm slashes *its* prices. The acquired firm's market share would increase if its rivals were to stand pat. Matching conduct by downstream rivals eager to protect their market shares would please the consumer all the more.

§ 4

THE DEVELOPING ANTITRUST LAW OF MERGER. Suffice it to say that the Brown Shoe case of 1962,[5] expressing adamant hostility to vertical merger in general, has been amply supported by subsequent Supreme Court decisions. When one takes into account the growing hostility of the courts to conglomerate mergers as well, one must sense a juridical trend which is economically misled.

Of course, vertical integration can occur without merger. For some strange reason both the courts and prominent academic authorities have been favourable to building *de novo* whilst hostile to vertical merger. Why should it be legal for Ogre Corporation to batter Tom Thumb to death, but illegal for Ogre to buy out Thumb at a price exceeding the value of Thumb's business assets to Thumb himself? Furthermore, a rule of law sealing off markets for existing physical assets leads to distorted investment programmes, an inevitable result under roughly-competitive conditions of preventing transfers of resources to more valuable uses.

4. THE BOTTLENECK CASE

The argument is set within monopoly theory only for simplicity and brevity: in this way, interdependence of conjectures can be avoided.

I have previously developed a theme which might unify much of the empirical evidence *and* which conflicts with the developing American antitrust law of merger.[6]

Monopoly-like pricing ordinarily leads to inefficient use of resources, which in turn reduces the monopolist's own potential profits below the level which it could enjoy, if only it could exercise its powers without inducing inefficient production. Think of a monopoly price as a tax imposed upon the public. (That is the surcharge above the competitive equilibrium price is to be regarded as a tax.) Then tying-sales, full-line forcing, and vertical merger can be viewed as an elaborated taxation network, both increasing exploitable revenues and attracting more revenues into the monopolist's coffers. Vertical integration, whether by merger or otherwise, is a particularly simple device towards this end: an integrated productive channel can use internal accounting prices appropriately rigged by the monopolist's headquarters.

Light is shed on a difficult problem first turned up by Professor Bork: bottleneck theory.[7] A bottleneck occurs when a firm can exert influence on costs of production of rival producers in contrast with the cases of Section 3. A bottleneck obviously exists when an upstream ingredient is priced so high that it ceases to be used downstream. The upstream firm's pricing policy then clearly affects the terms of minimum-cost production downstream. In this way we contemplate the possibility that a vertically integrating upstream firm can take over the entire downstream market by forcing up the costs of other downstream producers to prohibitive levels.

There is another ground for forward integration by a bottleneck holder: its recognition that its potential profits cannot be realized if it charges tariffs which do not reflect true costs!

'Reflect' has a broad connotation. In our sense, transfer of the excise tax to a product completely price-inelastic in demand leads to reflexion of true costs by prices.

Thus a company controlling a crucial isthmus might find that its high charges divert some traffic. If the Canal Company could gain control of firms using the isthmus, it could increase its profits: the integrated company could concern itself with the true costs of products laid down at the doors of final buyers. Obvious candidates for takeover would be shipping lines. Acquired lines could choose between the Company's and other straits in terms of true costs (at least if other charges are determined as in competitive equilibrium). The Canal Company, then, is encouraged to bring about a more efficient use of its facilities so that there is a bigger melon for it to slice.

It remains to explain how vertical integration by bottleneck holders can lead to higher *downstream* prices. Assume that unintegrated Firm Aleph has been selling a patented input V used by competitive producers. Input V competes with unpatented inputs Z, produced by firms in competition. Aleph's pricing policy has to take account of possibilities for substitution between V and Z. As a result the price of the final product is below the price maximizing composite profits.

That is, Aleph cannot take full account of elasticity of demand for the final product because of the elasticity of substitution between its intermediate product and inputs Z.

A group of competitive firms never maximizes *joint* profits.

However, Aleph can effectively take over the downstream sector by acquiring one or more downstream firms or by building new plant, simultaneously putting up the price of V to outsiders to a prohibitive level *and* charging less for the final-product than can firms confined to inputs Z. It is possible that the new final-product price will exceed the old. Aleph no longer will be constrained by possibilities for substitution against V in downstream production.

Conglomeration cannot cure the bottleneck case. Aleph can achieve its results through its irrefragable grip on downstream costs of production.

REFERENCES

1. Cf. R. G. D. Allen, *Mathematics for Economists* (London: Macmillan & Co.; 1938), Chap. 20. Also R. Bellman and S. Dreyfus, *Applied Dynamic Programming* (Princeton: Princeton University Press; 1962), Chap. 5.
2. Cf. L. Pontryagin and coworkers, *The Mathematical Theory of Optimal Processes* (New York: John Wiley & Sons Inc.; 1962), esp. Chap. I. Also, K. Fox, J. Sengupta and E. Thorbecke, *The Theory of Quantitative Economic Policy* (Amsterdam: North-Holland Publishing Co.; 1966), pp. 203–213 (contributed by T. K. Kumar) and their splendid bibliography, pp. 236–238.
3. M. Burstein and coworkers, *The Cost of Trucking: Econometric Analysis* (Dubuque, Iowa: Wm. C. Brown for the Transportation Center at Northwestern U.; 1965), pp. 106–137.
4. Cf. A. Alchian, 'Uncertainty, Evolution, and Economic Theory,' 58, *Journal of Political Economy*, 211 (1950).
5. Brown Shoe versus U.S., 370 U.S. 294 (1962).
6. Cf. M. L. Burstein, 'The Economics of Tie-In Sales,' 42 *Review of Economics and Statistics*, 68 (1960), 'A Theory of Full Line Forcing,' 55 *Northwestern University Law Review*, 62 (1960).
7. Cf. Robert Bork, 'Vertical Integration and the Sherman Act: The Legal History of an Economic Misconception,' 22 *University of Chicago Law Review*, 157 (1954).

CHAPTER 8

Oligopoly and Strategy

1. INTRODUCTION

Chapter 8 picks up themes first projected in the $N-M$ analysis of Chapter 3 and at least suggested in Chapter 6 and 7. Its *Leitmotiv* is *conjectural interdependence*: firms must form *strategies* in order to maximize their objective functions. No longer are reactions of other firms simply to be buried in functional notation.

¶8.2 recasts the Redland–Blueland discussion of ¶3.6, establishing the main problems of oligopoly theory. ¶8.3 takes up the theory of games, the signal formal technique of oligopoly theory. ¶8.4 considers attempts to link up oligopoly theory with the traditional theory of the firm.

2. OLIGOPOLY AND COLD WAR DIPLOMACY

What does it mean for a cold war to dissolve into a détente? Leaders, hitherto concerned about ruin, perhaps forced to contemplate pre-emptive strategies, begin, tacitly or overtly, to explore possibilities of cooperation in achieving joint goals. In the language of ¶8.3, *minimax* strategies become dislodged in favour of joint-maximization.

§ 2

Analogies between diplomacies of nations and firms are acute. Surely, facets of business strategy include:

1) war-chests of fungible assets which can offset pressures of adverse cash flow due to price wars or outside aggression;

A Stackelberg follower (cf. ¶8.4) maximizing short run profits might be in too delicate a position to try to trade off current for future profits.

2) overhead-cost positions, affecting how badly firms would bleed if sales were to fall off;

3) potentials for realization of economies of large size, partly determining the attractiveness of aggressive sales strategies, risking inflammation of the business game;
4) diversification. Does Firm Aleph have its eggs in one basket? If it does, it might be vulnerable to a quick thrust;
5) intensity of customer loyalty;
6) patent positions. A firm dependant upon another's patents might be peculiarly vulnerable;
7) can Firm Beth, if hard pressed, call up political allies?

Strategic and tactical considerations necessarily influence behaviour. A vulnerable firm is likely to cultivate only remote markets not regarded as rich prizes. A well-armoured firm with a rule-or-ruin spirit might try to smash up opponents, risking protracted periods of depressed prices and irregular order books, hoping to emerge as unchallenged top dog. Others might be capable of brief violent campaigns, but have poor resistance to a war of attrition. Accordingly, they would be alert to opportunities to launch *Blitzkriegs* whilst avoiding slogging matches. Again, consider basically-weak firms who have studied the tactics of children and guerrillas. They might yelp at the heels of powerful rivals, forcing them either to make concessions or to escalate the conflict to an unacceptable level of violence.

§3

Our first concrete problem is *kinky oligopoly demand*. Fig. 1 is drawn up for a one-product, non-discriminating oligopolist at date *t*. DD is best interpreted as showing maximum prices consistent with achievement of various sales levels, *taking account of reactions of other firms*. DD pertains to a subjective probability distribution revealing moral expectations and is *not* an adjunct to the objective demand functions of Chapter 7.

Kinked demand curves and their associated marginal-revenue curves are *discontinuous*: marginal revenue from sales greater than OA is negative; attempts to increase price above OB will lead to serious sales-losses.

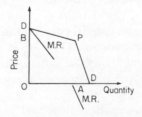

Fig. 1   Kinky Oligopoly Demand.

This implies that other members of the industry are anxious to maintain market penetrations. They would penetrate farther if able to do so passively, e.g. by maintaining their prices whilst others announce price increases.

Firms might be anxious to protect their penetrations (market shares) because lumpinesses have led to excess capacity or perhaps they are eager to exert leverage on a greater mass of capitalization.

What determines the position of the kink, P? The strategic considerations of ¶8.2 §§2 are important, as is the condition of entry. Thus even if a rate of return on invested capital of 10 per cent, expected with certainty, would induce entry, existing firms might be able to remain unchallenged as long as their rates of return did not exceed 13 per cent. 13 per cent might not offer enough breathing space to a prudent potential interloper in a stochastic universe.

If the ratio of invested capital to annual sales were $4:1$, and if the rate of return on capital were 13 per cent, price OB would imply a 52 per cent per annum rate of profit on sales. (If the capital-sales ratio were $1:4$, price OB would imply a 3·25 per cent per annum annual profit-rate on sales for a 13 per cent rate of return on capital.) If a drastic improvement in inventory management were to permit the ratio of capital to annual sales to fall to $2:1$, our argument urges that the kink would shift, that the 'kink price' would fall below OB. In the new solution the gross rate of profit on sales might become 26 instead of 52 per cent. (26 per cent is an approximate figure: the new condition will change firms' optimal capacities.)

POINT. Kinky-oligopoly-demand theory describes certain features of stabilized oligopoly conduct, but is incomplete: the theory cannot determine the position of the kink.

3. OLIGOPOLY AND THE THEORY OF GAMES

¶8.3 §§2–4 sketch an approach to oligopoly strategy based on the theory of *zero-sum* games whilst the laconic ¶8.3 §§5 touches on *non-zero-sum* game theory.

As it happens, *non-zero-sum* game theory, on the surface rich in promise, has not much influenced economics. The data it calls for are largely unavailable and probably could not be generated except in enervatingly artificial experiments. Its formal criteria are questionable, intuitively and philosophically.

Nor is *zero-sum* game theory the philosopher's stone. It is hard to set up a sensible model of business conduct which can be reduced, like bridge, to a state in which one partnership's gain is the other's loss. Agreed, if Nature—the environment in which business strategists are to swim—can appropriately be deemed to be the opponent, then *two-person zero-sum* game models might usefully describe coalesced behaviour against Nature. However, if Nature is thus the true opponent, only paranoic businessmen would seek the ruin of any but helpless opponents or assume that their *confrères* seek their harm.

Having said these things, the basic theory of *two-person zero-sum* games is to be studied with measured attention. ¶8.3 §§2 evokes game theory through military scenarios. Then, after reflexion in ¶8.3 §§3, ¶8.3 §§4 summarizes some of the results through matrix algebra.

§ 2

Countries *A* and *B* are at war. Their commanders in Sector Yellow must select one of two strategies: deploy in well-prepared defensive positions (formation 1); form up for an assault which, if it is to have hope of success, must achieve tremendous concentration on a narrow front (formation 2). Pay-offs, it is assumed, can be measured objectively in terms of effects on military potentials. Indeed a single index suffices: a pay-off of $+1$ for *A* yields -1 for *B*. The 2×2 contingency table of Fig. 2 describes pay-offs of the four possible strategic constellations, suggesting that *A* can hurt *B* more than vice versa, if *A* can attack an unprepared *B*.

		A	
		Formation 1	Formation 2
B	Form. 1	0	-10
	Form. 2	$+10$	$+20$

Fig. 2   Pay-offs to *A* in Sector Yellow.

A fully informed *B* will defend. Defence *dominates* for *B*. If *A*'s commander, Aleph, believes that his opponent, Beth, is perfectly informed and *N–M* rational (athough, here, 'non-masochistic' doubtless suffices), he also should defend: an attack loses 10 to a prepared *B*. If Aleph believes that Beth, perhaps not knowing the facts, is likely to be in his formation 2, Aleph might attack. (An *N–M* Aleph will attack if the probability of Beth's adopting formation 2 is as low as 0·34.) If Aleph believes that Beth is fully informed and, for example, is *N–M* rational, then Aleph may just as well minimize his maximum loss: he may just as well *minimax*.

Here a compulsively defensive commander of B forces would act like a fully informed
$N - M$ rational commander. It is not uncommon in Life to do the right deed for the wrong
reason.

Assume that A does *minimax*. Both defend. Both adopt *pure strategies*:
each defends with probability 1. The *expectation* of the game is zero for
both players: it is a *fair game*.

The game has a *saddle point* even in the absence of more complex
strategies: A's minimized maximum losses are equal to B's maximized
minimum gains. Hence the game has a *solution*. Neither player, even if
the other promises *never* to alter his strategy, can gain by altering his own
strategy when they are in state (1/1). Then a change in strategy must lose.
So it is that players, convinced that they face fully-informed, $N–M$ rational
opponents, immediately would fall into the (1/1) pattern. Both would
defend.

It is possible that, if only pure strategies are considered, even a *two-
person zero-sum* game does not have a saddle point. But *mixed strategies*
can be defined which surely will permit a *two-person* 'matrix' game between opponents obeying $N–M$ axioms to be solved. In a mixed strategy,
moves are made according to a prearranged probability scheme. A mixed
strategy is in fact a convex linear combination of pure strategies. For
example, a mixed A strategy would find Aleph tossing a coin (which
might be loaded), attacking on heads and defending on tails. Note how
a mixed strategy can improve one's expected pay-off. What if a puncher
faces a smart boxer, surely able to tie up the puncher if he goes into a
fixed pattern? If the puncher can develop a random pattern, he has a
chance, his only chance: he may be able to pop the boxer if the boxer
guesses wrong (and now he *must* guess) and weaves when he should bob.

Game theory and linear-programming are ineluctably linked. A mixed strategy can be
interpreted as a combination of basic vectors spanning an activity space and the value of a
game as the value of a corresponding programme, saddle-point theory being the link.

'...[a]n arbitrary "matrix" game can be solved by solving a certain
related linear programme ... [and] it is possible ... to associate with any
pair of dual standard programmes a certain symmetric game whose solutions provide solutions of the given programmes if such exist.'[1]

Fig. 3 describes a game which can be solved only through mixed
strategies. The strategic situation in Sector Orange differs from that in
Sector Yellow. Time is on A's side: A profits from a phoney war. A also
profits from mutual bashing: A can win a war of attrition. However, B
can earn a draw in a set-piece battle. If B commits himself to either of his
pure strategies, A can gain simply by matching B. If A becomes committed to either of his pure strategies, B can earn a draw by taking the

A

Formation 1   Formation 2

		Formation 1	Formation 2
B	Form. 1	10	0
	Form. 2	0	10

Fig. 3   Pay-offs to *A* in Sector Orange.

opposite stance. But, if *B* randomizes his strategy, he can assure himself of an expected loss of only 5, even if *A*, who must commit himself simultaneously, knows exactly what is *B*'s strategy. (Of course, the game is unfair.) Thus if Beth tosses a fair coin to determine his move, Aleph's best strategy is also to toss a fair coin. If either *A* or *B* then deviates from his mixed strategies, he must accept a lower expected pay-off. Surely if the players can be described by *N–M* utility functions, they will not change their mixed strategies as above? A solution to the game will have been obtained.

§3

Reflecting on heuristic bases for *minimax* strategy, we turn again to war. Paradoxical as it might seem, a strategist with well nigh overwhelming material superiority over a shaky enemy often will *minimax* whilst the latter must turn to wild play. Thus was Pearl Harbour: Japanese hopes depended on American failure to give optimum response. Again recall the campaign in Western Europe from D-Day in June 1944 to the Battle of the Bulge in December 1944–January 1945: once firmly positioned across the Channel, the Allies, possessed of overwhelming material superiority, could be basically cautious. If the Allies avoided massive blunders, they could surely win even against perfect German strategy. Of course, the desperate German Ardennes attack was made by a player who, by December 1944, knew he would lose if the monstrous machine opposite him always would be perfectly led (relative to perfect information, of course).

Minimax would be encouraged by the rude, but governing, American neglect of the political, as against the purely military, strategic manifold.

The dual proposition is that a *N–M* Hitler would toss in his hand if convinced that the Allies were rational, perfectly informed, and able to achieve the convex hull of their opportunity set.

Next consider a paradox emerging from a business phantasy. If a group of rival firms agree, tacitly or overtly, to behave as if each thought his rivals to be leagued against him in a Manichean conspiracy to bring about his ruin and to play *minimax* strategies in the game against Nature thus defined, each will behave stolidly and predictably, much reducing the likelihood of destructive business war and strengthening the basis for eventual détente (joint maximization).

§4

¶8.3 §§2–3 considered special cases of *two-person* 'matrix' games. If player Aleph has m pure strategies open to him $(r = 1, 2, \ldots, m)$ whilst Beth has available n pure strategies $(s = 1, 2, \ldots, n)$, there results an $m \times n$ pay-off matrix $\mathbf{A}$. The element of $\mathbf{A}$, a_{rs}, shows the pay-off to Aleph from the collision of his rth strategy with Beth's sth. Aleph's problem (corresponding perfectly with Beth's) is to choose proportions $x_1, x_2, \ldots, x_m$,

$$\sum_{r}^{m} x_r = 1$$

in which to play his strategies, the vector $(1, 0, \ldots, 0)$ being associated with a choice only to play the first strategy, for example. Denote Aleph and Beth plans by vectors $\mathbf{x}$ and $\mathbf{y}$, $\mathbf{y}$ being an n-vector of non-negative fractions such that

$$\sum_{s}^{n} y_s = 1$$

Note that $\mathbf{x}'$ is a row vector, the transpose of $\mathbf{x}$. The expected value of the game to Aleph, then, is $\mathbf{x}'\mathbf{A}\mathbf{y}$, $\mathbf{x} \in \mathbf{X}$, $\mathbf{y} \in \mathbf{Y}$, $\mathbf{X}$ being the set of all vectors meeting the requirement that a plan be comprised of non-negative fractions (m for Aleph) summing to 1. The expected value of the game can be written $E(\mathbf{x}, \mathbf{y})$.

A game is said to have a solution if there exists a saddle point defined by vectors $\mathbf{x}^*$ and $\mathbf{y}^*$, i.e.:

$$E(\mathbf{x}, \mathbf{y}^*) \leq E(\mathbf{x}^*, \mathbf{y}^*) \leq E(\mathbf{x}^*, \mathbf{y}) \tag{1}$$

The pay-off to Aleph for any admissible plan against $\mathbf{y}^*$ must be no greater than that afforded by $\mathbf{x}^*$; the pay-off to Beth in this *zero-sum* game for any admissible plan against $\mathbf{x}^*$ must be no greater than that afforded by $\mathbf{y}^*$.

Inequality (1) can be written:

$$\mathbf{x}'\mathbf{A}\mathbf{y}^* \leq (\mathbf{x}^*)'\mathbf{A}\mathbf{y}^* \leq (\mathbf{x}^*)'\mathbf{A}\mathbf{y} \tag{2}$$

Inequalities (1) and (2) require that there exist vectors $\mathbf{x}^*$, $\mathbf{y}^*$ such that $\mathbf{x}^*$ is the optimal *minimax* strategy against $\mathbf{y}^*$ and $\mathbf{y}^*$ that against $\mathbf{x}^*$. Thus let us define $\max_{\mathbf{x}} \min_{\mathbf{y}}$ as the value of the game anticipated by Aleph on the assumption that Beth will always do precisely that which minimizes Aleph's expected pay-off. Denote the plan associated with this pay-off, $\hat{\mathbf{x}}$. Similarly define $\hat{\mathbf{y}}$. It can be proved that:

$$\max_{\mathbf{x}} \min_{\mathbf{y}} = \min_{\mathbf{y}} \max_{\mathbf{x}} = E(\mathbf{x}^*, \mathbf{y}^*) \tag{3}$$

and that, where $E(\mathbf{x}, \mathbf{y})$ is of the form $\mathbf{x}'\mathbf{A}\mathbf{y}$, as here and as in any 'matrix' game, $\mathbf{x}^*, \mathbf{y}^*$ exists: *minimax* strategists in *two-person zero-sum* games anticipate the same expected value for the game. (This is not to say that the game is fair, that $E(\mathbf{x}^*, \mathbf{y}^*) = 0$.) Indeed, since $\hat{\mathbf{x}} = \mathbf{x}^*$ and $\hat{\mathbf{y}} = \mathbf{y}^*$, each anticipates the other's *minimax* strategy (we abstract from strategies yielding ties).

$\mathbf{x}^*, \mathbf{y}^*$ is known as an *equilibrium point*. At $\mathbf{x}^*, \mathbf{y}^*$ each maximizes his expected pay-off relative to the other's strategy; each only can lose by changing his plan. So $\mathbf{x}^*, \mathbf{y}^*$ is a stable solution of a *two-person, zero-sum,* 'matrix' game.

Professor Baumol has succinctly summarized '*minimax* and *equilibrium*': 'Equilibrium points therefore possess an element of inner stability in that if one player adopts a strategy consistent with the attainment of such a point, the other player also is motivated to do so.'[2] From this it follows that it always is possible to achieve a *security value* by *minimax*. However, keep in mind that in life, unlike textbooks, strategies are not worked out against stipulated (albeit subjective) probability distributions. Instead, in life, there must be concern for 'production functions' relating information-search to the statistical properties of these estimates. As I have suggested in my review of S-Ch Kolm, *Les choix financiers et monétaires* (Paris: Dunod; 1967), not only in bridge is a peek worth two finesses. (Cf. *American Economic Review*, 1968.)

§ 5[3]

Following J. D. Williams,[4] we conceive that duopolists Red and Blue are playing against each other or against Nature—here the public. There results either a *non-zero* or *zero-sum two-person* game: between Red and Blue in the first instance; between Red–Blue and Nature in the second. Let the pay-offs to Blue relative to Red strategies be

		Red		
		1	2	3
Blue	1	1	6	2
	2	3	0	3
	3	4	2	0

Fig. 4   Pay-offs to Blue.

Pay-offs to Red relative to Blue strategies are

Red

		1	2	3
Blue	1	−6	0	−3
	2	−5	−4	−3
	3	0	−1	−4

Fig. 5　Pay-offs to Red.

If Blue considers itself to be in a *zero-sum* game against a perverse Nature, conceived to hold Red's hand, he will adopt the oddments 4:6:1 (his three-sided die will be loaded so as to produce expected proportions $\frac{4}{11}, \frac{6}{11}, \frac{1}{11}$ in re his strategies 1, 2, and 3) leading to an expected pay-off of $2\frac{4}{11}$ whilst similar reasoning will lead Red to oddments 0:1:3 and an expected pay-off of $-3\frac{1}{4}$. *But* the coalition Red–Blue can achieve an expected pay-off of 6(6B + 0R) by adopting pure strategies 1 (Blue) and 2 (Red). Turning now to Williams,

> 'This leads us squarely into difficulties. There is the problem, classic among thieves, of how to divide the loot.... What system of side payments should be made among the players to ensure that the Coalition will prosper....? When will a player accept a less-favourable pay-off in order to penalise the other player?...'[5]

The upshot has been described, more formally by McKinsey, following von Neumann and Morgenstein themselves.[6] It can be shown that, if Nature pulls up a chair in an *n-person non-zero-sum* 'matrix' game, there can be defined over the set $N_n = \{1, \ldots, n\}$ the amounts that coalitions of *n* or fewer players can expect to win from Nature. Thus occurs the *N–M characteristic function* of a game. Next we consider an *N–M imputation* for a game, nothing more than a division of spoils (and there may be many), such that the characteristic function is exhausted and no player receives less than he could achieve unaided.

Of course, no serious implication has been developed here as to how the spoils will be divided, nor how the respective threat-powers and personalities will work out. Indeed *N–M* theory appears to leave us in even worse shape than does raw intuition. Thus consider one of McKinsey's examples. For a *two-person* game Aleph has only one strategy and Beth two pure strategies so that the pay-offs to Aleph are (0, 10) and to Beth (−1000, 0). *N–M* imputations encompass with equanimity results giving each at least zero and Aleph *cum* Beth 10. How much should Aleph be willing to let Beth rake off merely because Beth can threaten to blow out his own brains, soiling Aleph's new tie? If you were Aleph, would you not be fairly confident that you could induce Beth to play his second strategy for a very small bribe indeed? Still $N-M$, confined to their characteristic function, cannot do more than repeat woodenly that 'the solution of this game is the set of all ordered non-negative couples whose sum is 10'.

This vapid result reflects no discredit on $N-M$, but rather the emptiness of axiomatic approaches to conjecturally independent nexi. This is too bad: as a result, theoretical, and hence operational, progress in a key sector of economics has been paralysed.

4. OLIGOPOLY AND TRADITIONAL THEORY

In traditional theory the competitive firm does not at all consider how its actions affect other firms, whilst 'monopolists'' calculations of such effects are not explicitly analysed. Furthermore, outputs are equated with sales: demand functions take the form $\mathbf{y}^d = \mathbf{f}(\mathbf{p})$ which, at least for the one-product firm, can be written $p = f^{-1}(y)$.

Following Stackelberg, a natural extension of traditional theory into the field of conjectural interdependence treats some firms' policies as reflecting impact on other firms. Thus some are *leaders*. Their counterparts are *followers*. A *follower* simply seeks to discover what the *leader* plans to do and then optimizes relative to that datum. A follower never tries to influence the leader.

¶8.4 §§3 ff develop a version of traditionally-orientated oligopoly theory after Stackelberg. Special heed is given to 'Cournot industries' comprised of two or more firms, each maximizing short run profits and behaving like a *follower*, and to 'Stackelberg duopolies' in which one firm leads and the other follows.

§2

Cournot–Stackelberg theory has obvious limitations. Only polarized, highly-specialized cases are tractable. Almost the entire range of oligopoly behaviour, concerning moderately powerful firms in strategic play over *n* periods, often falling into overt or tacit partial joint-maximization, is inaccessible to the theory. An oligopoly theory cannot be credible if, as in Cournot–Stackelberg theory, rival productions are treated as homogeneous products. The *raison d'être* of promotional expenditure is differentiation of cars, soaps, cigarettes, etc.

Still Cournot–Stackelberg theory penetrates into life. Sophisticated protagonists might choose simple strategies in order to reduce the chance of cosmic misunderstanding (failsafe). Cf. the Cournot analysis of ¶8.4 §§6–8. A financially vulnerable firm might *have* to practise short run profit maximization. Cf. the Stackelberg analysis ¶8.4 §§3–5.

§ 3

The Stackelberg Analysis: Elements

Strategies are defined on outputs (sales) y_{ij}. In the duopoly case, profits are defined as functions of one's own and one's rival's outputs:

$$\pi_{1t} = \Phi(y_{1t}, y_{2t}) \tag{4}$$

S1

$$y_{2t} = y_{2t-1} \tag{5}$$

$$\pi_{2t} = \Psi(y_{1t}, y_{2t}) \tag{6}$$

S2

$$y_{1t} = f(y_{2t-1}) \tag{7}$$

S1 concerns the *follower*: his profits for the tth period, π_{1t}, depend upon his output, y_{1t}, and that of the *leader*, y_{2t}. The *follower*, trying to ascertain what is His will, comes to adopt the rule: He will produce this period whatever He produced last period. Presumably the leader has established that this is the rule the follower must adopt. It follows that the optimal value for y_{1t} is a function of y_{2t-1}. S2 concerns the *leader*. Since equation (7) describes the follower's *reaction function*, equation (6) can be rewritten:

$$\pi_{2t} = \Psi[f(y_{2t-1}), y_{2t}] = F(y_{2t}, y_{2t-1}) \tag{8}$$

For stationary cost and demand conditions, S1 and S2 can be solved together for steady-state outputs $\bar{y}_1, \bar{y}_2$.

§ 4

The Stackelberg Analysis: 'Is it not passing brave to be a king, and ride in triumph through Persepolis?'

A Stackelberg leader always acts more profitably relative to his data than does a Stackelberg follower: the leader takes account of follower reaction whilst the follower ignores effects of his decisions on leader decisions. One result is that a leader will tend to produce more relative to his data than will a follower. The former's marginal revenue for output y^* exceeds that of the follower: the leader knows that $dy_1/dy_2 < 0$, or, better, acts in the knowledge that $dy_1/dy_2 < 0$. Let us prove the profitability proposition. Assume that the demand law is:

$$p_i = \phi(y_1 + y_2) \qquad i = 1, 2 \tag{9}$$

and that cost conditions are identical. Indeed generality is not lost if we assume that both produce at zero cost. The *follower* acts as if his marginal revenue (here equal to marginal profit), $d\pi_1/dy_1$, were:

$$d\pi_1/dy_1 = \phi + y_1\phi' \tag{10}$$

The leader's marginal revenue, recalling equation (7), is:

$$d\pi_2/dy_2 = \phi + y_2(\phi' + \phi'f') \tag{11}$$

Note that equation (10) does not correctly specify the *follower's* marginal revenue: he does not maximize his profits relative to his true data. Pursuing further the stipulations, since $\phi' < 0$ and $f' < 0$, then $\phi'f' > 0$. For $y_1 = y_2$, $MR_2 > MR_1$. In equilibrium the notional marginal revenues will be equated with zero. Hence, $\bar{y}_2 > \bar{y}_1$. The leader gets the larger share of the market and the profits.

If the *follower* has lower costs or more favourable demand conditions, it might be the more profitable firm. We only argue that *leadership* is more profitable relative to a firm's data.

Consumers do not distinguish the firms' productions: for $p_1 \neq p_2$, there would be no planned demand for the higher-priced output. The market is assumed to operate under a *tâtonnement* mechanism: each producer informs the 'auctioneer' that he wishes to receive the maximum price consistent with his output plan; the 'auctioneer' invariably must cite the same price to both.

The text overlooks a number of *non-tâtonnement* possibilities, including one in which producers would announce output *and* price plans: the higher-priced producer now might make sales to persons at the end of the other's queue. This model describes some restaurant behaviour: I might charge high prices, being satisfied to handle only the overflow from *Le Bistro* next door. The tactic might be especially successful if the restaurants are at an isolated road junction some miles from town.

Finally, ϕ^1 and ϕ^2 need not be identical in a more general Stackelberg analysis, but the analysis is rooted in equal prices and hence identity of produce.

§5

The Stackelberg Analysis: Incompleteness

Consider some alternative stipulations for a leader-follower nexus. A dominant firm, not as wooden as one *à la* Stackelberg, might be able to say to the follower: 'On the average you may have 8 per cent of the market. Whenever your share definitely rises above 8 per cent, you are to raise prices, retract promotions, etc., until it falls back to 8 per cent.' Again, in a differentiated-product context, the dominant firm might instruct the follower to charge 10 per cent more than it does and might restrict follower promotional expenditure to 20 per cent of its own. Still followership is not single-faceted: followers need not be thralls. Properly, a follower merely makes clear exactly what will be his moves in response to the leader's, stating that he will initiate no departures from *status quo ante*. Thus a follower might say to the leader: 'I will produce during any month 1·1 times as much as you produced in the preceding month.' The follower, perhaps a powerful firm, will have surrendered initiative, but, indeed, might simply have *thrust* leadership upon a hated rival.

Above all, the leader–follower nexus must be subjected to the full armoury of the theory of strategy.

Post-1945 American diplomacy, especially in its containment phase, might have emphasized followership even when the United States had decisive nuclear superiority. On the other hand, the Americans surely did not *thrust* leadership on Stalin.

§6

Cournot Duopoly: Equilibrium

¶8.4 §§6 analyses a *follower–follower* relationship. Again generality is not sacrificed if costs are neglected, as A. Cournot recognized more than 130 years ago when he placed the problem in a zero-cost mineral-spring setting:

$$p_i = \phi(y_1 + y_2) \qquad i = 1, 2 \tag{12}$$

Each producer, a *follower*, maximizes short run profits relative to his expectation of the other's output, leading to first-order conditions described by equations (13) and (14), omitting subscripts *t*, as in equation (12):

$$y_1 \phi' + \phi(y_1 + \hat{y}_2) = 0 \tag{13}$$

$$y_2 \phi' + \phi(\hat{y}_1 + y_2) = 0 \tag{14}$$

where $\hat{y}_2$ is the expectation of the second producer's output held by the first producer.

First, a steady-state solution is sought. In a steady state, $y_{it} = \hat{y}_{it} = y_{it-1}$. On inspection of equations (13) and (14), the steady-state solution is:

$$\bar{y}_1 = \bar{y}_2 = \phi(\bar{y}_1 + \bar{y}_2)/\phi'(\bar{y}_1 + \bar{y}_2) \tag{15}$$

Further inspection of equations (13) and (14) yields equation (16):

$$\bar{y}/\bar{p} = (1/|b|)n \tag{16}$$

where the inverse demand law is:

$$p = a + by \tag{17}$$

and where $\bar{y}$ is equilibrium industry output, $\bar{p}$ equilibrium price and n the number of firms in the industry. For a monopolist, $\bar{y}/\bar{p}$ is $1/|b|$. In the pure-competition case, $\bar{p}$ tends towards zero; marginal cost is zero. $\bar{y}/\bar{p} \to \infty$ as $n \to \infty$. Finally, the equilibrium output of each firm, $\bar{y}^*$ is shown by equation (18):

$$\bar{y}^* = -a/b(1+n) = \frac{a}{|b|(1+n)} \tag{18}$$

§ 7

Cournot Duopoly: Stability

The stability process is that of the cobweb. Cf. Chap. 9 *infra*.

Consider a linearized Cournot system in which producer Aleph's estimate of Beth's current production is y_{2t-1} and where $\hat{y}_{1t} = y_{1t-1}$. 'Equilibrium' in the tth period is determined by solving equations (19) and (20), noting that y_{it-1} enters as a parameter in the tth period:

$$by_{1t} + a + b(y_{1t} + y_{2t-1}) = 0 \qquad (19)$$

$$by_{2t} + a + b(y_{1t-1} + y_{2t}) = 0 \qquad (20)$$

A steady-state solution is:

$$y_{it} = y_{it-1} = a/3|b| = a/3e \qquad e = |b| \qquad (21)$$

Substituting the value of y_{2t-1} required by equation (20) for y_{2t-1} in equation (19), there results equation (22):

$$y_{1t} - 0.25y_{1t-2} = k \qquad (22)$$

k being a constant term. Equation (22) is a second-order linear difference equation in y_1. Recalling equation (21), the general solution of equation (22) is:

$$y_{1t} = a/3e + A(0.5)^t \cos(\theta t - \varepsilon) \qquad (23)$$

where θ and ε are structural parameters and A is an arbitrary constant to be determined by initial conditions. Equation (21) establishes a/3e as a particular solution of the difference equation (22). Since $(0.5)^t \to 0$ as $t \to \infty$, y_{1t} tends towards $\bar{y}_1$ through a damped oscillatory motion, as does y_{2t} towards $\bar{y}_2$ ($= \bar{y}_1$), whatever might be initial outputs y_{10} and y_{20}. A sufficient condition for local stability of our Cournot solution is that the underlying demand function be subject to linear approximation in the neighbourhood of the solution point.

§ 8

Cournot Theory: Reflexion

On the surface Cournot strategists are fools: despite repeated evidence that rival productions are influenced by their own, Cournot strategists insist upon behaving as if their rivals were leaders. Reflexion softens the judgement. Departure from defensive follower postures could inflame a tranquil industry as dormant hostilities and fears revive. Halting but steady progress towards substantial joint maximization might become a setback. Thus, business strategists depicted in more complex models might settle upon Cournot-like behaviour in order to make credible their willingness to lead the quiet life, their renunciation of *revanche* or dreams of empire. Failure to achieve jointly maximized profits might become viewed as part of the cost of a merely partial détente, a small cost indeed when compared with the consequences of renewed warfare.

REFERENCES

1. D. Gale, *The Theory of Linear Economic Models* (New York: McGraw-Hill Book Co.; 1960), p. 218 and note Chap. 7, esp. pp. 216–220.
2. W. J. Baumol, *Economic Theory and Operations Analysis* (Englewood Cliffs, N.J.: Prentice-Hall Inc.; 1965), 2nd ed., p. 533.
3. Cf. J. McKinsey, *Introduction to the Theory of Games* (New York: McGraw-Hill Book Co.; 1952), Chap. 17 and M. Shubik, *Strategy and Market Structure* (New York: John Wiley & Sons; 1959). Also R. Luce and H. Raiffa, *Games and Decisions* (New York: John Wiley & Sons; 1957).
4. J. D. Williams, *The Compleat Strategyst* (New York: McGraw-Hill Book Co.; 1954), pp. 213–214.
5. J. D. Williams, *The Compleat Strategyst* (New York: McGraw-Hill Book Co.; 1954), p. 214.
6. J. McKinsey, *Introduction to the Theory of Games* (New York: McGraw-Hill Book Co.; 1952), Chap. 17, esp. pp. 347 353.

PART III

General-equilibrium

CHAPTER 9

Existence and Stability
of Competitive Equilibrium;
the Fixprice Approach

1. INTRODUCTION TO PART III

Chapters 1–5 flow into Part III whilst Chapters 6–8 flow into Part IV, Macrodynamics. Chapters 9 and 10 (*Optimality*), with Chapter 11 (*Socialism*), comprising Part III are as withdrawn from everyday life as Chapter 6, and perhaps Chapter 8, were immersed in it. Part III deals with abstractions which, unlike the variables of Part IV, do not have familiar counterparts.

After existence and stability properties of equilibria of isolated and multiple competitive markets have been analysed in Chapter 9, optimality of equilibria is studied in Chapter 10. Chapter 10 also considers efficiency criteria for paths of capital accumulation, easily subsumed under the rubric of *moving* competitive equilibrium. *En passant*, Chapter 9 bridges the gap between neo-classical theory and statical versions of Keynesian theory. Chapter 11 explores the considerable reach of the theorems of neo-classical economics, including activity analysis, in socialized economies. Indeed, the stability analysis of Chapter 9, arid in ongoing capitalist contexts, becomes vital for idealized socialist control centres flashing signals to branch managers.

2. INTRODUCTION TO CHAPTER 9

¶9.3–¶9.8 are an extension of the theory of pure-competition and nothing else. ¶9.3 takes up the existence of equilibrium of isolated competitive markets, rather clumsily introducing fixed-point theorems. ¶9.4 concerns the stability of isolated equilibria in the sense of *tâtonnement* and in the sense of the cobweb (*la toile d'araignée*). ¶9.5 concerns multimarket equilibria. ¶9.6 analyses their stability for a special case: *tâtonnement* in an

195

economy described by a system of simultaneous equations. ¶9.7 syn-
thesizes the comparative-statics operations of Parts I and II. ¶9.8 extends
general-equilibrium analysis to the holding of and dealing in incorporeal
assets, including equities and money-fixed claims. ¶9.9 extends ¶9.8,
developing a statical pseudo general-equilibrium model based on the
fixprice method introduced by Keynes and elegantly formalized by
Hicks and Tinbergen.

3. COMPETITIVE EQUILIBRIUM IN ISOLATED MARKETS

Considering only the rth commodity and not specifying the precise
conditions surrounding its production and consumption, we define E_r
as its excess supply. (Strictly, the object of sale or purchase is a *contract*
for present or future delivery of specified services.) E_r can be thought of
as a flow-rate measuring, say, the annual rate of excess of offers to sell
from stocks and current output over offers to purchase for stock-accumula-
tion and current consumption. Again, E_r can be a cumulant measuring
the number of units by which planned supply exceeds planned demand
over the next year, or day. In either case, suppliers' and demanders'
plans are made relative to a price announced by an unspecified 'auctioneer'
and parametric for traders.

In ¶9.3 only p_r varies. All other prices are to be held fixed. Does there
exist $p_r = \bar{p}_r$ such that $E_r = 0$, such that supply equals demand for the
rth commodity?

Consult Fig. 1:

Negative prices are excluded. For example, disposal costs are to be zero.

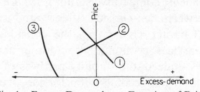

Fig. 1   Excess-Demand as a Function of Price.

Surely $\bar{p}_r$ exists in the cases yielding curves 1 and 2. Surely not in the case of
curve 3. ¶9.3 focuses on curves 1 and 3; curve 2 is significant for the
stability of market equilibrium, the topic of ¶9.4.

Figs. 2 or 3 could underlie curve 1 of Fig. 1. But, unlike the straightforward Fig. 2, Fig. 3 poses difficulties: it features decreasing supply price:
the minimum price necessary to induce a given aggregate offer falls with
the size of the offer.

Figs. 4a and 4b are inconsistent with the existence of isolated
equilibrium: Fig. 4b could underlie curve 3 of Fig. 1.

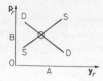

Fig. 2   A Well-behaved Isolated Market.

Fig. 3   A Less Well-behaved Isolated Market.

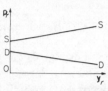

Fig. 4a   A Malignant Isolated Market.   Fig. 4b   Another Malignant Isolated Market.

How can it come about that the minimum price necessary to induce a given offer falls as the amount to be supplied is to increase? The answer is bound up in increasing returns to scale or lumpinesses-and-indivisibilities.

Contracts are being negotiated at date t for deliveries in future. Equilibrium prices reflect possibilities of fuller adjustment of production and consumption techniques. Projected sales and purchases of future goods reflect projected adaptation.

A backward-bending supply curve [)] shows maximum offers induced by stated prices and comes about through the superiority of 'leisure'. On the other hand, the supply curve of Fig. 3 can be interpreted either as showing minimum prices necessary to induce given offers (*à la* Marshall) or minimum offers which would be made at given prices (*à la* Walras).

Carefully distinguish between increasing returns to scale and decreasing unit costs due to lumpinesses and indivisibilities. Keep in mind that the text's problem is statical: lower costs through learning as the cumulant of output increases, etc., are ignored. Also distinguish the text's case from one in which external technical economies permit aggregate output to increase more than to scale.

Income effects can intrude upon supply curve analysis only when the theory of the firm is allowed to miscegenate with that of the household contrary to the strict *apartheid* imposed in Chapters 3 and 4. (Of course, income-effects can lead to curve 2 of Fig. 1 via the demand-orientated *Giffen* route.)

Violating *apartheid*, assume that a commodity is consumed by its representative producer, a household-firm, perhaps a family farm. That is to say disobey the insistence of Chapters 3 and 4 that demand by farmers for their own produce is a distinct household consumption activity, the transfer being accomplished by a 'shadow' purchase from a producer *alter ego*. If the commodity is superior for its bastard producer-consumers, planned producer-demand might increase more than planned output as price is imagined to increase over certain ranges. Amounts *offered* by producers might decrease as price increases. The text of Chapter 9, maintaining *apartheid*, avoids this messy case.

Increasing Returns to Scale in a simple case are described by inequality (1):

$$f(k\tilde{y}_1, \ldots, k\tilde{y}_m) > kf(\tilde{y}_1, \ldots, \tilde{y}_m) \tag{1}$$

Output y increases more than k-fold when inputs $\tilde{y}$ are increased k-fold.

198   *Economic Theory*

Of course, firms facing fixed input prices and enjoying increasing returns to scale will have lower supply prices for larger outputs. Increasing returns for firms over significant ranges are obviously inconsistent with pure competition.

In a hypothetical statical economy in which inputs are perfectly divisible in continuous *perfectly specified* production processes, inequality (1) could not apply.

Lumpinesses and Indivisibilities may lead to supply prices falling as aggregate output increases.

Inspecting the traditional U-shaped average-cost curve of a single-product firm, if the decreasing-average-cost segment is large relative to the size of the market, pure-competition becomes impossible. Thus falling unit costs over wide ranges of output of car producers result from large lumps of cost which first must be incurred.

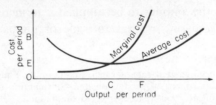

Fig. 5   A U-shaped Average Cost Curve Based on Specified Plant and Depicting only Costs which are Avoidable in the 'Length of Run' Being Considered.

The offer curve of a firm in pure competition is the marginal-cost curve over the output domain OC →. The firm would prefer to shut down rather than produce at a price less than OE and would offer OC at OE. At price OB it would offer OF, its rule being to equate marginal cost with price, subject to the price being at least as great as the appropriate average cost. And supply price rises over the domain OC →.

Considering next Fig. 6, the representative firm's unit cost is minimized at capacity output OH: marginal cost is constant at OG once the required lump of overhead expense is coughed up; *a fortiori*, unit cost is minimized at OH if marginal cost decreases with output. However, Fig. 6 leads to a flat industry supply curve; supply is perfectly elastic at price OJ.

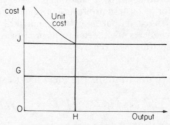

Fig. 6   A Fixed-capacity Case.

If Fig. 6 depicted a plant, discontinuities implicit in the stipulations can be ignored only if there are so many plants that the interval between outputs $n(OH)$ and $(n+1)(OH)$ is very small relative to equilibrium quantities. The following diagram suggests a queer possibility: price exceeds average cost in equilibrium although all plants are identical; $(n-1)$ plants produce at capacity whilst the nth produces short of capacity.

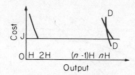

Fig. 6a   A Queer Possibility.

We are yet to conjure up a downward-sloping offer curve for a competitive *industry* (i.e. $\partial p^s/\partial y < 0$).

Putting aside external technical economies, cases in which the larger is the qth firm's output the better are the technological terms of transformation for the vth firm, only *pecuniary* economies external to the firm are to be considered.

Production of the rth commodity may require an input supplied by an energy company operating under decreasing unit costs. Perhaps the company's prices would reflect its falling unit costs as aggregate output of the rth commodity, and so the quantity of gas demanded, increases. (Effects of the qth firm's output on input prices are of a higher order of smalls.)

So in order to derive a case in which supply price falls as output increases in a purely-competitive industry we must specify that at least one input is produced by a firm *not* in competition. Otherwise the latter firm would not be maximizing its profits. (The second-order ('stability') condition that the second differential of profit be negative would not then be obeyed.) However, if any firm is a price quoter there cannot be general competitive equilibrium.

Figs. 3 and 4 describe cases in which there does not exist a rate of output for which the minimum price necessary to induce such supply is as great as the maximum price at which demanders would take it off the market. (¶9.5 is confined to completely vertically-integrated processes.)

§ 2

The results obtained in ¶9.3 §§1 must be generalized if the theory of general-equilibrium is to be grasped. The necessary theoretical tool is that of *fixed-point theorems*.[1]

The number x is an element of the set $\mathbf{X}$; $x \in \mathbf{X}$. $\mathbf{X}$ is the set of positive real numbers. Apply some transformation f to x such that $f(x) \in \mathbf{X}$; $f(x)$

maps x into **X**. If $f(x)$ has a fixed point, there exists $\bar{x} \in \mathbf{X}$ such that $f(\bar{x}) = \bar{x}$. Thus, if $f(x) = 2x - 1$, $\bar{x} = 1$.

Fig. 7 graphs the simple case. Recall that any point belonging to a 45° line has equal ordinate and abscissa intercepts.

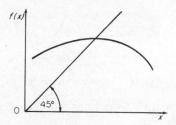

Fig. 7   Existence of a Fixed Point of a Transformation.

What are the requirements for existence of fixed points of transformations? Considering only the simple example thus far offered, pending ¶9.5, it can be proved that any function of one variable, $f(x)$, has a fixed point if $f(x)$ is continuous, never negative, and never larger than a predetermined number N.

Applying the fixed-point concept to ¶9.3 §§1, consider the non-negative real numbers **P** and $p^* \in \mathbf{P}$. p^* is a supply price indicating the minimum price necessary to induce output y^*. What is the maximum price consistent with y^* being demanded? i.e., what is the demand price for y^*? Answer, p^{**}. In this way the demand price can be derived as a function of the supply price. Existence of equilibrium in an isolated market depends upon the transformation having a fixed point. The case of Fig. 1 is appealing. The continuous function Φ, defined on supply-prices **P**, reaches a maximum at $p^d = \mathrm{N}$, the limiting demand price as $y \to 0$. Compare Fig. 8. $\Phi(p)$ steadily rises from a value arbitrarily close to zero as we move from *right to left*.

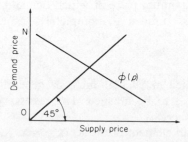

Fig. 8   Existence of a Fixed Point in the Case of Fig. 1.

4. STABILITY OF ISOLATED COMPETITIVE EQUILIBRIUM

Stability in the Sense of Walras

Recalling that Chapter 9 is placed within a context of auction markets, inequality (2) describes the dynamics of the 'auctioneer's' behaviour:

$$\dot{p}_r \gtreqless 0 \quad \text{as} \quad (D_r - D_s) \gtreqless 0 \tag{2}$$

The time derivative of the price quotation for any commodity is positive, zero, or negative as excess demand is positive, zero, or negative. Now the sense in which the equilibrium of a Walrasian market is unstable or stable is the sense in which the hypothetical 'auctioneer' does or does not go crazy. That is to say, he is not or is able again to declare the equilibrium price, if he has departed from it. Time as ordinarily perceived, calendar time, stands still during the imaginary process. The *tâtonnement* occupies only a notional- or meta-time. Economic events are conceived to transpire only at equilibrium prices. Acts of production or consumption at non-equilibrium or 'false trading' cannot be interpreted by the theory of competitive equilibrium.

The stability of the *tâtonnement* process depends on inequality (3):

$$\dot{p} \gtreqless 0 \quad \text{as} \quad (p_r - \bar{p}_r) \lesseqgtr 0 \tag{3}$$

The process is stable only if the 'auctioneer' always cries down p_r when it is in excess of $\bar{p}_r$ and cries up p_r when it is less than $\bar{p}_r$.

As in ¶9.6 only the stability of the process in the neighbourhood of an equilibrium price is considered. Global stability is not considered.

Inequalities (2) and (3) yield inequality (4), the criterion for stability of the isolated *tâtonnement*:

$$(D_r - S_r) \gtreqless 0 \quad \text{as} \quad (p_r - \bar{p}_r) \lesseqgtr 0 \tag{4}$$

The condition of inequality (4) is met if the slope of the demand curve is more negative than that of the supply curve at $\bar{p}_r$, since, for $p_r > \bar{p}_r$, $(S_r - \bar{S}_r) > (D_r - \bar{D}_r)$, recalling that $\bar{S}_r = \bar{D}_r$.

In 'Walrasian' analysis a negatively-sloped supply curve associated *minimum* supplies with prices. Thus outputs 100 to ∞ might be offered at \$1, and 40 to ∞ at \$2. If demand exceeds 40 at \$2 and, indeed, exceeds the minimum offer for all prices more than \$1, the equilibrium price will be \$1 with $\bar{y}_r \geq 100$—unless, of course, supply and demand both are zero.

Defining $(S_r - D_r)$ as E_r, excess supply of the rth commodity, the stability condition for an isolated market boils down to:

$$E_r \gtreqless 0 \quad \text{as} \quad (p_r - \bar{p}_r) \gtreqless 0 \tag{5}$$

in the neighbourhood of $\bar{p}_r$. Hence:

$$dE_r/dp_r > 0 \tag{6}$$

in the neighbourhood of $\bar{p}_r$ is the stability condition for the isolated *tâtonnement*.

A more formal analysis of the local stability of the equilibrium of an isolated competitive market can be based on Liapounoff's first method. (¶9.6 discusses how Liapounoff's second method may be applied to the analysis of multimarket stability.)[2]

Linearizing the excess-demand $f(p)$, around $\bar{p}$ and then transforming the origin so that $\bar{p} = 0$, our dynamic law becomes:

$$\dot{p} = ap \tag{7}$$

and the integral:

$$p = ce^{at} \tag{8}$$

We note that $a < 0$ if the excess-demand is a decreasing function of price and that $a = \lambda$ in the more general expression for the integral:

$$p = ce^{\lambda t} \tag{9}$$

'Liapounoff affirms that, if $\lambda < 0$, the equilibrium state is stable; if $\lambda > 0$, the equilibrium is unstable; if $\lambda = 0$, the equation of the first [i.e. linear] approximation is inadequate for determining stability.'[3]

To carry on with some of the pure theory of stability analysis, in economic theory it may be said that systems typically are *conservative*. (This book does not deal with inter-national trade theory. In this, positive or negative dissipation, relative to any sub-sector, can be decisive in determination of the system's motion.) A conservative physical system is one in which 'one assumes the law of conservation of energy'.[4] In economics, this follows naturally from closure.

Keeping in mind the last paragraph, and referring to Andronow and Chaikin, pp. 99–101, it might be interesting to adapt an example, due to Volterra, thus exhibiting the scope of the mathematical method, if nothing else. Our setting is a two-sector economy, including a self-sufficient argicultural sector and an industrial sector, also self-sufficient *except* that its labourers must ingest agricultural produce. Both sectors are identified by their populations y_1 (agriculture) and y_2. It is assumed that sectorial outputs are directly proportional to their populations. Furthermore, each sector has an inherent dynamic, expressed by coefficients ρ_1 and ρ_2

$$\dot{y}_1 = \rho_1 y_1 \qquad \rho_1 > 0 \tag{10}$$

$$\dot{y}_2 = -\rho_2 y_2 \qquad \rho_2 > 0 \tag{11}$$

Equation (11) says that the industrial sector would decay in isolation, sucking its own juices until it crumbled.

Now we stipulate that the two sectors are to live together, forming a semi-symbiosis, so that ρ_1 becomes a decreasing function of y_2 and ρ_2 of y_1. If we assume that functions $f(y_j)$ in $\rho_i = f(y_j)$ are linear-homogeneous, we get

$$\dot{y}_1 = y_1(\rho_1 - \gamma_1 y_2) \tag{12}$$

$$\dot{y}_2 = -y_2(\rho_2 - \gamma_2 y_1) \tag{13}$$

γ_1 and γ_2 also are positive constants. The appropriate non-linear differential equation is

$$\gamma_2 \dot{y}_1 + \gamma_1 \dot{y}_2 - \rho_2 \frac{d}{dt}(\log y_1) - \rho_1 \frac{d}{dt}(\log y_2) = 0 \tag{14}$$

The law of variation of y_1 and y_2 is periodic. For specified initial conditions, regular cycles of different amplitude, frequency, and phase develop for the two sectors. The symbiosis drives the economy's trade cycle, all perhaps vaguely descriptive of the soviet economy.

§ 2

Stability of a Cob-Web Process

In cob-web processes current supply is predetermined whilst current demand is a decreasing function of current price. Compare agriculture. Then compare equation (15), dropping the subscript r:

$$f(p_t) = g(p_{t-1}) \tag{15}$$

Equation (15) is to be solved for p_t^*, the market-clearing price in the tth period. The graphical counterpart is Fig. 9. Obviously, the equilibrium of Point Q is stable in the sense of Walras:

$$E_t = k - D_t; \qquad dE_t/dp_t > 0 \tag{16}$$

Excess supply in the current period increases with current price; the *tâtonnement* is stable in any period.

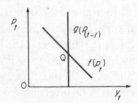

Fig. 9 A Cob-web Process in the tth Period.

There is, however, a sense in which a cob-web process can be unstable, a sense which becomes emphasized in the *multiplier-accelerator* analysis of Part IV. Solve equation (17):

$$f(p) = g(p) \tag{17}$$

The solution value, $\bar{p}$, yields a steady state: $p_t^* = p_{t+1}^* = \ldots = p_{t+\infty}^* = \bar{p}$ and always satisfies equation (15).

Consider now a linearized version of equation (15):

$$a + bp_t = c + dp_{t-1}, \qquad p_t - (d/b)p_{t-1} = (c-a)/b \tag{18}$$

Hence:

$$\bar{p} = \frac{c-a}{b-d} \tag{19}$$

$\bar{p}$ is a particular solution of the first-order difference equation, equation (18). Since $\bar{p}$ satisfies equation (18), then equation (20) holds.

i.e., $\bar{p}-(d/b)\bar{p} = (c-a)/b$. This equation can be subtracted from $p_t - (d/b)p_{t-1} = (c-a)/b$.

$$(p_t - \bar{p}) - (d/b)(p_{t-1} - \bar{p}) = 0, \qquad \pi_t - (d/b)\pi_{t-1} = 0 \qquad (20)$$

Try $\pi_t = A(-d/b)^t$, A being an arbitrary constant to be determined by an initial condition, as a solution for equation (20). (If π_0 were 10, $A = 10$.) Substituting this expression into equation (20):

$$-A(d/b)^t + A(d/b)(d/b)^{t-1} = 0 \qquad (21)$$

Of course, equation (21) is an identity. Indeed, $(-d/b)^t$ is a solution to equation (20). It follows that the general solution of equation (18) is:

$$p_t = \bar{p} - A(d/b)^t, \qquad (22)$$

noting that p_t is *defined* as the sum of $\bar{p}$ and π_t and that d is positive and b negative.

If $|b| > d$, the value of π_t will tend to zero as $t \to \infty$. Specifically, the positive-negative alterations around $\bar{p}$ will damp down over time. If $|b| < d$, the alternations will increase over time. (For $|b| = d$ there will be regular undamped alternations. This case also is unstable in the special sense of ¶9.4 §§2.) Thus for $|b| > d$, whatever is the initial state of the system, it will tend towards the bench-mark path $p_t = \bar{p}$ whilst for $|b| \leq d$, unless the initial condition permits $A = 0$, the process will not converge on $p_t = \bar{p}$ and if $|b| < d$, it will in fact alternate more and more violently. The case of $|b| \leq d$, although determinate, is dynamically unstable: the system's stable *tâtonnement* process will not converge.

5. EXISTENCE OF MULTI-MARKET EQUILIBRIUM

Finally the components of a hypothetical competitive economy are to be considered simultaneously. We must first establish a broader fixed-point theorem, unless we simply are to count equations and unknowns, praying that equilibrium outputs will be positive, that inputs will be negative, etc.

§2

The fixed-point theorem of Kakutani is quite formidable:

> 'If S is a non-empty, compact, convex subset of $\mathbf{R}^m$ and if ϕ is an upper semi-continuous correspondence from S to S such that for all $\mathbf{x} \in S$ the set $\phi(\mathbf{x})$ is convex (and non-empty), then ϕ has a fixed point.'[5]

Take up the words of art one by one. If a subset of S is to consist of elements of S with a given property, then, if no element of S has that property, the property P is said to define the empty subset of S, $\varnothing$. Compactness and convexity were discussed in Chapter 3. A correspondence need not be single-valued. A function is a single-valued correspondence. Paraphrasing *DOSSO* (vide note preceding ¶5.2), upper semi-continuity rules out situations in which a mapping or function associating $\mathbf{x} \in \mathbf{X}$ with a set $\mathbf{H_x}$ is such that $\mathbf{H_x}$ might 'contract all of a sudden' for continuous variation in $\mathbf{x}$.[6] Specifically, a correspondence ϕ is upper semi-continuous at $\mathbf{x}^0$ if, as $\mathbf{x} \to \mathbf{x}^0$ and—where $\mathbf{y} \in \phi(\mathbf{x})$—$\mathbf{y} \to \mathbf{y}^0$ as $\mathbf{x} \to \mathbf{x}^0$, then $\mathbf{y}^0 \in \phi(\mathbf{x}^0)$. (The symbol $\in$, rather than $=$, because a correspondence need not be single-valued. It need not be a function.) Finally $\mathbf{R}^m$ is a set of m-dimensional real numbers so that the price vector $(p_1, \ldots, p_m)$ belongs to $\mathbf{R}^m$.

$\mathbf{R}^m$ is an m-dimensional Euclidean space, the coordinates being referred to a 'normal orthogonal basis' for R^m. Outputs, prices, values of actions, etc. are defined as subsets of $\mathbf{R}^m$.[7]

§3

Incorporating into ¶9.5 assumptions about producers and consumers made in ¶3.3 and ¶4.2, we reconsider the concepts of *resources* and *shares*.[8] At a given date the jth consumer (household) possesses a pre-determined collection of commodities $\boldsymbol{\omega}_j$. The jth consumer's resources are $\boldsymbol{\omega}_j$. The firms are owned by the consumers so that $\Sigma_j \theta_{jq} = 1$, θ_{jq} being the proportion of the qth firm owned by the jth consumer.

The only non-physical assets considered are shares. These have precisely the value of the discounted net proceeds of issuing firms' production plans, including planned 'final' stock positions. Resources ω need not be for date 0: the jth consumer could enter the *tâtonnement* with initial futures positions.

In the 'axiomatic' model consumers at once transform current resources not intended for current consumption: holding a bag of peanuts over one day is an act of production.

In a private ownership economy firms will attempt to maximize their profits relative to prices $\mathbf{p}$. Contracts are tendered for future as well as current deliveries of commodities: profit maximization implies a present-value criterion. Accordingly, the wealth of the jth consumer, w_j is defined as:

$$w_j = \mathbf{p} \cdot \boldsymbol{\omega}_j + \sum_q \theta_{jq} \Pi_q(\mathbf{p}) \tag{23}$$

$\Pi_q(\mathbf{p})$ determines the qth producers profits as a function of $\mathbf{p}$.

At date t each customer will draw up a plan equating the present value of his consumptions and 'final' commodity holdings with his wealth. Of course, an equilibrium price vector must lead to zero excess demand for all commodities and to plans consistent with all constraints.

The model can interpret realized productions and consumptions only relative to an equilibrium price vector $\bar{\mathbf{p}}$. Need it exist? Yes. ¶9.5 §§4 collects properties of the private ownership economy emerging from

Chapters 3 and 4 and from ¶9.5 §§1–4. ¶9.5 §§5 suggests how the fixed-point result of ¶9.5 §§2 can be used to establish the existence of p̄ up to a normalization, i.e. to establish the existence of equilibrium relative prices.

§ 4 [9]

Each of the consumers, obeying its wealth constraint, chooses a consumption relative to **p**. Each set of feasible-consumptions is closed, convex and bounded from below. Cf. ¶3.3 §§4. At least one consumer is insatiable. Each preference ordering is convex.

Each producer (firm) is shared out amongst the consumers: shareholdings satisfy the requirement that $\Sigma_j\theta_{jq} = 1$ for all q. Each producer can, if it wishes, produce nothing. The set of aggregate outputs is closed and convex.

A number of recondite points should be made.

In this non-stochastic model one firm's shares will not be preferred over another's. Each firm's profits are known, prices for all spot and future deliveries being at least tacitly determined in 'today's' *tâtonnement*. At least the theory requires that producers and consumers act as if this is true. This essentially is to require that there need never be another *tâtonnement*. How distressing! Agreed, if the consumers were immortal eunuchs, there need be but one *tâtonnement* for all time, but, otherwise, the 'basis' of the consumption sets must be changed each day as some reach majority and others die. Indeed, once mortality is recognized, metaphysical underpinnings crumble. How can my unborn heir make his decisions now? If he cannot, what can 'certainty' mean intertemporally? So, retreating into a shell, we must simply assert that the theory requires that producers and consumers act as if today's *tâtonnement* will be the last, otherwise the postulation of certainty cannot be sustained.

Although financial assets and liabilities are not to be objects of choice, the sum of nominal values of commodity supplies of a specified dating can exceed that of demands for the same date, 'Say's Law' is *not* part of the theory.

Recalling ¶4.1, the concept 'producer' is abstract. In the first approximation at least, a producer is a production set on which profits are being maximized. Thus Ford and General Motors never properly could be classified as one producer: the aggregate of the two firms does not maximize profits on the aggregate production set. (In a linear model of competition any aggregate in equilibrium profits relative to p̄.)

Positive profits are possible for the qth producer, although the possibility of null action precludes negative profits in equilibrium. Since consumers' incomes are payments by firms, positive profits are accounted for by transfers of endowments between consumer-shareholders. On net, *dis-saving* consumers pay for their 'excess' consumptions by transferring endowments to shareholders. This is not done directly: securities transfers are not necessary in a once-and-for-all *tâtonnement*. Rather is it done indirectly: *dis-savers* spend more than they earn. Correspondence of profits with a class of shareholder expenditure takes one back to the Widow's Cruse of Keynes's *Treatise*.[10]

§ 5

Recalling that 'commodities' include labour services provided by consumers, let **P** be a set of price vectors, none of which has negative elements or all of its elements zero, ordered so that $(p_1, p_2, \ldots, p_m)$ defines the prices of the first, second, ... mth commodity. (Negative prices are excluded by the free-disposal assumption.) The jth consumer will select consumption $\mathbf{x}_j^*$ optimal for $\mathbf{p}^*$, adhering to its wealth constraint in turn reflecting planned profits (at $\mathbf{p}^*$) of producers in which he owns shares. Producers, maximizing profits relative to $\mathbf{p}^*$, will plan productions $\mathbf{y}_q^*$ consistently with the feasible-output set.

Now draw a correspondence between points $\mathbf{p} \in \mathbf{P}$ and $\mathbf{z} \in \mathbf{Z}$, $\mathbf{Z}$ being a set of excess demands: $\mathbf{z} \in \phi(\mathbf{p})$.

Next, the wealth constraints imbedded in the model are to be used to yield up a result analogous to Walras's Law in 'traditional analysis'. Compare inequality (24):

$$\mathbf{p} \cdot \mathbf{x}_j \leq \mathbf{p} \cdot \mathbf{\omega}_j + \sum_q \theta_{jq}(\mathbf{p} \cdot \mathbf{y}_q) \qquad \text{for all } j \tag{24}$$

Households may not contemplate expenditures beyond receipts from service sales in excess of their wealth.

Sets X and Y comprise a single commodity space: services 'produced' by households are recorded by firms as negative inputs.

En passant, investment over any interval is encompassed by accomplished household increases in non-consumption components of vectors $\mathbf{\omega}_j$. In so far as user cost is ignored, equilibrium requires that firms plan to increase intakes of such items, always bearing in mind that underlying commodity specifications are to be extremely precise. For example, an oil well becomes defined in terms of the stream of services yielded over its life.

Since $\sum_j \theta_{jq} = 1$ for all q, if inequality (24) is summed over indexes j and q:

$$\mathbf{p} \cdot \mathbf{x} \leq \mathbf{p} \cdot \mathbf{\omega} + \mathbf{p} \cdot \mathbf{y} \tag{25}$$

Defining the value of excess demand for the rth commodity as:

$$p_r z_r = p_r x_r - p_r y_r - p_r \omega_r \tag{26}$$

$$\mathbf{p} \cdot \mathbf{z} \leq 0 \tag{27}$$

The inner product $\mathbf{p} \cdot \mathbf{z}$ can be at most zero. Vectors $\mathbf{p}$ and $\mathbf{z}$ either make a right angle (are orthogonal) or a larger angle (are obtuse).

§6

Proof of the existence of competitive equilibrium hinges on there existing $\mathbf{p}^* \in \mathbf{P}$ such that $\phi(\mathbf{p}^*) \in (-\Omega)$ where Ω is the non-negative orthant of R^m, i.e. $\phi(\mathbf{p}) \cap (-\Omega)$ is not empty. A non-negative orthant of a set of real numbers of dimension m, $\mathbf{R}^m$, is the set of non-negative m-vectors without negative elements:

$$\Omega = \{\mathbf{x} \in \mathbf{R}^m | \mathbf{x} \geq \mathbf{0}\} \tag{28}$$

$$-\Omega = \{\mathbf{x} \in \mathbf{R}^m | \mathbf{x} \leq \mathbf{0}\} \tag{29}$$

§ 7

In the economy of ¶9.5 it can be proved that:

$$\phi(\mathbf{p}) \cap (-\Omega) \neq \varnothing \tag{30}$$

That is, for $\mathbf{p} \in \mathbf{P}$, there is at least one $\mathbf{z} \in \mathbf{Z}$ which has no positive elements. The proof is based on Kakutani's fixed-point theorem.

Define $\xi(\mathbf{p})$ as an excess-demand correspondence:

'... with each price system $\mathbf{p}$ in $\mathbf{P}$ is associated the non-empty set $\xi(\mathbf{p})$ of excess demands compatible with the selection by every consumer of a consumption optimal for his wealth constraint and by every producer of a production optimal for that price system.[11]

Already it has been established by inequality (27) that $\mathbf{p} \cdot \xi(\mathbf{p}) \leq 0$. It is to be proved that there exists a non-negative vector $\mathbf{p}^*$ such that each and every element of a corresponding vector of excess demands, $\mathbf{z}^*$, is negative or zero, i.e. that $\mathbf{z}^* \leq 0$.

Let $\zeta(\mathbf{z})$ determine the set of price vectors maximizing $\mathbf{p} \cdot \mathbf{z}$ on $\mathbf{P}$, noting that $\mathbf{P}$ is to be restricted by a normalization requiring, for example, that the sum of prices be unity. Then let $\psi(\mathbf{p}, \mathbf{z}) = (\zeta(\mathbf{z}), \xi(\mathbf{p}))$. ψ is defined in R^{2m} space.

$\psi(\mathbf{p}, \mathbf{z})$ belongs to the *Cartesian product* of sets $\mathbf{Z}$ and $\mathbf{P}$. The Cartesian product of sets $\mathbf{X}$ and $\mathbf{Y}$, where $\mathbf{x} \in \mathbf{X}$ is an abscissa- and $\mathbf{y} \in \mathbf{Y}$ an ordinate-value in 2-space. In fig. 10, $\mathbf{X}$ and $\mathbf{Y}$ are confined to the non-negative orthant.)

Fig. 10   Example in 2-space.

Indeed the transformation ψ has a fixed point $(\mathbf{p}^*, \mathbf{z}^*)$ so that $\mathbf{p}^* \in \zeta(\mathbf{z}^*)$, $\mathbf{z}^* \in \xi(\mathbf{p}^*)$. That is, for $(\mathbf{p}^*, \mathbf{z}^*)$ the transformations take us back to $(\mathbf{p}^*, \mathbf{z}^*)$.

The relation $\mathbf{p}^* \in \zeta(\mathbf{z}^*)$ implies that $\mathbf{p} \cdot \mathbf{z}^* \leq \mathbf{p}^* \cdot \mathbf{z}^*$. $\mathbf{p} \cdot \mathbf{z}^*$ is maximized at $\mathbf{p}^*$. The relation $\mathbf{z}^* \in \xi(\mathbf{p}^*)$ implies that $\mathbf{p}^* \cdot \mathbf{z}^* \leq 0$ by inequality (27). Hence, $\mathbf{p} \cdot \mathbf{z}^* \leq 0$. Next choose $\mathbf{p}$ so that p_k, the price of the kth commodity, is 1 and $p_h = 0$ for $h \neq k$. It follows that the requirement $\mathbf{p} \cdot \mathbf{z}^* \leq 0$ will be falsified unless $z_k^* \leq 0$. However, k can be chosen arbitrarily. Hence $\mathbf{z}^* \leq 0$.

§ 8

Proof of the existence of competitive equilibrium for the economy of ¶9.5 is based on the fixed-point result of ¶9.5 §§7. ¶9.5 §§7 can be used to establish the existence of a fixed-point of the price/excess-demand mapping, once appropriate production and consumption sets are defined.

An important complexity, ignored above, arises from the possibility that some of the feasible-output sets might not be closed, convex or bounded (although increasing returns are barred) and some of the feasible-consumption sets might be unbounded. The rigorous proof (cf. Debreu, *Theory of Value*) overcomes these difficulties by substituting the closed convex hull of Y_q for Y_q. (The convex hull of **S** consists of points belonging to all of the convex sets containing **S**. The closed convex hull of **S** contains the adherence of **S**, i.e. all points which are limiting values of sequences which can be constructed from points belonging to **S**.) Then 'well-chosen' compact convex subsets of X_j and of the closed convex hulls of Y_q are constructed. Existence of general-equilibrium is established for the surrogate economy. Finally, it is proved that the equilibrium vector $\bar{\mathbf{p}}$ of the surrogate economy is an equilibrium price system for *the* economy.[12]

It remains to show that fixed-point excess demands $\mathbf{z}^*$ all are zero. If $\mathbf{z}^* = 0$, the proof of existence of competitive equilibrium for the ¶9.5 economy will be completed: $\mathbf{z}^*$ results from operations conforming to all constraints and responding to the admissible price vector (price system) $\mathbf{p}^*$. Equations (31) and (32) are implicit in the analysis and yield equation (33).

$$\Sigma_j \mathbf{x}_j^* - \Sigma_q \mathbf{y}_q - \mathbf{\omega} = \mathbf{z} \qquad (\Sigma_j x_{1j}^* = x_1^*) \tag{31}$$

$$\Sigma_q \mathbf{y}_q^* = \mathbf{z} + \mathbf{y} \tag{32}$$

$$\mathbf{z}^* = \mathbf{y}^* - \mathbf{y} \tag{33}$$

Taking up equation (31), it has been shown that at $\mathbf{p}^*$, a fixed-point element, $\Sigma \mathbf{x}_j^* - \Sigma \mathbf{y}_q^* - \mathbf{\omega} = \mathbf{z}^*, \mathbf{y}^* \in \mathbf{Y}, \mathbf{z}^* \in \mathbf{Z}$. Equation (31) is satisfied by $(\mathbf{y}^*, \mathbf{z}^*)$. Taking up equation (32), it has been shown that, since $\mathbf{z} \in (-\mathbf{\Omega})$ and disposal is free, there exists $\mathbf{y} \in \mathbf{Y}$ satisfying the equality. Now substituting $\mathbf{y}^*$ and $\mathbf{z}^*$ for $\mathbf{y}$ and $\mathbf{z}$ in equation (31) and $\mathbf{z}^*$ for $\mathbf{z}$ in equation (32), and then subtracting equation (32) from equation (31), there follows equation (33). Note again that $\mathbf{z}^*$ is defined as $\mathbf{x}^* - \mathbf{y}^* - \mathbf{\omega}$. And, of course, for $\mathbf{y} = \mathbf{y}^*, \mathbf{z}^* = 0$!

It has been proved, then, that there exists amongst admissible price vectors $\mathbf{p}^* = \bar{\mathbf{p}}$, such that all constraints are observed, all microbehaviour is *optimal* relative to $\bar{\mathbf{p}}$, and all excess demands are zero. There exists a general competitive equilibrium.

For a meticulous and extended treatment of the topics of ¶9.5 see Robert E. Kuenne, *The Theory of General Economic Equilibrium* (Princeton: Princeton University Press; 1963), Chap. 9, pp. 512ff. For a proof of existence of general equilibrium in an economy with an indefinitely large number of traders, cf. R. Aumann, 'Existence of Competitive Equilibrium in Markets with a Continuum of Traders,' *Econometrica*, Jan., 1966 (Vol. 34, No. 1), pp. 1–17.

§9

Is the equilibrium unique? If the weak axiom of revealed preference holds, the answer is yes. Thus assume that there are two solutions $(\bar{\mathbf{p}}, \bar{\mathbf{y}})$[1]

and $(\bar{\mathbf{p}}, \bar{\mathbf{y}})^2$ where $\bar{\mathbf{y}} = \bar{\mathbf{x}} - \omega$. Producers' equilibrium requires that:

$$\mathbf{p}^1 \cdot \mathbf{y}^1 > \mathbf{p}^1 \cdot \mathbf{y}^2 \tag{34}$$

$\mathbf{y}^1$ maximizes $\mathbf{p}^1 \cdot \mathbf{y}$ for feasible $\mathbf{y}$. Similarly:

$$\mathbf{p}^2 \cdot \mathbf{y}^2 > \mathbf{p}^2 \cdot \mathbf{y}^1 \tag{35}$$

The weak axiom of revealed preference requires that, if a collection of goods A is bought when B costs less, A must be preferred to B. However, if $\mathbf{y}^1$ and $\mathbf{y}^2$ both are equilibrium outputs, it follows from inequalities (34) and (35) that $\mathbf{y}^1$ is preferred by consumers to $\mathbf{y}^2$ *and* that $\mathbf{y}^2$ is preferred to $\mathbf{y}^1$. Hence obedience to the weak axiom of revealed preference implies uniqueness of general competitive equilibrium.

6. STABILITY OF MULTI-MARKET EQUILIBRIUM[14]

A special case of a competitive private ownership economy can be depicted by a set of excess-demand functions, one for each of n commodities, each function being equated with zero. The economy's producers and consumers choose their actions relative to prices $\mathbf{p}$. The households obey budget constraints. Walras's Law applies. Cf. ¶2.4 §§4. The economy can be described by equations (36), noting that $\mathbf{p}_n = 1$ by stipulation:

$$f^i(\mathbf{p}) = 0 \qquad i = 1, 2, \ldots, n-1 \tag{36}$$

Consider the equilibrium vector $(\bar{p}_1, \bar{p}_2, \ldots, \bar{p}_{n-1})$. Evaluate partial derivatives at $\bar{\mathbf{p}}$, writing the excess-demand function as:

$$f^r(\mathbf{p}) \simeq \sum_{i}^{n-1} f^r_i \pi_i \tag{37}$$

f^r_1 being the rate at which excess demand for the rth commodity changes with p_1 at $\bar{p}$ and π_s being defined as $(p_s - \bar{p}_s)$. Of course:

$$f^r(\bar{\mathbf{p}}) = 0 \tag{38}$$

Denote f^r_i as a_{ri} and the excess *demand* for the rth commodity as E_r. Equation (37) then is written:

$$E_r = \sum_{i}^{n-1} a_{ri} \pi_i \qquad r = 1, \ldots, n-1 \tag{39}$$

§2

¶9.6 also deals with the notional behaviour of a Walrasian 'auctioneer' whose dynamic law is:

$$\dot{p}_r = -\mu_r (S_r - D_r) \tag{40}$$

Prices are cried up when demand exceeds supply and down when supply exceeds demand. 'Supply' and 'demand' are actions *planned* by households and firms. 'Stability' pertains to the 'auctioneer's' conduct. Will he be able to cry out $\bar{\mathbf{p}}$ if initially he cries out $\mathbf{p} \neq \bar{\mathbf{p}}$?

§3

The scalar μ in equation (40) transforms a disparity of supply from demand into a time-rate of change of price, $\dot{p}_r$. Measure p_r so that $\mu_r = 1$ for all r. This procedure is legitimate either if μ_r is invariant against E_r or if the analysis is confined, as it is, to the neighbourhood of $\bar{p}_r$.

§4

The argument up to this point leads to equations (41):

$$\dot{\pi}_r + \sum_{s}^{n-1} a_{rs}\pi_s = 0 \qquad r = 1, 2, \ldots, n-1 \tag{41}$$

Equations (41) are a system of simultaneous homogeneous differential equations. An integral of equations (41)—the specification of price disparities $\boldsymbol{\pi}$ as functions of time—may be written analogously to the solution of an 'isolated' first-order differential equation:

$$\pi_r = k_r\, e^{-\lambda t} \qquad r = 1, \ldots, n-1 \tag{42}$$

where we are to solve for λ and the vector $\mathbf{k}$. Substitute equation (42) into equation (41) obtaining:

$$\begin{bmatrix} a_{11}-\lambda & a_{12} & \ldots a_{1n-1} \\ a_{21} & a_{22}-\lambda \ldots a_{2n-1} \\ \cdots\cdots\cdots\cdots\cdots\cdots\cdots\cdots \\ a_{n-11} & \qquad a_{n-1n-1}-\lambda \end{bmatrix} \mathbf{k} = \mathbf{0} \qquad \mathbf{S1} \tag{43}$$

S1 can be solved only if the determinant of $(\mathbf{A}-\mathbf{I}\lambda)$ is zero: the characteristic equation of the matrix is to be solved for values of λ consistent with its determinant being zero. (If $\mathbf{A}$ in $\mathbf{Ax} = \mathbf{0}$ has linearly-dependent columns, there exists vector $\boldsymbol{\lambda}$ such that $\mathbf{A}\boldsymbol{\lambda} = \mathbf{0}$. Thus $\mathbf{x} = \boldsymbol{\lambda}$ solves $\mathbf{Ax} = \mathbf{0}$.)[15] This done, the general solution of **S1** can be written:

$$\pi_r = \sum_{s=1}^{n-1} c_s k_{rs} e^{-\lambda_s t} \qquad r = 1, \ldots, n-1 \tag{44}$$

Each *eigenvalue*, λ_s, is a solution of $|\ | = 0$ and associates with an *eigenvector* $\mathbf{k}_s$, a solution for the equation system relative to λ_s. The vector $\mathbf{c}$ is to be determined by $\bar{\mathbf{p}}$ initial conditions.

'... the *general* solution ... may be obtained by taking the general linear combination of the solutions to equations (44).' The weights c, determining the linear combination above, are themselves determined by initial conditions.[16]

§ 5

In general (a_{rs}) is not symmetrical and rather little can be said about the system's stability properties.

Many motions are possible, depending on whether all of the eigenvalues are real and on the signs of real parts of complex roots.[17]

However, consider the special case in which (a_{rs}) is symmetrical so that $a_{rs} = a_{sr}$, precisely the case which emerges when income effects of price changes are neglected: substitution effects have been proved to be symmetrical.

In the symmetrical case all the eigenvalues are real numbers. Stability, i.e. $\pi_r \rightarrow 0$ as $t \rightarrow \infty$ for all r, requires that these values be positive as well as real, as will be true if the quadratic form $\mathbf{x}'\mathbf{Ax}$ is positive definite, i.e. is positive for any vector $\mathbf{x}$ not zero. Thus:

$$a_{11} > 0; \quad \begin{vmatrix} a_{11} & a_{12} \\ a_{12} & a_{22} \end{vmatrix} > 0; \ldots; \quad \begin{vmatrix} a_{11} \ldots a_{1s} \\ \ldots \ldots \ldots \\ a_{1s} \ldots a_{ss} \end{vmatrix} > 0; \ldots \quad (45)$$

The conditions imposed by inequalities (45) are known as *Hicksian conditions*.[18]

Of course, the analysis rigorously pertains only to the behaviour of an 'auctioneer' in a *tâtonnement* market-adjustment process.

§ 6[19]

¶9.6 §§1–5 comprise a conventionally-informal treatment of *multi-market* stability centred on an extension of the first method of Liapounoff to normalized price vectors. ¶9.6 §§6 dips into Karlin's superb chapter 9[20] for a more general discussion of *multi-market* stability, using non-normalized price vectors (on the whole more satisfactory, at least so long as the theory of money is being neglected).

¶9.6 §§7 refers to an application of the second method of Liapounoff. Throughout this treatment, the discussion is abstract. No effort is made to offer calendar-time interpretations of the meta-time 'events' of the theory.

A number of preliminary concepts are crucial. A *strictly-positive* price vector $\mathbf{p}$ finds $\mathbf{p} > \mathbf{0}$. The (r, s)th element of the matrix $\mathbf{A}(\mathbf{p})$ is $\partial f_r/\partial p_s$, $\mathbf{f}(\mathbf{p})$ being a vector of excess-demand functions. If $\mathbf{A}$ is a M(Metzler) matrix $a_{rs} > 0$ for $r \neq s$. *Weak gross substitutability* finds $\partial f_r/\partial p_s \geq 0$, whilst *strict gross substitutability* finds $\partial f_r/\partial p_s > 0$. Finally, since rational behaviour has been shown to require that $\mathbf{f}(\mathbf{p})$ is zero-order homogeneous in $\mathbf{p}$,

'... local stability shall mean that if $\mathbf{p}$ is a price vector near the ray Γ, then $\mathbf{p}(t)$ tends to some equilibrium vector situated on the ray Γ.'[21]

The crucial theorem on local stability is:

Let $A(\bar{p})$ be a strict M-matrix. If $\bar{p}$ is strictly positive and p is sufficiently close to Γ, then $p(t)$ converges to an equilibrium point of Γ.[22]

The theorems on global stability flow from a lemma, always stressing that we take $\bar{p}$ to be strictly positive:

If $\bar{p}$ is strictly positive and if $f(p) > 0$ for all vectors p, not $\bar{p}$, 'then the non-normalized price adjustment process is globally stable.'[23]

Some global theorems are:

'If the excess-demand functions satisfy the weak axiom of revealed preference, then the process . . . is globally stable'[24] (i.e., the lemma is satisfied).

Noting that: 'the axiom of revealed preference is usually verified only in the neighbourhood of an equilibrium point and need not hold in the large,'[25] the theorem states that: 'if the excess-demand functions satisfy the property of strict gross substitutability in the interior of the positive orthant [i.e. in the open subset excluding any zero-prices or "if excess demands defined on such prices satisfy . . ."], then the process . . . is globally stable.'[25]

'If the excess demand functions $f(p)$ are defined, can be differentiated for $p \geqslant 0$, are homogeneous, and if they satisfy the Walras Law and possess the property of weak gross substitutability, then the price-adjustment process [characterized as below] is stable.'[26]

The process referred to leads up to a differential equation system somewhat different from that employed hitherto in ¶9.6, viz., $dp_i/dt = H_i[f_i(p)]$ 'where $H_i(x)$ is continuous and sign-preserving, i.e., sign $H_i(x) =$ sign x for all real x.'[27]

Needless to say, continuing work in the analysis of *multi-market* stability will evolve from the materials taken up in ¶9.6 §§6–7.

§ 7[28]

¶9.6 §§7 is little more than a methodological note on *the second method of Liapounoff*: the systematic approach to the stability of general competitive equilibrium of ¶9.6 §§6 takes another tack.

One prop for our discussion (i.e. Newman's discussion) is the concept of the norm of a vector x. The norm, $N(x)$, is any scalar-valued function $N(x)$ satisfying the following four requirements:

1) $N(x) \geq 0$, for all x.
2) $N(x + y) \leq N(x) + N(y)$, for all x and y [y being another vector of course].
3) $N(\alpha x) = |\alpha| N(x)$, for all x and any complex constant α [$|\alpha|$ being its real part].
4) $N(x) = 0$ if each component of x is zero.[29]

We note that these properties are satisfied by the 'Euclidean Norm' $(\sum x_i^2)^{1/2}$.

A second prop is Liapounoff's theorem underlying his second method, namely that the solution $\bar{x}$ for the system $g(x) = 0$, so that $\dot{x} = f(\bar{x}) = 0$, is stable if 'there exists a scalar function V with continuous first partial derivatives such that $V(0) = 0$, and:

1) $V(\pi) > 0$ for all $\pi \neq 0$;
2) $\dot{V}(\pi) < 0$ for all $\pi \neq \mathbf{0}$;
3) $V(\pi) \to \infty$ as $N(\pi) \to \infty$,'[30]

where, departing from Newman's notation, as it happens, π is a vector of deviations from $\bar{x}$ such that, for $\pi = \mathbf{0}$, the system is in state $\bar{x}$.

The stage thus being set, we can consider the stability of the system:

$$\dot{p} = Ap \qquad\qquad (46)$$

We at once transform the variables so that the system becomes:

$$\dot{\pi} = A\pi \qquad\qquad (47)$$

Adopting the Euclidian norm as above, 'V conditions' 1) and 3) are seen to be satisfied on inspection. Condition 2) proves to be satisfied if A is negative quasi-definite, that is the elements of A are no greater than zero. In this way, the analysis of *multi-market* stability becomes both enlarged and simplified.

7. COMPARATIVE STATICS

¶9.7 §§2 generalizes 'Walrasian' comparative statics. ¶9.7 §§3 takes up the statical theory of economic policy, a topic pursued in ¶9.9 and extended in Part IV. Considering how slender is ¶9.7, the reader might reflect:

> In this last of meeting places
> We grope together
> An avoid speech
> Gathered on this beach of the tumid river,

or, more familiarly:

> This is the way the world ends
> Not with a bang but a whimper.

But, in truth, the method of comparative statics is extremely straightforward.

§2

The underlying system can be written:

$$f(p;z) = 0 \qquad\qquad (48)$$

i.e.,

$$f^1(p_1, p_2, \ldots, p_{n-1}; z_1, z_2, \ldots, z_m) = 0$$

$$\cdots\cdots\cdots\cdots\cdots\cdots\cdots\cdots\cdots\cdots\cdots\cdots\cdots\cdots\cdots\cdots \tag{49}$$

$$f^{n-1}(p_1, \ldots, p_{n-1}; z_1, \ldots, z_m) = 0$$

Solve for $\bar{\mathbf{p}}$ relative to parameters $\mathbf{z}^0$. The parameters include measures of taste, availability of land, etc. Evaluate the partial derivatives of the excess-demand functions at $(\bar{\mathbf{p}}, \mathbf{z}^0)$. The differentiated equilibrium conditions (49) then can be written:

$$a_{11}\,d\bar{p}_1 + \ldots + a_{1n-1}\,d\bar{p}_{n-1} = b_{11}\,dz_1^0 + \ldots + b_{1m}\,dz_m^0$$

$$\cdots\cdots\cdots\cdots\cdots\cdots\cdots\cdots\cdots\cdots\cdots\cdots\cdots\cdots\cdots\cdots\cdots\cdots \tag{50}$$

$$a_{n-11}\,d\bar{p}_1 + \ldots + a_{n-1n-1}\,d\bar{p}_{n-1} = b_{n-11}\,dz_1^0 + \ldots + b_{n-1m}\,dz_m^0$$

i.e.,

$$\mathbf{A(dp)} = \mathbf{B(dz^0)} \tag{51}$$

The elements of matrices $\mathbf{A}$ and $\mathbf{B}$ are first-order partial derivatives (adjusted for sign in the case of $\mathbf{B}$) evaluated at the initial equilibrium point. Thus:

$$\mathbf{d\bar{p}} = \mathbf{A}^{-1}\mathbf{B(dz^0)} \tag{52}$$

or

$$dp_i/dz_j = \sum_j \Delta_{ji}/\Delta \tag{53}$$

In this way a change in the techniques available to shoe-making leads to a change in the equilibrium level of the wages of pastry chefs.

Intuition can mislead in general-equilibrium analysis. When all interactions are considered, perhaps a reduction in non-reproducible resources specialized to phonograph-needle production will *not* lead to a decrease in disc prices even in a purely-competitive economy.[31]

§3

The static theory of economic policy emerges from ¶9.7 §§2. Chapter 12 dynamizes the theory of economic policy. Consider child-labour laws, factory-safety acts, zoning restrictions and other variables under the control of an unspecified Government. Assume that these official actions can be measured by continuous variables $\mathbf{z}$, instruments. Noting that $\bar{\mathbf{p}}$ associates with equilibrium productions and consumptions $\bar{y}_q$ and $\bar{x}_j$, given $\mathbf{z} = \mathbf{z}^*$, the officials ideally could work with reduced-form equations:

$$\bar{\mathbf{p}} = \Phi(\mathbf{z}) \tag{54}$$

For simplicity, assume that there are but two prices and three instruments:

$$\bar{p}_1 = \Phi^1(z_1, z_2, z_3) \tag{55}$$

$$\bar{p}_2 = \Phi^2(z_1, z_2, z_3) \tag{56}$$

Now assume that the officials are dissatisfied with $(\bar{p}_1, \bar{p}_2)^0$ associated with $(z_1, z_2, z_3)^0$ and wish to obtain $\bar{p}_1^1 = \bar{p}_1^0, \bar{p}_2^1 \neq \bar{p}_2^0$. An algebraic solution treats the prices as parameters, regaining lost degrees of freedom by treating two of the instruments, say the first and second, as variables:

$$z_1 = \Psi^1(z_3^0, \bar{p}_1^0, \bar{p}_2^1) \tag{57}$$

$$z_2 = \Psi^2(z_3^0, \bar{p}_1^0, \bar{p}_2^1) \tag{58}$$

Having thus solved for the appropriate instrument levels, $\mathbf{z}^1$, the officials can set $\mathbf{z} = \mathbf{z}^1$. Market forces (alas, rigorously the *tâtonnement!*) will yield up $\bar{\mathbf{p}}^1$. Traders might be conscious only of 'free' market forces leading up to $\bar{\mathbf{p}}^1$. Indeed the officials might emphasize their dedication to the free market.

8.   MULTI-MARKET MODELS INCLUDING FINANCIAL ASSETS AND LIABILITIES: STATICS[32]

The economy is to be described by equations (59) to (61):

$$f^i(\mathbf{p}, \boldsymbol{\pi}, \mathbf{r}; \mathbf{K}) = 0 \qquad i = 1, 2, \ldots, n \tag{59}$$

$$f^j(\mathbf{p}, \boldsymbol{\pi}, \mathbf{r}; \mathbf{K}, \alpha) = 0 \qquad j = 1, 2, \ldots, m \tag{60}$$

$$f^k(\mathbf{p}, \boldsymbol{\pi}, \mathbf{r}; \mathbf{K}, \alpha) = 0 \qquad k = 1, 2, \ldots, q \tag{61}$$

Equations (59) pertain to the n commodities: f^i is an excess-demand function. Equations (60) pertain to the m money-fixed, interest-bearing 'bonds': f^j is the excess-demand function for the jth bond, perhaps promising to pay the bearer \$1 in 30 days. Equations (61) concern common shares.

The variables to be determined within the system include vectors $\mathbf{p}$, $\boldsymbol{\pi}$, and $\mathbf{r}$. The price of commodity 1, p_1, is to be set equal to 1. Commodity 1 is a standard of value, traditionally gold or silver. Its price is fixed at 1 by a law requiring that tender of authenticated standard quanta of commodity 1 discharge debt valued at \$1.

Non-monetary gold (or silver) is a separate commodity bearing a separate price: coinage is a distinct activity and surely involves costs different to jewellery preparations for example.

$\boldsymbol{\pi}$ is a vector of share prices. $\mathbf{r}$ is a vector of interest rates. $\mathbf{K}$ is a vector of initial commodity holdings including physical means of production.

Since all contracts are for delivery at the end of the market period, there is no need to distinguish between 'old' and 'new' capital markets, certainly not after it is specified that depreciation is to be ignored and the 'commodity basis' is to be fixed. α is the nominal value of a special asset, held only by banks and used only as an interbank means of payment.

Financial institutions, including banks, usually would hold both gold and *alpha-credit*. Gold and *alpha-credit* are not perfect substitutes. *Alpha-credit* does not discharge claims presented by the public. The analogy to Special Drawing Rights-type reform schemes for the International Monetary Fund system is very strong.

The authorities are assumed to certify certain firms as 'banks', entitled to hold *alpha-credit*. However, banking functions also are performed by unchartered firms.

The reserve asset is issued or called in by the otherwise unspecified Government. Financial operations are unregulated: institutions specializing in issue of short-term liabilities against longer-term assets take account of penalties attached to insolvency.

Some of the 'bonds' will be means of payment: demand deposits (current accounts), theoretically and sometimes in practice, interest bearing, are amongst the 'bonds'.

Since Walras's Law applies, there are no more than $n+m+q-1$ independent equations to determine the $n+m+q-1$ prices ($n-1$ commodity prices, m yields, and q share prices).

§2

Rational behaviour precludes *money illusion*: production and consumption decisions of optimizing traders are unaffected by all-inclusive proportional price changes, analogous to measuring in inches instead of feet. If the vector $(\bar{p}, \bar{\pi}, \bar{r}; K, \alpha^0)$ is an equilibrium vector, so will be $(\lambda\bar{p}, \lambda\bar{\pi}, \bar{r}; K, \lambda\alpha^0)$.

Monetary neutrality includes the substance of the *quantity theory of money* as a proposition in comparative statics. If the monetary base, α, together with *all* commodity prices were increased by the positive factor λ, all nominal values would, in equilibrium, increase by the factor λ whilst all real values would be unaffected. In this case the price of the *numéraire*, monetary gold, must become λ instead of 1.

If α were held fixed, there would not be sustained the initial proportion between the equilibrium general price level and the value of the monetary-gold stock. Similarly, a change in the supply of *alpha-credit* would not be neutral unless the price of the *numéraire* were appropriately altered.[33]

§3[34]

The reader may be disturbed by the falling off of rigour in the analysis from ¶9.5 to ¶9.8. For example, 'convexity', 'continuity', 'compactness', etc., central to ¶9.5, have melted away. Not that this book is singularly at fault:

> 'Recent work on the existence of an equilibrium has been concerned with a world without money while all work in monetary theory has ignored the "existence" question.'[34]

However, being unable myself to fill in this gap in the formal theory of a monetary economy, I shall merely gloss Professor Hahn's interesting discussion, noting that he is on a lonely, if somewhat depressed, eminence.

Hahn is able to show that rigour can be preserved in general-equilibrium theory even if there is introduced non-interest-bearing fiat paper money, and no other financial asset (liability), thus ensuring against the possibility of nominally-fixed indebtedness. We must note, however, that:

1) such a monetary model can be only trivially interesting from the standpoint of monetary theory;
2) Hahn requires a number of unspecified auxiliary 'purely technical assumptions' (p. 132) to get his results.

Professor Hahn—and, it would appear, everyone else as well—is stonewalled in his efforts to infuse rigour into models including varieties of financial assets (liabilities). However, he offers a provocative speculation about what might be one source of difficulty:

> 'One of the main problems faced in establishing the existence of an equilibrium is to find acceptable assumptions which will ensure that the excess demand functions are continuous over the relevant domain.... [L]et us suppose that our individual has initial endowments which include debt fixed in terms of money at a rate of interest also so fixed. Then [as money-prices become] lower and lower ... he will go bankrupt.... The possibility of bankruptcy is therefore also a possibility for the occurrence of some rather sharp discontinuities.'[35]

§4

It is our position, of course, that the problems of sustaining the rigour of the theory of general competitive equilibrium, augmented by financial assets, are interesting only as *Dogmengeschichte*. After all, ¶1.5 §§5–6 exhaustively explained that the processes of the theory of general competitive equilibrium, unlike the processes of post-Keynesian empirical-economics, do not unfold in calendar time. Chapter 6 showed how the characteristically imperfect competition of Life makes it impossible to treat the representative trader as a price taker.

So it is: again and again it is found to be impossible to reconcile neo-classical and Keynesian theory, a point that will be sharpened in ¶9.9, which exposits Keynesian statics, but only by standing neo-classical procedures on their heads.

9. THE FIXPRICE APPROACH TO GENERAL-EQUILIBRIUM THEORY[36]

Consider the behaviour of an economy in which prices are held fixed but in which a sense of equilibrium can be preserved. The amount traded in each market is governed by supply or demand whichever is the less. Traders, including workers and *entrepreneurs*, make their consumption plans contingent on the amount of work they can get, on the sales they can achieve, or on the availability of commodities they wish to purchase. Once certain parameters are specified, an equation system can be solved for such quantities as employments and outputs.

The *fixprice* method thus leads to a determinate result for what is essentially a disequilibrium state of a competitive private ownership economy. It accommodates the fact that normally buyers and sellers are not acting optimally relative to prices **p**, i.e. they are not taking actions which would be optimal if **p** defined the only relevant constraints.

¶9.9 emphasizes disequilibrium states featured by excess supplies of commodities. But the analysis accommodates states of excess-demand. Granted, complexities arise when supplies are not elastic.

§2

The *fixprice* method analyses movements of *gross national product, investment, employment*, etc. Despite its simplicity, it leads to implications which may be falsified. The *fixprice* method is sensitive to the fact that on a given date $\bar{\mathbf{p}}$ hardly can govern an ongoing economy: parameters are ceaselessly changing as accumulation transpires and tastes change. Indeed it is natural in *fixprice* theory to jettison pure-competition altogether and simply to specify that sellers and buyers quote prices for commodities in which they deal. Nor is the *fixprice* assumption unrealistic: at each point in time, the economy's prices are predetermined by its history. The fact that the *fixprice* method explains 'today' by flashing a stroboscope does not mean that tomorrow's prices will be the same. Admittedly, the *fixprice* method *is* thoroughly statical.

§3

¶9.9 is amenable to *aggregation*. Since prices are fixed, automobiles, wheat, carpets, etc., can be lumped together and measured in dollars, as can be labour offers and demands. Now stipulate that all income elasticities of demand are unity and that 'redistribution effects' can be ignored: at fixed prices, the same mix of goods always will be demanded. Next recall the Hicksian group-of-goods theorem: goods whose prices always maintain the same proportions can be treated as a single good. Ours becomes a degenerate case of this theorem. These stipulations having been made, changes in national income can be rigorously measured in dollars at fixed prices.

§4

Fixprice theory has a Keynesian flavour. Since all relevant commodity supplies are perfectly elastic at prevailing prices, commodity productions and sales are determined by demand. *The* rate of interest in the crude financial sector is determined by the authorities who feed out or draw back as much money as is necessary to make the public and banks satisfied relative to the rate of interest. (The supply of 'money', the model's only specified financial asset, is determined by the authorities.) All outputs are lumped together. All interest rates are represented by a single number.

The *fixprice* model is 'open': only as many markets are specified as are of immediate interest.

The text's money is non-interest bearing.

Interest rates are to be policy-determined. The open-market operator is willing to sell and buy securities in unlimited amounts at the fixed rates. A correlative problem centres on the possibility that the public would be unwilling to hold for any length of time bonds at yields as low as those quoted by the official operator. This is the *liquidity trap*.

If for any reason the officials wish arbitrarily to determine M, they must declassify an r-value as a policy-determined variable, at least if the system is to remain statically determinate.

§5

The *fixprice* economy is described by equations (62) and (63):

$$Y = f(Y, r^0, \gamma) + A \tag{62}$$

$$L(r^0, Y) = M \tag{63}$$

Equation (62) requires that total output, Y, be equated with aggregate demand. (Strictly, 'aggregate demand' should read 'demand for all goods'.) Aggregate demand has induced and autonomous components. The autonomous component is A, including expenditures uninfluenced by feedback, expenditures exogenous to the system. Exports and imports temporarily are to be neglected.

Feedback amongst international economies is neglected, although it easily could be encompassed. Cf. the appendix to Chapter 9: *Markov Chains and Financial Equilibrium*.

Induced expenditure is determined by $f(Y, r^0, \gamma)$, γ being the rate of income taxation. The functional relationship encompasses a famous scheme of association of expenditure with income: the *consumption function*. In the theory of competitive equilibrium households *choose* their incomes, whilst in *fixprice* theory they choose levels of consumption expenditure *according* to their incomes. Equation (63) is more in accord with tradition: demand for money, determined by function L, is to be equal to the supply of money, M.

Taking both γ and the Government's revenues as zero, solve equations (62) and (63) for equilibrium values $\overline{Y}$, $\overline{M}$. Then totally differentiate the system in the neighbourhood of $(\overline{Y}, \overline{M})$:

$$(1 - f_Y)\,d\overline{Y} \qquad = \qquad f_r\,dr + dA \qquad (64)$$

$$L_Y\,d\overline{Y} - d\overline{M} = -L_r\,dr \qquad (65)$$

§6

The *investment multiplier* measures the effect of a change in autonomous expenditure on equilibrium national income, *ceteris paribus*, all within the statical framework of *fixprice* theory:

$$d\overline{Y}/dA_{dr=0} = 1/(1 - f_Y) \qquad (66)$$

The determinant of the left-hand side of the system, Δ, is:

$$\Delta = \begin{vmatrix} (1 - f_Y) & 0 \\ L_Y & -1 \end{vmatrix} = -(1 - f_Y) \qquad (67)$$

f_Y is a marginal propensity to spend, i.e. the rate at which planned expenditure increases with income at $(\overline{Y}, \overline{M}; r^0)$ and $0 < f_Y < 1$. Otherwise, in the framework of the model, demand-forces would impose no upper bound on national income (or $\overline{Y} = A$ would result from $f_Y = 0$).

Bank Rate, here a portmanteau term for interest rates, is to be held fixed. Accordingly the authorities must obey equation (68) in determining the stock of money:

$$d\overline{M}/dA = \begin{vmatrix} (1 - f_Y) & 1 \\ L_Y & 0 \end{vmatrix} \div \Delta = L_Y/(1 - f_Y) \qquad (68)$$

Since *demand-for-money* can be expected to increase with transactions activity, L_Y is taken to be positive and $d\overline{M}/dA > 0$.

Next consider how Bank Rate might affect $\overline{Y}$:

$$d\overline{Y}/dr^0 = -f_r/\Delta < 0 \qquad (69)$$

To the extent that demand for goods is negatively sensitive to interest rates, monetary policy can be used as a lever for income determination.

Cf. ¶9.9 §§8 for an extension of Bank Rate analysis to international systems.

§7

Exercise: analyse $d\overline{Y}/d\gamma_{dA=dr=0}$. This problem's empirical counterpart aroused intense interest in the United States circa 1963–1964.

Automatic stabilization is to be analysed, adopting a simplifying assumption: induced consumption is to be determined by the linear expression $\beta(Y-\gamma Y)$, γY being stipulated as *tax-take* so that $(Y-\gamma Y)$ is *disposable income*, governing formation of consumption plans. Induced investment expenditures are to be determined by $\Phi(Y, r)$. Next we are to calculate $d\bar{Y}/dA_{dr=0,\,dy=0}$ for $0 \le \gamma < 1$ and $\beta > \gamma$. Equations (70) and (71) are required:

$$Y = \beta(1-\gamma)Y + \Phi(Y, r) + A \tag{70}$$

$$L(r^{0}, Y) = M \tag{71}$$

Again differentiate the system in the neighbourhood of $(\bar{Y}, \bar{M})$:

$$(1 - \beta + \beta\gamma - \Phi_Y)\,d\bar{Y} = \Phi_r\,dr + dA - \beta\bar{Y}\,d\gamma \tag{72}$$

$$L_Y\,d\bar{Y} - d\bar{M} = -L_r\,dr \tag{73}$$

Hence:

$$d\bar{Y}/dA_{dr=dy=0} = \frac{1}{(1-\beta)+\beta\gamma-\Phi_Y} \tag{74}$$

For $\gamma = 0$, equation (74) is written:

$$d\bar{Y}/dA_{dr=dy=0} = \frac{1}{1-\beta-\Phi_Y} \tag{75}$$

Since $\beta\gamma > 0$, the denominator of the equation (74) expression is larger than that for the equation (75) expression. Income taxation reduces the multiplier. The system becomes less volatile. It absorbs shocks better.

§8

The final exercise in manipulation of *fixprice general-equilibrium* models introduces the balance of payments. We introduce an exogenous component, autonomous exports (X), together with induced imports and capital inflow so that there now can be defined a net foreign balance, B. But tax policy is deleted. Since exchange rates are to be fixed, equations (76) to (78) follow:

$$Y = F(Y, r) + A + X \tag{76}$$

$$L(Y, r) = M \tag{77}$$

$$B = X - \Psi(Y) + \phi(r) \tag{78}$$

Demand for domestically produced goods is determined by $F(Y, r)$. The net foreign balances describe the excess of 'flow' demand for 'our' currency over that for foreign currency, noting that demands for foreign goods and securities give rise to corresponding requirements for foreign tenders. Import demand is determined by $\Psi(Y)$. Net demand for 'our' securities is to depend on 'our' rate of interest, 'theirs' being held fixed: hence $\phi(r)$.

Totally differentiate equations (76) to (78) in the neighbourhood of an equilibrium $(\bar{Y}, \bar{M}, \bar{B})$:

$$(1 - F_Y)\,d\bar{Y} = F_r\,dr + dA + dX \tag{79}$$

$$L_Y\,d\bar{Y} - d\bar{M} = -L_r\,dr \tag{80}$$

$$\Psi_Y\,d\bar{Y} + d\bar{B} = \phi_r\,dr + dX \tag{81}$$

We assume that the Government is committed to maintaining B at $\bar{B}$ and that $dA = 0$: Bank Rate is to be the only instrument. Finally we assume that there has been a shift, dX, in export-demand.

Effects on income, interest rates, etc., can be analysed. First we rewrite equations (79) to (81) in accordance with the stipulations:

$$(1 - F_Y)\,d\bar{Y} - F_r\,d\bar{r} \qquad = dX \tag{82}$$

$$L_Y\,d\bar{Y} + L_r\,d\bar{r} - d\bar{M} = 0 \tag{83}$$

$$\Psi_Y\,d\bar{Y} - \phi_r\,d\bar{r} \qquad = d\bar{X} \tag{84}$$

Defining the system's determinant as Δ:

$$\Delta = \begin{vmatrix} 1 - F_Y & -F_r & 0 \\ L_Y & L_r & -1 \\ \Psi_Y & -\phi_r & 0 \end{vmatrix} = -\phi_r(1 - F_Y) + \Psi_Y F_r < 0 \tag{85}$$

Hence:

$$d\bar{Y}/dX = (\Delta_{11} + \Delta_{31})/\Delta = (-\phi_r + F_r)/\Delta > 0 \tag{86}$$

It is left as an exercise to show that ordinary economic reasoning requires $d\bar{r} < 0$ in this thought experiment. This result, together with equation (82), permit us to establish and analyse equation (87):

$$d\bar{Y} = dX/(1 - F_Y) + (F_r/(1 - F_Y))\,d\bar{r} \tag{87}$$

For $d\bar{r} < 0$, both right-hand terms must be positive. Now if the Government did not insist on $dB = 0$, but, instead, on keeping unchanged all of its instrument levels, equation (87) would be written:

$$d\bar{Y} = dX/(1 - F_Y) \tag{88}$$

The right-hand side of equation (88) is less than that of equation (87). Thus national authorities complying with the *writ of the gnomes of Zurich* might have to adopt policy mixes making their system especially volatile with respect to external disturbance. In the case put forward in ¶9.9 §§8, authorities, observing a decline in demand for their exports, would put up their Bank Rate, further deflating the economy, in order to defend their balance of payments.

CHAPTER 9—APPENDIX: MARKOV CHAINS AND EQUILIBRIUM THEORY[37]

Markov chain theory can treat existence and stability of equilibrium for models spanning such diverse fields as international economics, banking, and cash-balance distribution. In the simplest case the state of the sub-economy can be described by a vector of proportions summing to unity: fractions of the global stock of monetary gold held in France, Germany, America . . . ; the fraction of the money stock held by households as against that held by large corporations; etc. Markov theory shows how hypothetical systems switch from one state to the next. Is there a state which switches into itself? If so, will $\bar{S}$ be attained regardless of the system's initial state? In Markov chain theory, steady-state equilibrium falls out as a special case of a dynamical formulation.

§2

¶9. App. §§3 states certain definitions. ¶9. App. §§4 states some theorems without proof. ¶9. App. §§5 et seq. offer economic interpretations of the theorems.

§3

A *stochastic matrix* is a square matrix with row sums of unity. A row vector is called a *probability vector* if it consists wholly of non-negative components summing to unity. (The mathematical results do not in any way depend on the underlying system being stochastic. Indeed no stochastic interpretation is offered here.) The probability vector t is a *fixed point* of the *transformation* P if $t = tP$, P being a *transition matrix*. t becomes an *absorbing state*. The stochastic matrix P is *regular* if all of its elements are positive. Any regular matrix is *ergodic*; not all *ergodic* matrices are regular.

§4

In this appendix the symbol x represents a row vector. Unless noted to the contrary x is a column vector elsewhere in the book whilst a row vector is designated x'.

If P is a regular stochastic matrix, P^n approaches a matrix T as n becomes indefinitely large. ($P \times P = P^2$; $P^2 \times P = P^3$; etc.) Each row of T is the same probability vector **t**, each component of **t** being non-negative. Furthermore, if **p** is any probability vector, $\mathbf{pP}^n$ approaches **t** and **t** is the unique fixed point probability vector of **P**.

§5

Consider a system containing two banks, Banks 1 and 2. The flow of funds from Bank 1 customers to other customers of Bank 1, together with that from Bank 1 customers to Bank 2 customers, is shown by equations (89) and (90). Equations (91) and (92) similarly pertain to Bank 2:

$$0{\cdot}8D_1 = X_{11} \tag{89}$$

$$0{\cdot}2D_1 = X_{12} \tag{90}$$

$$0{\cdot}8D_2 = X_{21} \tag{91}$$

$$0{\cdot}2D_2 = X_{22} \tag{92}$$

If Bank 1 deposits initially were \$100, \$20 would flow out to Bank 2 during the period. If Bank 2 deposits initially were \$100, \$80 would flow out to Bank 1 during the period. Thus:

$$\mathbf{P} = \begin{bmatrix} 0{\cdot}8 & 0{\cdot}2 \\ 0{\cdot}8 & 0{\cdot}2 \end{bmatrix} \tag{93}$$

Consider an initial vector of deposit proportions:

$$\mathbf{p} = (0{\cdot}5, 0{\cdot}5) \tag{94}$$

The theorems assert that the system will come into stationary equilibrium at $\mathbf{p}^n = (0{\cdot}8, 0{\cdot}2)$, a fixed-point probability vector of the transformation **P**. ($\mathbf{p}^n$ simply is the probability vector for the nth period.) Since **P** is a matrix of class **T**, the system becomes stationary after a single transition:

$$(0{\cdot}5, 0{\cdot}5)\begin{bmatrix} 0{\cdot}8 & 0{\cdot}2 \\ 0{\cdot}8 & 0{\cdot}2 \end{bmatrix} = (0{\cdot}8, 0{\cdot}2) \tag{95}$$

$$(0{\cdot}8, 0{\cdot}2)\begin{bmatrix} 0{\cdot}8 & 0{\cdot}2 \\ 0{\cdot}8 & 0{\cdot}2 \end{bmatrix} = (0{\cdot}8, 0{\cdot}2) \tag{96}$$

After a single transition, $\mathbf{pP} = \mathbf{t}$, the absorbing state.

Let the appropriate stipulations be made, as here. The theorems require that $\mathbf{p}^0\mathbf{P}^n$, the state of the system after n transitions from arbitrary initial position $\mathbf{p}^0$, approach **t** and $\mathbf{P}^n$ approach **T**. Thus, if n is large enough, the $(n+1)$st state can approach the limiting value **tT** as closely as is desired.

Thus Markov chain theory pulls the theory of economic equilibrium into the orbit of scientific method.

REFERENCES

1. Cf. W. J. Baumol, *Economic Theory and Operations Analysis* (Englewood Cliffs, N.J.: Prentice-Hall; 1965), 2nd ed, pp. 493–496.
2. A. A. Andronow and C. E. Chaikin, *Theory of Oscillations* (Princeton: Princeton University Press; 1949), Chap. 6, § 6, pp. 147–148.
3. A. A. Andronow and C. E. Chaikin, *Theory of Oscillations* (Princeton: Princeton University Press; 1949), p. 147.
4. A. A. Andronow and C. E. Chaikin, *Theory of Oscillations* (Princeton: Princeton University Press; 1949), p. 61.
5. G. Debreu, *Theory of Value* (New York: John Wiley & Sons; 1959), p. 26.
6. *DOSSO*, p. 372, fn. 2.
7. Cf. G. Birkhoff and S. MacLane, *A Survey of Modern Algebra* (New York: Macmillan & Co.; 1965), 3rd ed., p. 180.
8. Cf. G. Debreu, *Theory of Value* (New York: John Wiley & Sons; 1959), pp. 78ff.
9. 'Households' = 'Consumers'. G. Debreu, *Theory of Value* (New York: John Wiley & Sons; 1959), pp. 79–86.
10. Cf. M. Burstein, *Money* (Cambridge, Mass: Schenkmann Publishing Co. Inc.; 1963), pp. 684–694.
11. G. Debreu, *Theory of Value* (New York: John Wiley & Sons; 1959), p. 80.
12. Cf. G. Debreu, *Theory of Value* (New York: John Wiley & Sons; 1959), Chap. 5.7, 83ff.
13. Cf. *DOSSO*, pp. 374–375, especially their footnote 2.
14. Cf. T. Negishi, 'The Stability of a Competitive Economy: A Survey Article,' *Econometrica*, Oct. 1962 (Vol. 30, No. 4), pp. 635–669. Negishi discusses non-*tâtonnement* processes and the global stability of *tâtonnement*. The text above is confined to the standard Hicks–Samuelson stability analysis.
15. Cf. R. G. D. Allen, *Mathematical Economics* (London: Macmillan & Co.; 1964), 2nd ed., p. 455. Also Chap. 14.6.
16. D. Bushaw and R. Clower, *Introduction to Mathematical Economics* (Homewood, Ill.: Richard D. Irwin Inc.; 1957), p. 310.
17. R. G. D. Allen, *Mathematical Economics* (London: Macmillan & Co.; 1964), 2nd ed., pp. 482–483.
18. Cf. J. R. Hicks, *Value and Capital* (Oxford: The Clarendon Press; 1946), 2nd ed., pp. 315–319.
19. Cf. S. Karlin, *Mathematical Methods and Theory in Games, Programming, and Economics* (Reading, Mass.: Addison-Wesley Pub. Co. Inc.), Vol. I, pp. 301–335.
20. S. Karlin, *Mathematical Methods and Theory in Games, Programming, and Economics* (Reading, Mass.: Addison-Wesley Pub. Co. Inc.), Vol. I, Chap. 9.
21. S. Karlin, *Mathematical Methods and Theory in Games, Programming, and Economics* (Reading, Mass.: Addison-Wesley Pub. Co. Inc.), Vol. I, p. 308. An early analysis of the stability of *multi-market* equilibrium in the presence of homogeneous excess-demand functions is O. Lange, *Price Flexibility and Employment* (Bloomington, Indiana: Principia Press; 1944). Lange leads this analysis into Keynesian economics. Cf. also M. L. Burstein, *Money* (Cambridge, Mass.: Schenkman Pub. Co. Inc.; 1963), pp. 528–533.
22. S. Karlin, *Mathematical Methods and Theory in Games, Programming and Economics* (Reading, Mass.: Addison Wesley Pub. Co. Inc.), Vol. I, p. 308.
23. S. Karlin, *Mathematical Methods and Theory in Games, Programming and Economics* (Reading, Mass.: Addison-Wesley Pub. Co. Inc.), Vol. I, p. 310.

24. S. Karlin, *Mathematical Methods and Theory in Games, Programming and Economics* (Reading, Mass.: Addison-Wesley Pub. Co. Inc.), Vol. I, p. 311.
25. S. Karlin, *Mathematical Methods and Theory in Games, Programming and Economics* (Reading, Mass.: Addison-Wesley Pub. Co. Inc.), Vol. I, p. 312.
26. S. Karlin, *Mathematical Methods and Theory in Games, Programming and Economics* (Reading, Mass.: Addison-Wesley Pub. Co. Inc.), Vol. I, p. 318.
27. S. Karlin, *Mathematical Methods and Theory in Games, Programming and Economics* (Reading, Mass.: Addison-Wesley Pub. Co. Inc.), Vol. I, p. 316.
28. Cf. Peter Newman, 'Approaches to Stability Analysis,' *Economica*, February 1961, pp. 12–29.
29. Peter Newman, 'Approaches to Stability Analysis,' *Economica*, February 1961, p. 24.
30. Peter Newman, 'Approaches to Stability Analysis,' *Economica*, February 1961, p. 25.
31. Cf. H. Hotelling, 'Edgeworth's Taxation Paradox, etc.', *Journal of Political Economy*, Vol. 40 (1932), pp. 577–616.
32. Cf. Don Patinkin, *Money, Interest and Prices* (New York: Harper, Row & Co.; 1965), 2nd ed. Also J. G. Gurley and E. S. Shaw, *Money in a Theory of Finance* (Washington: The Brookings Institution; 1960).
33. Cf. M. L. Burstein, *Money* (Cambridge, Mass.: Schenkmann Publishing Co. Inc.; 1963), Chap. 2, appendix.
34. Cf. F. H. Hahn, 'On Some Problems of Proving the Existence of an Equilibrium in a Monetary Economy,' in Hahn and Brechling (eds.), *The Theory of Interest Rates* (London: Macmillan & Co. Ltd.; 1965), pp. 126–135. Also the discussion of Hahn's paper, pp. 309–313.
35. F. H. Hahn, 'On Some Problems of Proving the Existence of an Equilibrium in a Monetary Economy,' in Hahn and Brechling (eds.), *The Theory of Interest Rates* (London: Macmillan & Co. Ltd.; 1965), p. 134.
36. The term *'fixprice* method' is due to Sir John Hicks. Cf. J. R. Hicks, *Capital and Growth* (Oxford: The Clarendon Press; 1965), Chap. 7, p. 76ff.
37. Cf. J. Kemeny, J. Snell, and G. Thompson, *Introduction to Finite Mathematics* (Englewood Cliffs, N.J.: Prentice-Hall; 1957), Chaps. 4 and 7. Also J. Kemeny and J. Snell, *Mathematical Models in the Social Sciences* (Boston: Ginn & Co.; 1962), Chaps. 5 and 6 and appendices. See also M. L. Burstein, *Money* (Cambridge, Mass.: Schenkmann Publishing Co. Inc.; 1963), pp. 140–146.

CHAPTER 10

Optimality

1. INTRODUCTION

May one economic state be said to be more optimal than another? This question preceded formal economic theory and provoked the development of economics as a science.

Chapter 10 exemplifies serendipity. Its major conclusion is that economic theory cannot resolve conflicts about the ethics of distribution, *but* techniques developed in the quixotic quest for economic justice have revolutionized management of multi-branch enterprises and illuminated intertemporal relations in production and consumption.

§ 2

Chapter 10's substance is presented in seven sections after further reflexion on welfare economics and the bourgeois world-view (¶10.2). ¶10.3–¶10.5 are strictly statical. ¶10.3 takes up efficiency properties of formal competitive equilibria. ¶10.4 informally derives the well-known Pareto-optimum conditions. ¶10.5 imposes still more *caveats*. ¶10.5–¶10.9 concern intertemporal allocations of resources with special emphasis on capital accumulation. Analytically ¶10.6–¶10.9 hardly differ from ¶10.3–¶10.5. ¶10.6 simply makes explicit a piece of the market system of ¶10.3, namely contracting for sale and purchase of future-dated commodities in a once-and-for-all *tâtonnement* under perfect certainty. The programmes analysed in ¶10.7–¶10.9 easily could be interpreted as engineering solutions of production-planning problems subject to boundary conditions. Thus Chapter 10 is, on the whole, not properly dynamical: it does not analyse general motions of economic variables but, instead, works out properties of selected 'equilibrium' paths.

¶10.6–¶10.9 focus on *intertemporal* decisions and actions. After the subject is glossed in ¶10.6, intertemporal production models are built up from a *Leontief system* base in ¶10.7 and from a *von Neumann* base in ¶10.8. Then, adhering to the resulting linear structures, concepts of *optimality* of growth paths are explored in ¶10.9.

2. WELFARE ECONOMICS AND THE BOURGEOIS WORLD-VIEW

Economics might never become divorced from the hedonistic (pleasure–pain) calculus of Benthamite utilitarianism. Perhaps this is because the atomized structure of price theory, viewing the economy as a network of relationships between optimizing decision units, so easily is interpreted as a model of *society*. *Optimal* social choice speciously seems to emerge from weighted averages of individual values. In this way, economists tacitly have adopted social-contract theories *à la* Locke and have been unable to accommodate organic theories of the state *à la* Hegel or Fichte.

It is not holist fallacy to state that social actions cannot be reconstructed by summing up individual component actions.

Note that the atomistic–individualistic approach is especially unviable in an urban society where massive consumption services are provided by huge lumps of socialized or naturally-monopolized capital, such as water-works, sewage plants, underground railways, parks, etc. Lumpiness and indivisibility, together with felt needs of social cohesion preclude your or my opting out of such programmes—or consider defence![1]

§2

As it happens, 'democratic' criteria of social choice, criteria based on 'just' weighted voting, are fatally inconsistent. Does not the government stand *in loco parentis* to minors and unborn persons? Is not a Premier charged with altering the character of national life? What if the fears of ordinary men lead to time preferences deemed by the Government to be too high? Is the Government supposed serenely to add up preferences of genocides, nudists, sybarites and others, together with yours and mine?

But concentrate the attack along simple lines. Since the contemporary public are in an intertemporal tussle with their children and the unborn, 'individualism' disenfranchises persons whose interests possessive-individualist libertarians agree should be considered.

Consulting ¶3.4 §§3, note that the decision units of economic theory or Lockeian society are *living adults*. The Government, i.e. the President-in-Congress, together with ancillary power residing in the courts and amongst the states, in its very nature and under ancient precedent established by Common Law and King-in-Parliament, is trustee for unborn persons and indeed has wide discretion to protect people against themselves.

More metaphysically, my tastes and preferences at this moment are changing in ways I do not understand and leading to positions I cannot anticipate: I do not know what will be the effects of biological aging processes on me or on others, nor do I know what will be the experiences of myself and others. Indeed, 'I' tomorrow am not 'I' today. (Cf. first note at the end of ¶3.4 §§3.) Worse yet, the Ruler's actions today will affect the judgements of 'I' tomorrow about past, present, and future: the mountaineer, unhappily driven north by effects of minimum-wage legislation on low-yield Appalachian industries, might later be glad that he was exiled. Perhaps so will be his children. Speaking of children, note that thoroughgoing Benthamite individualism reduces children to kerns of their 'free' parents. What worse tyranny ever has existed than that of the tribal patriarch?

Future historians might write a brief for J. Stalin who imposed his preferences on the Russians of his day, perhaps to their regret. However, today's Russians enjoy whatever were the fruits of his *Terror*. Perhaps Stalin will be viewed through historical mists as the Protector of future Russians against the short sighted materialism of his contemporaries. Perhaps not— but surely this was the rôle of such 'good' absolute and hated rulers as Moses, Lincoln and, indeed, Yahveh.

3. FORMAL ANALYSIS OF OPTIMALITY OF COMPETITIVE EQUILIBRIA

Refer back to ¶5.3 §§8–§§10, elaborating a sense in which the equilibrium of a competitive economy operating linear production activities is efficient. The value of aggregate output was found to be maximized relative to prices $\bar{\mathbf{p}}$. The equilibrium vector of activity levels, $\bar{\mathbf{x}}$, led to efficient outputs $\bar{\mathbf{y}}$. Furthermore, there must exist in such an economy an equilibrium price vector making a given efficient vector of activity levels, $\mathbf{x}^*$, an equilibrium vector: for $\mathbf{x}^*$ there must exist $\mathbf{p}^*$ such that $\mathbf{p}^* \cdot \mathbf{y}^* \geq \mathbf{p} \cdot \mathbf{y}^*$, $\mathbf{p} \geq \mathbf{0}$ (for $\Sigma p_i = 1$ for example). Of course $\mathbf{y}^*$ concerns outputs associated with $\mathbf{x}^*$. The theorem may be stated, 'for $\mathbf{x}^*$ there must exist $\mathbf{r}^*$ such that $\mathbf{r}^* \cdot \mathbf{x}^* \geq \mathbf{r} \cdot \mathbf{x}^*$.'

§2

The ¶5.3 §§8–10 analysis was incomplete. Optimality ignored consumer preferences. Furthermore the stipulation of linear production was restrictive. However, it is possible to show that more general competitive equilibria are in a sense optimal, albeit without empirical counterparts and confined by underlying continuity and convexity assumptions.

The sense of optimality is that of Vilfredo Pareto and is well stated by Debreu:

> 'given two attainable states of an economy, the second is considered to be at least as desirable as the first if every consumer desires his consumption in the second state at least as much as his consumption in the first. An optimum is thus defined as an attainable state such that, within the limitations imposed by the consumption sets, the production sets, and the total resources of the economy, one cannot satisfy better the preferences of any consumer without satisfying less well those of another.'[2]

Two crucial theorems, climaxing neo-classical economics, can be proved along lines suggested here:

1) a competitive equilibrium of the private-ownership economy of Chapter 9 is optimal;
2) any optimum state can be a competitive equilibrium.

§ 3

1) Optimality of a Competitive Equilibrium[3]

A set of outputs cannot be *optimal* if it is possible to increase one output without decreasing any other, recalling that aggregate consumption is to be insatiable. One set of outputs cannot be said to be at least as efficient as a second, unless each output in the one set is at least as great as the corresponding element of the other. Hence, we must first show that a competitive equilibrium attains the feasible-production *frontier*.

Consider the elementary feasible-production set Y and its frontier TT below. Any point belonging to Y and not on TT (say Q) is inferior to some point on TT (say P)

Fig. 1   An Elementary Production Set.

Recall that the aggregate set of feasible-outputs is convex, that inputs are included in Y as negative outputs, and that in a competitive equilibrium the sum $\bar{\mathbf{p}}. \Sigma \mathbf{y}_q = \bar{\mathbf{p}} \cdot \mathbf{y}$ was maximized.

The argument now moves onto mathematical ground. A theorem due to Minkowski again is stated: if Y is a convex set belonging to the set of m-dimensional real numbers $\mathbf{R}^m$, and $\mathbf{y}$ is an m-dimensional real number, there is a hyperplane $\mathbf{H}$, bounding for Y through $\mathbf{y}$, if $\mathbf{y}$ is not interior to (i.e. if $\mathbf{y}$ is on the *frontier* of) Y.

What is a bounding hyperplane to a set? It is a set of points $\mathbf{Z}$ such that for $\mathbf{z}^* \in \mathbf{Z}$, $\mathbf{p}^* \cdot \mathbf{z}^* \geq M$ whilst $\mathbf{p}^* \cdot \mathbf{y} \leq M$, where $\mathbf{p}^*$ is a selected vector and M is a real number. A bounding hyperplane to Y, then, is a supporting plane to Y at $\mathbf{y}^*$ if $\mathbf{y}^* \in \mathbf{Z}$.

Supporting planes are common in economics. Consider Fig. 2. The *tangent* to the frontier of Y at P defines two half spaces such that all points belonging to the shaded area either belong to Y (P is the only such point)

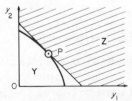

Fig. 2   An Example of a Supporting Plane.

or are 'greater' than a point belonging to the hull of **Y**. All points in the unshaded area either belong to **Z** (**P** is the only such point) or are 'less' than a point belonging to **Z**. **Z** is a supporting plane to the set of feasible-outputs **Y** at **P**. One knows intuitively the connexion between convexity and the existence of supporting planes: convex sets bend back on themselves.

Let us pause to consolidate the argument. If **Y** is convex, then there exist pairs $(\hat{\mathbf{p}}_r, \hat{M}_r)$, $\hat{\mathbf{p}}_r$ being a vector $\geq 0 (\hat{\mathbf{p}}_r \neq 0)$ and $\hat{M}_0$ a scalar, such that $\hat{\mathbf{p}}_r \cdot \mathbf{y} \leq \hat{M}_r$ for $\mathbf{y} \in \mathbf{Y}$. Furthermore, only if **y** is not interior to **Y** can $\hat{\mathbf{p}}_r \cdot \mathbf{y} = \hat{M}_r$. *Now* interpret **p** as a price vector. In competitive equilibrium $\bar{\mathbf{y}}$ maximizes the inner-product $\bar{\mathbf{p}} \cdot \mathbf{y}$ over the set of feasible-outputs. i.e., for $\mathbf{y} \in \mathbf{Y}$ but $\mathbf{y} \neq \bar{\mathbf{y}}$, $\bar{\mathbf{p}} \cdot \mathbf{y} \leq \bar{\mathbf{p}} \cdot \bar{\mathbf{y}}$. Therefore, if **Z** is a supporting hyperplane to **Y** at $\bar{\mathbf{y}}$, $\bar{\mathbf{y}} \in \mathbf{Z}$: $\bar{\mathbf{p}} \cdot \bar{\mathbf{y}} = M$ where $\bar{\mathbf{p}} \cdot \mathbf{z} \geq M$ for $\mathbf{z} \in \mathbf{Z}$. Outputs $\bar{\mathbf{y}}$ are on the frontier of $\mathbf{Y} : \bar{\mathbf{y}}$ *is an efficient set of outputs.*

Turn now to consumption, following *DOSSO*, pp. 411–412, and recalling that labour services are in consumptions **x**. (For a more rigorous proof, see *Theory of Value*.)[4] Each household is subject to a budget constraint requiring that its expenditure shall not exceed the value of its initial endowment plus its income. Postulating that *no* household has a satiation consumption, each household will exhaust its budget constraint. Consider equilibrium consumptions $(\bar{\mathbf{x}}_j)$. If $(\bar{\mathbf{x}}_j)$ is not a Pareto-optimum set of consumptions, there must exist a different set of feasible-consumptions $(\mathbf{x}_j^*)$ such that the alternative consumptions are not cheaper for any household and cost more for at least one household at $\bar{\mathbf{p}}$. If $\bar{\mathbf{p}} \cdot \mathbf{x}_r^* < \bar{\mathbf{p}} \cdot \bar{\mathbf{x}}_r$, the rth household would be revealed to prefer $\bar{\mathbf{x}}_r$ to $\mathbf{x}_r^*$. (If the alternative consumptions were indeed preferred to consumptions $(\bar{\mathbf{x}}_j)$, they would be selected, if they could be afforded.) This would be to say that there exists a feasible configuration of outputs which is valued at more than $\bar{\mathbf{p}} \cdot \bar{\mathbf{y}}$, again noting that services sold by households are inputs (negative outputs) for firms and that firms' outputs are inputs for households. Such cannot be the case if $\bar{\mathbf{y}}$ is efficient—but $\bar{\mathbf{y}}$ *is* efficient.

POINT. It can be proved that a competitive equilibrium is a Pareto-optimum.

§4

2) 'Competitiveness' of a Pareto-Optimum[5]

We merely gloss the difficult proof. Thus we assume that initial endowments are nil, that $\boldsymbol{\omega} = \mathbf{0}$. Consider consumptions which each household prefers to $\bar{\mathbf{x}}_j$. Each such set must be convex. Compare the suggestive two-commodity, fixed income example of Fig. 3: **Z** is a convex set. Consider next the set of *aggregate* consumptions $\mathbf{X}^*$ at least as preferred as $\bar{\mathbf{x}}$. $\mathbf{X}^*$ includes 'bundles' $\Sigma \mathbf{x}_j$ consistent with at least one household, say the rth, enjoying a position preferred to $\bar{\mathbf{x}}_r$ and no household experiencing a less preferred position than $\bar{\mathbf{x}}_s$ $(s \neq r)$.

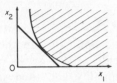

Fig. 3   The Set of Consumptions Preferred to $\bar{\mathbf{x}}_j$.

$\mathbf{X}^*$ is a convex set. By hypothesis $\bar{\mathbf{x}}$ is a Pareto optimum: no point in $\mathbf{X}^*$ preferable to $\bar{\mathbf{x}}$ in the sense of Pareto can be produced. That is to say that $\mathbf{X}^*$ and points no more preferred than $\bar{\mathbf{x}}$ can be divided by a separating plane. However, we have seen that, if $\mathbf{x} \in \mathbf{X}$ supports a bounding hyperplane, there must exist a vector $\bar{\mathbf{p}}$ such that $\bar{\mathbf{p}} \cdot \bar{\mathbf{x}} \geq \bar{\mathbf{p}} \cdot \mathbf{x}$. In other words, at $\mathbf{p} = \bar{\mathbf{p}}, \bar{\mathbf{x}} = \bar{\mathbf{y}}$ becomes the optimum set of outputs for profit-maximizing competitive producers.

The demonstration reaches a crescendo through *dualism*, in many ways the yeast of neo-classical theory, emerging as it does from interaction of utility-maximizing and cost-minimizing decision units bounded by convex opportunity sets. It can be proved that $\Sigma \bar{\mathbf{y}}_q$, belonging to $\mathbf{Y}$ and maximizing $\bar{\mathbf{p}} \cdot \Sigma \mathbf{y}_q (\Sigma \mathbf{y}_q \in \mathbf{Y})$ is equal to $\Sigma \bar{\mathbf{x}}_j$, belonging to $\mathbf{X}$ and minimizing $\bar{\mathbf{p}} \cdot \Sigma \mathbf{x}_j$ for $\Sigma \mathbf{x}_j \in \mathbf{X}^*$. That is, it can be proved that each component, $\bar{\mathbf{y}}_q$, of the efficient vector of feasible-outputs, $\bar{\mathbf{y}}$, maximizes its producer's profits at $\bar{\mathbf{p}}$ and each component of the vector of feasible-consumptions $\bar{\mathbf{x}}$ costs less than would any consumption at least as much preferred as $\bar{\mathbf{x}}_j$. There exists, then, $\bar{\mathbf{p}}$ such that each producer's profits are maximized at $\bar{\mathbf{y}}_q$ and no consumer can afford consumptions preferred to $\bar{\mathbf{x}}_j$ and at which efficient outputs $\bar{\mathbf{y}}$ are equal to aggregate consumptions $\bar{\mathbf{x}}$.

POINT. It can be proved that a Pareto optimum can be a competitive equilibrium.

If initial endowments are nil, feasible-consumptions must have zero cost for each household: revenues from sales of services (negative consumptions) must be equal to the cost of purchases. To say that more-preferred consumptions would cost more is to say that the jth consumer would have to earn more income to achieve a position preferred to $\bar{\mathbf{x}}_j$.

A number of accounting relationships can be inferred. Since firms are owned by households earning all of their incomes by selling services to firms, and since financial dealing is excluded, the present value of income payments to households must equal that of total household expenditure. Profit must be zero for each firm (recalling the possibility of inaction) in general competitive equilibrium excluding initial resource endowments. However, if $\boldsymbol{\omega} \neq \mathbf{0}$, positive profits are possible. (Cf. note at the end of ¶9.5 §§4.)

International trade is ignored. Of course, a global (i.e. 'all-earth') optimum cannot be achieved unless all trading opportunities are fully exploited. However, subsets of traders can gain, if able to form coalitions without experiencing retaliation. Finally, to the extent that some are unfavourably affected by enlargement of trading zones, the usual 'compensation' problems arise.

4. PARETO OPTIMALITY

The criteria for economic optimality in the sense of Pareto can be developed through the calculus. ¶10.4 works out some of the necessary conditions for Pareto optimality and then shows how a competitive equilibrium assures their fulfilment, always excluding 'externalities' or interdependence of utilities. The model serves another purpose. It introduces *socialism* and shows that the concept, competitive equilibrium, need not be confined to private ownership economies.

§2

There are to be two households, each consuming two commodities. The means of production are fully automated and owned by the state. The households, not able to contemplate working, receive subventions from the state. ¶10.4 §§2–3 concern technocratic criteria. ¶10.4 §§4 deals with a competitive economy within the technocratic framework of ¶10.4 §§2. ¶10.4 §§5 compares the market-equilibrium results of ¶10.4 §§4 with the technocratic criteria.

The ordinal utility function of the second household is to be maximized subject to that of the first standing at at least 100.

$$\max U(x_{12}, x_{22}) \tag{1}$$

subject to:

$$u(x_{11}, x_{21}) = 100 \tag{2}$$

$$x_1 = f(x_2) \tag{3}$$

$$x_1 = x_{11} + x_{12} \tag{4}$$

$$x_2 = x_{21} + x_{22} \tag{5}$$

Consumption of the second commodity by the first household is denoted x_{21}.

Form the Lagrange function, V:

$$V = U - \lambda_1(u - 100) - \lambda_2(x_1 - f) - \lambda_3(x_1 - x_{11} - x_{12})$$
$$- \lambda_4(x_2 - x_{21} - x_{22}) \tag{6}$$

Repeat the constraints and set the other partial derivatives equal to zero, obeying the convention that partial derivatives with respect to $x_{11}, x_{12},$ $x_1, x_{21}, x_{22},$ and x_2 are indexed by subscripts $1, 2, \ldots, 6$:

$$-\lambda_1 u_1 + \lambda_3 = 0 \tag{7}$$

$$U_2 + \lambda_3 = 0 \tag{8}$$

$$\lambda_2 + \lambda_3 = 0 \tag{9}$$

S1

$$-\lambda_1 u_4 + \lambda_4 = 0 \tag{10}$$

$$U_5 + \lambda_4 = 0 \tag{11}$$

$$\lambda_2 f' - \lambda_4 = 0 \tag{12}$$

§3

Some interesting economic implications follow from inspection of **S1**. Thus a necessary condition for Pareto optimality, for it being impossible to increase U without decreasing u, is that:

$$U_5/U_2 = \lambda_4/\lambda_3 = u_4/u_1 \tag{13}$$

The rate of substitution in consumption between the commodities must be the same for each household. Equation (13) cannot be observed if the households face different prices.

Next recall that the rate of substitution in production, dx_2/dx_1, is given by $-f'(x_2)$:

$$dx_2/dx_1 = -f'(x_2) \tag{14}$$

S1 requires that:

$$-f' = \lambda_4/\lambda_3 = U_5/U_2 = u_4/u_1 \tag{15}$$

In an optimum state, rates of substitution in production and consumption must be the same.

Introduce a third commodity, fixed in supply: $x_3 = k$; $x_{31} + x_{32} = x_3 = k$. Indexing its partial derivatives as 7 and 8, the problem is to be redefined:

$$\max U(x_{12}, x_{22}, x_{32}) \tag{16}$$

st

$$u(x_{11}, x_{21}, x_{31}) = 100 \tag{17}$$

$$x_1 = f(x_2) \tag{18}$$

$$x_{31} + x_{32} = k \tag{19}$$

$$\sum_j x_{ij} = x_i \qquad i = 1, 2 \tag{20}$$

The corresponding Lagrange function is

$$U - \lambda_1(u - 100) - \lambda_2(x_1 - f) - \lambda_3(x_1 - x_{11} - x_{12}) - \lambda_4(x_2 - x_{21} - x_{22}) - \lambda_5(k - x_{31} - x_{32}) \tag{21}$$

The first-order conditions include:

$$-\lambda_1 u_1 + \lambda_3 = 0; \tag{22}$$

$$U_2 + \lambda_3 = 0; \tag{23}$$

$$-\lambda_1 u_7 + \lambda_5 = 0; \tag{24}$$

$$U_8 + \lambda_5 = 0. \tag{25}$$

It follows that:

$$-\lambda_1 u_7 = U_8; \tag{26}$$

$$u_7/u_1 = U_8/U_2: \tag{27}$$

the rate at which each household is willing to exchange the third commodity for the first (or second) must be the same. For Pareto optimality, each household must face the same price for each commodity fixed in supply. Competition assures that this will happen. Competition also assures that nobody is willing to pay more for increments to his holdings or consumptions than other users of the commodities are willing to pay at their margins.

§4

Assume that the production-possibilities relation $x_1 = f(x_2)$ takes the form $x_1 + 2x_2 = K$, K being the aggregate stock of capital, and that production is managed by a large number of disembodied profit-maximizing directors bidding for the right to lease out capital. A competitive market organization is to be established. The subventions from the state M_1 and M_2 comprise household purchasing power. Budget constraint requires $p_1 x_{1j} + p_2 x_{2j} = M_j$. Competition amongst directors will assure $p_2 = 2p_1$ and that:

$$p_1 x_1 + p_2 x_2 = M_1 + M_2 = rK \tag{28}$$

Total revenues will be determined by the total of subsidies paid out to the households. Total rents, defining r as 1, will exhaust total revenues. Exhaustion of revenues by rental payments follows from equations (29) and (30):

$$p_1 = r = 1 \tag{29}$$

$$0 \cdot 5 p_2 = r \tag{30}$$

Hence, in equilibrium, each competitive producer equates marginal revenue with marginal cost and here average cost and marginal cost are equal, as are marginal and average revenue.

The 'competitive' general equilibrium boils down to equations (31) to (33):

$$F^1(1, 2; M_1, M_2) = f(x_2) \tag{31}$$

$$F^2(1, 2; M_1, M_2) = x_2 \tag{32}$$

$$M_1 + M_2 = K \tag{33}$$

F^1 and F^2 determine demand for the first and second commodities. At prices $(1, 2)$ producers are indifferent about the mix of their outputs. Equation (33) follows from equation (28).

Note that the aggregate supply-price of output is K dollars. Since budget constraint requires that the aggregate demand-price also be K dollars, it follows that, if equation (31) is satisfied, so must be equation (32): $p_1 F^1 + p_2 F^2 = M_1 + M_2$ (by budget constraint); $p_1 \cdot f(x_2) + p_2 x_2 = K$ (stipulation of competition assures that the aggregate supply-price will equal the aggregate cost of production). Hence the system can be reduced to a locus, $\psi(M_1, M_2) = 0$, associating 'equilibrium' subventions. Each point of the locus is associated with an 'equilibrium' pair of ordinal utilities. Each admissible distribution (M_1^*, M_2^*) associates with an ordinal utility pair (u^*, U^*).

§5

The competitive equilibrium achieves a Pareto optimum. Since prices are the same for each consumer, rates of substitution in consumption must be equal. The price, equal to marginal costs, conform to the rate at which commodities can be substituted in production. Specifically, $\bar{\lambda}_4/\bar{\lambda}_3$ can be interpreted as the price ratio p_2/p_1.

The λs *cannot* be interpreted as prices. The objective function, i.e. the function to be maximized, is expressed in units of ordinal utility. Accordingly, in the solution the λs give marginal valuations of constraint relaxations in terms of U.

The production frontier is attained: capital-capacity is exhausted and, so long as demands are insatiable, must remain exhausted.

If demands are satiable and the capital stock unlimited, for example, the 'competitive' market processes will establish rent at zero.

In the competitive equilibrium U is maximized, given $u = u^*$.

The Pareto-optimum conditions boil down to: $f' = \lambda_4/\lambda_3 = U_5/U_2 = u_4/u_1$, relative to the constraints: $x_1 = f(x_2)$, $x_1 = x_{11} + x_{12}$; $x_2 = x_{21} + x_{22}$. A competitive equilibrium can be described precisely by these equations. Remember, then, that the ratio $\bar{p}_2/\bar{p}_1$ is equal to $\bar{\lambda}_4/\bar{\lambda}_3$.

Next consider a generalization of the text's argument based on G. Hadley, *Nonlinear and Dynamic Programming*, Chap. 3.7 and 3.8, pp. 72–75. (Cf. also ¶5.2 §§5.) The dual of the primal problem defined by equations (1) to (5) is closer to hand if these equations are re-written:

$$\max U(x_1 - x_{11}, x_2 - x_{21}) \tag{34}$$

st

$$u(x_{11}, x_{21}) - 100 = 0 \quad \text{i.e., } g^1(\mathbf{x}) = 0 \tag{35}$$

$$x_1 - f(x_2) = 0 \quad \text{i.e., } g^2(\mathbf{x}) = 0 \tag{36}$$

The primal problem's solution occurs at a point at which the constraints are obeyed and at which:

$$\partial U/\partial x_j - \sum_{i=1}^{2} \lambda_i\, \partial g^i/\partial x_j = 0 \qquad j = 1, 2, \ldots, 4 \tag{37}$$

Observe the obvious condensation of notation, and note that any relative maximum can be characterized in just such a way. Denote the solution of the primal problem as $(\bar{x}, \bar{\lambda})$.

Referring back to ¶5.2 §§5, the dual problem is to *minimize* the Langrange function $U - \lambda_1 g^1 - \lambda_2 g^2 = F(x, \lambda)$ with respect to λ subject to equation (37). Just as the first- and second-order conditions of the primal problem can be satisfied at a relative maximum, so will the dual function achieve a relative minimum at such a point. Its value will be that of the primal function at its relative maximum.

Since $\bar{x}$, associated with $\bar{\lambda}$, obeys equations (35) and (36), $F(\bar{x}, \bar{\lambda}) = U(\bar{x})$. It can be shown that equation (37) can be solved uniquely for x^* upon λ^* being specified: F can be written as a function of λ. Also, it can be shown that F reaches a relative minimum at $\bar{\lambda}$ subject to equation (37). That is, subject to equation (37), there holds inequality (38):

$$F(x, \lambda) \geq F(\bar{x}, \bar{\lambda}) = U(\bar{x}) \tag{38}$$

for (x, λ) in the neighbourhood of $(\bar{x}, \bar{\lambda})$. In this neighbourhood the primal and dual problems have the same value.

The argument has developed that in the neighbourhood of a relative extremum

$$\min_{\lambda} F(\lambda) = \max_{x} U(x) \tag{39}$$

subject to constraints (37) for the dual problem and equations (35) and (36) for the primal problem. Thus the Lagrange function has a saddle point at $(\bar{x}, \bar{\lambda})$. This is $U(\bar{x}) = \min_\lambda \max_x F(x, \lambda)$ when the variation in x is restricted to the region defined by equations (35) and (36). (Note that min $F(\lambda)$ is less heavily constrained.)

Criteria for *global* extrema are neglected here, but sources are cited in ¶5.2 §§5. Needless to say, *neighbourhood* properties of global extrema are adequately described above.

Again recalling ¶5.2 §§5, observe that dualism here does not lead to a neatly-dichotomous pair of problems. There is no elegant shibboleth such as 'maximization of total revenue versus minimization of imputed resource value' emerges. (Cf. first note in this section supra.)

5. CAVEATS TO THE OPTIMALITY OF COMPETITIVE EQUILIBRIUM: 'SECOND BEST'

¶10.5 §§2 points out that usually 'efficient allocation' is not altogether relevant politically. ¶10.5 §§3 recalls the scepticism of ¶10.2 about utility-orientated approaches to social decision making. ¶10.5 §§4 recalls the 'externalities' of ¶4.3 §§11. ¶10.5 §§5 is concerned with 'second best', pointing out that, if there is a departure somewhere in the system from Pareto optimality, 'correction' of yet another deviation can make things worse instead of better.

More thoroughgoing deflation of 'optimality of competitive equilibrium' would be required, except that already it has been made clear that 'competitive equilibrium' and 'optimality' are mathematical ideas rather than descriptions of economic organizations and performance in life.

§2

Tickets for the heavyweight boxing championship are to be sold at auction. The result will be efficient: nobody outside the arena will be willing to pay more than anyone inside. Is it fair? Only rich men might be inside. Perhaps non-negotiable tickets should be distributed by lot amongst fans and the promoters reimbursed by the state. The alternative is inefficient: persons outside the arena would be glad to bribe spectators, who would wish they could take the bribes. Might not the tickets be distributed by lot and then sold in a free ticket-market? The third scheme is efficient and might satisfy the scruples of the first's critics.

In the 'real world' perhaps only schemes 1 and 2 can be considered. Alas, welfare economics can only suggest that scheme 3 is to be preferred to scheme 2 if one is willing to subject fight tickets to the market place. Once the lottery is over, nobody can have a less-preferred position under scheme 3 than under scheme 2. (Neglecting possibilities of *interdependence of utilities*. Cf. ¶10.5 §§3.) Welfare economics cannot discriminate between schemes 1 and 3 or between schemes 1 and 2: in neither instance does one scheme's distribution of welfare dominate the other's. In these instances, as in the case of alternative grain-distributions in countries threatened by famine, and in a myriad other significant problems, economic theory can only develop sets of technologically-feasible productions and consumptions and predict measurable consequences of alternative programmes.

§3

What if I am your sworn enemy, consumed with hatred of you? What if our utilities are *interdependent*? Moral judgement cannot be avoided in setting up criteria for economic distribution. Should the gods consider my attitude towards you? Indeed moral judgement *has* been important in the problem received by ¶10.5 §§3: presumably the consumption sets X_j have been bounded away from opium-smoking, radioactive watch dials, etc.

§4

Thus far Chapter 10 has dealt with models in which actions of one producer or consumer do not change terms of transformation experienced by others. Aleph's preference ordering has been defined independently of Beth's actions. One's production possibilities has been defined independently of any other's actions. ¶4.3 §§11 showed that such assumptions are restrictive, but suggested that the optimality criteria of ¶10.4 can be recast to accommodate *externalities*.

The sense of dependence is that in which terms of transformation are affected by 'outside' actions, *not* that in which consumers would be sunk if producers went on strike, for example.

That is to say, 'dependence' is a state in which producers must contemplate 'outside' activity levels in calculating their own input-output possibilities.

Externalities detach private from social costs: an upstream producer dumping waste into a river need not be concerned with social effects downstream. Still, unless the commodity spaces were redefined, competitive equilibrium no longer would satisfy Pareto optimality. Redefine the commodity space(s)? If one conjures up zoning ordinances or markets in which stream polluters, builders of garish signboards, and others are bought off, then commodities must be redefined. The analysis must be changed categorically.

More rigorously, if wastes, odours, uglinesses, etc., are to be sold in markets, 'discommodities' bearing negative prices must be defined. In a sense, to introduce technical 'diseconomies' is to drop the zero-disposal-cost assumption: the 'disaesthetics' of the American Embassy at London or the Pan-Am building at Grand Central (N.Y.C.), Britain's massive retaliation for the Golden Eagle of Grosvenor Square, cannot costlessly be buried.

It requires some ingenuity to set up a model in which 'disaesthetics' are auctioned off at negative prices. However, it can be done. Are there any amongst us who believe that the door to unfettered private enterprise in life would thus be opened?

§5

'Second Best'

Say that the social cost of rail service of a specified type is 2¢ per ton–mile whilst that of motor truck service is 10¢. Assume that the price of rail service has irrevocably been set at 12¢. A competitive motor-haulage market would settle on a 10¢ price, leading to a diversion of traffic into socially-more-expensive mode. Here a ring amongst motor truck hauliers, leading to a 20¢ price, might be welcomed.

POINT. Upon violation of Pareto optimality in one sector of the economy, it cannot be guaranteed that satisfaction of Pareto-optimum conditions in other sectors is conducive to economic efficiency in the sense of Pareto. The 'second-best' optimum might call for further departure from, say, marginal-cost pricing.

Consider another example, based on Fig. 4. The context might be provided by excise taxation. The Pareto-optimum is at P. A *permanent*

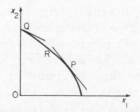

Fig. 4   An Excise-tax Example

excise tax is to be imposed on commodity 1 making it artificially expensive relative to commodity 2, leading to the 'non-optimal' equilibrium, Q. An appropriate counter-excise tax on commodity 2 could restore equilibrium at P. More interestingly, a sub-optimal counter-excise tax on commodity 2, leading to R, might be desirable. R might be preferable to Q, to the extent that persons achieving more-preferred positions at R could afford fully to compensate persons with less-preferred positions at R—and still be better off than at Q.

POINT. Once there is stipulated to be a violation of Pareto optimality, actions inefficient relative to a Pareto optimum can be desirable relative to the non-optimum state. Thus, in a sense they are efficient relative to the non-optimum state.

6. INTERTEMPORAL EFFICIENCY: INFORMAL DISCUSSION

The analysis evolves from a simple observation: today's actions generate results which must be accepted tomorrow as predetermined. Thus future terms of trade in production between metals and cloth will be affected by allocation of current output between blast furnaces and looms. Examining Fig. 5,[6] let us revert to phantasy. The economy produces two commodities. Curve I describes the frontier of the set of feasible-current-outputs, whilst consumption requirements are described by P so that the shaded area describes feasible-productions for stock(s). Now consider points A and B. Each associates with different production possibilities in the next period: each yields a different stock-carry-out position (recall the metals-textiles example). Assume that Gabriel's trumpet will sound out at the end of the second period. Judgement will be at hand. Priests, having examined entrails and witnessed auguries, have determined upon the optimal proportion, described by angle $\hat{\theta}$, of the transcendental burnt offering, comprising all capital goods, to be tendered to the brooding gods.

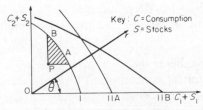

Fig. 5 Intertemporal Efficiency

The economic problem is well defined: obeying requirements imposed by production possibilities and consumptions P, maximize r in $(r, \hat{\theta})$. The criterion calls for B, not A.

In a sense productions A and B both are efficient: neither dominates the other with respect to current outputs. However, relative to the *stipulated* criterion, B is to be preferred.

§2

We move towards algebra.[7] ¶10.6 §§3 et seq. introduce some of the material of ¶10.7–¶10.9, building up to dual interpretations of closed consumptionless systems.

§3

An abstract economy contains but one scarce commodity, one which can reproduce itself. The product available in period 1 is $(1+i)$ times the stock carried out of period 0. Since output either is to be consumed or stocked, inequalities (40) to (42) follow, K being interpreted as an initial endowment of *the* commodity:

$$(1+i)y_t \geq C_{t+1} + y_{t+1} \tag{40}$$

$$C_n + y_n \leq (1+i)^n K - (1+i)^n C_0 - (1+i)^{n-1} C_1 - \ldots - (1+i)C_{n-1} \tag{41}$$

$$C_0 + C_1/(1+i) + C_2/(1+i)^2 + \ldots + C_n/(1+i)^n \leq K \tag{42}$$

Inequality (40) asserts that, if $i = 0\cdot10$ and if 100 units of stock are carried out of the tth period, total product available in period $t+1$ will be 110, if efficient procedures are followed, and that the product is to be allocated between consumption and investment. Inequality (41) follows from inequality (40). Inequality (42) is derived from inequality (41) in an especially obvious way.

§4

Two points of general economic interest are close to the surface of the argument:

1) inequality (42) looks very much like a present-value formula and, indeed, the analogy has deep purport;
2) rates of substitution between outputs of different dating easily are calculated.

Taking 1) and 2) together, a theory of price emerges.

Pursuing 2), a unit of consumption foregone during period t can be converted into $(1+i)^h$ units of consumption in period $(t+h)$: the technological rate of substitution between consumptions in periods t and $(t+h)$ is

$(1+i)^h$. It hardly is surprising that ¶10.9 reveals the implication that in competitive equilibrium, if $\bar{p}_t = 1$, then $\bar{p}_{t+h} = 1/(1+i)^h$, $\bar{p}_{t+h}$ being the equilibrium price at date t for delivery during period $(t+h)$.

§5

Some themes pertaining to the *von Neumann* model of ¶10.8 can be sounded now.

Preclude consumption: the growth (or decay) factor is to be net. Then equation (43) follows:

$$y_t = K(1+i)^t \tag{43}$$

The maximum attainable product available in the tth period is, in this discrete model, calculated by compounding the initial stock K and its increments. Indeed a pretentious, but eventually significant, assertion can be made now: the maximum attainable rate of growth of the embryonic system is $100i$ per cent per period.

The argument cries out to be fulfilled by insertion of its dualistic potential. Provide a (competitive) market-oriented interpretation and then compare the resulting equilibrium 'rental rate' with the technologically-determined rate of growth.

A grand *tâtonnement* is to occur at period 0. The large group of potential producers are to bid for the power to hire capital. The standard-form lease requires that lessees have possession of increments to capital, as well as initial acquisitions. They are to take this into account when bidding.

If the price of a unit of capital is defined as \$1, competition amongst producer-lessees will force up the equilibrium rent to \$i per period. No producer could profitably commit himself to a higher rental. The equilibrium rental can be transformed into a rate of interest: any lease can be interpreted as a loan.

POINT. The competitive equilibrium appurtenant to the simple closed consumptionless system of ¶10.6 §§5 finds the rate of interest equal to the maximum attainable rate of growth and finds output growing at the maximum attainable rate.

Define the primal problem as maximization of y_T subject to the system's technology and $K_0 = \hat{K}$. The dual problem is to minimize total rental payments st profits not being positive. The resulting 'shadow' interest rate is the minimum interest rate consistent with the dual constraints. Hence it is equal to i, the maximum rate of growth—the rate of growth chosen by profit-maximizing *entrepreneurs*.

7. LEONTIEF SYSTEMS

¶10.7 is largely self-contained, although its main purpose is to lay a foundation for the accumulation problems of ¶10.8 and ¶10.9. It is based on the massive work of Professor Wassily Leontief.

§ 2

In the beginning is technology. The central idea is *production of commodities by means of commodities.* Each unit of final product is produced by a unique linear combination of commodities and 'labour'. If the final outputs are treated more or less as consumptions, rather than merely as a basis for future activity, the model is said to be *open.* Otherwise it is *closed.* Since ¶10.7 is to lead into ¶10.8 and ¶10.9, it will come to focus on *closed* Leontief systems.

In order to fix ideas, consider a system comprised of steel, automobiles, and textiles. Two automobiles can be produced by combining 2 units of steel, 3 units of textiles and 1 automobile (which must die if 2 automobiles are to emerge at the end of the period). We adopt the convention of subtracting automobiles used up in the production of automobiles from final output so that, as a matter of accounting convention, the automobile-input requirement in automobile production will be recorded as zero. If 100 automobiles are to be produced on net, there must be used up 200 units of steel and 300 units of textiles. Equivalent calculations for steel and textiles permit computation of commodity requirements for any bill of final demands. Labour requirements are similarly built up.

Turning to algebra, an *input coefficient,* a_{rs}, the amount of the rth commodity required in the production of a unit of net output of the sth, can be calculated in this linear single-technology system by dividing the total amount of the rth commodity used in production of the sth, x_{rs}, by the total output of the sth, y_s, that is to say $a_{rs} = x_{rs}/y_s$, noting that a_{rr} has been established as 0. The *input matrix* $\mathbf{A}^* = (a_{rs})$ follows at once, keeping in mind that each activity yields but one output. Equation (44) defines the *technology matrix,* $\mathbf{A}$:

$$\mathbf{A} = \mathbf{I} - \mathbf{A}^* \tag{44}$$

$\mathbf{A}$ is a $(n+1) \times (n+1)$ matrix, proper commodities running from 1 to n and labour being the $(n+1)$st. $\mathbf{I}$ is an $(n+1) \times (n+1)$ matrix with unit diagonal elements and zero off-diagonal elements:

$$\mathbf{A} = \mathbf{I} - \mathbf{A}^* = \begin{bmatrix} 1 & -a_{12} \ldots & -a_{1n+1} \\ -a_{21} & 1 & \ldots -a_{2n+1} \\ \cdots\cdots\cdots\cdots\cdots\cdots\cdots\cdots \\ -a_{n+11} & & \ldots & 1 \end{bmatrix} \tag{45}$$

In Leontief's *open* system fuel for the labour force is ignored: $a_{1n+1} = a_{2n+1} = \ldots = a_{nn+1} = 0$. The labour requirement for unit output of the rth commodity is a_{n+1r}. Denote $(a_{n+11}, \ldots, a_{n+1n})$ as $(c_1, \ldots, c_n)$ but put aside vector $\mathbf{c}$ so that the matrix $\mathbf{A}$ gives way to the $n \times n$ matrix $\hat{\mathbf{A}}$ of equation (46) in Leontief's *open* system. (The model will be reinterpreted when Leontief's *closed* system is taken up in detail.)

$$\hat{A} = \begin{bmatrix} 1 & -a_{12} \ldots -a_{1n} \\ \cdots\cdots\cdots\cdots\cdots \\ -a_{n1} & \ldots & 1 \end{bmatrix} \tag{46}$$

It follows that a basic equilibrium condition in such an *open* Leontief system is:

$$\hat{A}y = x \tag{47}$$

The vector y describes total outputs and x is a vector of final demands. Of course, we are especially interested in total commodity-input requirements associated with a given bill of final demands, noting that the total labour requirements are:

$$c'y = c_1 y_1 + c_2 y_2 + \ldots + c_n y_n \tag{48}$$

Commodity-input requirements are:

$$y = \hat{A}^{-1}x \tag{49}$$

The matrix inversion of equation (49) is vital for a number of practical problems: thus compare determination of the economic impact of military procurements.

It is assumed that the Leontief models are *productive*. Matrix A is productive if a nonnegative vector z exists such that $z > Az$. Obviously, if it takes more than 1 automobile as input to produce 1 automobile, a model including automobiles as an output is unproductive. The Hawkins–Simon conditions would not then be met. (Cf. *DOSSO*, pp. 215–218, 234–237, for an excellent discussion of the Hawkins–Simon conditions and their relation to Böhm–Bawerkian capital theory.) Finally, we assume that Leontief systems are *indecomposable*: each industry either directly or indirectly is both supplier to and buyer from each other. (An industry using automobiles, but not buying steel as such, is an indirect customer of the steel industry.) Cf. *DOSSO*, pp. 254–260.

§3

We next develop a value-orientated counterpart to the technocratic 'equilibrium condition' of equation (47). Defining the nominal wage unit (*money wage rate*) as 1, construct a vector of prices $(p_1, \ldots, p_n)$ so that the wage bill becomes allocated amongst the net outputs, i.e. final demands, x, and so that each commodity's total labour costs (direct- plus indirect-labour-costs) are equal to its price:

$$\hat{A}'p = c \tag{50}$$

In words, when commodity–input costs are subtracted from the corresponding commodity price, the difference is to be equal to its direct labour cost. The value of each activity, exclusive of direct labour cost, is to be exhausted by direct labour cost. Since the value of each net output (final demand) is accounted for by direct labour costs, it follows that:

$$\mathbf{p} \cdot \mathbf{x} = \mathbf{c} \tag{51}$$

Equation (51) conforms to general economic reasoning: labour is the only possible scarce resource under the model's specifications. If labour were available in unlimited quantities, there would be no limit to attainable productions. Of course, this labour theory of value would break down if some other *primary resource* were introduced or if the system were closed up so that no one input (i.e. output) could be singled out as a primary resource. If indeed a number of primary resources were to exist, economically sound accounting practice would allocate the value of final outputs amongst the scarce primary resources.

§ 4

The equilibrium conditions for the *closed* Leontief system are:

$$\mathbf{Ay} = \mathbf{0} \tag{52}$$

$$\mathbf{A'p} = \mathbf{0} \tag{53}$$

The concept of final demand is abandoned. Instead coefficients $(a_{1n+1}, \ldots, a_{nn+1})$ are interpreted as requirements of the first, second, ... commodity necessary to sustain and thus in a sense to produce a unit of labour. Thus the last of the 'equilibrium conditions' of equations (52) becomes expressed:

$$y_{n+1} = \sum_{i}^{n} a_{n+1i} y_i \tag{54}$$

The rth equilibrium condition of equations (53) can be written:

$$p_r = a_{1r} p_1 + \ldots + a_{r-1r} p_{r-1} + a_{r+1} p_{r+1} + \ldots + a_{n+1} p_{n+1} \tag{55}$$

p_{n+1} being the *wage rate*. Prices, thus determined up to a factor of proportionality, will lead to exhaustion of value products and to zero-profit production.

Equations (52) and (53) cannot be solved unless the rank of the $(n+1) \times (n+1)$ matrix $\mathbf{A}$ does not exceed n. Therefore, the solution of equations (52) defines achievable *structures* of outputs: the scale is *not* determined.

§ 5

The analysis of Leontief's *open* system can be reduced to that of a particularly simple linear programme in which the primal problem is:

$$\text{min. wage bill} = z = \mathbf{c'y} \text{ subject to } \hat{\mathbf{A}}\mathbf{y} = \mathbf{x}, \mathbf{y} \geq \mathbf{0} \tag{56}$$

and its dual is:

$$\text{max. value of output} = \mathbf{x}'\mathbf{p} \text{ subject to } \mathbf{\hat{A}}'\mathbf{p} = \mathbf{c}, \mathbf{p} \geq \mathbf{0} \qquad (57)$$

Vectors $\mathbf{x}$ and the technology $\begin{pmatrix} \mathbf{\hat{A}} \\ \mathbf{c}' \end{pmatrix}$ are given. A feasible solution to the primal problem has been shown to be:

$$\mathbf{y} = \mathbf{\hat{A}}^{-1}\mathbf{x} \qquad (58)$$

and a feasible solution to the dual problem has been shown to be:

$$\mathbf{p} = (\mathbf{\hat{A}}')^{-1}\mathbf{c} \qquad (59)$$

However, if there exist feasible solutions to these problems, the solutions will be the same and optimal: there are n variables and n side relations in both the primal and dual problems. Of course, the optimal values of the problems being the same, the value of final demands (net outputs) is equal to the value of factor payments in equilibrium. National income equals national expenditure for optimal feasible input–output combinations.

§6

Are the reported Leontief results sensitive to the stipulation that producers can consider only one technology for the production of the rth commodity? No. A remarkable *substitution theorem* gives the following result. If a very large number of Leontief techniques, each yielding one output, are available, and if $\mathbf{S}^*$, a particular set of techniques—one for each requirement—is optimal relative to final demands $\mathbf{x}^*$, then $\mathbf{S}^*$ will be optimal for any vector of final demands $\mathbf{x} \in \mathbf{X}$, where $\mathbf{X}$ is the set of final demands which can be produced under the labour-capacity limitation. Hence the set $\mathbf{S}^{**}$ of all available techniques excluding $\mathbf{S}^*$ can be neglected.

A sketch of a proof can be drawn up following Gale.[8] *First*, there can be proved a lemma arising from the following problem:

minimize $\mathbf{y} \cdot \mathbf{c}$ subject to $\mathbf{Ay} = \mathbf{b}^*$. ($\mathbf{b}^*$ can be interpreted as a vector of final demands and $\mathbf{c}$ as a vector of labour requirements.)

Consider a set of independent rows $\mathbf{S}_i$ comprising $\mathbf{A}$. $\mathbf{S}_i$ is an *optimal feasible basis*, if there exists an optimal feasible vector $\mathbf{y}$ relative to $\mathbf{S}_i$. The lemma is:

if $\mathbf{S}_i$ is an optimal feasible basis for the original problem, then $\mathbf{S}_i$ is an optimal feasible basis for a different problem, viz. to minimize $\mathbf{y} \cdot \mathbf{c}$ subject to $\mathbf{Ay} = \mathbf{b}^{**}$.

Secondly, the concept of *output space* is to be defined. An *output space* is simply the set of all feasible-outputs. *Thirdly*, specify the bill of final demands as **b*** and set out to minimize labour-utilization $\mathbf{y} \cdot \mathbf{c}$. Denote $\bar{\mathbf{y}}$ as a basic optimal solution for this problem. The n-vector $\bar{\mathbf{y}}$ can depend on n activities at most. There never can be more basic activities in the solution of a linear programme than there are binding constraints. In this way a particular basis, $\bar{\mathbf{A}}$, is established: $\bar{\mathbf{A}}$ is the technology matrix associated with $\bar{\mathbf{y}}$. *Fourthly*, since $\bar{\mathbf{A}}$ is known to be *productive*:

$$(\mathbf{I} - \bar{\mathbf{A}})\mathbf{y}^{**} = \mathbf{b}^{**} \qquad (60)$$

b** being another bill of final demands. The lemma asserts that **y**** is an optimal feasible vector relative to the set of all bases which can be erected for productions **Y**.

§ 7

In ¶10.7 §§8 a *closed* Leontief system is dynamized. *Time-paths* of productions involving stocks of capital are analysed. As it happens, ¶10.7 §§8 uncritically depicts a simple Leontief model in order to fix ideas. Certain crucial reservations are postponed until ¶10.7 §§9.

§ 8

In addition to the technology matrix **A**, consider the matrix $\mathbf{B} = (b_{rs})$. The element b_{rs} is the accelerator coefficient for the rth capital (including working capital) requirement for the sth output. A unit increase in y_s requires an increase in the rth capital stock of b_{rs}. (Thus automobile production requires that there be steels held in stock in addition to requiring that steel be used up in automobile manufacture.) Permitting continuous variation in time:

$$\mathbf{Ay} = \mathbf{B\dot{y}} \qquad (61)$$

Equations (61) comprise a set of simultaneous linear differential equations. Try as a solution:

$$\mathbf{y} = \mathbf{k}e^{-\lambda t} \qquad (62)$$

so that:

$$\dot{\mathbf{y}} = -\mathbf{k}\lambda e^{-\lambda t} \qquad (63)$$

Substituting into equations (61):

$$(\mathbf{A} + \lambda\mathbf{B})\mathbf{k} = \mathbf{0} \qquad (64)$$

The next steps have become familiar. Solve for λ so that $|A + \lambda B| = 0$; solve for **k** up to factors of proportionality, satisfying the resulting set of simultaneous linear equations whose $(n+1) \times (n+1)$ matrix now has rank no greater than n. Solving the characteristic equation, vector λ, includes conjugate-complex values, since A and B are not symmetric. The general solution is of the form:

$$y = \sum_{s}^{n} A_s k_s e^{-\lambda_s t} \qquad (65)$$

i.e.:

$$y_r = A_1 k_{r1} e^{-\lambda_1 t} + A_2 k_{r2} e^{-\lambda_2 t} + \ldots + A_n k_{rn} e^{-\lambda_n t} \text{ for all } r \qquad (66)$$

Values A_s are arbitrary constants to be determined by initial conditions. A vector, such as $(k_{1s}, \ldots, k_{ms})$, is an *eigenvector* corresponding to the *eigenvalue* λ_s. There is one such vector for each root of the characteristic equation. It is *not* arbitrary. It is determined, up to a factor of proportionality, by the system's structure and satisfies an appropriate set of homogeneous linear equations (cf. equations (64)). Finally, any pair of conjugate-complex roots can be combined into an expression of the form $A k_r e^{-\alpha t} \cos(\omega t - \varepsilon)$, A and ε being arbitrary constants.

There is a sense in which a dynamic *closed* Leontief system has an equilibrium, namely if it tends towards *balanced growth* so that:

$$\dot{y}_r/y_r \to -\lambda_m \quad \text{and} \quad y_r/y_s \to k_{rm}/k_{sm} \quad \text{as } t \to \infty \qquad (67)$$

λ_m being the dominant root of the system and taken to be real and negative. If the system is stable, it will tend towards balanced growth at the rate $-\lambda_m$ regardless of the initial configuration of stocks and outputs. In any event, equation (65) plots the future of a dynamic *closed* Leontief system once initial conditions are specified.

The system's technological requirements must be satisfied in the solution. Cf. ¶10.7 §§9.

In a dynamical *open* Leontief system, final demand paths are defined on time. There then remain to be calculated output paths which will obey the technology, produce the final demands, and minimize labour utilization.

§9

DOSSO, pp. 295–300, point out that, for a fixed Leontief technology, arbitrarily-prescribed initial stocks will only exceptionally be consistent with obedience of the equalities of ¶10.7 §§8. In general, determinacy requires an inequality formulation.

The intertemporal indeterminacy of the dynamized Leontief system, as against the strict determinacy of statical Leontief systems, results from possibilities for intertemporal substitution in production. Future consumption requirements can be produced ahead of time. Intertemporal Leontief production possibilities are not locked in.

Still there does exist an initial stock-configuration permitting steady growth without excess capacities. This balanced-growth rate is the greatest which can be achieved. It exceeds any balanced-growth rate requiring excess capacities.

Finally, ¶10.9 shows that a programme based on the maximum attainable balanced-growth rate is efficient, more or less in the sense of Pareto, but that any other balanced-growth programme is inefficient.

8. THE VON NEUMANN MODEL AND STEADY GROWTH[9]

¶10.8 attempts a concise summary of the late J. von Neumann's remarkable growth model, partly because modern growth theory cannot be understood without it and partly to complete the foundation for the analysis of optimality of accumulation paths suggested in ¶10.6 and completed in ¶10.9.

§ 2

The von Neumann model is a general linear model of production. There is specified a set of activities, each yielding a number of outputs; there are specified alternative procedures for commodity productions. Specifically, there are m activities operated at levels $\mathbf{x}$, $\mathbf{x}$ being the vector $(x_1, \ldots, x_m)$. The rth activity, operated at unit level, is associated with two non-negative n-vectors, (a_r) and (b_r): an input vector $(a_{r1}, \ldots, a_{rn})$ and an output vector $(b_{r1}, \ldots, b_{rn})$. The input matrix $\mathbf{A} = (a_{rs})$ consists of m rows (one for each activity) and n columns (one for each commodity) as does the $m \times n$ output matrix $\mathbf{B}$. Total input and output requirements are given by the column vectors yielded by $\mathbf{A}'\mathbf{x}$ and $\mathbf{B}'\mathbf{x}$.

The model is *closed*: 'there is no flow of goods to or from the model'.[10] We recall the sociology of *closed* models of production from ¶10.7.

Feasibility requires that the model produce its own inputs and is assured by assuming that:

1) $(b_{1s}, \ldots, b_{ms}) \geq 0$ for all s

2) $(a_{r1}, \ldots, a_{rn}) \geq 0$ for all r

Each commodity is an output of some activity. Each activity must have at least one input.

The expansion of the model can be defined in terms of its input and output matrices:

$$\mathbf{B}'\mathbf{x} \geq \alpha \mathbf{A}'\mathbf{x} \tag{68}$$

Each of outputs $\mathbf{B}'\mathbf{x}$ is at least α times as great as each of corresponding inputs $\mathbf{A}'\mathbf{x}$: the n-vector $\mathbf{b}$ is at least α times as great as the n-vector $\mathbf{a}$. But:

1) the scalar α need not exceed unity. The system can decay;

2) each commodity appears in the same order in vectors a and b;

3) it is possible for $a_s = b_s = 0$.

§3

Defining the *technological* expansion problem, find an m-vector x and a scalar α such that α is maximized subject to $\mathbf{B}'\mathbf{x} \geq \alpha \mathbf{A}'\mathbf{x}$, $\mathbf{x} \geq 0$. The solution is $(\bar{\alpha}, \bar{\mathbf{x}})$. It can be proved that there exists $\bar{\alpha} > 0$ for models of this specification.

§4

Defining the *economic* expansion problem, find an n-vector $\mathbf{p}$ and a scalar β such that β is minimized subject to $\mathbf{Bp} \leq \beta \mathbf{Ap}$. Denote the solution values $\bar{\beta}$ and $\bar{\mathbf{p}}$. Call $\bar{\mathbf{p}}$ an optimal price vector. It can be proved that there exists $\bar{\beta} > 0$ for models of this specification.

It is natural to interpret β as an interest- or profit-factor. We sense that the economic problem is the *dual* of the technological problem.

$\mathbf{Bp}$ defines a revenue vector and $\mathbf{Ap}$ a cost vector. For $\bar{\beta} = 1 \cdot 05$, the inequality $\mathbf{Bp} \leq \beta \mathbf{Ap}$ requires that:

$$\frac{\text{revenue from } r\text{th activity}}{\text{cost of } r\text{th activity}} \leq 1 \cdot 05 \tag{69}$$

The minimum rate of profit on sales, consistent with the constraint that net revenues must not grow more rapidly than $100(\bar{\beta} - 1)$ per cent per period, is 5 per cent per period.

If the economic interpretation is to hold up under competitive stipulations, the rate of profit must be the same in each operated activity. Now consider *opportunity cost*: rational *entrepreneurs* consider profits of foregone opportunities as a cost of operating the rth activity. The constraint $\mathbf{Bp} \leq \beta \mathbf{Ap}$ requires that marginal ($=$ average) profits, properly interpreted, be non-positive. Since profits are zero for non-operated activities, the economic interpretation requires that profits, properly interpreted, be zero in each operated activity. In competitive equilibrium opportunity costs must absorb net revenues in linear-homogeneous models of production.

§5

Can the economic interpretation hold up? Yes. However, the explanation requires deeper probing into the economic expansion problem as the dual of the technological expansion problem. We first note that the constraints of both the primal (technological) and dual (economic) problems are non-linear in the unknowns $(\alpha, \mathbf{x})$ or $(\beta, \mathbf{p})$. The possibilities are richer and the proofs harder than in linear programming, although the expansion-model and linear programming both belong to convex programming.

The following lemma can be proved:

$$\bar{\beta} \leq \bar{\alpha} \tag{70}$$

Inequality (70) leads to the desired result, $\bar{\alpha} = \bar{\beta}$ (the duality theorem) through another fundamental theorem, due to von Neumann, asserting that, under the stipulations of the ¶10.8 model, there must exist non-negative vectors $\bar{\mathbf{x}}$ and $\bar{\mathbf{p}}$ and a scalar γ such that:

$$\mathbf{B}'\bar{\mathbf{x}} \geq \gamma \mathbf{A}'\bar{\mathbf{x}} \tag{71}$$

and if:

$$b_{1s}\bar{x}_1 + \ldots + b_{ms}\bar{x}_m > \gamma(a_{1s}\bar{x}_1 + \ldots + a_{ms}\bar{x}_m) \quad \text{then} \quad \bar{p}_s = 0; \tag{72}$$

$$\mathbf{B}\bar{\mathbf{p}} \leq \gamma \mathbf{A}\bar{\mathbf{p}} \tag{73}$$

and if:

$$b_{r1}\bar{p}_1 + \ldots + b_{rn}\bar{p}_n < \gamma(a_{r1}\bar{p}_1 + \ldots + a_{rn}\bar{p}_n) \quad \text{then} \quad \bar{x}_r = 0. \tag{74}$$

Expressions (72) and (73) assert that equilibrium prices of commodities whose outputs are increasing more than γ times their inputs will be zero—expression (72)—and that activities unable to earn rates of profit as great as $100(\gamma - 1)$ per cent per period will not be operated—expression (74). More precisely, the suggested economic interpretations make these assertions.

Expression (72) requires additional glossing: if the rate of growth of the sth output exceeds its requirement as an input in this *closed* consumptionless system, it is redundant. The only objective of production in a consumptionless system is to provide inputs.

It follows from the lemma that $\bar{\alpha} \geq \gamma$; $\bar{\beta} \leq \gamma$: inequalities (71) and (73) are identical with constraints $\mathbf{B}'\mathbf{x} \geq \alpha\mathbf{A}'\mathbf{x}$ and $\mathbf{B}\mathbf{p} \leq \beta\mathbf{A}\mathbf{p}$, except that γ replaces α and β. The lemma imposes upper and lower bounds on α and β. It remains to establish stipulations under which $\bar{\alpha} = \bar{\beta}$. The controlling duality theorem reads: if the model defined by $(\mathbf{A}, \mathbf{B})$ is *irreducible*, then $\bar{\alpha} = \bar{\beta}$. An *irreducible* model of production is one which cannot be partitioned, so that a subset of commodities can be produced without resort to commodities excluded from the subset. Accordingly, if all commodities are required in the production of any one commodity, model $(\mathbf{A}, \mathbf{B})$ is *irreducible* and $\bar{\alpha} = \bar{\beta}$.

POINT. In the *irreducible* von Neumann model, the maximum attainable rate of balanced growth is equal to the minimum rate of profit consistent with secularly-stationary relative prices under competition. These profits are equal to 'opportunity rent' of employed capital. The maximized rate of balanced growth characterizing von Neumann equilibrium is equal to the rate of profit in the von Neumann equilibrium.

'Balanced growth' should be glossed. A more precise locution might be 'balanced growth of scarce outputs' or 'balanced growth after disposal'. It is possible that the rate of growth of some outputs, priced at zero, will tend to exceed $(\alpha - 1)$ 100 per cent per period. However, the underlying zero-cast-of-disposal assumption permits us to ignore disposal-economics and to specify that in the *closed* consumptionless von Neumann system excess outputs are discarded, so that net outputs all grow at the same rate, which is the gross rate of growth of scarce (non-zero-priced) outputs.

Since no limits on primary resources are specified, only relative prices and relative activity intensities are determined in von Neumann equilibrium. The scale is left open.

§ 6

It is shown in ¶10.9 that a von Neumann path is in some sense efficient, and that no path of balanced growth, other than one exhibiting the maximized rate of growth can be efficient. It is shown in ¶10.9 that a von Neumann path can be a path of moving competitive equilibrium.

'Efficiency' is technocratic: tastes and preferences are not consulted. Thus if military matériel were amongst the commodities, an inefficient and, as it happens, an unbalanced path might be chosen, along which armaments become less and less important. The objective might be to maximize in some sense the rate of decay of the armaments sector, subject to various constraints.

¶10.8 §§6 then modulates to ¶10.9 which focuses on certain queries. How can efficient-production criteria be applied to dynamic models of production? In such dynamic models does the theory of competitive equilibrium continue to be linked up with that of economic optimality? Yes. The explanation climaxes and completes the book's primary objective: it shows how modern economic theory spans almost the whole range of resource-use problems with a few theorems of great power.

9. OPTIMALITY AND ACCUMULATION[11]

The neo-classical model of ¶10.4 is to be extended to two periods in ¶10.9 §§2, yielding Pareto-optimum results which are easily generalized.[12] It becomes obvious that the optimality of competitive equilibrium is preserved in intertemporal analysis. Then ¶10.9 §§3 analyses criteria for efficiency in *closed* consumptionless systems, ¶10.9 §§4 works out efficiency properties of a particular (von Neumann) mode of balanced growth, ¶10.9 §§5 collects some results on the efficiency of various modes of accumulation, ¶10.9 §§6 briefly analyses *turnpike theory* and ¶10.9 §§7 makes two final qualifications.

§2

Let us revise the model of ¶10.4. Only one commodity is to be considered, one which either can be consumed in the first period or stocked and used as productive capital in the second. It cannot directly be carried over for consumption in the second period: compare eggs which, if not eaten today, can be used only as 'cooking eggs' tomorrow. Utility functions are to be defined on consumptions in each of the periods and on end-period stocks. (Only *final* stocks are attributed to households. Intermediate stocks, productive agents, are the state's property.) Output in the first period is predetermined by the specified socialized basic apparatus and by the stock of 'cooking eggs' carried into the period. System **S1** results:

$$\max U(x_{12}, x_{22}, S_2) \tag{75}$$

subject to:

$$u(x_{11}, x_{21}, S_1) = 100 \tag{76}$$

$$y_2 = F(z) \tag{77}$$

S1

$$y_1^0 = x_{11} + x_{12} + z \tag{78}$$

$$y_2 = x_{21} + x_{22} + S_1 + S_2 \tag{79}$$

Here x_{21} and x_{22} are second-period consumptions, y_1 and y_2 are outputs, z is a carry-over of period 1 production into the second period, and S_1 and S_2 are final stocks. Partial derivatives with respect to $x_{11}, x_{12}, x_{21}, x_{22}, S_1, S_2, y_2$ and z are to be indexed $1, 2, \ldots, 8$.

The Lagrange function is:

$$U(x_{12}, x_{22}, S_2) - \lambda_1(u - 100) - \lambda_2(y_2 - F)$$
$$- \lambda_3(y_1^0 - x_{11} - x_{12} - z) - \lambda_4(y_2 - x_{21} - x_{22} - S_1 - S_2) \tag{80}$$

Amongst the first-order conditions are:

$$-\lambda_1 u_1 + \lambda_3 = 0 \tag{81}$$

$$U_2 + \lambda_3 = 0 \tag{82}$$

$$-\lambda_1 u_3 - \lambda_4 = 0 \tag{83}$$

$$U_4 - \lambda_4 = 0 \tag{84}$$

$$-\lambda_1 u_5 - \lambda_4 = 0 \tag{85}$$

$$U_6 - \lambda_4 = 0 \tag{86}$$

$$-\lambda_2 + \lambda_4 = 0 \tag{87}$$

$$\lambda_2 F' + \lambda_3 = 0 \tag{88}$$

On inspection it is required that $u_3 = u_5$ and $U_4 = U_6$. Marginal utilities of second period consumption and *final* stock carry-out must be the same for each household, noting that utility functions are being defined *now* in contemplation of current and future activities.[13] Equations (81) to (84) require that $u_1/u_3 = U_2/U_4$. Intertemporal rates of substitution in consumption must be the same for all households. Equation (88), together with equations (83) and (84), require that the intertemporal rate of substitution in consumption be equal to that in production, that $F' = U_2/U_4 = u_1/u_3$, i.e. $U_4F' = U_2$. In words, optimality requires that, if households are willing at the margin to give up 1·5 units of current consumption for 2·0 units of second period consumption, 'firms' should at the margin be able to obtain 2·0 units of second period output with an incremental 'cooking egg' input of 1·5 units.

A competitive equilibrium assures that intertemporal substitution rates will be the same for both households and that *final* stocks will be valued by each household on a par with second period consumption: prices will be the same for each. Prices of final period stocks and consumption will be the same since their costs are the same. (The *tâtonnement* is to be held 'now'. Prices of future goods are properties of contracts drawn up now and calling for future deliveries.) Finally, profit maximization by branch managers will assure that the value of incremental sales of goods for delivery in the second period will be equal to the minimum cost of production of an incremental unit, i.e., $p_z = p_1 = F'(z) \cdot p_2$.

The system's implicit rate of interest is $100(F'(z) - 1)$ per cent per period. The rate of time preference in equilibrium is $100(F'(z) - 1)$ per cent per period. Define time preference as $100((u_1/u_2) - 1)$ per cent per period.

Thus in a competitive equilibrium $u_1/u_3 = U_2/U_4 = p_1/p_2 = F'(z)$.

POINT. The Pareto-optimality of competitive equilibrium is preserved when intertemporal production of commodities by means of commodities is introduced.

§ 3[14]

Focus now on *productive* efficiency, recalling that, whatever sequence of outputs is conceived to be yielded up by tastes *cum* technology, there always exists a productively efficient sequence which is at least as preferable as the stipulated sequence.

Production continues to be in the manner of ¶10.9 §§2: current-output possibilities depend upon stocks carried over from past outputs. However, consumption is excluded. Choice concerns selection of an optimal path of intermediate stocks. Consumption, in the ordinary sense, is encompassed within input requirements. Taking up a two-commodity, T period system, define a point belonging to an efficient (and mathematically very well behaved) intertemporal set as in equation (89):

$$S_{2T} = F(S_{1T}; S_{1T-1}, S_{2T-1})$$ (89)

More generally:

$$S_{2t} = F(S_{1t}; S_{1t-1}, S_{2t-1})$$ (90)

Specifying the *final* stock of the first commodity at the level $\hat{S}_{1T}$ and obeying the production function F, applicable to all periods, maximize the *final* stock of the second commodity, S_{2T}, the constraints being:

$$F(S_{1t}; S_{1t-1}, S_{2t-1}) - S_{2t} = 0 \qquad t = 1, 2, \dots, T-1$$ (91)

$$S_{1T} = \hat{S}_{1T}$$ (92)

After setting up the standard Lagrange function and putting partial derivatives equal to zero, the representative first-order condition is found to be:

$$\frac{-F^{t+1}_{S_{1t}}}{F^{t+1}_{S_{2t}}} = F^{t}_{S_{1t}}$$ (93)

The symbol, $F^{t}_{S_{1t}}$, represents the rate of substitution between outputs of the second and first commodities in the tth period. Since F is invariant against dating, superscripts merely identify the times at which F and its partial derivatives are to be evaluated. Thus $F^{t+1}_{S_{1t}}$ represents the marginal productivity of the first commodity as an agent of production of the second in the $(t+1)$st period. Let an increment of the first commodity be abjured in this period: an increment of the second commodity becomes available in the next period. Now equation (93) shows that the increase in next period's availability of the second commodity, achieved by producing the first commodity in this period and transforming it into the second commodity next period, must equal the alternative increment.

Equations (90) and (93) comprise a pair of first-order, non-linear difference equations in S_1 and S_2, their solutions giving paths of efficient production of the two commodities. Note that optimal paths generally depend on initial stocks S_{10} and S_{20} and on the required level of S_{1T}, i.e. $\hat{S}_{1t}$.

It already has been established that moving, idealized competitive equilibria achieve loci required by the solution of equations (90) and (93). It remains to study the efficiency properties of a particular mode of growth—*balanced* growth.

§4

Many growth criteria become observationally indistinguishable under *balanced* growth. Recalling the 'Marxian' analysis of Chapter 2, if workers do not save, the rate of growth of the wage bill is an increasing function of the rate of profit. Again, consider a system with fixed techniques of production in which workers' biological requirements can be met only by a certain quantum *per caput* per period of *the* consumer good—perhaps a fortified mush. The Stalinist Tsar might care only to maximize the rate of growth of capital. But what does it matter? The system's technology demands that consumer good production grows at the same rate as that of capital. A neo-Malenkov, concerned to maximize the rate of growth of consumption, would adopt a policy which would be observationally indistinguishable from that of a neo-Stalin. (Of course, growth modes in which inputs and outputs obey rigid proportions, including balanced growth, lend themselves to extreme aggregation.)

In *balanced* growth, stocks maintain fixed proportions with each other. In ¶10.9 §§3 terms, if $100(g-1)$ per cent per period were the rate of *balanced* growth and if the two stocks were in proportion b:

$$S_{1t} = S_{10}g^t \qquad (94)$$

$$S_{2t} = bS_{10}g^t \qquad (95)$$

Substituting these values into equation (90):

$$bS_{10}g^t = F(S_{10}g^t; S_{10}g^{t-1}, bS_{10}g^{t-1}) \qquad (96)$$

It is to be assumed that F is first-order homogeneous in its arguments, that if the variables $S_{1t}, S_{1t-1}, S_{2t-1}$ were changed in proportion k, S_{2t} would change in proportion k. Choose $k = 1/S_{10}g^{t-1}$:

$$bg = F(g; 1, b) \qquad (97)$$

By Euler's theorem, the partial derivatives of F are zero-order homogeneous: they are invariant against the choice of k. Accordingly, upon stipulation of a balanced mode of growth, equation (93) can be written:

$$F^t_{S_{1t}}(g; 1, b) \cdot F^{t+1}_{S_{2t}}(g; 1, b) + F^{t+1}_{S_{1t}}(g; 1, b) = 0 \qquad (98)$$

Equation (97) is to be interpreted as a locus of feasible pairs of *balanced* growth-rates and capital structures. Now if we index the partial derivative of F^t with respect to S_{1t} and of F^{t+1} with respect to S_{1t} and S_{2t} by 1, 2, 3 so that $F^t_{S_{1t}} = F^t_1$, superscripts can be dropped. Next differentiate equation (97) with respect to g and b, noting that $F_g = F_1$ and $F_b = F_3$. g and b are merely values which can be substituted for S_{1t} and S_{2t-1} at date t because of the first-order homogeneity of F. Equation (99) follows:

$$dg/db = (F_3 - g)/(b - F_1) \qquad (99)$$

Deviously, we note that $dg/db = 0$ for $F_3 = g$: an extreme value for g and its associated capital structure (b) can be obtained by solving equations

(100) and (101), denoting F_3 as $\phi(g, b)$:

$$bg = F(g, b) \tag{100}$$

Cf. equation (97).

$$g = \phi(g, b) \tag{101}$$

It can be proved that the solution of equations (100) and (101) defines a unique maximum *balanced* growth rate g^*. Considering pairs (g, b), for $b = b^*$, $g = g^*$, the maximum rate of *balanced* growth which can be achieved. Note well that only a particular capital endowment at $t = 0$ makes feasible the greatest of all attainable rates of *balanced* growth (and, of course, any mode of *balanced* growth keeps intact the initial capital structure).

Recall equation (99) and calculate the second derivative d^2g/db^2, taking g as the dependent variable:

$$d^2g/db^2 = \frac{F_{11}(dg/db)^2 + 2(F_{13}-1)(dg/db) + F_{33}}{b - F_1} \tag{102}$$

Since some of one output must be given up in order to get more of another at any time, $F_1 < 0$ and, since $b > 0$, $(b - F_1) > 0$. For $dg/db = 0$, the right-hand expression boils down to $F_{33}/(b - F_1)$. Since production possibilities are to be convex, i.e. since the law of variable proportions is to hold, $F_{33} < 0$. Hence $dg/db = 0$, $d^2g/db^2 < 0$ at (g^*, b^*). The maximum value of g is g^*.

Recalling the first note at the end of ¶10.8 §§5 supra, since disposal of redundant stocks is to be economically trivial, the operative capital structure can remain balanced as any redundant outputs are effortlessly sloughed off in a von Neumann mode.

Is the mode g^* *efficient*? Yes. First restate equation (97), evaluating the function at (b^*, g^*):

$$b^*g^* = F(g^*; 1, b^*) \tag{103}$$

By Euler's theorem, evoking a bygone *cause célèbre* in the history of economics, the 'adding up' problem, we have:

$$F(g^*; 1, b^*) = F_1g^* + F_2 + F_3b^* \tag{104}$$

noting that the surrogate of S_{1t-1} at date t is the number 1. It follows, since $g^* = F_3(g^*; 1, b^*)$ by equation (99), that:

$$b^*g^* = F_1 \cdot F_3 + F_2 + b^*g^* \tag{105}$$

i.e.:

$$F_1 \cdot F_3 + F_2 = 0 \quad \text{(evaluated at } (g^*, 1, b^*)) \tag{106}$$

Recall the necessary condition for intertemporal efficiency stated in equation (98):

$$F_1 \cdot F_3 + F_2 = 0!$$ (107)

POINT. The highest possible rate of *balanced* growth permitted by the set of possible initial capital structures is efficient. This rate, g^*, is feasible only if the initial capital structure is described by b^*.

The analysis easily can be extended to n commodities: each stock at date t can be defined as a multiple of some initial stock. A vector $\mathbf{b}^*$ replaces the scalar b^* and the system of difference equations is correspondingly enlarged.

§5

Recall again that the analysis of ¶10.9 §§3–4 was confined to consumptionless systems. In that context we established that a von Neumann mode of growth is efficient.[15] It can be established that the *only* efficient mode of balanced growth is that at the maximum attainable rate of *balanced* growth. But g^* is capable of achievement only if the initial capital structure is just right. *In general balanced growth is inefficient.* In all but one of an indefinitely large number of cases, efficient programmes of accumulation exclude *balanced* growth.

Looking forward to Chapter 12, growth along an equilibrium path of a *multiplier-accelerator* or Harrodian model generally is inefficient. (However, compare the case in which the warranted- and natural-rates are equal.)

Under the *fixprice* method of Chapter 12, relative prices are held constant. Since producers and consumers are constrained by feasible-sales regions and 'income', it cannot be implied that constant relative prices are either necessary or sufficient for *balanced* growth even for a stipulated technology.

Finally, many efficient unbalanced paths associate with a given set of initial conditions. In the special case $b = b^*$, growth at g^* leads only to one of a number of efficient trajectories. Nor is there any reason for the capital structure defined by b^* to be the most preferred.

DOSSO discuss intertemporal efficiency of dynamized Leontief systems at pp. 335–345, concluding that if a 'Leontief trajectory' is feasible it is efficient. That is to say, if in a dynamical Leontief system it is possible to achieve a *balanced* growth-mode, the resulting path will be efficient. Furthermore, a consumptionless dynamic Leontief system is a special case of a von Neumann model: thus in such a Leontief system $\mathbf{B\bar{x}} = \bar{\alpha}\mathbf{A\bar{x}}$.[16]

§6

Is then the analysis of *balanced* growth only trivially interesting? No.

'... *maximal* steady growth, growth at the von Neumann rate and in its particular proportions *is* special. For one thing it is efficient. In fact, even more is true. In the very long run, maximal *balanced* growth is in a sense *the* best way for the economy to expand.'[17]

Thus the turnpike theorem! Consider a case like that of ¶10.6 and its Fig. 5, consulting Fig. 6. Assume that the objective (whose objective?) is to 'go as far in direction θ_1 as is possible, given initial stocks and transformation possibilities and that the programme's terminal date is in the very distant future'. The initial capital structure is described by angle θ_3 and that permitting a von Neumann path by θ_2. The turnpike theorem states that, under the stipulations of ¶10.9 §§4–5, the economy could best satisfy the criterion by first programming for a von Neumann capital structure and then following a von Neumann path for a very long time, before finally veering off towards the θ_1 structure. In this way *balanced* growth in the von Neumann mode becomes highly important despite the fact that optimal paths virtually always are unbalanced.

Why should the result be called a turnpike theorem?

> 'It is exactly like a turnpike paralleled by a network of minor roads ... If origin and destination are close together and far from the turnpike, the best route may not touch the turnpike. However, if origin and destination are far enough apart, it will always pay to get on the turnpike ... even if this means adding ... mileage at either end.'[18]

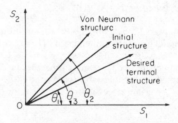

Fig. 6   Graphics for *Turnpike Theory*

§7

The work of Chapter 10 has been completed, but consider these postscripts.

1) Remember that the stipulations attached to growth models in Chapter 10 go far to strip them of empirical significance and to disqualify them as guides to social action. After all, development of new ways of doing things, diversification of consumption experience, cultural richness and, for that matter, having fun all are important. The life of a society cannot properly be reduced to grim pursuit of material goods whilst adhering to accumulation plans which, even if feasible, cannot reflect mechanical and aesthetical revelations still to occur.

The first postscript does not, of course, diminish capital theory in its many correct applications.

2) The logical significance of a model as a scheme of explaining data is different from that as a guide to distributive justice. Thus a certain community utility function might, together with other structural specifications, lead to remarkably high correlation of consumption data with tariff changes. This utility function might register especially high when tariffs on corn importations are high and tariffs on coal are low. Still, regardless of the goodness of data-fit and exactness of identification of the underlying econometric model, the high corn-tariff, low coal-tariff policy cannot properly be said thus to have scientific sanction. What if farmers supported the music of Wagner whilst miners adored Mozart?

For an excellent discussion of what must be the very narrow sense in which an econometric model can be said to be identified, together with sophisticated discussion of 'science and economics', see F. M. Fisher, *A Priori Information and Time Series Analysis* (Amsterdam: North Holland Publishing Co.; 1966).

CHAPTER 10—APPENDIX: SUPPLEMENTARY REMARKS

Chapter 10 is so fragile, and was so hard to construct, that I have decided simply to tack on some supplementary remarks—mostly suggested by criticisms of late drafts—rather than once again to tear it up.

§ 1

¶10.6 and ¶10.9 probably give the impression that the economic theory of intertemporal efficiency is almost exclusively concerned, at least in concrete form, with end-of-horizon stock positions. This is not true, especially since the application to economics of Pontryagin theory. I own that I would have avoided this bias if I had been familiar with the Principle earlier and I urge readers to become familiar with it.

Still ¶10.3's orotund generalities cover at least as much intertemporal efficiency material as non-holistic, neo-classical welfare economics commands.

§ 2

Taking up *holism* and recalling ¶7.5 there is no reason either for an intertemporal competitive equilibrium to maximize an integral such as:

$$J = \int f[\rho(t), p(t)] \tag{108}$$

where ρ_t is the rate of growth of Gross National Product and p_t is the price level at date t, or for there to exist a competitive equilibrium, relative to feasible controls, capable of such a maximization. For example, a Pareto-inefficient growth-path might be called for. This emphasizes the tenuousness of the connexion, if any, between Pareto-optimality and the theory of the state. It does not offer moral sanction for such a functional, whatever might be its interest for cardinal problems such as those cast up by the theory of the firm. 'Democratic consensus' does not produce 'just' functionals and the Holy Spirit's indifference prevents their revelation. We repeat what was stated in ¶7.5: carefully-hedged, non-teleological interpretations of so-called collective utility functions can be useful for positive economics.

Taking up *neo-classicism*, Pareto-optimality obviously is not a useful criterion in Life: competitive equilibrium is not descriptive of market data; *Realpolitik* must be considered; macroeconomic formulation is essential for criteria to be operable, as is recognition of non-price constraint.

REFERENCES

1. Cf. Karl R. Popper, *The Poverty of Historicism* (London: Routledge and Kegan Paul; 1960).
2. G. Debreu, *Theory of Value* (New York: John Wiley & Sons; 1959), p. 90.
3. Cf. G. Debreu, *Theory of Value* (New York: John Wiley & Sons; 1959), Chap. 6 and *DOSSO*, Chap. 14.
4. G. Debreu, *Theory of Value* (New York: John Wiley & Sons; 1959), pp. 94–95.
5. Cf. G. Debreu, *Theory of Value* (New York: John Wiley & Sons; 1959), pp. 95–96 and *DOSSO*, pp. 412–415.
6. Fig. 5 is based on *DOSSO*, Chap. 11.
7. Cf. *DOSSO*, Chap. 11.2, pp. 267 ff.
8. Cf. D. Gale, *The Theory of Linear Economic Models* (New York: McGraw-Hill Book Co.; 1960), pp. 303–306.
9. Cf. D. Gale, *The Theory of Linear Economic Models* (New York: McGraw-Hill Book Co.; 1960), pp. 310–315.
10. D. Gale, *The Theory of Linear Economic Models* (New York: McGraw-Hill Book Co.; 1960), p. 310.
11. Compare *DOSSO*, pp. 303–345.
12. Compare Irving Fisher, *The Theory of Interest* (New York: Kelley & Millman; 1954).
13. Cf. R. H. Strotz, 'Myopia and Inconsistency in Dynamic Utility Maximization,' *Review of Economic Studies*, Vol. XXIII, No. 3, 1955–1956.
14. Cf. *DOSSO*, Chap. 12, esp. pp. 326–329.
15. Cf. J. R. Hicks, *Capital and Growth*, Part III, for a largely non-mathematical discussion of optimality-and-accumulation, esp. Chap. 19.
16. D. Gale, *The Theory of Linear Economic Models* (New York: McGraw-Hill Book Co.; 1960), p. 317.
17. (*DOSSO*, p. 329.) See *DOSSO*, pp. 329–331. *DOSSO* are the parents of the theorem.
18. *DOSSO*, p. 331.

CHAPTER 11

Socialism

1. INTRODUCTION

Chapter 11 concerns an abstract economy whose resources are not under private ownership, but not any existing economy which is called socialist. The analysis focuses on properties of competitive equilibrium as a mathematical concept. In this way it establishes the full generality of earlier results.

§2

Two themes dominate Chapter 11: prices under socialism (¶11.2); decentralization under socialism (¶11.3). Whilst neither the theory of optimizing economic behaviour nor that of valuation devices in organizing economic activities depends on particular forms of economic organization, there are substantive differences even between abstract private ownership and socialist economies.

1) In a private ownership economy prices and distributive shares of households are inextricably linked, subject only to tax-subsidy schemes. In an idealized socialist economy ('to each according to his needs...') pricing and distribution are separated out, subject to the influence of the income incentive on productiveness. A facet of 1), leading into 2), suggests that the dynamics of pricing can be very different in private ownership and socialist economies. This is partly for sociological reasons: political-social effects of falling wage rates are quite different when shadow- instead of market-wages are at stake. Cf. Chapter 7— appendix.
2) As the 'decomposition' analysis of ¶11.3 makes clear, stability properties of Walrasian *tâtonnement* can be important in abstract socialist systems, just as are their *disequilibrium* characteristics. Indeed the dynamics of socialist economics are, if anything, more amenable to neo-classical economics than are those of capitalism.

Human productivity almost always appears partly to depend on what the agent is being paid. Agricultural productivity surely depends on whether one is tilling one's own land. However, we neglect relationships between productivity and remuneration, including *piecework* remuneration. In this we follow theorists who prefer to treat sources of labour services and labour services symmetrically with non-human counterparts. In formal theory a labour contract arranges a rental of a human source and producers compare internal- with market-valuations of services of human sources. Thus we stipulate brazenly that *piecework* remuneration schemes are simply elaborate ways of announcing demand-prices for labour services and that production sets are to be defined purely technocratically.

2. PRICES UNDER SOCIALISM

¶10.4 concerned a fully automated socialist system orientated towards consumers: the authorities simply served the tastes of Household 2, subject to achievement by Household 1 of a minimum goal. A price-mechanism interpretation was offered.

The authorities might, in the manner of feudal lords realizing feudal rights through the *taille*, appropriate certain resources prior to our problem, leaving us only a residual.

§ 2

Considering next a somewhat elaborated version of the ¶10.4 model, each of the households possesses factors 1 and 2 and offers them in fixed quanta so that:

$$\tilde{y}_i^0 = \sum_j \tilde{y}_{ij} \qquad i = 1, 2 \tag{1}$$

The households are not paid for their productive services. Rather the state determines 'money valued' demand through its aggregate transfer payments, Y, and the proportion of payments going to the first household, c. All chits are to be spent currently. The plant managers are 'Mamelukes', consuming nothing and not forming households. The 'Mamelukes' behave like capitalists, maximizing profits and bidding for factors at state conducted auctions. The only scarce productive agents are factors 1 and 2.

Money can be ignored. 'Mameluke'/state transfers are strictly accounting transactions. Chits expire during the economic day.

Walras's Law does not apply. Aggregate nominally-valued demand is not implicitly constrained to equal the aggregate supply-price of production.

$$f(p_1, p_2, w_1, w_2; Y, c) = 0 \tag{2}$$

$$F(p_1, p_2, w_1, w_2; Y, c) = 0 \tag{3}$$

$$g(p_1, p_2, w_1, w_2; \tilde{y}_1^0) = 0 \tag{4}$$

$$G(p_1, p_2, w_1, w_2; \tilde{y}_2^0) = 0 \tag{5}$$

S1

It is left as an exercise to show that the equilibrium of **S1** is Pareto-optimal and that, for example, profit-maximizing competitive 'Mamelukes', operating linear processes, necessarily will minimize the value of scarce resources relative to $\bar{p}$. This would be subject to the usual dual constraints and that $\bar{y}$ maximizes $\bar{p} \cdot y$ amongst feasible-outputs.

The excess-demand functions for the two commodities (here final products) and for the two factors, equated with zero, determine the unknowns p_1, p_2, w_1, and w_2, given parameters c, Y, $\tilde{y}_1^0$, and $\tilde{y}_2^0$. Equations (2) and (3) reflect commodity demands and supplies by households and 'firms' each treating prices, including w_1 and w_2, as parameters. Equations (4) and (5) require that planned demands for factors by 'firms' equal predetermined supplies.

S1 reflects heavy decentralization. Command decisions are taken only on Y and c, thus determining only the distribution of income and the general price level. The authorities cannot take more command decisions if there is to be a competitive equilibrium. Additional command decisions could lead only to shortages and redundancies, so long as consumer sovereignty reigns.

3. DECENTRALIZATION UNDER SOCIALISM

The abstract socialist economy of ¶11.3 more resembles known socialist systems. Decentralization in the new scenario is to be a mere administrative device in a commanded economy. However, in the modified economies of ¶11.3 §§3 et seq., plant managers are permitted considerable latitude. It is not crystal clear at what point *la dirigiste* gives way to *laissez faire*, if at all.

§2

Assume first that fully informed authorities, having selected outputs y^* as targets from efficient outputs belonging to the feasible set of outputs Y, wish to avoid day-to-day managerial problems whilst assuring that y^* will be produced. Along the lines of ¶5.3 §§9, they need *only* compute and then publish p^*, noting that in Life, y^* must be defined for each microinterval as must be p^*. At p^* productions y^* maximize $p^* \cdot y$ on the set of feasible outputs. Indeed $p^* \cdot y^* = 0$, recalling that inputs (negative outputs) are assigned negative numbers.

A programme for efficient production must make precise specifications of commodities. Tomorrow's production possibilities depend on where exactly goods produced today or yesterday are to be and have been. The light notation of Chapter 11 glosses over the extraordinary complexity of programming interpretations of 'socialist equilibrium'. The formal general-equilibrium theory of Chapter 9 determined prices for millions of future deliveries and programmes for intricate intertemporal procedures. However, simple programming models dealing with isolated chunks of time are not always valid algorithms for real planning problems. Surely rational central planners would not wish their branch managers to do one-period profit-maximization, nor would optimal technological choices emerge from temporal calibration so coarse that sequential production problems became obscured and the programming formulation became as vague as the neo-classical production function.[1]

An important specification problem can be crudely limned. Production possibilities ideally are described *in posse*, the *tâtonnement* determining the distribution, spatially and otherwise, of productive agents. In Life this is impossible: at date *t* things are where they are. What if all machine tools of type alpha are at *location Z* whilst the central programme calls for at least some of them to be at *A*? (At 'Moscow' planners deal with production set **Y** remember.) How can alpha tools end up at *A* if the authorities were merely to cry prices up and down? How much more difficult would be the instrumentation of the socialist *tâtonnement* than the fact of real capitalist Life, in which a holder of redundant equipment simply throws it onto the market, marking down *his* price quotation on it.

§3

What is to be done with the positive outputs amongst $\mathbf{y}^*$? Let us treat consumption more meaningfully. Without specifying factor-reward and money-payment procedures, define a modified competitive equilibrium problem: the authorities command only that outputs $(y_1^*, \ldots, y_r^*)$ be produced, but do not command levels for $(y_{r+1}, \ldots, y_n)$. If computationally and administratively feasible, it would seem that 'Moscow' either should manipulate a heavily constrained version of the ¶10.4 model or simply choose from amongst vectors **p**, permitting general competitive equilibrium with $(\bar{y}_1, \ldots, \bar{y}_r) = (y_1^*, \ldots, y_r^*)$. Note that degrees of freedom are provided by the ability of the authorities to determine arbitrarily the equivalent of initial collections of shares and physical assets. Certainly there are theorems showing that there must exist $\mathbf{p}^{**}$ for which $\mathbf{p}^{**} \cdot \mathbf{y}^{**}$ maximizes $\mathbf{p} \cdot \mathbf{y}^{**}$ where $\mathbf{y}^* = (y_1^*, \ldots, y_r^*, y_{r+1}^{**}, \ldots, y_n^{**})$ is both feasible and efficient. (Of course, the non-commanded equilibrium outputs are $(y_{r+1}^{**}, \ldots, y_n^{**})$.) On the other hand, if 'Moscow' were to insist on $(y_1^*, \ldots, y_r^*)$ *and* on more or less arbitrary prices p^+, difficulties would ensue. The resulting vector $(y_1^*, \ldots, y_t^*, y_{r+1}^+, \ldots, y_n^+)$ most likely would be productively inefficient and surely would not be an equilibrium vector. Demands and supplies for commodities $(r+1), \ldots, n$ would be unbalanced.

§4

Professor Lieberman of Kharkov University has urged that Soviet factory managers be allowed more leeway in production planning and that output should become more orientated towards profit criteria whilst, as it happens, prices continue to be determined centrally. An article by Professor Lieberman appears in *The Economist* (London: 26 Feb. 1966), pp. 782–786. See also *Le Monde* (Paris: 10 Mar. 1966), p. 4 for an interesting discussion of 'Liebermanism'.

Here is where Professor Lieberman comes in. Professor Lieberman has emphasized the immense variegation of the vector **y**, putting aside problems of dating: y_s might pertain to blue smocks at Moscow; y_{s+1} to yellow smocks at Leningrad; y_{s+2} to red smocks at Vladivostok, etc. Variegation being inevitable, possibilities for chaos consequent to arbitrary specifications of productions and prices are myriad.

Recognizing specifically the imperfect nature even of pseudo-competitive processes in Life, Professor Lieberman has urged that factory- and store-managers be more free to use profitability criteria in planning outputs and placing orders, so that supplies and demands will better be matched.

§5

Of course, Lieberman managers putatively respond to centrally determined prices. Does the fact that its prices are authoritatively determined at date t necessarily mean that a system is doomed to *disequilibrium* and technological inefficiency? No. The upshot, as in *real life* capitalism, depends on the dynamic laws shaping price paths, e.g. $\dot{\mathbf{p}} = \mathbf{f}(\mathbf{E})$. There is no reason why 'Moscow' might not attempt to accomplish the dynamic of ideally competitive markets. There is no theoretical barrier against it surpassing the performance of many clogged capitalist markets. Thus 'Moscow' might use investment criteria requiring that resources always move towards activities in which their 'shadow' prices are highest, that price velocities be directly related to excess demands, etc.

The connexion of socialism with Pareto optimality depends on the laws of motion obeyed by prices and on incentive systems, rather than on the socio-legal framework in which prices and outputs are determined. The theory of general equilibrium transcends sociology and politics.

§6[2]

¶11.3 §§6, concerning *decomposition of linear programmes*, is more than a coda, but has been postponed lest its dense matter obscure the main line of argument.

The discussion of ¶11.3 §§4–5 leads into a model in which central authorities, although determined to govern by *diktat* under criteria not thrown up by consumer sovereignty, admit to imperfect information and, sometimes, ignorance. Accordingly, they may be attracted by a computational procedure under a decomposition principle permitting them to deal with smaller, simpler programmes whilst branch-managers solve sub-programmes, subject to centrally decreed prices. More realistically, quite specific input–output goals would be imposed on branches by authorities, who would be sensitive to reported profits in subsequent reformed programmes. In the one case, the theory of the dynamics of *tâtonnement* would apply, in the other, the laws of motion governing price-output behaviour of ongoing economies. In both cases, we are interested in whether iterative procedures can lead to an optimum from some other initial state. In both cases, it is obvious that economic theory is unconscious of forms of ownership.

In order to fix ideas, a caricature of a socialist economy will be set up.[3] A small Islamic socialist state is entirely specialized to the production of four pork products. The authorities' criterion is simply to maximize the value of national output at externally-determined final-product prices, since the entire national product is to be exported. Thus the criterion:

$$\max z = x_1 + 8x_2 + 5x_3 + 6x_4 \tag{6}$$

Of course, the external price vector is $(1, 8, 5, 6)$. There are two prototype plants, one producing products 1 and 2, absorbing two *self-contained* capacities in accordance with the sub-technology matrix

$$\begin{bmatrix} 2 & 3 \\ 5 & 1 \end{bmatrix}$$

and the other producing products 3 and 4 and also absorbing two *self-contained* capacities, under the sub-technology matrix

$$\begin{bmatrix} 1 & 0 \\ 0 & 1 \end{bmatrix}$$

Plant 2 also uses a class of labour which is redundant. For political reasons it is required that at least 12 units of this labour be absorbed. Hence the constraints:

$$2x_1 + 3x_2 \le 6 \tag{7}$$

$$5x_1 + x_2 \le 5 \tag{8}$$

$$x_3 \le 4 \tag{9}$$

$$x_4 \le 3 \tag{10}$$

$$3x_3 + 4x_4 \ge 12 \tag{11}$$

$$x \ge 0 \tag{12}$$

Finally, the activities absorb a 'social' capacity—non-reproducible like the others—which is portable and is to be allocated between the plants:

$$x_1 + 4x_2 + 5x_3 + 2x_4 \le 7 \tag{13}$$

Inequality (13) ties up the branch managers with the central authorities and, of course, inequalities (7) to (13) comprise the problem's constraints.

Now assume that the central authorities, while fully cognizant of inequality (13) have not estimated the structures of inequalities (7) to (11). Indeed they do not wish to undertake so expensive and probably so fruitless a task. However, there are certain theorems which, together with appropriate initial data, may permit them not only to issue feasible instructions, but eventually to arrive at an optimal solution, without ever estimating the structures of inequalities (7) to (11).

The central theorem is that solutions of sub-problems calling for maximization of plant profits (managers rent the social resource from 'Mecca' and sell final products to 'Mecca')[4] and not explicitly recognizing the social constraint comprised a close, convex set in the four-dimensional activity space which, if strictly bounded, as here, may cast up convex combinations of extreme points, i.e. weighted combinations of extreme points, the non-negative weights ρ summing to 1.

The central statistical bureau can provide the necessary data, as many past activity-level sets as are required, may satisfy *all* of the constraints and, *a fortiori*, satisfy inequalities (7) and (8) (re plant 1) and inequalities (9) to (11) (re plant 2).

The tacit underlying simplex solution procedure assures that the reports of the central statistical bureau can be processed to cast up extreme points of the relevant set.

These stipulations having been made, the authorities can work with a new problem, one consistent with their limited information but having the same solution-value as the original problem:

$$\max\ z = \rho_1(x_1^1 + 8x_2^1 + 5x_3^1 + 6x_4^1) + \rho_2(x_1^2 + 8x_2^2 + 5x_3^2 + 6x_4^2) + \ldots \quad (14)$$

Where there are K extreme points in the set of feasible sub-solutions, $J \le K$. Of course, the superscripts index these extreme points.

$$\rho_1(x_1^1 + 4x_2^1 + 5x_3^1 + 2x_4^1) + \rho_2(x_1^2 + 4x_2^2 + 5x_3^2 + 2x_4^2) + \ldots \le 7 \quad (15)$$

$$\Sigma\rho_i = 1 \quad (16)$$

There emerges a set of extreme points $(\mathbf{x}^1, \ldots \mathbf{x}^J)$ and multipliers $(\rho_1, \ldots, \rho_J)$,[5] together with shadow price, $\bar{\lambda}$, of the social resource, at which excluded activities make losses and included activities zero profits. (Again, outputs are sold to and the social resource is rented from 'Mecca'.)

It happens that standard computational procedures will lead to a prompt solution of our problem:

$$\bar{x} = 0{\cdot}125(0, 2, 0, 3) + 0{\cdot}875(0, 0, 0, 3) = (0, 0{\cdot}25, 0, 3) \quad (17)$$

Passing over to more general prospects, including huge activity vectors and technology matrices, in Life, even under our statical postulations, a solution might be excruciatingly delayed. In exploring this remark, we are to consider a number of possibilities, always keeping in mind private-ownership-economy counterparts.

In the (notional) meta-time of a *tâtonnement*, successive iterations would lead to corresponding shadow declarations, λ, in turn evoking different sub-solutions. These, as they became available, would enlarge the ascertained subset of the set of basic feasible sub-solutions, leading to further iterations. 'Finally', observing that all of this is to transpire at a point in calendar time, the optimal solution and its mate $\bar{\lambda}$ are discovered. Of course, such an adjustment process is just as unrealistic as its capitalist counterpart, but no more so.

More realistically, as feasible, but non-optimal, directives are issued, leading to non-optimal ongoing dispositions, shadow prices for the social resource will be circulated to branch managers instructed to report what they regard as optimal responses relative to $(\lambda^*, \mathbf{p})$. This will yield up notional, but useful, elements of $(\mathbf{x}^1, \ldots, \mathbf{x}^K)$. An iterative optimizing procedure would unfold alongside feasible, non-optimal Life. There is excellent correspondence with more realistic, albeit statical, capitalist models although sociological differences would generate quite different price-output paths. For both economies, theoretical complications leaping out upon removal of statical underpinning are overwhelming. Dreadful difficulties develop if ongoing events work changes in parameters of the optimization problem: if today's acts affect tomorrow's constraints—including tomorrow's knowledge; if there is an investment sector; if optimal strategy must be defined relative to time-paths of external prices; etc. These possibilities stress the narrowly abstruse character of formal economic theory and evoke twinges of concern that its equanimity towards forms of ownership of economic resources stems from its emptiness.

REFERENCES

1. Cf. R. Bellman and S. Dreyfus, *Applied Dynamic Programming* (Princeton: Princeton University Press; 1962).
2. Cf. G. Dantzig, *Linear Programming and Extensions* (Princeton: Princeton University Press; 1963), Chap. 23, esp. pp. 462–466 (contributed by C. Almon), and G. Hadley, *Linear Programming* (Reading, Mass.: Addison-Wesley Pub. Co.; 1962), pp. 400–411. Needless to say, the decomposition principle is interesting in any context in which there can be conceived a centre and subordinate decision-units.
3. What follows is an interpretation of an example: G. Hadley, *Linear Programming* (Reading, Mass.: Addison-Wesley Pub. Co.; 1962), pp. 407 ff., fn. 7, enriched by C. Almon's analysis.
4. Cf. J. Carew, *Moscow is not My Mecca* (London: Secker & Warburg; 1964).
5. For a discussion of the necessary finiteness of the iterative process under various circumstances cf. G. Dantzig, *Linear Programming and Extensions* (Princeton: Princeton University Press; 1963), Chap. 23.1.

Macrodynamics

CHAPTER 12

Multiplier-Accelerator Theory and Extensions

1. INTRODUCTION TO PART IV AND CHAPTER 12

Part IV diverts the stream of Chapters 6–8 into macroeconomics, emphasizing dynamic models geared to the social accounts. So it deploys differential and difference equations in order to consider laws of motion, which may be obeyed by such aggregates as Gross National Product, employment, and *the* price level. Part IV is connected only tenuously with optimization and is ripped from the theory of general competitive equilibrium.

The decision to dissociate income theory from the theories of competitive industry and general competitive equilibrium is inevitable, I think, for a Keynesian and isolates us from an extensive domain of macro-analysis.[1] Thus we eschew marginal-productivity theories of factor pricing: the objective notion, value of marginal-product, gives way to subjective marginal-revenue products. Models of competition are cast off. Nor are aggregate production functions to be considered. Ours is a theory of diverse subjectivity, rather than one of homogeneous objectivity (for example, competitive models with aggregate Cobb–Douglas production functions). So we hold fast to models in which producers hold subjective sales expectations. Financial prospects are tractable only to moral expectation, thus stressing non-price, non-technocratic constraints on realizations.

It may seem reactionary at this time to eschew multi-sectoral macro-economic models, vintage production functions, 'distributional' savings functions, technical-progress models, etc., let alone holistic approaches to optimal paths of economic growth verged upon in Chapter 10. Reflexion suggests that much of more-recent work, in as far as it differs qualitatively from older Keynesian economies comprises a neo-classical revival, a renaissance of optimizing calculus. It is a search for an avenue of escape

273

from the inherently anti-welfare-economic properties of Keynesian economics. After all, to eschew models of competition is to eschew Pareto optimality as a tool of analysis of alternative economic states. To spurn holism in the form of collective welfare functions is virtually to discard welfare economics in the macroeconomic sphere. We have done both, gladly. So we have little incentive to squeeze macroeconomics into models of competition and Cobb–Douglas technologies, a purposeless action unless normative implication is sought.

Not all of recent work revives neo-classicism. Far from it! Important steps have been taken to accomplish more disaggregation and to build more flexibility into savings functions. We can only apologize for our neglect of such work, demurring that Chapter 12 in particular is concerned to establish the categorical differences between neo-classical economic theory and Keynesian theory. The former views general economic equilibrium as a solution to an optimization problem generated by responses to objective data (including prices). In the latter, price-quoters, responding to moral expectations, generate curves in phase-space, but not states which can be properly called equilibria.

This the chapter does without having to enlarge its present scope. Of course, Chapter 12 does not comprise a proper course in modern macroeconomic theory, just as Chapter 13 is not a course in monetary theory. Both are frankly methodological in emphasis.

2. DYNAMICAL THEORIES OF ECONOMIC POLICY

We begin simply by gumming up the version of the static theory of economic policy of equations (1):

$$\phi^i(y_1, \ldots, y_n; z_1, \ldots, z_m) = 0 \qquad i = 1, 2, \ldots, n \tag{1}$$

Equations (1), determining general equilibrium in n independent markets, permit the authorities m degrees of freedom. There are m instruments $\mathbf{z}$.

There are obvious switches in notation from Chapters 10 and 11. Allocation of variables between vectors $\mathbf{y}$ and $\mathbf{z}$ reflects worldly administrative facts. However, do not confuse mundane and mathematical logic. The authorities might care about the price of sausage, but not a fig about the level of the instrument, Bank Rate. Still they will *announce* Bank Rate and merely contemplate, perhaps with smug satisfaction, the emergent price of sausage. Cf. the text *infra*.

Now assume that, for whatever reason, the authorities wish to establish the values $(y_1^*, \ldots, y_m^*)$. The system becomes:

$$\phi^i(y_{m+1}, \ldots, y_n, z_1, \ldots, z_m; y_1^*, \ldots, y_m^*) = 0 \qquad i = 1, \ldots, n \tag{2}$$

The instruments are to be treated mathematically as unknowns, together with the $n-m$ remaining endogenous variables of equations (1).

There is a sense, admittedly violating general equilibrium *à la* Walras, in which the authorities have many more degrees of freedom than is implied by equations (1) and (2). It is this sense which leads to dynamization of the theory of economic policy so that, once initial conditions are supplied, models can trace out predicted values for data. Perhaps the most signal feature of such dynamized models is that they can properly be interpreted in ordinary calendar time instead of only the logical- or meta-time of the dynamics of Walrasian *tâtonnement*.

§2

Returning to equations (1), assume that there has been established a general equilibrium in the sense of Chapter 9 relative to $\mathbf{z}^*$. Then postulate that z_k^*, the yield basis on which the official open-market operator has been buying and selling 20-year-Government-bond maturities, is put up to z_k^{**}—say to 9 per cent. Perhaps, when boundary conditions on money-wages and other prices are considered, general-equilibrium will be precluded, at least temporarily. The fact that the notional state, general-equilibrium, is inconsistent with a given policy specification is vital neither politically nor empirically. Economic data generated by disappointed or surprised consumers and producers can be statistically explained relative to well-defined instrument levels.

High Bank Rate should not indefinitely prevent general-equilibrium in the sense of Chapter 9. Once clogs on price adjustment have been removed, secular effects of restrictionary policies become registered, not in unemployment, but rather in low rates of growth or the return of workers to subsistence farming—to the bush.

A stronger case can be made out for a *disequilibrium* approach than for the pure-competition assumptions bottoming equations (1). Life concerns firms making decisions from subjective probability-density distributions of demands conditional on quoted prices, effects of promotional schemes on quantities demanded, etc. So we move to a policy space in which official actions correspond with persistent inflation or deflation, excess demand for labour, unemployment, etc., within 'real-world' industrial organizations. Of course, ¶9.1 already has developed a statical theory of disequilibrium policy. ¶12.2 §§3 makes an extension to dynamics.

Be sure to distinguish between inflation accompanied by persistent excess demand in uncleared markets and continuous equilibrium at ever high prices.

In Chapter 13 of *Money*,[2] I dealt with a general-equilibrium system so simple that it could be reduced to:

$$\psi(r) = 0$$

the rate of interest being r so that $\bar{r}$ may be called the 'natural rate of interest', $\psi(r)$ being assumed to have the positive root $\bar{r}$. If the authorities insist upon $r^* \neq \bar{r}$, there must result persistent inflation or deflation, side-stepping 'real' versus nominal interest rates *à la* Irving

Fisher. (Cf. Chapter 13 *infra*.) The case of $r^* < \bar{r}$ associates with a Wicksellian cumulative inflation, that of $r^* > \bar{r}$ with cumulative deflation. The latter case makes the transition from Wicksell to Keynes: when $r^* > \bar{r}$, outputs become adjusted to lower levels than are called for by purely-competitive profit maximization and households must tailor their consumptions to fit incomes yielded by sub-optimal factor sales.

§3

Although policy theory should be econometric, a deterministic formulation suffices here. The determinism is of a special sort: the actors base their decisions on current data and multi-valued expectations built up in ways known to the model-builder, but not to them.

At least the actors are unable to divine exactly the expectational patterns of their fellows. Clearly their behaviour would be affected by knowledge of the model used by the authorities and almost certainly will reflect guesses about what is the model. No such problem confronts geologists or astronomers. Zoologists?

Once an initial state is supplied, the model-builder can grind out the future. Since the solution is defined relative to *time-paths* of instruments, the officials presumably will select instrument-paths leading to maximization of some criterion, a criterion that will in general be unrelated to Parcto-optimum theory unless holistic welfare criteria are inserted into the analysis. It is obvious that the argument is virtually on all fours with the Pontryagin analysis of Chapter 7, at least in its normative aspects. However, we shall proceed 'positively'.

Stating the argument symbolically, chop up the time axis into discrete intervals, noting that peculiarities of differential versus difference equations easily are accommodated. The time-paths of the m instruments, controls, **z** are defined by difference equations, equations (3):

$$\mathbf{z} = \boldsymbol{\phi}(t) \tag{3}$$

The instruments (controls) include tax rates, bond-support prices, defence spending, etc., and are bounded by various political and social, as well as technocratic limitations. However, feedback is not being considered. (Cf. ¶12.6.)

Having defined the vector $\boldsymbol{\phi}(t)$, we are to obtain a time integral for endogenous variables **y** (including prices of commodities and securities, outputs, etc.):

$$\mathbf{y} = \boldsymbol{\psi}(t) \tag{4}$$

Again, the price components of **y** are quotations by sellers and buyers.

A behavioural framework now must be supplied. In period θ, price quotations, demands, stock-building plans, etc., will be affected by previous experience. Attainable outcomes will be governed by requirements that realized sales occur at the lower of sellers' or buyers' quotations, that capacity constraints be observed, etc. Accordingly it is useful to set up 'potential functions' at date θ defining actions planned for that date: then departures of realized from desired positions can be measured.

In Chapter 12 it is important to distinguish between the date θ and the replacement set from which it is drawn, t, i.e., $\theta \in t$.

Capacity constraints are to be defined in terms of the system's history up to date θ. It may be well to stipulate that demand- and supply-prices at date θ are predetermined. There emerge high-ordered, doubtless very messy, difference equations for variables $\mathbf{y}$:

$$\mathbf{f}(y_t, y_{t-1}, y_{t-2}, \ldots; z_t, z_{t-1}, z_{t-2}, \ldots) = \mathbf{0} \tag{5}$$

The integral of equations (5) is equations (4).

3. MULTIPLIER MODELS

¶9.9 defined the statical *multiplier* as $d\bar{Y}/dA$, the rate at which equilibrium expenditure (income) changes with autonomous expenditure. ¶12.3 concerns a multiplier relation tracing out over time effects of alternative autonomous expenditure paths on income paths.

Multiplier models have heavily dampened feedback: propensities to spend out of income are specified to be less than unity whilst expenditure is not directly related to the rate of change of income. So the economy described by a standard multiplier model, unlike that described by many *multiplier-accelerator* models, is not hypersensitive. Its agitations are not fed back into its central nervous system.

§2

Multiplier processes are inherently stable. Taking up a generalized case of lagged response to economic stimuli, assume that expenditure plans have two components, an autonomous component, A and an induced component, C, determined by equation (6):

$$C_t = c_1 Y_{t-1} + c_2 Y_{t-2} + \ldots + c_n Y_{t-n}$$
$$c_i \geq 0, \qquad 0 < \Sigma c_i < 1 \tag{6}$$

Equation (6) describes a *distributed-lag* relationship and could develop from formation of expectations from experience. Next assume that autonomous expenditure always is A^0 so that:

$$Y_t = C_t + A^0 = \sum_{i=1}^{n} c_i Y_{t-i} + A^0 \tag{7}$$

Equation (7) is an n-th order linear difference equation.

Define Σc_i as c. A particular solution of equation (7), a function defined on time satisfying the equation, is:

$$\overline{Y}_t = \frac{A^0}{1-c} \tag{8}$$

Substitute $A^0/(1-c)$ for Y in equation (7): $A^0/(1-c) = cA/(1-c)+A^0$. i.e. $1/(1-c) = c/(1-c) = (c+1-c)/(1-c) = 1/(1-c)$. Q.E.D.

The statical result of ¶9.9 falls out as a special case of the dynamical analysis.

In general $Y_t \neq \overline{Y}$. Accordingly, form equation (10) by subtracting equation (9) from equation (7), recalling that $\overline{Y}$ is a solution of equation (7). Then study equation (11).

$$\overline{Y} = \Sigma c_i \overline{Y} + A^0 \tag{9}$$

$$y_t = \Sigma c_i y_{t-i} \tag{10}$$

$$y_t = Y_t - \overline{Y} \tag{11}$$

y_θ is the deviation of income for the 0-th period from the particular value $\overline{Y}$. Upon discovering $y = \Phi(t)$ satisfying equation (10), the general solution of equation (7) can be written:

$$Y_t = A^0/(1-c) + \Phi(t) \tag{12}$$

The system is stable relative to the benchmark path $Y = A/(1-c)$ if $\Phi(t) \to 0$ as $t \to \infty$. In fact it can be proved that a solution for equation (10) is:

$$y_t = k_1 \overline{\lambda}_1^t + k_2 \overline{\lambda}_2^t + \ldots + k_n \overline{\lambda}_n^t \tag{13}$$

where $(\overline{\lambda}_1, \ldots, \overline{\lambda}_n)$ are roots of the auxiliary equation:

$$\lambda^n - c_1 \lambda^{n-1} - \ldots - c_n = 0 \tag{14}$$

and where $(k_1, \ldots, k_n)$ are arbitrary constants to be determined by initial conditions.[3]

Initial conditions determine arbitrary constants as follows. Begin with a general solution of the form $y_t = \Sigma k_j \lambda_j^t$. The initial conditions require that $y_i = y_i^0$. $i = 1, 2, \ldots, n$. (Initial values can in fact be selected for any n periods in the range of t.) There emerge equations of the form:

$$y_1^0 = k_1 \overline{\lambda}_1 + \ldots + k_n \overline{\lambda}_n$$
$$\cdots\cdots\cdots\cdots\cdots \qquad \mathbf{S1} \quad (15)$$
$$y_n^0 = k_1 \overline{\lambda}_1^n + \ldots + k_n \overline{\lambda}_n^n$$

The λs being roots of the auxiliary equation, $\mathbf{S1}$ is merely a system of n equations linear in $\mathbf{k}$.

Furthermore, it can be proved that the dominant root of equation (14), the value for $\bar{\lambda}(=\hat{\lambda})$ which, as $t \to \infty$, determines y_t, lies between zero and c:

$$0 < \hat{\lambda} < c \tag{16}$$

In the limit, $\Phi(t)$ approaches zero: the *multiplier* relation is stable.

§3

Consider next a special case, the basis for the subsequent macro-dynamics of Chapter 12:

$$Y_t = cY_{t-1} + A^0 \tag{17}$$

Equation (17) describes the simplest of the possibilities encompassed by equation (7). It is bottomed on equation (18), a simple version of equation (6):

$$C_t = c_1 Y_{t-1} \qquad c_2 = c_3 = \ldots = c_n = 0, \qquad c_1 = c \tag{18}$$

Of course, the particular solution of equation (18) is:

$$\bar{Y} = A^0/(1-c) \tag{19}$$

Since $\bar{Y}$ is a solution of equation (17),

$$y_t = cy_{t-1} \tag{20}$$

Try as a solution of equation (20):

$$y_t = kc^t \tag{21}$$

Substitute kc^t for y_t in equation (20):

$$kc^t = c(kc^{t-1}) = kc^t! \tag{22}$$

The general solution of equation (17) is:

$$Y_t = A^0/(1-c) + kc^t \tag{23}$$

Of course, $y_t \to 0$ as $t \to \infty$.

§4

We have done operational macrodynamics: upon plugging in initial conditions, determinate sequences of measurable outcomes have been generated. (Perfectly elastic supply leads to demand-determined results.) However, work remains to be done: only trivial paths converging on $\bar{Y}$ have been developed; even the complicated motions implied by equations (13) and (14) are defined relative to a stationary path. A model must be worked up which satisfies at least casual empirical observations of fluctuations around positive trends.

4. MULTIPLIER-ACCELERATOR MODELS[4]

An *accelerator* relation is to be tacked onto a slightly extended ¶12.3 model. In equations (24) and (25), expenditure has both *multiplier* and *accelerator* footings:

$$C_t = c_1 Y_{t-1} + c_2 Y_{t-2} \tag{24}$$

$$I_t = v(Y_{t-1} - Y_{t-2}) \tag{25}$$

Customarily C_t and I_t label 'consumption' and 'induced investment' expenditure, naive characterizations happily soon to disappear. Autonomous expenditure, of course, obeys its own law:

$$A_t = f(t) \tag{26}$$

Three possibilities are especially interesting:

$$A_t = A_0 \tag{27}$$

$$A_t = A_0(1+g)^t \tag{28}$$

$$A_t = A_0 \cos(\delta t - \gamma) \tag{29}$$

Equations (27) to (29) respectively describe stationary autonomous expenditure, log-linear growth of autonomous expenditure, and regular oscillations, δ and γ being fixed coefficients.

In any event, the appropriate difference equation is:

$$Y_t = c_1 Y_{t-1} + c_2 Y_{t-2} + v(Y_{t-1} - Y_{t-2}) + A_t \tag{30}$$

which can be rearranged as:

$$Y_t = c Y_{t-1} + w(Y_{t-1} - Y_{t-2}) + A_t \tag{31}$$

and then as:

$$Y_t - (w - s + 1)Y_{t-1} + w Y_{t-2} = A_t = f(t) \tag{32}$$

where $s = (1 - c)$ and $w = (v - c_2)$.

§2

The particular solution $\bar{Y} = A_0/s$ obviously holds for equation (32) when autonomous expenditure obeys equation (27). It can be proved that the particular solution $\bar{Y} = (A_0/s)\cos(\delta t - \gamma)$ holds for equation (32) when autonomous expenditure obeys equation (29) and that equation (28) leads to $\bar{Y} = (A_0/s)(1+g)^t$.[5]

The steady log-linear growth case, establishing a positive trend as a bench-mark path, is especially interesting, accommodating as it does at least crude contours of 'real world' data. Admittedly the steady-growth case is rooted in a blatant contrivance, the forcing term $A_0(1+g)^t$.

§ 3

The argument will focus on the 'remainder parts' of the general solutions.

Professor Harwitz has shown that the stability properties of *multiplier-accelerator* models with autonomous expenditure components are not invariant against time measure (day, quarter, etc.). Cf. M. Harwitz, 'On the Invariance of the Stability of Dynamic Equilibrium', *Oxford Economic Papers*, Mar. 1964 (Vol. 16, No. 1), p. 70 ff. It follows that time measure choice should be governed by empirical considerations: a one-day measure, for example, would imply a very large *accelerator* coefficient. If the resulting model were to yield a falsified inference of instability, then a longer period should be chosen.

Since equation (32) is satisfied by a particular integral in each of the three cases of ¶12.4, we can write:

$$y_t - (w - s + 1)y_{t-1} + wy_{t-2} = 0 \tag{33}$$

Equation (33)'s class of second-order linear difference equations will now be analysed with special concern for possibilities of oscillatory motion.

¶12.4 does not lead to a satisfactory theory of economic cycles in capitalist countries, partly because feedback-orientated official interventions are neglected and partly because:

1) the model develops steady oscillations only under special structural specifications. Otherwise it calls for explosiveness or damping. Observation suggests that a sound theory would call for regular oscillation under a wide range of structural specifications;
2) any one oscillation in the model's solution is symmetrical, contradicting empirical observation;
3) amplitudes of oscillations should be structurally determined, but here are determined by initial conditions;
4) ceilings and floors for 'real' outputs are ignored, but empirical and theoretical work suggest that (a) bottlenecks often induce 'downturns' and (b) limits on disinvestment imposed by *postponement of replacement and maintenance* possibilities buttress the economy against downward pressure;
5) the model's complete aggregation blots out empirically-significant effects of relative price changes;
6) monetary factors, including interest rates and credit-availability, are suppressed.

Note how 6) might be moderated. If functions **g**(*t*) describe behaviour of *bank rate* instruments, the laws obeyed by autonomous expenditure **f**(*t*) and the *accelerator* coefficient, *v*, can be modified to reflect alternative bank rate policies. After all, a variable is autonomous only relative to the setting in which it is placed.

Taking up oscillatory motion, equation (34) is the auxiliary equation of equation (33):

$$F(\lambda) = \lambda^2 - (1 - s + w)\lambda + w = 0 \tag{34}$$

Consider this possibility:

$$(1 - \sqrt{s})^2 < w < \sqrt{(1+s)^2} \tag{35}$$

If inequality (35) holds, the roots of $F(\lambda)$ are a conjugate-complex pair:

$$\tfrac{1}{2} \times [(w-s+1) \pm \sqrt{4w-(w-s+1)^2}] \tag{36}$$

Write $\tfrac{1}{2}(w-s+1)$ as α and $\tfrac{1}{2}\sqrt{4w-(w-s+1)^2}$ as β. Note that i, that is $\sqrt{-1}$, can be written as $(0, 1)$ in the complex plane, the abscissa being the real line and the ordinate the imaginary axis.

Under inequality (35), the solution of equation (33) becomes:

$$y_t = B_1(\alpha+i\beta)^t + B_2(\alpha-i\beta)^t, \tag{37}$$

B_1 and B_2 being arbitrary constants to be determined by initial conditions.

§5

It is useful to switch to polar coordinates (r, θ), consulting Fig. 1. The cartesian coordinates of point P are (0A, 0B). P also can be defined in (r, θ) space: each pair (x_1^*, x_2^*) maps into a pair (r^*, θ^*). The transformation is defined in trigonometry:

$$x_1 = r \cdot \cos \theta \tag{38}$$

$$x_2 - r \cdot \sin \theta \tag{39}$$

Equations (38) and (39) suffice to determine (r, θ) relative to (x_1, x_2).

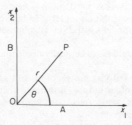

Fig. 1   Polar and Cartesian Coordinates.

Perhaps more rigorously, the transformation can be accomplished through the circular functions

$$\cos \theta = 1 - \theta^2/2! + \theta^4/4! - \theta^6/6! + \ldots \tag{40}$$

$$\sin \theta = \theta - \theta^3/3! + \theta^5/5! - \theta^7/7! + \ldots \tag{41}$$

θ need not be interpreted as an angle.

§6

Solve equations (42) and (43) for r and θ:

$$r \cdot \cos \theta = \tfrac{1}{2}(w-s+1) \tag{42}$$

$$r \cdot \sin \theta = \tfrac{1}{2}\sqrt{4w-(w-s+1)^2} \tag{43}$$

The solution of equations (42) and (43), (r^*, θ^*) is to be substituted into equation (37):

$$y_t = r^{*t}[B_1(\cos \theta^* t + i \cdot \sin \theta^* t) + B_2(\cos \theta^* t - \sin \theta^* t)] \tag{44}$$

The notation can be lightened, now that it has been established that we are dealing with particular values for r and θ established by the behavioural parameters of the system:

$$y_t = r^t[B_1(\cos \theta t + i \cdot \sin \theta t) + B_2(\cos \theta t - i \cdot \sin \theta t)] \tag{45}$$

Keep in mind that the underlying algebra requires that:

$$(r \cdot \cos \theta)^t = r^t \cdot \cos \theta t; \qquad (r \cdot \sin \theta)^t = r^t \cdot \sin \theta t \tag{46}$$

§7

It is desired that y_t be a real number. Accordingly, B_1 and B_2, the arbitrary constants, are chosen to be a conjugate-complex pair.

$$B_1 = b_1 + ib_2; \qquad B_2 = b_1 - ib_2 \tag{47}$$

Hence

$$(b_1 + ib_2)(\cos \theta t + i \cdot \sin \theta t) + (b_1 - ib_2)(\cos \theta t - \sin \theta t) = b_1 \cos \theta t + ib_2 \sin \theta t + ib_2 \cos \theta t$$
$$+ i^2 b_2 \sin \theta t + b_1 \cos \theta t - ib_1 \sin \theta t - ib_2 \cos \theta t + i^2 b_2 \sin \theta t = 2b_1 \cos \theta t - 2b_2 \sin \theta t \tag{48}$$

Furthermore, equation (45) can be written more compactly if B_3 and B_4 are substituted for B_1 and B_2. B_3 and B_4 are determined by equations (49) and (50):

$$B_3 = B_1 + B_2 \tag{49}$$

$$B_4 = i(B_1 - B_2) \tag{50}$$

B_3 and B_4 will have real values and the solution can be written:

$$y_t = r^t(B_3 \cos \theta t + B_4 \sin \theta t) \tag{51}$$

Consulting equations (47), $B_1 = b_1 + ib_2$ and $B_2 = b_1 - ib_2$ and consulting equations (49) and (50), $B_3 = B_1 + B_2$ and $B_4 = i(B_1 - B_2)$:

$$y^t = r^t(2b_1 \cos \theta t - 2b_2 \sin \theta t) = r^t(B_3 \cos \theta t^2 + B_4 \sin \theta t) \tag{52}$$

Indeed yet another switch in arbitrary constants, determined by equations (53) and (54), leads to the compact equation (55):

$$B \cos \varepsilon = B_3 \tag{53}$$

$$B \sin \varepsilon = B_4 \tag{54}$$

$$y_t = Br^t \cos(\theta t - \varepsilon) \tag{55}$$

Alternatively,

$$B_3 + B_4 = B(\cos^2 \theta + \sin^2 \theta) = B; \qquad \tan \varepsilon = \frac{\sin \varepsilon}{\cos \varepsilon} = \frac{B_4}{B_3}$$

In either formulation:

$$Br^t(\cos \theta t \cdot \cos \varepsilon + \sin \theta t \cdot \sin \varepsilon) = Br^t[\cos(\theta t) - \varepsilon)] \tag{56}$$

The parameters r and θ are determined by the system's structure whilst B and ε are determined by initial conditions.

§8

Thus a *multiplier-accelerator* process has been reduced to an integral defined on time and comprising an oscillatory motion imposed upon a particular solution. The emergent result is empirically orientated: upon being supplied with initial conditions, the model grinds out falsifiable implications for the indefinite future. Granted the stipulations are rude and the potential motions are not rich.

§9

There should be noted a few properties of the integral:

$$Y_t = \overline{Y}_t + Br^t \cos(\theta t - \varepsilon) \tag{57}$$

recalling that Chapter 12 centres on damping versus explosiveness. The oscillations of y_t are damped, regular, or explosive as $r < 1, r = 1$, or $r > 1$.

Models formulated in years and accordingly with structures estimated from annual data, imply rather more volatility than experience confirms. This suggests that expenditure responses should be smeared out rather more than in the ¶12.4 system and that *non-linear* constraint should be introduced. Cf. J. R. Hicks, *Trade Cycle*.

Of course, damped oscillations imply that $Y_t \rightarrow \overline{Y}_t$ as $t \rightarrow \infty$. The *period* of an oscillation of equation (57) is defined by $2\pi/\theta$: the system recycles every $2\pi/\theta$ 'days': $0 < \theta < \pi/2$.

If the period of an oscillation is 5·2 weeks, its *frequency* can be defined as 10 per annum.

The *amplitude* of the oscillation at $t = 0$ (initial amplitude) is B, amplitude being the maximum distance during an oscillation from the benchmark path $\overline{Y}_t$. Finally the *phase* of the initial oscillation, the time it takes for the initial oscillation to reach its peak or trough, measured in the appropriate time unit, depends on B and ε.

The general solution for the case of regularly-oscillating autonomous investment is

$$Y_t = (A/s) \cos(\delta t - \gamma) + Br^t(\cos \theta t - \varepsilon)$$

Assume that $\delta < \theta$. The period of the forced oscillation—that of the autonomous or forcing term—$2\pi/\delta$, then is longer than that of the inherent oscillation, $2\pi/\theta$. The system becomes reduced to superimposed oscillatory motions. As additional factors are considered, there develops a Fourier series, which, if elaborate enough, can depict any motion representable by a polynomial defined on t.

¶12.4 ignored monetary factors: it was assumed that necessary finance was always available. However, this might not be so. Consider reduced United Kingdom and United States construction activity in 1966 resulting from curtailment of flows of funds through building societies and of expansion of bank portfolios.

Possibilities for *accelerated* decumulative effects of current inability to accomplish commodity-purchase plans are fairly obvious, provided that there is not straightforward current redeployment of demand.

Finally, prompt recircuiting of financial flows might prevent official attempts to bring about tight money or might offset endogenous disturbances (say of the flow of funds through building societies).

5. STABILIZATION[6]

There are deep connexions between the theory of economic policy and electric-circuit theory, but ¶12.5 §§1 is confined to a crude depiction of *feedback* in economics, followed by a gloss of Professor Phillips's elegant stabilization model in ¶12.5 §§2–6.

Consider Fig. 2. It concerns an elementary system with autonomous expenditure, A, a class of induced expenditure, X, and another such class, G. A feeds into Y (say Gross National Product) but receives no guidance from Y. The symbol $\boxed{1}$ indicates the 1-for-1 correspondence between ΔA (or ΔC or ΔG) and ΔY. X also feeds into Y, but there is no feedback from Y to X: X can be written $f(Y)$. Of course, if in an unmitigated case, one could write $Y \rightarrow \boxed{1\cdot5} \rightarrow X$, the system soon would overheat and then burst into flames.

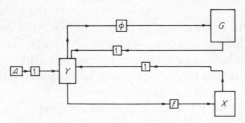

Fig. 2   Simplified Feedback.

Ignore the possibility of outright instability, together with more sophisticated specifications of Y as a function of time. Instead simply consider the way in which changes in A would be able to agitate less febrile systems: feedback could massively amplify static.

Now consider G. The function ϕ defines the Government's stabilization policy, $G = \phi(Y)$. When the economy threatens to overheat, G falls.

When business seems to be turning sour, G rises. (In life the official feed-back processes would not be confined to the $Y-G-Y$ circuit.) Of course, 'real world' authorities are likely to measure the economy's performance against a trend line. Perhaps they will build their policy around the goal of achievement on the average of a certain rate of growth of national income per head.

§2[7]

¶12.5 §§2–6 develop an algebraic approach (Phillips's) to the stabiliza-tion problem limned in ¶12.5 §§1. Two themes are stressed: the categorical difference between neo-classical and post-Keynesian approaches to general-equilibrium; the way in which characteristically lagged responses by stabilizing authorities almost inevitably impart an oscillatory torque to the motion of national output. For the last time neo-classical general-equilibrium theory, concerning constellations of notional economic variables permitting consonance of planned actions, is contrasted with post-Keynesian macrodynamics, which concerns laws of motion obeyed by economic variables reflecting interaction of disappointments and surprises in moving economies with imperfect markets.

§3

Happily the analysis can be nested in a simple *multiplier* model.
Equations (58) and (59) emphasize *disequilibrium*:

$$Z = (1-s)Y + A \qquad (58)$$

$$dY/dt = \lambda(Z - Y) \qquad (59)$$

Defining Z as the value of aggregate demand (at fixed prices of course), equation (58) defines aggregate demand on Gross National Product, i.e., Y, and autonomous expenditure. In equation (59), λ converts excess demand for commodities, $Z - Y$, into a time derivative of supply, $\dot{Y} = dY/dt$.
Substituting $[(1-s)Y + A]$ for Z in equation (59):

$$dY/dt + \lambda s Y = \lambda A \qquad (60)$$

The solution of equation (60) is:

$$Y = A/s(1 - e^{-\lambda st}) + Y_0 e^{-\lambda st} \qquad (61)$$

Y_0 being an initial value for Gross National Product. The solution tends to A/s as $t \to \infty$, by now a familiar result.

§4

We now consider differential operators, a remarkable contrivance due to the engineer Heavyside. Referring back to equation (59), denote the symbol d/dt as D:

$$DY = \lambda(Z - Y) \tag{62}$$

And D can be manipulated algebraically! Specifically:

$$Y(D + \lambda) = \lambda Z \tag{63}$$

$$Y = (\lambda/D + \lambda)Z \tag{64}$$

The eccentric equation (64) is to be put aside for now.

§5

Any number of stabilization rules might be set up. Government expenditure at a given date might be *proportional* to a shortfall of actual or intended income. Again Government expenditure might be based on an *integral* stabilization rule:

$$G = -\int_0^t y \, dt \tag{65}$$

y being a deviation of actual from target income. There are *many* other possibilities.

§6

Consider a proportional stabilization rule:

$$DG = -\gamma y \tag{66}$$

i.e.,

$$G = -\frac{\gamma y}{D} \tag{67}$$

Government expenditure immediately reflects deviations from planned income-levels, *but* response is smeared out; expenditure increases in proportion γ to the potential response—the response which presumably would result if the authorities were altogether confident of their data. And $G = 0$ for $y = 0$: 'equilibrium' Government expenditure is encompassed in A. It follows that the time derivative of the deviation of planned expenditure from the desired level, (A/s) is:

$$Dy = \lambda\left[(1-s)y - \frac{\gamma y}{D} - y\right] = -\lambda s y - \frac{\lambda \gamma y}{D} \tag{68}$$

since

$$Dy = \lambda(z - y) \qquad (69)$$

For $z = y = 0$, $Dy = 0$ and $Z = Y = A/s$.

i.e.,

$$D^2 y + \lambda(sDy + \gamma y) = 0$$

Two points have surfaced already—admittedly, 1) is closer to the surface than is 2):

1) the stabilization procedure can lead to oscillatory motion which otherwise would not be present in the system;
2) if there has been a departure of income from its target level, A/s, of, say, \$100 because of a permanent shortfall of autonomous spending of \$20 from its previous level (where $s = 0.2$), then the proportional stabilization policy leads to a basic income-shortfall, around which oscillation may occur, of $\$20/(0.2 + 0.3) = \$40$ for $\gamma = 0.3$.

The proportional stabilization policy can be only partially successful. A more-powerful policy would take into account additional inter-dependent economic forces. However, no feasible policy could account for all of the forces working to determine general economic states.

Cf. K. Fox, J. Sengupta and E. Thorbecke, *The Theory of Quantitative Economic Policy* (Amsterdam: North-Holland Publishing Co.; 1966), Chap. 8, for a 'control theory' approach to stabilization policy. A contribution to this chapter by T. K. Kumar applies Pontryagin's Principle and related methods to optimal growth policy. The authors then apply the Principle and other methods to 'Phillips theory'.

REFERENCES

1. For an excellent summary of recent work in what the text calls a revived neo-classical vein cf. R. G. D. Allen, *Macro-Economic Theory* (London: Macmillan; 1967), esp. Chaps. 10–16.
2. M. Burstein, *Money* (Cambridge, Mass.: Schenkmann Publishing Co. Inc.; 1963).
3. Cf. R. G. D. Allen, *Mathematical Economics* (London: Macmillan & Co. Ltd.; 1964), 2nd ed., p. 205.
4. Again compare R. G. D. Allen, *Mathematical Economics* (London: Macmillan & Co. Ltd.; 1964), 2nd ed., Chaps. 1, 2, 5–9, for an excellent extended treatment of macrodynamics and its associated mathematics. For ¶12.4 cf. pp. 210 ff.
5. Compare J. R. Hicks, *A Contribution to the Theory of the Trade Cycle* (Oxford: The Clarendon Press; 1950), mathematical appendix. I have worked out some simple illustrations of this case in M. L. Burstein, *Money* (Cambridge, Mass.: Schenkmann Publishing Co. Inc.; 1963).
6. Cf. R. G. D. Allen, *Mathematical Economics* (London: Macmillan & Co. Ltd.; 1964), 2nd ed., Chap. 9, for an excellent discussion of 'closed-loop control systems'. Also R. G. D. Allen, *Macro-Economic Theory* (London: Macmillan & Co. Ltd.; 1967), Chap. 18.
7. Cf. R. G. D. Allen, *Mathematical Economics* (London: Macmillan & Co. Ltd.; 1964), 2nd ed., pp. 262–279.

Money-supply Theory and Central-bank Policy

Chapter 13, abridging an essay, admittedly is not wholly integrated into the book. Still it augments the book usefully. Chapter 13 deepens the austere discussion of Chapter 12 with material dredged up from Life. Its results are based on some of the book's central propositions. Furthermore, a book on economic theory, if reasonably comprehensive, must treat money.

1. INTRODUCTION: THE NINE PROPOSITIONS

Two central conclusions flow from nine propositions.

1) Monetary policies bottomed on rules to be obeyed by the time-profile of the monetary base cannot be buttressed by economic statics.
2) Proper money-supply theory is nested in *disequilibrium* dynamics.

The propositions are:

1) In neo-classical models effects of monetary policy are mediated only through prices changed through *tâtonnement* so that effects of monetary measures on equilibrium are subsumed under 'neutrality of money.' Indeed reflexion vitiates even 'real balance' effects of changes in the stock of fiat currency.
2) In a statical Keynesian model, which admittedly is not neutral against the monetary base, it would be better to assign interest rate rather than monetary base (let alone M!) targets, leading up to 'a suggested simplification of Mr. Hicks.'
3) Observed time-paths of interest rates will differ, relative even to identical money-supply time-paths, depending on whether credit markets typically clear. In turn this hinges on decision rules of *lenders of last resort*. The more efficient are lenders of last resort the less significant is money-supply theory!

4) Static-stability analysis properly does not intersect monetary dynamics because the former is bound up in general-equilibrium theory, which is itself uncongenial to monetary dynamics.

5) The quantitative importance of *disequilibrium* phenomena, and hence the importance of monetary theory (dynamic when useful), keys on the degree of perfection and speed of adjustment of credit-markets. Balance-sheet switching, sometimes offsetting official actions, falls under this rubric. So the theory of deposit switching from banks to non-banks is important for money-supply theory.

6) Noting the links between monetary dynamics and credit availability, established in the proofs of the first five propositions, the core of the *Radcliffe Report* is quite valid.

7) The Bank of England's grip on short run movements of British money-supply is more fragile because the Bank is a *lender of last resort*. Still the Bank is not made *hors de combat*.

8) Distinction between 'active' and 'passive' official operations on the cash base leads up to certain methodological problems, and then to the conclusion that structural identification is important in monetary econometrics.

9) Money-supply régimes are sapped by recent international financial developments (witness Eurodollars) and the relative importance nowadays of *covered*, as against *uncovered*, movements of funds. These developments, whilst sometimes permitting more autarkical Bank Rate régimes, also undermine Bank Rate's traditional influence over balances of payments.

§ 2

Abstract as is some of this chapter's discussion, a higher level of generality is required than is thus far suggested. We are to merge the theory of money with the theory of finance (long suggested by Professors Gurley and Shaw) employing a hypothetical *laisser-faire* economy. Thus imagine an economy in which the only monetary legislation was a legal tender act, specifying that debts stated in money of account could be satisfied at a given rate by tender of standardized quanta of gold or fiat paper money. However, in this economy, anyone can carry on functions we identify with clearing banks, merchant banks, insurance companies, etc. Only *ad hoc* criteria could distinguish between banks and non-banks. More intriguingly, perhaps it would be impossible to separate out certain liabilities as 'the supply of money'. After all, current account (demand–deposit) liability may be a feature of the representative trader's balance-sheet in much the same way as production activities are attributed to him in the neo-classical theory of welfare economics.[1] Nor would there be any need for peculiar financial substances to discharge means-of-payments functions. (Not that they do now.) Then the endogeneity of whatever is to be called money-supply becomes obvious. Indeed the model may be described as an idealization of Radcliffe monetary philosophy.

The *laisser-faire* system's statics preserve the properties of more conventional systems. Standard neo-classical stipulations, foreclosing money illusion for example, make the real properties of a standard statical general-equilibrium representation of the *laisser-faire* model invariant against the nominal value of, say, a fiat paper legal tender base. However, we choose to centre on the system's laws of motion without reference to notional states of full equilibrium.

All traders are to be price quoters in all markets in which they trade: the scheme verges on all-round monopoly and has appeal in the 'real world' of imperfect competition *cum* oligopoly *cum* monopoly. Quotations and programmes today reflect expectations flowing from experienced disappointment and surprise. Realized transaction levels are governed by quantities offered for supply or demand, whichever is the less. So the economy is to be represented by a system of differential equations like that of ¶12.2. Turning to the model's financial aspects we become concerned always with portfolio choice, i.e. portfolio *change*. Indeed, from a 'micro' point of view, investment programmes treat physical and financial actions in just the same way. Does the *j*th trader, in the light of experience, wish to expand his physical capital, by issuing new debentures? Does the *k*th trader wish to acquire 30-year maturities by issuing 10-day claims which, as it happens are means of payment? Again, perhaps the *i*th trader, calling itself the Chase Manhattan Bank, can be forced out of portfolio balance if authorities sell securities to its customers. Perhaps some—not we—will characterize the *k*th plan as increasing the quantity of money.

Keep our *laisser-faire* model in mind. It underlies most of the chapter's analysis from ¶13.2 onwards.

2. MONEY AND INTEREST IN NEO-CLASSICAL THEORY

Consider a system rather like that of Dr. Lange's *Price Flexibility and Employment*.[2] Recalling, ¶13.1 §§2, the *laisser-faire* economy is to have a unique legal tender (also to be the standard of value), the aggregate value being M^0 (measured in money of account) and determined by otherwise unspecified authorities. We do not specify the extent to which one or another of $n-1$ privately issued securities exercise monetary functions. It does not matter:

$$f^i(p_1, \ldots, p_m; r_{m+1}, \ldots, r_{m+n}) = 0 \qquad i = 1, 2, \ldots, m \qquad (1)$$

$$F^j(\mathbf{p}, \mathbf{r}, M^0) = G^j(\mathbf{p}, \mathbf{r}, M^0) + K^j \qquad j = m+1, \ldots, M+n-1 \qquad (2)$$

$$f^{m+n}(\mathbf{p}, \mathbf{r}, M^0) = 0 \qquad\qquad \mathbf{S1} \quad (3)$$

$$\Sigma K^j = M^0 \qquad\qquad (4)$$

The authorities are to supply an *inside* 'money' of nominal value M^0 in exchange for privately issued securities of the same value. Equilibrium requires that the value of the private securities held by the authorities be precisely equal to that of the official securities, viz. M^0, held by the private sector. This is to be a model of *tâtonnement* either without 'history' or in which 'history' is constrained by equation (4). Official demand for each of securities $m+1, \ldots, m+n-1$, defined by terms to maturity, is K^j, subject to $\Sigma K^j = M^0$. Thus, in equilibrium, the supply of the jth security, measured in money of account, must be equal to private demand, G^j, plus official demand, K^j. Equation (3) requires that excess demand for 'money' be zero whilst equation (1) requires that excess demand be zero for each of the m commodities.

S1 then is a system of $m+n+1$ equations in the variables $\mathbf{p}$ (a m-vector), $\mathbf{r}$ (a n-vector), M, and $\mathbf{K}$ (a $n-1$ vector). Walras's Law removes one of the $n-1$ excess degrees of freedom and the specification that M be policy-determined another, so that $n-3$ degrees of freedom remain: for example arbitrary decisions can be taken on all but two of official holdings K^j under a crude 'equations-equal-unknowns' criterion.

Consider now a solution state of **S1**, $(\bar{\mathbf{p}}, \bar{\mathbf{r}}, \bar{K}^{m+1}, \bar{K}^{m+2}, M^0, K^{m+3*}, \ldots K^{m+n-1*})$. Rational behaviour here precludes money illusion: functions $1, 2, \ldots, m$ are zero-order homogeneous and the others first-order homogeneous in $\mathbf{p}$. Hence **S1** also is solved by $(\lambda\bar{\mathbf{p}}, \bar{\mathbf{r}}, \lambda\bar{K}^{m+1}, \lambda\bar{K}^{m+2}, \lambda M^0, \lambda K^{m+3*}, \ldots, \lambda K^{m+n-1*})$. That is: $\partial\bar{\mathbf{p}}/\partial M = \mathbf{k}$ and $\partial\bar{\mathbf{r}}/\partial M = \mathbf{0}$.

Such is the analytical content of the quantity theory of money neo-classically formulated. What are its implications for policy? None, if we postulate that the equilibrium structure of interest rates is invariant against the term structure of public debt. If we postulate otherwise, it is still clear that monetary measures would have to work their effects through interest rate changes in equilibrium.

§2

Two pockets of resistance have been by-passed. One concerns 'the burden of the money supply,' the other '*tâtonnement* and monetary theory.'

§3

The Burden of the Money-Supply

Consider two classes of property, A and B. A-property consists of rights to exact the *taille* from certain persons. B-property yields a perpetual stream of scarce consumer services. Surely in a closed system B-property properly is part of national wealth, somehow calculated. What about A-property, specified to be non-negotiable and ineligible as collateral? Would not the value of *taille*-rights then be precisely that of the burden of the *paysans*? Is not financial property, liquidity aside, precisely like A-property, imposing duties *pari passu* with conferring of rights?

Liquidity aside! Financial arrangements affect production possibilities and are the object of preferences. Still, once qualitative effects of the existence of monetary arrangements are built into the analysis, *fiat* money can be deemed to have the zero-sum (or dual) properties of the *taille*. After all, 'real balance' effects traditionally have been studied through simple budget equations. Is not your power to command commodities with currency our liability? Indeed may one distinguish the usual *closed* case from international (or other *open*) systems? Thus an economy comprising n traders may be deemed to be any one of n combinations, 'they' being 1 or 2 or ... or n, 'we' being $(2, \ldots, n)$ or $(1, 3, \ldots, n)$ or ... In each instance net financial wealth is zero within groups and, taking up the first combination, if 1's case balance were increased, the wealth of $1 + (2, \ldots, n)$ would be unchanged even in terms of aggregates of private calculations. Distribution effects become the *sine qua non* of monetary theory.

§4

Tâtonnement and Monetary Theory

First reread ¶1.5 §§5. Then note, at the risk of repetition, that, upon dropping *tâtonnement*, the analysis verges upon that of all-round monopoly. Traders must reckon that they may not be able to accomplish desired sales or purchases. They must work out programmes against back-drops of subjective probabilities attributed to quantities they may be able to buy or sell at quoted prices. Thus, once auction markets are put aside, neoclassical monetary formulations recede in favour of Keynesian economics. The bulk of Chapter 13 is concerned to establish a rôle for money-supply theory in a new, Keynesian context centring on properties of non-*tâtonnement* dynamics.

3. SOME KEYNESIAN STATICS; A DYNAMICAL WICKSELLIAN EXTENSION

Consider system **S2**, taken from the *fixprice* analysis of ¶9.9:

$$Y = f(Y, r^0) \tag{5}$$
$$M = L(Y, r^0) \tag{6}$$

S2

Observe that some would find **S2** to be unorthodox: the unknowns are
Y and M, not Y and r: *the* rate of interest is to be defended by official
operators dealing freely between securities and money. Indeed **S2** is in a
sense a 'suggested simplification of Mr. Hicks': its graphics can be confined
to that segment of IS not foreclosed by the '*liquidity trap*'.

Unorthodox or not, **S2** comes to the heart of the matter: since in statical
Keynesian models, money-supply influences real income only through
effects on interest rates. Authorities focus on what counts and merely
accommodate whatever portfolio mix the public wish at r^0. Indeed in a
stochastic version of **S2** it would be stupid to frame policies in terms of
money-supply instruments: econometric would then be imposed on substantive (i.e. specification) error. Interest rate targets, perhaps wrongly
selected, might not be achieved.

§2

Keynesian statics, bottomed on the *fixprice* mode of analysis, lead up to
a statical theory of economic policy *à la* Tinbergen.[3] An underdetermined
equation system is written out. Excess degrees of freedom are absorbed by
stipulations of some of the solution values. Policy, thus defined, is executed
through such instruments as surtax rate, reserve requirements, central-
bank investments, etc. Usually instrument levels do not enter into preference functions being maximized; usually excess degrees of freedom are
exhausted by selection of target levels for such non-instruments as prices
and employment. Statical policy-theory, an extension of **S2**, does not
offer a rôle to money-supply theory.

§3

There is a sense, admittedly violating general-equilibrium, in which
policy models possess many more degrees of freedom than would be
suggested by **S2** and its extensions. Dynamic models can be projected
which, upon being supplied with initial conditions, trace out projected
values for data generated by *disequilibrated* systems. And why should the
notional state, general-equilibrium, dominate the theory of economic
policy?

§4

Wicksell leads directly to modern macrodynamics but not to a rôle for
money-supply theory, whatever Wicksell may have said. Consider **S3**,
a much simplified form of **S1**.

$$\Phi(r) = 0 \tag{7}$$
$$\Psi(p; M^0) = 0 \tag{8}$$

S3

There is to be a pure-credit money. Equation (8) may be based on a Cantabrigian formulation of money-demand.

Solve S3 for $(\bar{r}, \bar{p})$, observing that $\bar{r}$ is invariant against the monetary base. Now assume that the authorities insist on $r \neq \bar{r}$. Cumulative inflation or deflation must result.

Why does not Wicksell succour money-supply theory? Because S3 implies that the officials deal freely at r^0. If they select $r^0 = \bar{r}$, they can arbitrarily select M, thus determining the scale of prices. Agreed, for $r^0 \neq \bar{r}$, the time-profile of money-supply would have to obey a system such as that of equations (12.1) and (12.2) if securities markets were to be cleared continuously: The general price level might not be arbitrarily determinable by officials opting for $r^0 \neq \bar{r}$. Still there would be no rôle for money-supply theory: the lever is r; M merely is chosen to validate r^0. However, if S3 were queered so that securities markets were persistently in substantial *disequilibrium*, perhaps because the monetary base were abruptly moved about, *then* prevailing interest rates would reflect monetary *disequilibrium* and the relevant domain of analysis would become availability (of credit) theory. This last theme is to be enlarged in ¶13.4.

4. THE LENDER OF LAST RESORT IN ALTERNATIVE MODES OF ANALYSIS; MONEY-SUPPLY AND INTEREST RATE TIME-PATHS IN ALTERNATIVE MODES OF ANALYSIS

It is a commonplace in elementary texts—albeit correct only in a *fixprice* context—that a decision on M is a decision on **r** and vice versa. This dictum is supported by S2 but contradicted by systems S1 and S3, as well as by the system of equations (12.1) and (12.2). Still there need logically be no collision.

§ 2

Consider first Régime A: the central bank's rôle as lender of last resort is complete and passive (cf. the Ideal Wife). Assume that the A authorities determine on *time-paths* of interest rates which they stand ready to defend with all of their resources:

$$\mathbf{r} = \mathbf{f}(t) \tag{9}$$

There emerges an observed path of money-supply:

$$M = g(t) \tag{10}$$

Now consider Régime B: it has no lender of last resort. Its authorities decide upon a money-supply path. Indeed they decide on the very path $g(t)$. We contend that, under Régime B, quite different time-paths of interest rates can be expected, doubtless more turbulent than $f(t)$:

$$\mathbf{r} = \mathbf{h}(t) \tag{11}$$

Under Régime *B*, severe contractionary pressures, perhaps induced by massive open-market sales over a brief interval, can lead to involuntary liquidation-attempts in imperfect non-auction markets by debtors. Frustrated, they become hammered, albeit they are happy to pay going rates of interest. Again, when the authorities' purchases flood the banks with liquidity, interest rates may plummet as bankers trudge home unable to acquire securities on the terms fixed for today—terms which they doubtless will make more generous tomorrow, perhaps unavailingly. Under Régime *B*, necessarily there is frequent, if not persistent, *disequilibrium* in the securities markets. The history of interest rates in *B* should be different from that in *A*, where securities markets always are in equilibrium.

§ 3

Why estimate parameters of money-demand under Régime *A*? *A*-officials merely defend target yields. Régime *B* is more interesting to students of 'the demand for money,' but only in *disequilibrium*. Thus the long run elasticity of demand for money is probably only trivially interesting even under Régime *B*. To the extent that *B*-authorities contemplate a tranquil state in which all securities markets are cleared, we have shown that they would be better advised to work to interest rate targets, supplying whatever monetary base becomes necessary. However, the speed and magnitude of cash-balance adjustments, necessarily reflecting the speed and magnitude of *desired* adjustments, can be very important in a *disequilibrium* context. For example, if their speed and, magnitude were very great indeed, effects of official contractionary action quickly might be offset by transitions in the *matrix of claims* (cf. ¶13.6–7).

5. STATIC-STABILITY AND MONETARY DYNAMICS

Recall that static-stability analysis transpires only in logical- or meta-time. Since the underlying functional relationships must be kept rigidly fixed, the trading processes must be notional, otherwise expectations could not be invariant against trading experience for example. Hence the relevance of static-stability analysis to monetary economics becomes that of models of *tâtonnement*. Chapter 13 already has suggested that the guts of monetary economics are not contained in *tâtonnement* models. The sequel is to make this even clearer. If indeed the sequel thus succeeds, our little syllogism forces us out of static-stability and into study of the dynamics of ongoing systems, conceding that the upshot well may be intractable to classical methods.

6. SWITCHES IN THE MATRIX OF CLAIMS, MONETARY DISEQUILIBRIUM AND MONEY-SUPPLY THEORY

First consider the *matrix of claims*. Construct a huge grid on which all conceivable indebtednesses can be recorded disaggregatively. Economic transactions then can be conceived to comprise a non-stationary transitions matrix $\mathbf{T}_t$ switching the *matrix of claims* $\mathbf{C}_t$ into $\mathbf{C}_{t+h}$—being careful to read $(\mathbf{C}_t)$, *not* $(\mathbf{C})_t$. In statics one asks whether the transformations lead up to an absorbing state. However, a theory of monetary policy, concerned as it must be with irregularly growing, sometimes decaying, never orderly ongoing economies, can by-pass this query.

After analysing in ¶13.6 §§2, a hypothetical episode of monetary contraction, easily generalized, we pass over in ¶13.6 §§3 et seq. to implications for money-supply theory. We focus on a practical problem, deposit switching between banks and non-banks. Monetary effects will come to be seen as 'availability' phenomena divorced from static-stability theory.

§2

Credit stringency induced by official open-market sales easily is explained through balance sheets. Ignoring all finance sources but banks for the nonce, banks will find their reserves to be deficient and, accordingly, will come under pressure to sell assets (non-renewal of customer loans are to be treated as sales by banks). Although each bank may associate asset sales with reserve accretions, collectively reserves would not thus be increased if there is no *lender of last resort* to whom to make sales and if currency influx and efflux are ignored. Bank-portfolio balance cannot be restored until the banks have sold enough securities, paid for by cheques drawn against current accounts and reducing deposit liability *pari passu*, to restore desired ($\geq$ customary or legal) reserve ratios. At the same time, the public's collective balance-sheet must come to show less cash *and* less indebtedness to banks. In a system of auction markets with a *tâtonnement* dynamic these balance sheet changes would reflect interest rate changes: the open-market sales would be simply an elaborate device for affecting interest rates. In Life 'availability' effects, peculiar to monetary action, appear. Thus interest rates will not ration credit while bank-portfolios are contracting, nor when securities markets are congested as banks are unable to expand portfolios rapidly enough during booms. Sellers' quotations are marked down only as securities markets fail to clear day after day—as sellers become convinced that it was no accident that they could not move their stock yesterday at a price they are shaving today.

We now propose to deal with extended matrixes **C** and **T**; we are to take account of switches which, amongst other things, cause flows of non-bank finance to move in counterphase to bank finance. After a brief general statement, we will consider trade credit. This accomplished, ¶13.6 §§3 will loom up.

Consider a non-bank financier balance-sheet switch in a setting of official contractionary inpulse. (Perhaps the reader will think of a merchant banker, e.g. Lazard Brothers.) Doubtless motivated by attractive lending terms, the financier might try to attract additional capital and perhaps will succeed in inducing hoarders to disgorge cash on his recognizance, thus countervailing official policy. A similar effect could be caused by an insurance company able to sell Government stock for cash. More complicated effects ensue from deposit switches or from trade credit.

Brechling and Lipsey[4] show that expansion of gross trade credit can, for a while, finance increased nominally-valued transactions activity and that expansion of net trade credit can do so indefinitely.

> '... trade credit shows definite signs of reacting to monetary policy; both credit periods tend to rise in times of monetary squeezes and to fall in times of easy money. This evidence is clearly consistent with the theory that the quantity effect of monetary policy is definitely felt by firms and that they take active steps to avoid it by running up their credit taken.'[5]

A firm's net trade credit position is defined by the difference between the amount of trade credit it has given and that which it has taken. Its gross position by the amount which it has given.

The *sustained* inflationary impact of trade credit expansion is another matter. Under a rough *ceteris paribus*, if the volume of trade credit is x, then $\dot{p} > 0$ requires $\ddot{x} > 0$. It is not the volume of trade credit, but its rate of increase, which contributes to the demand for goods. For the demand for goods to increase, so must the rate of increase of trade credit. It follows that, for inflation ($\dot{p} > 0$) to be sustained in this way, the expansionary impulse must persistently accelerate. However, red flags hoisted by credit managers, together with growing exigency caused by increasing demand for currency, are likely quite soon to halt the process. So the significance of trade credit changes is transitory. Still our central contention is that transitory displacements from stock equilibria are the *sine qua non* of monetary theory.

§3

Now we are to explain the economic significance of shifts by depositors between different classes of monetary institutions, inevitably assessing the meaning and utility of alternative money-supply definitions. The discussion has 'spin-off'. It suggests that the true interest of commercial banks is for competing financial institutions also to be hamstrung by regulations rather than for the banks to be permitted to become more competitive. ¶13.6 §§4, like ¶13.6 §§5 is in an American context. The former may be called 'Regulation Q and Competition for Deposits', the latter, 'Some Implications for Money-Supply Theory'.

§ 4

(Federal Reserve) Regulation Q permits the Federal Reserve Board of Governors to establish maximum member-bank deposit rates. Easement of a binding Regulation Q stimulates growth of commercial-bank interest-bearing deposits whilst perhaps stunting that of non-banking financial houses, *and* leads, *ceteris paribus*, to contractionary effects on liquid asset supply and to lower commercial-bank profits.

1. CONTRACTIONARY EFFECTS ON LIQUID-ASSET SUPPLY. Consult equation (12) together with the following glossary of symbols. Then note the austere stipulations.

$$\Delta D = -1 + (k_1 - k_2)/k_1 \tag{12}$$

Glossary
1) $\Delta D =$ change in total deposit liability of commercial banks *plus* that of non-banks.
2) $k_1 =$ reserve requirement against demand deposits of commercial banks.
3) $k_2 =$ reserve requirement against interest-bearing deposits of commercial banks.

Stipulations
1) There is to be a transfer of \$1 by a non-bank depositor into an interest-bearing bank deposit, in response to higher deposit rates offered by commercial banks responding to an eased Regulation Q.
2) The aggregate of interest-bearing deposits is to be held fixed.
3) Non-bank reserves are held as demand deposits at commercial banks.
4) Currency holdings are to be neglected.
5) No distinctions are to be drawn between different types of interest-bearing deposits.
6) Excess and borrowed (and hence free) reserves of commercial banks are to be ignored.

Now analyse equation (12). At impact, transfer of \$1 in interest-bearing deposits from non-banks to banks reduces total deposits by \$1: if a building society loses $1 in deposits, it must write a $1 cheque against a commercial bank. Deposit of the cheque does not affect the total of commercial-bank deposits: demand deposits are reduced by $1; interest-bearing deposits are increased by $1. Building-society bank cash has been reduced by $1 and, as soon as the building-society attempts to restore its bank cash, there will be corresponding excess supply in securities markets, partially offset if $k_1 > k_2$. Commercial banks will have excess reserves of $(k_1 - k_2)(100)$ cents: commercial bank equilibrium dèposit-liability will be $(1/k_1)(k_1 - k_2)(100)$ cents greater than before the transfer.

If one accepts the model's stipulations, one must conclude that, whatever has been the expansion of American liquid assets since relaxation of Regulation Q in January 1962, it would have been greater if commercial banks had not thus been allowed to compete more effectively for interest-bearing deposits. To the extent that deposits absorb the monetary base, liquid asset expansion is deterred.

2. BANK-DEPOSIT EXPANSION AND BANK PROFITS. Focus on the *aggregate* of commercial banks: Bank Aleph, if it receives additional interest-bearing deposits, most likely will be increasing its reserves *pari passu*, *but* the cheque deposited with Aleph probably will be drawn against Beth.

Extend the glossary.

Extended glossary
4) r = the rate of return, adjusted for risk, which can be earned by commercial banks on incremental loans and investments (if $r = 0{\cdot}04$, the rate of return is 4 per cent per annum).
5) $\hat{r}$ = the commercial-bank deposit rate.
6) x = commercial-bank interest-bearing deposit liability.
7) $\lambda = [r(k_1 - k_2)/k_1] - \hat{r}$.
8) π = commercial-bank profits.
   Additional stipulations are required.

Additional stipulations
7) r and $\hat{r}$ are to be parameters.
8) Service costs are to be ignored.
9) Recalling stipulation 2), feedback effects on commercial-bank interest-bearing deposits are to be neglected, leading to overstatement of the algebraic value of $\Delta\pi$.

Inequality (13) must hold for $\Delta\pi > 0$. So we shall call inequality (13) the *profitability condition*:

$$[r(k_1 - k_2)/k_1 - \hat{r}]\,\Delta x - (\Delta\hat{r})x > 0 \qquad (13)$$

$$\lambda\,\Delta x - (\Delta\hat{r})x > 0 \qquad (14)$$

Subsequent to $\Delta\hat{r} > 0$, bank costs will increase: there will be an increment to interest-bearing deposits, interest cost on new deposits being approximately $\hat{r}\,\Delta x$, and more must be paid on initial interest-bearing deposits, the measure being $\Delta\hat{r} \cdot x$. On the other hand, more can be invested at yield r.

For $k_1 = 0\cdot12$ and $k_2 = 0\cdot04$, inequality (13) becomes:

$$r > 1\cdot5\hat{r} + 1\cdot5[\Delta\hat{r}(x/\Delta x)] \tag{15}$$

The order of magnitude of x in the United States is $\$100(10)^7$. So, under the stipulations, even if a $0\cdot0005$ increase in deposit rate brought in $\$10(10)^7$ in new interest-bearing commercial-bank deposits, the profitability condition requires $r > 0\cdot135$ for $\hat{r} = 0\cdot04$!

The rub is in stipulations 2), 7) and 8). As these stand, general-equilibrium reasoning requires that an eased Regulation Q should lead to higher interest rates and less credit availability. Surely more appropriate stipulations would centre on invariant official targets, defined on time, for market rates of interest on commercial and Government paper.

POINT. In a more interesting model, if Regulation Q were eased, commercial-bank reserves would increase more quickly. Larger reserves, *ceteris paribus*, permit more-profitable operation of commercial banks: leverage then can be exerted on larger masses.

So the next step is to relax the stipulations so that easement of Regulation Q can be accompanied by more-rapid expansion of bank-portfolios. Indeed imagine that non-banks had been prevented from increasing their deposit liabilities over the years 1956–1960. Reserve requirements and deposit rate limits could have been imposed (incidentally, then, leading to lower offer-prices for deposits). Suppose that the actual increase in non-bank deposits from 1956 to 1960, $\$38\cdot2$ billion, had been tacked onto the $\$24$ billion increase in commercial bank interest-bearing deposits which actually occurred. How much would have to have been $\Delta\hat{r}$ for the compound event to leave bank profits unaffected? Solve equation (17), following from equation (16), for $\Delta\hat{r}$. Note that equation (17) is supplied with 'real world' data:

$$(1-k_2)(\Delta x_1)(r) = (\Delta\hat{r})(x^0) + (\hat{r}+\Delta\hat{r})(\Delta x_1) + (\Delta\hat{r})(\Delta x_2) \tag{16}$$

$$(0\cdot96)(38\cdot2)(0\cdot06) = (\Delta\hat{r})(46\cdot3 + (0\cdot03+\Delta\hat{r})(38\cdot2) + (\Delta\hat{r})(23\cdot0) \tag{17}$$

i.e.:

$$(107\cdot5)\Delta\hat{r} = 1\cdot056 \tag{18}$$

$$\Delta\hat{r} \simeq 0\cdot01 \tag{19}$$

Clarifying equation (16), distinguish between increments to commercial bank interest-bearing deposits which are and which are not related to the new policy: Δx_1 is induced. Δx_2 would have occurred anyhow. Incremental

investment profits are measured by the left-hand sides of equations (16)
and (17). There are three kinds of incremental expense: increased interest
cost on initial deposits x^0; interest cost on incremental deposits generated
by the new policy Δx_1; increased interest cost on new deposits which would
have been received in any case Δx_2. Equation (17) shows that United
States commercial banks over the years 1956–1960 could have afforded to
offer only 1 per cent more for deposits, even if that would have permitted
them to attract the entire increment of non-bank deposits accruing over
1956–1960! Furthermore, a compliant monetary authority would have to
have fed additional reserves to the banks.

It is time to consider relaxing stipulation 7). If non-banks could be forced
to maintain larger reserves and to pursue more-conservative investment
policies, they would come to offer lower deposit rates, perhaps permitting
$\Delta \hat{r} < 0$, in which case we can quickly reach home. A new scenario unfolds:
docile authorities shackle competitors of banks whilst providing reserves to
be absorbed by additional bank deposits. Indeed, the authorities could
compel commercial bankers, facing hamstrung non-banks, to offer lower
deposit rates, leading up to the best of all possible commercial-banking
worlds.

§5

It follows from ¶13.6 §§4 that:

1) money-supply series restricted to deposit liabilities of commercial
   banks (together with currency) might be seriously misleading; and
2) once again, statical theories of economic policy logically focus on
   implementation of interest rate targets, rather than on effects of
   liquid assets on interest rates.

1. MONEY-SUPPLY SERIES. If money were defined as '*all* deposits of commercial banks' (ignoring currency), a policy causing bank deposits to
increase at the expense of non-bank deposits could lead to a sharp increase
in measured M, even if aggregate deposit liability were falling. A naive
observer might think that money-supply was being increased in order to
counteract developing excess-supplies of securities whilst the authorities,
bemused by their criterion, might be concerned about inflationary
pressures, evidenced by increasing M and excess supplies of securities,
suggesting that 'demand for funds is running ahead of savings.' In this
instance credit-market conditions better would be reflected by an M
confined to demand deposits.

Pursuing the possibility of M being restricted to demand deposits
of commercial banks, what if depositors at banks were to shift from
interest-bearing to demand deposits? Measured M would increase *and*

contractionary pressure would be building up. Here the 'all bank deposit' definition is better. The total of bank deposits would be declining, or falling below trend, at least if borrowed and unborrowed reserves increase according to a predetermined trend-dominated pattern.

2. LIQUID ASSETS AND INTEREST RATES. Of course there is no point in building up a collection of hypothetical cases favouring one and then another inadequate monetary criterion. So we will make our point of departure the theme that monetary dynamics are not so much concerned with properties of optimal portfolios as with 'release of cash.' We must recall that optimal-portfolio criteria are relevant, however, since disparities of actual from desired positions establish discharge-potentials. Ordinarily the significant events during episodes of monetary expansion and contraction are typified by *obstruction* of portfolio adjustment processes. Taking up a case of contraction, creditors' desires to change the forms of their portfolios, not necessarily into cash but surely in ways which require debtors to 'cough up' cash which they do not have—and soon will find that, collectively, they cannot get—lead up to *disequilibrated* credit-markets. These in turn force bankruptcies, cancellations of investment programmes, etc. Again, consider an expansionary episode in which banks, surfeited with new liquidity, seek to induce the public to take out more credit. This leads to cash flowing from the banks to the public, but during the decisive phase the public doubtless are *planning* to convert most of the cash into other assets. Agreed, restoration of tranquillity requires that cash balances be in harmony with optimizing calculations. However, the excess demands and supplies associated with cash-balance disparities ordinarily appear only in the 'Recessionals' of monetary episodes. Ordinarily! Important exceptions include pathological events such as the United States bank crisis of 1932–1933. These conclusions are supported by American colonial experience.[6]

Analogously, the dunning creditors on the 'downside' might be *planning* to convert the proceeds of liquidations into bank bills for example. Such plans cannot come to fruition unless the debtors can, in fact, 'cough up' cash. This leads up to certain differences between *tâtonnement* and *non-tâtonnement* dynamics: under the former calls can lead to a twisted yield curve, reflecting planned disposals of receipts; under the latter plans for disposal of receipts one cannot obtain are boiled off from the analysis. The analysis leads up to a correct statement of 'liquidity preference' versus 'loanable funds' theories of interest rates.

The formal background is supplied by a theory dealing with acute shifts or attempted acute shifts in matrix $\mathbf{C}$ (say towards substitution of short for long term debt) requiring rapid and drastic changes in transition matrices $\mathbf{T}$. In such a theory portfolio-choice analysis becomes subordinated to establishment of potential discharge positions, i.e. to prediction of matrix $\mathbf{T}_t$.

The model of ¶13.6 §§3, et seq., sharply distinguishes between banks and non-banks. The latter hold their reserves with the former. So a deposit switch from the former to the latter does not cost the banks reserves, whilst a reverse switch erodes the reserves of the non-banks. Thus is shown the inflationary character of an increased preference for non-bank deposits.

Once currency—even more ultimate than current accounts as a financial substance—is introduced, the banks (i.e. the clearing or commercial banks) lose their uniqueness amongst the economy's firms. Introduction of currency into the model poses reserve-loss problems for banks and, hence, leakage-dynamics. Note the analogy to the prevailing (November 1967) system of holding and management of international reserves: the gold-exchange standard now in force finds the United States at the apex of an inverted pyramid.

Taking up leakage, how does the rate, at which claims accruing against a sector come to be deposited within that sector, compare with the rate at which such accruals require the sector immediately to liquidate some asset? In the model of ¶13.6 §§3, claims against commercial banks are deposited within the commercial-banking sector, so that an increase in bank reserves leads rapidly to a multiplied expansion of bank deposits and investments. If banks expand their assets beyond equilibrium levels, they experience only a slow leak of reserves, so long as bank liabilities continue to be at the bottom of the inverted pyramid of reserves—as General de Gaulle has pointed out in another, closely tied, connexion. On the other hand, the building-societies lose reserves almost as quickly as accruals mount against them: claims against building societies are not at the bottom of the inverted pyramid. What if they were? What if commercial banks were not uniquely identifiable at the bottom of the inverted pyramid? Then our earlier dynamical distinctions would become dissolved in the melting pot already containing the theory of general-equilibrium of the financial sector.

7. RADCLIFFE HISTORICALLY CONTEMPLATED AND OTHERWISE VINDICATED

Recall the Banking School/Currency School controversy. The Currency School, favouring the Bank Charter Act of 1844, argued that British monetary policy should focus on note issue (currency). The Banking School, opposing the Act, argued that the separation of the Bank's issue and banking departments, called for in the Act, was chimerical for reasons well put by J. S. Mill:

> 'It is well known that, of late years, an artificial limitation of the issue of bank notes has been regarded by many political economists, and by a

large portion of the public, as an expedient of supreme efficacy for preventing, and when it cannot prevent, for moderating, the fever of speculation;
and this opinion received the recognition and sanction of the legislature
by the Currency Act of 1844. At the point, however, which our enquiries
have reached, though we have conceded bank notes a greater power over
prices than is possessed by bills or book credits we have not found reason
to think that this superior efficacy has much share in producing the rise in
prices which accompanies a period of speculation, nor consequently that
any restraint applied to this one instrument can be efficacious to the degree
which is often supposed, in moderating either that rise or the recoil which
follows from it. We shall be less inclined to think so when we consider that
there is a fourth form of credit transactions, by cheques on bankers, and
transfers in a banker's books which is exactly parallel in every respect to
bank notes, giving equal facilities to an extension of credit, and capable of
acting on prices quite as powerfully.'[7]

Mill is perfectly correct in arguing that switches in the *matrix of claims*
can lead to pronounced changes over considerable intervals in flow rates
of excess-demand in various markets, quite apart from the behaviour of
the currency base. Putting aside altogether the Banking School's celebrated principle of reflux, and centring instead on their negation of
Currency School dogma, we must support the Banking School, arguing
that 'the factor which monetary policy should seek to influence or control
is something that reaches far beyond what is known as the "supply of
money"'.[8]

The factor is as general as are matrices **C** and **T**: in Life. Control of a few
of the many determinants of credit expansion and contraction need not be
decisive.

Still there is a sense, rooted deep in general-equilibrium theory, in which
the Currency School may be correct—correct in the way in which Ricardo
often was correct whilst being incorrect in the way that he could be incorrect. Consider a simplified version of system **S1**:

$$f^i(\mathbf{p}, \mathbf{r}) = 0 \qquad\qquad i = 1, 2, \ldots, m \qquad\qquad (20)$$

$$g^j(\mathbf{p}, \mathbf{r}) = h^j(\mathbf{p}, \mathbf{r}) \qquad j = (m+1), \ldots, n \quad \textbf{S4} \quad (21)$$

$$F(r_{m+1}) \cdot h^{m+1}(\mathbf{p}, \mathbf{r}) = \mathbf{k} \qquad\qquad\qquad\qquad (22)$$

Equations (20) concern commodities markets, **p** and **r** being vectors.
$f^i(\mathbf{p}, \mathbf{r})$ determines excess demand in the ith commodity market; $g^j(\mathbf{p}, \mathbf{r})$
determines demand and $h^j(\mathbf{p}, \mathbf{r})$ supply of the jth security. As the analysis
of **S1** established, the zero-order homogeneity (in **p**) properties of the
commodity excess-demand functions, together with the first-order
homogeneity (in **p**) properties of the security excess-demand functions
(derived from functions g^j and h^j), make it possible to solve equations (20)

to (22) only up to a scale factor. However, once the nominal value of one of the securities, for example, is specified (with the aid of function F mapping yields into prices), the system's nominal equilibrium values also become specified, being determinable through control of the nominal value of the supply of a single stock. If as many as two such values were arbitrarily predetermined, real properties of general-equilibrium would cease to be invariant against the arbitrary nominal value of any one stock, although system S4's reduced form still would associate real solutions with nominal value vectors of the arbitrary stocks. Indeed authorities under the revised S4 would have more influence: the real equilibrium state of the system can be influenced by manipulation of nominal values of securities supplies in the revised, but not in the former, case.

The sense in which general-equilibrium theory can lend qualified support to the Currency School has been suggested by Clower and me:

> 'The emphasises... that the stock of bonds is "geared" to the stock of money via a market adjustment mechanism in such a fashion that changes in the aggregate stock of bonds are, *ceteris paribus*, directly proportional to changes in the stock of money.'[9]

Unfortunately, this logically-valid statical result does not contact day-to-day events, necessarily interpreted as *disequilibria* or without reference to *any* equilibrium state.

§2

Now leap forward more than 100 years. There developed a discussion, led by Professors Gurley and Shaw, strikingly like that of *circa* 1844. True, much of the new discussion was flawed. Relative magnitudes of liquid asset stocks or their relative growth rates concerned writers who would have done better to centre on deviations from trend in a context of 'release of cash'. Such queries as: 'what really is money?' and 'are non-banks really different from banks?' were more frequent than 'do shifts in bank and non-bank portfolio positions generate credit flows, which may offset contractions in bank credit induced by contraction of the monetary base, in ways which cannot easily be anticipated?' or 'what of the intensity and duration of "flow" impulses reflecting *disequilibrium* due to portfolio disturbance by open-market operations, reverse-requirement changes, etc.?' The latter queries reflect the thrust of this chapter, viz. that monetary authorities, outside of Bank Rate régimes, exert influence mostly to the extent that they can 'foul up' financial machinery. Success in thus 'fouling up the works' will depend on the financial system's adaptive responses, especially its ability quickly and massively to reroute credit circuits. Take it for all and all, *Radcliffe* comes closer to getting things right than does most money-supply theory.

8. MONEY-SUPPLY PRACTICE IN BRITAIN

¶13.8 concerns 'availability' or 'quantity' effects in *closed* systems rather than more traditional domains of the theory of Bank Rate.

British credit-markets communicate exceptionally well, partly because the discount facilities of the Bank of England are so easy to tap. To this extent it is harder for British authorities to displace credit-markets, in particular to affect credit availability at going rates. This leads up to a null hypothesis:

> official attempts to affect aggregate demand through induced stringency beyond the rubric of Bank Rate cannot succeed, short of directives or quantitative actions distinctly larger than those on record.

The alternative hypothesis is:

> British officials *can* importantly affect aggregate demand by manipulating the monetary ('cash') base.

Before carrying on, two facets of the alternative hypothesis should be explored. The first can be succinctly stated: the alternative hypothesis views Bank Rate as a tail wagged by a cash-base dog. Bank Rate, influencing other interest rates in well-known ways, is keyed to money-supply targets, M^* for example, so that:

$$(\dot{BR}) \gtreqless 0 \quad \text{as} \quad (M - M^*) \gtreqless 0 \tag{23}$$

Thus, if operations on the monetary base were being thwarted by recourse by the market to the Bank, Bank Rate would be pushed up. Of course, this facet of the alternative hypothesis is implausible: Bank Rate by tradition, and surely since 1961, has responded to the United Kingdom *Balance of Payments* and has *not* been a tail wagged by the money-supply dog. Indeed, since Bank open-market operations largely have reflected a mode of monetary policy inherent in system **S1** and **S2** (cash-base being a tail wagged by the Bank Rate dog), it is doubtful if British data allow a test of significance between our two hypotheses. Still there is doctrinal precedent for treating British monetary data as if they were generated in a closed system under the ægis of money-supply targets, including Keynes's *Treatise on Money*.

Turning to the second facet, *cognoscenti* will spy out the *cash-base* approach to the bank-deposit control mode. This is for two reasons:

1) the logic of the liquid-assets-base approach to bank-deposit control appears to be flawed;
2) its empirical implications appear to be falsified.[10]

Pursuing the matter of the flawed logic of liquid assets approaches, we take up the Coppock and Gibson critique of the late W. M. Dacey, the leading proponent of outright *New Orthodoxy*.[11] Dacey made the crucial simplifying assumption that all Treasury Bills are bank (*cum* discount market) held and also ignored commercial bills, eligible as liquid assets to apply against the 28 per cent liquidity ratio, together with short-bond holdings of the discount market. Unfortunately, these simplifications appear to be necessary for Dacey's results. Dacey's model excluded switches of bills between outside tenderers and banks and the market, together with shifts in bank holdings of commercial bills, processes which appear to be critical for the argument. Nor did he ponder on the fact that, to the extent that the market is in the Bank at Bank Rate, the discount houses are encouraged to liquidate certain of their assets and repay the Bank, thus cutting back the cash-base.

Continuing discussion of the logic of liquid assets approaches, we concede that Radcliffe *New Orthodoxy*, although also ignoring discount-market holdings of short-bonds, is more sophisticated than the Dacey version. The *Report* emphasizes official reluctance to tolerate wide movements in Bill Rate. It concludes that, as a result, a Bank sale of securities will be accompanied by free dealing by the Bank between Bills and cash, thus vitiating cash-base control. In other words, the Bank would draw back from the consequences for Bill Rate of its contraction of the cash-base and would undo its own acts. However, as Coppock and Gibson point out, this merely is to say that the Bank would become awed by the *efficacy* of open-markets operations. Furthermore they show that either a cash-base or a liquid assets mode has (in the context of a conventionally simple model) the same effect on equilibrium Bill Rate for a given net contraction of the Bank's total securities portfolio. As for expansionary operations on the monetary base:

> 'the existence of a minimum liquid assets ratio in addition to the conventional cash ratio means that there may be circumstances in which an increase in the cash-base may not be a necessary and sufficient condition for an increase in deposits because there are insufficient potential liquid assets to support the new level of deposits.... [I]f the central bank really desired an increase in the money supply, it could easily (disfund) to make the necessary liquid assets available.'[12]

The argument can be summarized more rigorously. Proceed first under a Bank Rate régime. There is to be a change in Bill Rate, assumed to be geared to Bank Rate, this change being $d\bar{r}$. We calculate the resulting changes in the public's desired Bill-holdings ($d\bar{x}_1$) and deposits ($d\bar{x}_2$) ignoring, *à la* Dacey, commercial bills. Profit-maximizing behaviour by the banks and market leads up to:

$$d\bar{x}_3 = f(d\bar{x}_2, d\bar{r}), \tag{24}$$

$d\bar{x}_3$ being the desired change in bank Bill holdings, $d\bar{x}_2$ and $d\bar{r}$ being predetermined as above. (Here we loosely aggregate banks and the discount market.) We pause to note that:

1) both the deposits which the banks wish to have outstanding and those the public wish to possess are endogenous variables, so that it makes no sense to treat either as influencing behaviour. We should not refer to the banks as responding to a reserve base, but instead to a constellation of interest rates such that banks engage in promotions and offers achieving deposit levels, which appear to be optimal under the circumstances and are consistent with available reserves, emphasizing that these are not parameters for any bank.
2) upon digesting 1), one concludes that money-supply theory of the M vintage is inconsistent with general-equilibrium theory whilst Bank Rate theory can live with general-equilibrium theory, at least if the latter is given a Wicksellian twist.

The authorities are to determine upon changes in bank-reserves (dz_1) and in the supply of Bills (dz_2) in the light of the inequalities

$$D \le k_1 z_1 \tag{25}$$

$$D \le (z_2 - x_1)k_2 \tag{26}$$

London practice is for inequality (25) to hold exactly (ignoring deposit liabilities of the market itself). The London call-loan system makes it pointless for banks to hold excess reserves. Highly-liquid bank reserves, above those held at the Bank, take the form of short loans to the market (subject to a remark hinging on development of interbank loans at London, but not affecting the exactness of inequality (25)). So dz_1 and dz_2, become determined as endogenous variables in a Bank Rate régime.

It might seem that a *cash-base* régime can be described by an initial determination on $d\bar{D}$, enforced by changes in Bank Rate, Bill issue, etc., required for financial equilibrium. But this is not true: for such a cash-base régime effects on aggregate demand would be generated entirely by interest rate changes. Any member of the public would deem his deposit position endogenous. *Quantity effects* can be developed only in a *disequilibrium* nexus. For example, substantial open-market sales by the Bank might be accompanied by a sharp increase in an already penal Bank Rate and rigid Bank refusal to give backdoor help to the market.

Then almost certainly interest rates would not ration credit for some time.

Now we sketch a 'Bank Rate and money supply' model for the United States, obviously being heavily indebted to Dr. Meigs. Macrovariables include:

r = market rate
r^* = Federal Reserve discount rate
ρ = deposit rate
z = aggregate unborrowed reserves
y_1 = required reserves = $\Phi(y_2)$
y_2 = aggregate bank deposits
y_3 = aggregate borrowed reserves

Microvariables include:

y_2^j = deposits of the jth bank, here predetermined
y_3^j = borrowings at the Federal Reserve Bank of the jth bank
y_4^j = reserves of the jth bank
y_5^j = investments of the jth bank all yielding r

Turning to the system's microstructure, we note that banks may borrow at the Federal Reserve Bank, in order to obtain resources with which to increase their investments, as well as to augment their reserves (in which case they would not draw down their fresh credits). There is no one-for-one correspondence between borrowed reserves and borrowings at the Federal Reserve Bank for the jth bank. In the preferred mode of analysis, the jth bank does not create deposits. Rather it receives deposits—gladly because this allows it to make investments. It also seeks resources from non-depositors, including the central bank and new shareholders.

The structure will lead to, amongst others, these reduced-form equations:

$$\bar{y}_3^j = f^3(r, r^*, \rho, y_2^j, \ldots) \qquad (27)$$

$$\bar{y}_4^j = f^4(\qquad\qquad) \qquad (28)$$

The analysis also determines $\bar{y}_2$. The equivalent to bank liquidity-preferences leads banks to enter securities markets, buying or selling off investments, and in that way affecting the aggregate of deposits. These steps being taken, we can write:

Free Reserves = Excess Reserves − Borrowed Reserves = $\psi(r^*)$ (29)

although deeper analysis reveals that the system's motion will depend on the relationship between desired and actual free reserves in ways which Meigs has developed.

So the money supply, on any usual definition, is a function of r^*. A change in the value of z will lead to adaptive responses such that $dy_3 \neq 0$. The significance of this adaptive response for the viability of *cash-base* policy will depend on its predictability, together with the appropriate organizational and political constraints on the policy space. Cf. ¶13.9.

§2

We now are ready to attempt a test of significance on the null and alternative hypotheses keyed to a modified cash-base interpretation of a policy-mode, attempting to achieve quantity effects via bank-deposit movements. There are two modifications:

1) in Britain, and, perhaps less obviously, in most places, such policy-controlled stocks as the total of Treasury Bills must move in consort with the cash-base. This is for reasons already elaborated;
2) policy-determined elements of the cash-base must be distinguished from passive elements, in particular the market's discounts at the Bank.

Pursuing 2), the London call-loan system makes the equivalent of excess reserves pointless in Britain: well-nigh perfect correlation of the British cash-base with clearing-bank deposits has no substantive significance. However, the degree of negative correlation between movements in the Bank's securities and the market's discounts at the Bank is highly interesting, as is the variability of discounts. The higher is the negative correlation, the less is the *apparent* ability of the Bank to displace the system through open-market operations (will the open-market operator's work be undone at the discount window?). The greater is the variability of discounts and the less is the negative correlation, the harder it is for the Bank to anticipate what will happen pursuant to open-market operations.

§3

Statistical investigations for 1959–1963, based on quarterly observations, suggest that, whilst 'perverse' recourse doubtless occurs in Britain, it is smaller and less sure in operation than has been suggested by the *New Orthodoxy*.

It is important to define a policy variable ingesting official response to shifts in the public's demand for currency, here taken to be exogenous. A well-defined policy variable would take on zero-value when open-market purchases correspond pound for pound with increases in the public's currency holdings. Thus we define the policy-determined change in the *net cash-base* (*net* because the public's currency holdings are deducted from the *gross cash-base*) as: 'the change in total securities of the

Banking Department of the Bank (*not* including discounts and advances) less the change in currency outstanding with the public, taking account of *special deposits* for June 1960–March 1963.'

Newlyn (1962) explains special deposits at pp. 36–37: 'This control consists in the Bank of England requiring the banks to deposit with it amounts, determined from time to time, which do not constitute liquid assets for the purpose of satisfying the liquid assets requirements.'[13] Increases in special deposits at the Bank lead, *pari passu*, to decreases in bank cash. But clearing banks have been allowed to replenish their reserves by, in effect, selling Bills to the Bank so that the net effect of special deposits requirements has been on liquid assets ratios.

Defining the quarterly first-difference in the Bank's adjusted securities as S, that of the currency holdings of the public as C and that of special deposits as D,

$$E = S - C - D \tag{30}$$

'My' officials are to respond continuously to the public's currency habits and to other basically seasonal forces in adjusted 'unborrowed bank reserves' in United States parlance. However, the discount market's borrowed funds at the Bank, B, are not in any usual sense (cf. ¶13.9) instrumental in the London system: these funds are passively supplied by the Bank in its traditional rôle as *lender of last resort*.

B was regressed on E, using the 17 differenced quarterly observations from June 1959 to June 1963. The point estimate of the regression coefficient is -0.07. The correlation coefficient, -0.47, is not significant at the 5 per cent level. Thus I estimate from this sample that a unit change in the policy-determined variable (at the sample mean) leads to a 0.07 unit change of opposite sign in the variable not under official control—the market's discounts at the Bank. I cannot deny at a conventionally secure level of confidence that the market's recourse is uncorrelated with Bank security-portfolio shifts. Still I would bet my Bayesian life that market discounts are so correlated.

§4

Quite recent changes in Bank of England procedures require that our experiment be substantially redesigned if later data are to be considered. It is not certain that the new circumstances permit any appropriate test. Specifically, the maturities of Bank loans to the market have become more varied. The Bank no longer views its advances to the market merely as a reflexion of its obligation as *lender of last resort*. Now it often gives help at market rates at the discount window. So Bank open-market operations and discounts-and-advances no longer can easily be distinguished functionally. Of course, the dynamic response of the market to falling into the

Bank will be quite different if help has been offered at market—as against penal—rates.

One effect of normal recourse below Bank Rate is to permit the authorities to keep the market on a short leash. Rather-drastic effects would follow Bank refusal to renew advances except at penal rate. Of course, habitual recourse long has characterized the United States, and the Federal Reserve Bank long has been able to exert that much more pressure along the same lines as those just described.[14]

9. SOME METHODOLOGY OF MONEY-SUPPLY POLICY

We have reckoned, at least as Bayesians, that an open-market sale by the Bank, postulated to be pursuing a cash-base policy, leads to increased Bank advances because of additional recourse. This suggests two conclusions:

1) high correlations between British cash-base and money-supply may be factitious since (a) the call-loan system precludes excess reserves and (b) the observed cash-base movements need not reflect official will;
2) if discount feedback is substantial, control of the money-supply through cash-base operations is jeopardized.

On reflexion the second conclusion is specious. Thus, if, because of feedback, an open-market sale of £10 would certainly lead to increased advances of £2, the authorities, wishing to reduce bank reserves by £100 simply could solve:

$$x - 0.2x = 100 \qquad (31)$$

i.e.,

$$x = 125 \qquad (32)$$

The appropriate securities sale is £125. Advances will increase by £25.

Moving into a stochastic frame of reference, two possibilities emerge— one quickly to be put aside:

1) the feedback coefficient, 0.2 in equation (31), may exceed unity, making the system explosive;
2) Bank securities and Bank advances may be badly correlated and the latter may be highly volatile as well, making the worst case for *cash-base* authorities.

1) is to be put aside: if economic policy is *inherently* destabilizing, why bother?

Pursuing 2), we consider 'adaptive response (roughly feedback) and the viability of régimes of economic policy'. First observe that policies based on models of the financial subsector of the economy surely will be buffeted about by massive disturbances—that is, massive in terms of such models. Changes in expectations and tastes, perhaps induced by labour disputes or innovations, together with growth and decay in excluded sectors, are likely to make for weak estimates of the structure of the financial subsector. So it is difficult for the monetary authorities either to ascertain how far off course present policies are taking the economy or what are the appropriate corrective actions. In other words, specification errors of manageable models, together with general problems of structural estimation, make it likely that adaptive responses will appear to be highly volatile in a sectoral model.

§2

¶13.9 §§3 and ¶13.9 §§4 are codas to ¶13.9 §§1. ¶13.9 §§3 is an excursion in *politics and money-supply policy*, resuscitating the methodologically discredited criticism of orthodox régimes anlysed through equations (31) and (32). ¶13.9 §§4 dips into *metaphysick and money-supply policy*, becoming concerned with the ways in which economic processes, moving uncertainly through time, can be expected to affect preferences and hence criteria in ways which cannot be predicted. Finally, ¶13.9 §§5 will develop further the central theme of ¶13.9 §§1, discussing *identification in money-supply theory*.

§3

Political realities often squeeze the feasible policy set into a small part of the space suggested by ordinary economics. Thus United States politics are unlikely to permit the United States Bill Rate to reach 8 per cent. Nor is it likely that massive tax increases can be enacted during election years. United States politics probably would not permit peacetime budget deficits as great as \$40 billion. United Kingdom open-market operations are confined within quite narrow limits, etc.

One illustration shows how critiques, seemingly crushed, may revive. Say that political constraints preclude policies which would cause interest rates to rise above stated levels over the next several months and that it is believed that open-market sales by the central bank in excess of x^* billion over that interval would push interest rates through the ceiling. Then stipulate that adaptive responses, reflected in Matrixes **C** and **T**, would reduce the impact of $x billion in sales to $0·33x$ billion. Now, if other constraints made it impossible to consider operations in excess of $2x^*$ billion, the officials could not, in practice, achieve the hypothetical ceiling. And, if truly deterrent rates exceeded the ceiling, monetary policy would have to be marked 'paid' anyhow.

§4

It is conventional in the theory of intertemporal optimization in economics to state criteria invariantly against the process under control, to ignore feedback which would cause the history of the process to affect preferences about future events (partly because views of the past would thus be changed). A crucial theorem, established by Karl R. Popper, saps this convention:

'I have shown that, for strictly logical reasons, it is impossible for us to predict the future course of history.... The argument may be summed up ...

1) The course of human history is strongly influenced by the growth of human knowledge....
2) We cannot predict ... the future growth of our scientific knowledge....
3) We cannot, therefore, predict the future course of human history....
4) This means that we must reject the possibility of a *theoretical* history; that is to say, of a historical social science that would correspond to *theoretical physics*. There can be no scientific theory of historical development serving as a basis for historical prediction....'[15]

Policy makers, whether they propose to be guided by consensus, God or the grandeur of France, thus cannot know what will be their or others' preferences in the future: all will come under the influence of unknown processes, throwing up experiences, new techniques, etc., of now incognizable consequence. So it is that evaluators of pay-off functions needs must be endogenous variables in dynamic processes.

§ 5

Now we restore the postulation that the relevant structures are to be invariant against the history of the process. Nor is *structure* used lightly. Proper money-supply theory is concerned with stochastic processes; the problem of *identification* soon comes to the surface.

Recall the model for the 'quantity effect' policy mode: money-supply theory then is swallowed up by Matrixes **C** and **T**. Now historical correlations between bank deposits and Gross National Product or multiple regressions regressing interest rates on vectors of financial assets are likely to cast little light on the values of the cell-elements of the matrices. The reason is in basic statistical theory. If the economy could be viewed as a stationary stochastic process, say repeated tossing of a hyper-die in a tranquil environment, then perhaps historical correlations could lead up to useful regressions of endogenous on policy-determined variables, so that identification of structural parameters could be by-passed. However, Life does not cast up data which can be viewed as an infinite replication of a stationary process *à la* our cosmic 'crap' game. In economics, each policy decision, quantitatively construed, is a unique event and can be judged only against a history comprised of unique events. For one thing the stochastic environments are not stationary. Agreed, the evidence against historical correlations as a basis for monetary policy throws up a harsh environment for structural estimation as well. Nevertheless, it is one thing simply to be deprived of an *a priori* basis and another to know, perhaps futilely, what should be done.

> '... Historical correlations may indeed be an easy way to forecast correctly so long as nothing happens to disturb the observed associations.... When something happens to alter the situation, however, structural information is indispensable. This may occur ... because it seems desirable to adopt a policy which will affect one or more variables of the system or because one enters a period in which historical co-movements are broken up—as when the economy encounters a turning point in the business cycle. Such occasions ... are likely to be just the ones, however, about which accurate prediction is crucial.'[16]

The *raison d'être* of monetary policy is to disturb the associations which would emerge from an uncontrolled process or which have emerged from whatever has been the process.

Professor Walters has ably shown that carelessness about structural specification has led to serious bias in estimates of parameters of demand-for-money functions.[17]

10. BANK RATE AND MONEY-SUPPLY IN THE INTERNATIONAL ECONOMY

Central bankers in open economies, i.e. in Life, respond to the *Balance of Payments* as well as to the 'closed' criteria already considered. Surely British central-banking practice has been in an open setting.

¶13.10 §§2, after establishing a ZZ/BB construction, considers Bank Rate régimes, centring on *covered* and *uncovered* movements of funds under fixed and flexible (floating) exchange. ¶13.10 §§3 concerns effects of Eurodollar and related markets on 'quantity effect', i.e. cash-base régimes of monetary policy, concluding that national monetary régimes may find it increasingly hard to execute autarkical policies. ¶13.10 §§4 concerns a conjecture.

§ 2

Fig. 1, the ZZ/BB construction may serve as a basis for the fixed-exchange discussion. The ZZ curve is a locus of Gross National Product growth rates and interest rates for a given country, which is divorced from general-equilibrium theory rather as is the celebrated Phillips curve. The ZZ curve emerges from a thought-experiment or from simulation associating growth rates and interest rates (all encompassed within the locution Bank Rate which, at a given date, would be experienced if foreign-exchange disequilibrium could be ignored, or, better, were soaked up by a buffering operation. The BB curve associates growth rates and interest rates permitting a specified surplus or deficit on Balance of Payments. There is of course a family of BB curves. (For that matter, so is there a family of ZZ curves. The ZZ curves are drawn up relative to fiscal policy specifications.)

The BB curve of Fig. 1 emphasizes *uncovered* movements of funds between financial centres,[18] whilst the BB curves of Fig. 2 concern *covered* movements, that is spot shifts accompanied by 'opposite' futures transactions. A covered 90-day movement from New York to London would

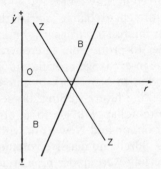

Fig. 1   The ZZ/BB Construction

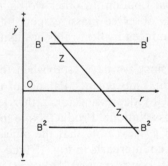

Fig. 2   ZZ/BB, Covered Movements

require that comparable amounts of sterling be sold 90 days forward for dollars. Turning to Fig. 1, we may stipulate that its BB curve calls for Balance of Payments equilibrium. If this or a more favourable balance is to be achieved, direct controls being locked in at a certain level, the authorities must accept the Bank Rate implied by the intersection of the two curves (or a higher Bank Rate) *and* a decaying growth rate of Gross National Product. Nor are fiscal remedies available. The BB curve implies that the rate of growth of imports increases relative to that of exports as the rate of growth of Gross National Product increases. Any fiscally expansionary policy must be accompanied by still higher Bank Rate. Of course, if foreign trade elasticities of demand are high enough and if retaliation can be put off, currency-devaluation, which effectively increases the costs of imports (that is to say makes foreign profit margins less attractive) and decreases export prices (that is to say makes profit margins for 'our' exporters more attractive), can shift the BB family leftwards. Essentially this describes the *raison d'être* of the November 1967 British devaluation (still unresolved in May 1968).

A word about the foreign exchange market behaviour underlying Fig. 2. Roughly speaking, interest *arbitrageurs*, shifting hot money between financial centres in order to profit from interest rate differentials, must become married to foreign-exchange speculators. A proposed net shift of spot funds from London to New York by interest *arbitrageurs* gives rise to future-dollars seeking future-sterling. If speculators do not offer future-sterling, the future-dollar will go to a discount, restoring the *interest parity* between London and New York with perhaps a miniscule movement of spot funds. Surely, no massive volume of such funds would come forward unless sterling were under *bear* attack. Unfortunately, in that instance the forward pound would already be at a discount, as speculators contracted to offer sterling for dollars in future to *arbitrageurs* shifting spot funds *from* London. In other words, if *covered* movements generally predominate, observed massive spot shifts are more likely to reflect haemorrhages induced by bear raids or flights, but *not* response to shifts in Bank Rate.

Turning to Fig. 2, since we have established that Bank Rate policy there cannot affect capital movements, Balance of Payments adjustment must be accomplished by depressing (or, rather less likely, expanding) the growth rate of Gross National Product. Note that, *à la* Phillips, wage behaviour is linked to $\dot{y}$. Next note that the officials have rather more autarky than did their counterparts in Fig. 1. True $\dot{y}$ is to be determined by Balance of Payments considerations. However, if we are permitted to enlarge the model's income determination features so that the set of admissible $\dot{y}/r$ values lie in a plane, the Bank Rate instrument becomes freed: taxes may be increased and money made cheap in order to encourage capital formation, for example.

Figs. 3 and 4 concern two of the three special cases concluding our discussion of Bank Rate régimes under fixed exchange. Fig. 3 depicts the first of three cases, that of a financially-atomistic economy in a world in which international flows typically are uncovered. Unless this economy adheres to global Bank Rate, either it will be overwhelmed with funds or

.uffer a fatal haemorrhage almost at once. However, Fig. 3 allows considerable fiscal leeway. Balances of Payments can be controlled by Bank Rate (indeed the authorities need only ascertain what is global Bank Rate. There will be a perfectly-elastic supply of funds at that rate). 'Our' economy can isolate itself from the global trade cycle.

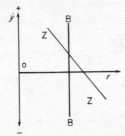

Fig. 3 Financial Atomism: Uncovered Movements

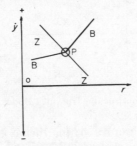

Fig. 4 Kinked BB Curves and the Salad Days of Bank Rate

Fig. 4 depicts Britain during the salad days of Bank Rate at London:

> 'Three circumstances were particularly favourable to this [Bank Rate] link in the chain of control [approximately between 1874 and 1914]. First, the internal effect of high rates in drawing cash from the country banks was probably at its maximum in the third quarter of the century . . . Secondly, London's foreign lending was large and extremely sensitive to market rate. Thirdly, the world's total stock of gold was increasing.'[19]
> '. . . [D]uring the eighties [London's net foreign lending] soared. . . . The pace at which new loans were floated was highly sensitive to interest rates. Borrowers were usually able to wait a few weeks in the hope that a spell of dear money would pass . . . or, if the bonds had already been issued, high interest rates [at] London would make them slow to remit the proceeds abroad. . . . So, in one way and another, a short spell of dear money would ease the strain on the exchanges before ever the balance of trade could be affected.'[20]

Starting at P, a substantial leftward shift of ZZ would not lead to much reduction in $\dot{y}$: lower interest rates quickly would offset effects on the

Balance of Payments of a reduced growth rate. Alternatively $\ddot{y} < 0$ would be accepted together with a larger Balance of Payments surplus. A substantial rightward shift in ZZ could be accommodated at only slightly higher Bank Rate without affecting the Balance of Payments: thus capital inflow could easily be increased.

The third special case concerns Country A. Other countries treat its 'IOUs' as fundamental liquid assets, as part of their national reserves. So A can be heedless of Balance of Payments deficits. A is free to move along whatever ZZ curve it is able to construct, quite without foreign interference.

Turning to flexible exchange, consider Fig. 5.

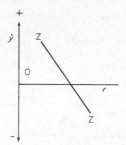

Fig. 5   The ZZ/BB Construction Truncated Under Flexible Exchange

Fig. 5 fits the case of Country A: the theme is flexible exchange and autarky. Reflexion supports the theme, qualifiedly. First a technical note. Under flexible exchanges, the foreign-exchange market and the commodities market, in Metzler's locution, are linked directly: the terms of trade directly affect exports and imports. The ZZ curve of Fig. 5 takes this into account. Why is there no BB curve in Fig. 5? The foreign-exchange market will, through price adjustments, accommodate *Balance of Payments* consequences of ZZ phenomena.

In a dynamic model of flexible exchange there are unbalances in international payments: undesired accumulations and decumulations of foreign exchange occur from day to day, from week to week, etc.

Considering qualifications to 'flexible exchange and autarky', centre on the Bank Rate instrument. What goes on behind the ZZ façade when the Bank Rate is reduced? Exports must increase more than imports in order to accommodate increased capital outflow. This outflow will be completely inelastic relative to the level of the exchange rate under unitary elasticities of expectation in the foreign-exchange market. Hence the terms of trade must become more adverse for 'us', at least if the traditional Marshall–Lerner condition is imposed. Hence, there are important real effects of Bank Rate movements generated by the foreign-exchange market.

Again consider a small country for whom foreign trade is very important and whose exports are highly specialized. Over fairly short time spans, demand for its exports may be almost totally inelastic, so that, under flexible exchanges, intolerable deterioration of its terms of trade could result from a substantial reduction in its Bank Rate.

It remains to take up Bank Rate autarky under flexible exchange in some detail. We consider four cases: $U \cdot \alpha$, $U \cdot \beta$, $C \cdot \alpha$ and $C \cdot \beta$. The symbol α signifies exchange-market subjective belief that, over the intervals under consideration, 'our' exchange rates are likely to fluctuate only within narrow intervals. The symbol β signifies the opposite. U and C are *uncovered* and *covered*, the context being obvious.

$U \cdot \alpha$. Note well that the main difference between cases $U \cdot \alpha$ and $C \cdot \alpha$ is that in the former instance non-speculators are willing to act on their convictions, but not in the latter. Then take up a hypothetical Toronto–New York nexus under an equally hypothetical global régime of flexible exchange. First focus on Toronto. Note that significant departure of Toronto from New York money market rates will *in posse* lead to massive flows of funds between the two centres. Recalling our portmanteau usage of 'Bank Rate', if Canadian Bank Rate exceeded United States Bank Rate, the demand for Canadian dollars would greatly increase. This would stem both from attempted placements of funds at Toronto and from attempts of Canadian debtors to secure finance at New York, converting the proceeds into Canadian dollars. It becomes clear that, under $U \cdot \alpha$ stipulations, it is impossible for Ottawa authorities to increase the Canadian cost of borrowing relative to that at New York. If Canadian Bank Rate were placed below the United States rate, Canadian authorities would have to engage in huge open-market purchases of paper offered by United States borrowers and then these gigantic sums would have to be taken up by speculators able to offer United States dollars spot. At least, these transactions would appear gigantic to the Canadians. The North American speculators would have to finance the United States economy! Nor is it helpful to take account of the fact that the United States economy is so large relative to the Canadian in building up the New York story. *Vis à vis* the rest of the world the United States is not *that* much bigger than Canada.

Finally we note that it is most unlikely that the stipulations of $U \cdot \alpha$ could hold up in Life. The order of magnitude of susceptible funds in foreign-exchange speculation from day to day does not appear to support $U \cdot \alpha$ stipulations.

$U \cdot \beta$. Why ask the arcane question: 'under what circumstances would risk-preferences be so strong that movements typically would be uncovered, even if subjective probability-density functions were highly dispersed?' We shall modify the stipulations of case $U \cdot \beta$: there simply are to be no forward-exchange facilities. The revision is not uninteresting: forward-exchange markets have been specialized to short maturities and have not been thick. The implications for the feasibility of global flexible exchange are sombre.

In brief, $U \cdot \beta$, as revised, finds national finance centres disconnected and thus restores Bank Rate autarky, doubtless at great cost to countries whose development requires substantial capital inflow. A single illustration suffices. Assume that Toronto's Bank Rate is put up. Now a potential Canadian borrower at New York faces a chilling prospect. If he has much company, the Candian dollar will go to a substantial premium over the United States dollar at the outset, as funds obtained at New York are repatriated to Toronto. Later, when repayments are being made, the Canadian dollar may become heavily discounted against the United States dollar. Thus there is a distinct prospect that Canadian dollars will be bought dear and sold cheap, perhaps raising the effective interest rate to a ruinous level. How much *long term* international finance would become generated under such circumstances? And note how the terms of trade are to fluctuate violently, doubtless discouraging international commerce.

$C \cdot \alpha$. The C cases are more interesting. If the foreign-exchange rates arc to bear the major burden of international financial adjustment, we can assume that β-type subjective probability-density functions will be common and that risk-neutrality or risk-avoidance will dominate in preferences of transactors in foreign-exchange markets. Cover will be demanded. This being done, it follows that a realistic C case leads to results much like those flowing from the flat BB curves of Fig. 2. Bank Rate becomes immobilized as a mechanism of international adjustment, here perhaps as a means of protecting the terms of trade. Furthermore, international flows of funds are likely to become clogged for reasons already explained.

Taking up case $C \cdot \alpha$, apologetically, its result are like those of case $U \cdot \alpha$, despite the fact that traders assume their own exchange risks in the latter instance and pay speculators to do this for them in the former instance. Under $C \cdot \alpha$ stipulations, speculators do not have to be paid much. So, of course, case $C \cdot \alpha$, like $U \cdot \alpha$ precludes autarkical régimes of Bank Rate. A single illustration suffices. Again assume that Toronto's Bank Rate is put up. Under $C \cdot \alpha$ stipulations, Canadians going to New York for finance, will be able to buy forward United States dollars at a small premium. Speculators, confident about the narrow range of likely foreign-exchange rate movements, can easily be induced to buy Canadian dollars forward against United States dollars. *Massive* flows must be contemplated: the realism of the analysis crumbles; alternatively, the upshot is to vitiate autarkical control of the cost of credit.

$C \cdot \beta$. In scenario $U \cdot \beta$, potential hot-money borrowers *worry* about having to pay the equivalent of ruinous interest charges in the end. In scenario $C \cdot \beta$ they *know* that they will have to pay ruinous interest charges. Again imagine that Toronto's Bank Rate is put up. Offers to buy United States dollars forward (and *pari passu* to sell Canadian dollars forward) are likely to be taken up only if the Canadian forward dollar is substantially marked down. β probability distributions are so dispersed that only a handful of plungers are likely to be willing to function as speculators unless paid, on the average, exorbitant fees. Short term forward markets are apt to be thin and long term forward markets non-existent.

Thus do Bank Rate régimes act under flexible exchange. We conclude that it is likely that considerable autarkical powers are likely to subsist within Bank Rate régimes under flexible exchange. The likely preponderance of β subjective probability-density functions, in turn makes it likely that international flows of funds would dry up.

§ 3[21]

Dr. Einzig has written:

'The control of the monetary system by central banks is likely to be weakened by the development of the *Eurodollar* market and of other foreign currency deposit markets in the following ways:

1) Monetary authorities have less control over the volume of liquid resources in their money market.
2) They have less control over the structure of national interest rates.
3) They have less control over the supply of credit available to their economy.
4) They have less control over the financing of unwanted imports.
5) They have less control over the influx and efflux of short term funds. ...
9) Discipline within the banking communities is less firm.'[22]

'The main reason why central banks are in a position to enforce discipline ... is that they are the main source from which banks can receive assistance in time of need. As a result of the development of the *Eurodollar* market, banks in many countries now are in a position to raise funds to tide them over difficult dates without having recourse to their central banks. ...'[23]

Briefly, the Eurodollar market has led to yet another way in which the *matrix of claims* can be switched, fuelling the system with additional credit. For example, a European deposit house can, upon reducing the dollar-claims deposited with it to negotiable funds, extend credit to Americans or can convert the dollars into funds capable of discharging debt at its own central bank. Furthermore, the Eurodollar nexus leads to an extension of a realistic analysis of the United States financial system to a network of deposit positions, sited *outside* of the United States and outside the *direct* control of the Federal Reserve authorities. Now, one must consider the possibility of a German portfolio manager selling Eurodollar deposits to a Hamburg importer, otherwise unable to obtain dollar finance. *Direct* control of the Federal Reserve? Open-market operations by consortiums of central banks in the Eurodollar market have become common.

§ 4

As financial dealing in international markets thickens, ominous portent for money-supply theory grows. Is it not possible that only official attitudes (expressed through controls of course) have confined the Eurodollar market to its present intermediary rôle? Thus, at present, British banks provide 'dollars' only in the form of a draft against funds reducible to United States legal tender: Lloyds Bank, having reduced a Eurodollar deposit to a sight obligation against New York, can transfer that sight obligation to me. However, it is conceivable that, in future, a cashier's cheque from Lloyds Bank, denominated in dollars, will be able to discharge debt payable in United States funds throughout the world. Then British clearing-bank balance-sheets would continue to value their deposit liabilities in British money of account, but the *de facto* distribution of this liability amongst pounds, dollars, francs, etc., would be a variable to be determined by the interaction of the global economy, as would be the distribution of bank assets between paper of various legal-tender properties denominated in pounds, dollars, etc.

How fanciful is the conjecture? After all, the *de facto* system of international monetary reserves is approaching such a state. Swaps between central banks and overdraft facilities at central banks now are at the centre of global liquidity whilst conventional international 'monies' such as gold and, more recently, dollars either are declining in quantitative importance or are under a cloud as uniquely monetary substances in international dealings. Nor is it likely that new International Monetary Fund contrivances such as Special Drawing Rights or Bancor *à la* Keynes–Triffin will come into play on a scale large enough to restore *l'ancien régime* (albeit in the name of 'Reform'). Indeed it is possible that the United States dollar's vast significance as an international liquid asset more reflects raw geopolitical power than it does inherent economic forces,—just as does the privilege of the Federal Reserve to influence the United States economy through its patents on cash-base creation. If the conjecture becomes fructified, how would we define M for Country A, let alone A's exogenously-determined cash-base? Alas, both concepts would truly have become meaningless. And so it would be that M would be heard no more.

REFERENCES

1. Cf. J. de V. Graaff, *Theoretical Welfare Economics* (Cambridge: Cambridge University Press; 1957).
2. Oskar Lange, *Price Flexibility and Employment* (Bloomington, Ind.: The Principia Press; 1944), esp. pp. 91–103.
3. J. Tinbergen, *On the Theory of Economic Policy* (Amsterdam: North Holland Publishing Company; 1963), 2nd ed.
4. R. Lipsey and F. Brechling, 'Trade Credit and Monetary Policy,' *The Economic Journal*, Dec. 1963, pp. 618–641. At pp. 618–620 they contrast *quantity* with *interest* effects of monetary policy.
5. R. Lipsey and F. Brechling, 'Trade Credit and Monetary Policy,' *The Economic Journal*, Dec. 1963, p. 635.
6. Cf. M. Burstein, 'Colonial Currency and Contemporary Monetary Theory,' *Explorations in Economic History*, 2nd Series, 1966, pp. 220–233.
7. J. S. Mill, *Principles of Political Economy*, Ashley Ed., Book III, Chap. 12 § 6, pp. 536–537.
8. Committee on the Working of the Monetary System, *Report* (London: HMSO; 1959), §981.
9. Clower and Burstein (1960), p. 36.
10. Cf. R. L. Crouch, 'The Adequacy of "*New Orthodox*" Methods of Monetary Control,' *Economic Journal*, Dec. 1964, pp. 916–934.
11. D. J. Coppock and N. J. Gibson, 'The Volume of Deposits and the Cash and Liquid Asset Ratios,' *Manchester School*, Sept. 1963, pp. 203–222. Also W. M. Dacey, *The British Banking Mechanism* (London: Hutchinson & Co.; 1962), esp. Chap. 10.
12. D. J. Coppock and N. J. Gibson, 'The Volume of Deposits and the Cash and Liquid Assets Ratios,' *Manchester School*, Sept. 1963, p. 222.
13. Cf. Bank of England *Quarterly Bulletin*, Dec. 1960, pp. 3–4.
14. Cf. R. S. Sayers, *Modern Banking* (Oxford: The Clarendon Press; 1967), 7th ed., pp. 319–330.
15. Karl R. Popper, *The Poverty of Historicism* (London: Routledge & Kegan Paul; 1960), pp. ix and x.
16. F. Fisher, *The Identification Problem in Econometrics* (New York: McGraw-Hill Book Co.; 1966), pp. 2–3.
17. Cf. A. A. Walters, 'Lags and the Demand for Money', *The Journal of Economic Studies* (London: Pergamon Press, 1967), pp. 3–22.
18. *The Economist* (London: 10 June 1967), pp. xv–xix, discusses what had been underpublicized uncovered international flows responding to 'interbank' interest differentials.
19. R. S. Sayers, *Central Banking After Bagehot* (Oxford: The Clarendon Press; 1957), p. 13.
20. R. S. Sayers, *Central Banking After Bagehot* (Oxford: The Clarendon Press; 1957), pp. 14–15.
21. Cf. *The Economist* (London: 8 July 1967), pp. 126–127. 'The Decade of the Euro-Dollar.' Also Holmes and Klopstock, 'The Market for Dollar Deposits in Europe,' Federal Reserve Bank of New York *Review*, Nov. 1960, and O. Altman, 'Recent Developments in Foreign Markets for Dollars, etc.', International Monetary Fund *Staff Papers*, Mar. 1963, referring to O. Altman, 'Foreign Markets for Dollars, etc.', Dec. 1961.

22. P. Einzig, *The Euro-Dollar System* (London: Macmillan & Co. Ltd.; 1964), pp. 113–114.
23. P. Einzig, *The Euro-Dollar System* (London: Macmillan & Co. Ltd.; 1964), p. 117.

Roma, Christmas 1965
Juan-les-Pins, April 1966
Birmingham, June 1966
Aspen, August 1968

Author Index

Subject Index

Subject Index